Routledge Revivals

Class, Politics and the Economy

This study, first published in 1986, provides a systematic account of the processes and structure of class formation in the major advanced capitalist societies. The focus is on the organizational mechanisms of class cohesion and division, theoretically deriving from a neo-Marxian perspective. Chapters consider the organization and structure of the 'corporate ruling class', the middle class and the working class, and are brought together in an overarching analysis of the organization of class in relation to the state and the economy. This title will be of particular interest to students researching the impact of recession on societal structure and the processes of political class struggle, as well as those with a more general interest in the socio-economic theories of Marx, Engels and Weber.

Class, Politics and the Economy

Stewart Clegg, Paul Boreham and Geoff Dow

Routledge
Taylor & Francis Group

First published in 1986
by Routledge & Kegan Paul

This edition first published in 2013 by Routledge
2 Park Square, Milton Park, Abingdon, Oxon, OX14 4RN

Simultaneously published in the USA and Canada
by Routledge
711 Third Avenue, New York, NY 10017

Routledge is an imprint of the Taylor & Francis Group, an informa business

© 1986 Stewart Clegg, Paul Boreham and Geoff Dow

Publisher's Note
The publisher has gone to great lengths to ensure the quality of this reprint but
points out that some imperfections in the original copies may be apparent.

Disclaimer
The publisher has made every effort to trace copyright holders and welcomes
correspondence from those they have been unable to contact.

A Library of Congress record exists under LC control number: 85008369

ISBN 13: 978-0-415-71547-8 (hbk)
ISBN 13: 978-1-315-88150-8 (ebk)
ISBN 13: 978-0-415-71562-1 (pbk)

Class, politics and the economy

Stewart Clegg

Paul Boreham

Geoff Dow

Routledge & Kegan Paul

London, Boston and Henley

First published in 1986
by Routledge & Kegan Paul plc

14 Leicester Square, London WC2H 7PH, England

9 Park Street, Boston, Mass. 02108, USA and

Broadway House, Newtown Road,
Henley on Thames, Oxon RG9 1EN, England

Set in 10/11 pt Times
by Columns of Reading
and printed in Great Britain
by T.J. Press (Padstow) Ltd,
Padstow, Cornwall

Library of Congress Cataloging in Publication Data

Clegg, Stewart.

Class, politics, and the economy.
Bibliography: p.
Includes indexes.
1. Social classes. 2. Elite (Social sciences)
3. Marxian school of sociology. 4. Marxian economics.
I. Boreham, Paul. II. Dow, Geoff. III. Title.
HF609.C62   1986   305.5   85-8369
British Library CIP Data also available

ISBN 0-7102-0452-3 (c)
ISBN 0-7102-0827-8 (p)

Contents

Acknowledgments

The production of this volume owes much to the following institutions: the School of Humanities, Griffith University; the Division of External Studies, University of Queensland; the Department of Sociology, University of New England; Macquarie University and Stanford University. Griffith and Queensland Universities generously provided us with financial support; while Macquarie, Stanford and Griffith made visiting scholar facilities available (to Geoff Dow, Stewart Clegg and Paul Boreham respectively) during the course of the project. The following people were a great help: Mike Emmison, Winton Higgins, Bob Hinings, John Mepham, Richard Bryan, Lyn Finch, Kate McGuckin and George Lafferty. We thank them all and absolve them from responsibility for any infelicities that remain.

Introduction

Contemporary themes developed in a diverse set of substantive contexts have important implications for the study of class. However, in a literature premised on conventional sub-disciplinary and disciplinary models, this relevance is not always apparent. *Class, Politics and the Economy* sustains its analysis by integrating what have hitherto all too frequently been distinct fields of enquiry.

Classical conceptions of class emerge with the birth of a concern within political economy with issues of macro-economic growth, accumulation, distribution and production, a mode of enquiry continued and extended by Marx. Subsequent sociological discussion of class frequently takes Marx's model of two major classes as a co-ordinate for constructing more complex analyses of the class structure than an essentially binary framework allows. These more recent innovations to Marx's classical framework have contributed valuable studies of specific classes, their structure, formation, ideology and politics, often derived from a more Weberian than Marxian framework. However, the opposition between Marx and Weber is illusory in some respects. Despite their quite different premises they concur on the determinant role and analysis of structures of economic domination. From this concurrence a model for class analysis may be constructed which integrates Marx's concerns for processes of class formation with Weber's more empirically developed categorization of class structure. However, what is invariably lost in the process of developing sociological models of class from the tradition of political economy, is the concern of the latter with macro-economic issues.

The framework which we construct for analysis is one which focuses not only on the arena of class structure but also on its

1

intersection with the state and civil society. The latter always intermediate the development of processes set in motion by the economic unfolding of capital-logic. Consequently, although one can note analytical tendencies based on a logic to capitalist development, notably in the nature of changing property relations, these are always unfolding in civil and political contexts which ensure that analytical 'logic' is always mediated.

Whereas those models derived from the classical tradition of political economy concentrate on the 'two great classes' of capital and labour, sociologists are more inclined to dissect the distinct modalities of strata such as the petty bourgeoisie, the corporate ruling class, the new middle class, and the working class.

The focus of this volume in chapters 1, 2 and 3 is precisely on these divergent traditions of political economy and sociological analysis of class. Chapters 4 to 7 each address in detail the social organization of the principal classes outlined. While not exhaustively complete, the main elements in the class structure of advanced industrial capitalist societies and the politics of macro-economic growth are considered. The scope of this volume meant omitting certain groups such as the judiciary or landowners. However, they are peripheral to our argument.

Underlying the emergent structure of classes are processes of institutional transformation in the sphere of private property relations. Increasingly, property forms have become more impersonal and institutional in character. Consequently, the nature of ruling-class formation and its mechanisms of coherence have changed markedly. Ownership and control may once have been personally fused, but this is no longer the case, nor has it been since the end of the last century. Contrary to conventional interpretations of these changes, we do not argue that the new middle classes are the controllers of industry. Instead, we note that no necessary capitalist interest will attach itself to all factions of the new middle class in an era in which personal surveillance and discipline give way to increasingly impersonal control. This theme has, as we show, been vigorously debated. Collectively, where capital assumes increasingly institutional forms, these can become a mechanism for quite different regimes of accumulation and control, articulated through the control of investment mechanisms such as pension funds as well as the development of economic democracy.

Policy issues such as these obviously have to be fought out in the political arena. In the majority of advanced industrial capitalist societies, this political infrastructure is dominated by parties which were forged in an earlier political economic conception of a basically two-class structure. There are some exceptions to this, of course, which we consider in an empirical context in the final chapter. An evident tension exists between a conception of society composed of a complex structure of classes and a primarily binary structure of parties, historically grounded in class. Political representation and class structure clearly do not correspond to each other in such a framework. Consequently, the relation between class and politics can never be one of correspondence. The expansion and growth of a new middle class, and the continuing, if much reduced, significance of the petty bourgeoisie, ensure this lack of correspondence.

The new middle class became the crucial political target for electoral mobilization and alliances by virtue of its numerical and strategic centrality to advanced capitalism. In chapter 6 we analyse how the new middle class has become divided both in its expression of political interests and in its fundamental attachment to capitalism as a system. The lack of a coherent political programme on the part of the new middle class imposes no allegiance on their part to particular strategies of accumulation, other than those which are supportive of the bureaucratic structures in which they occupy strategic locations. Such an interest in the reproduction of their own careers may lead some members of the new middle class to have less interest in the reproduction of capitalism *per se*, and more interest in sustained capital accumulation, irrespective of the mode of economic activity through which this is achieved. If capital accumulation can be achieved only through policies that undermine capitalist reproduction, this potential will be realized. Reconsideration of the classical tradition of political economy in its modern post-Keynesian forms suggests quite forcibly that the simultaneous reproduction of capital accumulation and long-term economic growth is incompatible with the reproduction of capitalism. Important political implications follow from this for an effectively two-party system. One analysis which we consider briefly and reject suggests that the new middle class's impact is likely to produce a crisis in the two-party system of representation. The concerns of this stratum of society with issues of personal identity and social responsibility located in civil society, it has been proposed, will produce a fragmentation of two-party systems into incommensurable single-issue politics. We would anticipate the probable detachment of some factions of the new middle class from bourgeois political parties, particularly those espousing monetarism. However, it is less likely that a 'new class' party will develop where a labour or democratic socialist party can formulate an alternative capital accumulation strategy.

Alternative accumulation strategies become feasible under

specific conditions. These can be empirically determined by a post-Keynesian analysis of macro-economic outcomes. Comparative data from the OECD allows the construction of an argument which demonstrates the efficacy of such an alternative accumulation strategy. On this basis we can anticipate the possibility of economic growth into a post-capitalist development. The central arena for the implementation of such polities is the political class struggle in and through the state. In the concluding chapter of this volume the comparative context of competing macro-economic policies is adumbrated in detail. A consequence of this analysis is a major reconceptualization of the significance of the state. Rather than propose a conventional 'corporatist' thesis, in which the working class becomes the invariable loser in a role cast by functionalist argument, we suggest that a more realistic conceptualization of these state forms regards them as potential conduits for class struggle. Such struggle, we maintain, is essential to any conception of class, politics and the economy.

1 Classes, accumulation and crisis

The earliest conceptions of class structure derive from political economy in its classical form in the eighteenth century. It is not merely an historical interest which recommends these concerns as an appropriate point of introduction. On the contrary, classical political economy's concern with the influence of social classes on the macro-economic performance of nations, we argue, should be an integral component in contemporary class analysis. Unfortunately, much analysis has moved away from a concern with the economic underpinning of the participation of different categories of collective actors in advanced capitalism. Consequently, structures of domination, premised on macro-economic patterns of activity, remain somewhat under-theorized in their effect on individual, collective and institutional action.

Our introductory remarks to this chapter should not be taken as either support or even qualified endorsement for versions of economic reductionism. This will become even clearer subsequently. Here, our concern is with processes of capital formation as implicitly processes of class formation, not to suggest a correspondence between the two, but to note the linkage. This linkage is effected through acknowledging that capital accumulation, whatever its mode, is always political. In other words, capital accumulation, under definite modes of rationality, always has differential, if opaque and unacknowledged, class effects.

These conceptions of the economy first came into currency with the break, in the eighteenth century, from a moral order premised on the possession and traditionally sanctioned disposition of surplus. Included were not only owners and producers, but also other social categories such as religious orders, the poor, the sovereign. The new moral philosophy was articulated most notably by Adam Smith and David Ricardo. Its break with

5

tradition resided in the construction of a new moral order whose pivot turned not on the distribution of a surplus already secured, but on its production. Henceforth, Smith and Ricardo signalled that the new order was no longer premised on tradition to be learnt but on a rationalizing instrument of production, to be mastered.

Smith and Ricardo

Early in the development of capitalist economies, the analysis of economic mechanisms was conducted in terms of the major classes, the different sources of the income which they received and the consequences for the whole society of the differential decisions classes were able to make about the use or disposal of these incomes. The French Physiocrats developed policy conclusions concerning desirable ways of increasing national wealth in a feudal system from analyses which observed that production of an agricultural surplus, and its subsequent appropriation by a class of non-producers, gave rise to very different categories of income for each of the producing and non-producing groups. Furthermore, societal development, in the sense of capacity to engage in manufacturing activities and capacity to devote some of the surplus ('net output') to ceremonial or 'unproductive' consumption, was regulated by the choices that were made by the surplus-appropriating classes. The higher the agricultural surplus (that is, the smaller the proportion of total production which was taken up by the necessary costs of peasant subsistence and costs of cultivation), the more there would be available to create a demand for the output of artisans and for what would later be called economic growth.

With classical political economy, notably the writings of Adam Smith (1723–90) and David Ricardo (1772–1823), this problematic became well established. In *An Enquiry into the Nature and Causes of the Wealth of Nations*, Smith considered an economy with three classes: landlords, capitalists and workers; but he was concerned to advocate the political rights and economic benefits of one class in particular (capitalists with 'self-interest') and to denounce the dominance of another (landlords, who 'love to reap where they never sowed'). Hence Smith urged that an enhancement of 'the wealth of nations' would accompany the emergence of an unrestricted, private enterprise economy. Smith produced a plea for the free play of self-interest to be unleashed from feudal and mercantilist restrictions, for competition and for the rights of individual entrepreneurs to engage in it. Pre-existing groups of merchants and traders had managed to impose the 'narrow defensiveness of mercantilist policies' which had become an impediment to more generalized economic development and national wealth (Robinson and Eatwell, 1973, p.15). Changes in the dominant forms of economic life required changes in the existing class structure.

For Smith, an economic system could be seen to have a dynamic of its own, laws could be discerned and, regardless of the will or intentions of those involved, the economic interaction and self-interest of individuals would create a self-regulating economic order. Economic liberty was expected to generate social harmony:

> It is not from the benevolence of the butcher, the brewer or the baker that we expect our dinner, but from their regard to their own self interest. We address ourselves not to their humanity, but to their self love, and never talk to them of our own necessities but of their advantages (Smith, 1961, p.15).

For Smith, market prices and competition would equate supply and demand and therefore provide the incentive for appropriate responses by both buyers and sellers, capitalists and labourers. An 'invisible hand' would guide diverse behaviours in such a way that 'natural prices', reflecting real conditions, would prevail. Self-interested individualism once liberated from pre-bourgeois inhibitions would maximize collective welfare.

This advocacy of laissez faire was in fact an opposition to established sectional interests and restrictive practices, especially those of the landowning classes whose rents increased as profits increased (thus restricting capital accumulation), and those of merchants whose riches were not reinvested to become accumulating wealth for the whole nation. Smith advocated a generalized process of industrial expansion and capital accumulation by seeking to legitimate the political rights of the bourgeoisie and to delegitimate the anti-competitive interventions of government. In addition, Smith argued that specialization and division of labour would enhance the processes of growth and accumulation. In so doing, he recognized that people could intervene in the world systematically to guarantee production and consumption and to help reduce arbitrary inequalities. Understandably, Smith did not dwell at great length on the potentially negative aspects of this way of organizing and improving social and material life. However, he did pose certain intellectual and political dilemmas for future generations.

He made much of the apparent distinction between productive and unproductive labour. In the absence of any contribution to production by accumulated capital, it should be the case, claimed

Smith, that natural exchange values of commodities should exactly reflect the amount of labour time involved in their production. This rudimentary formulation of a labour theory of value was very abstract, however, because tools and other produced equipment would normally be involved in production, thus affecting significantly the commensurate exchange values. Furthermore, different qualities of labour itself exist in a complex society; thus the productive activities of some interlock with the more or less productive activities of others. A concomitant of Smith's elaboration of the conditions for an increase in the wealth of nations necessarily involved the identification of a class element in production.

The system which Smith was attempting to analyse was not wholly analysable in terms of the categories he wished to deploy. The invisible hand would not eliminate all forms of unproductive labour. It was not a completed system, but one still emergent, still in the process of becoming. None the less, with Smith, a new emphasis on non-agricultural sources of surplus and accumulation, a critique of the emphases of the Physiocrats, was initiated.

The making of a market society, the form of society in which the potential of bourgeois freedoms would be revealed, was one which owed more to prolonged interventionism than to any innate 'propensity to truck, barter and exchange'. There has not been a unilinear evolution of market from non-market society, of specialized from non-divided labour, of wealth from poverty or of a free from an unfree workforce.

> Just as, contrary to expectation, the invention of labour-saving machinery had not diminished but actually increased the uses of human labour, the introduction of free markets, far from doing away with the need for control, regulation and intervention, enormously increased their range. ... Laissez faire was planned; planning was not (Polanyi, 1944, p.140).

However much Adam Smith's anthropological expectations were at fault, the force of his polemic and the terms of his analysis have survived. The historical and institutional questions canvassed by Adam Smith were the first systematic attempt to establish a science of political economy. As Therborn puts it: 'economic discourse emerged as a concomitant of the rise of what this discourse was about: the capitalist economy' (1976, p.77). Polanyi gives less credit to Smith, but does affirm the same conjunction: 'economic liberalism and the class concept were performed in these contradictions. With the finality of an elemental event, a new set of ideas entered our consciousness' (1944, p.85).

The analysis of capitalism and the science of political economy were both advanced by David Ricardo in a way which was also to contribute to an understanding of class formation and class behaviour. Compared with Smith, Ricardo was less sanguine about the untrammelled benefits of capital accumulation. Although he was as concerned as his predecessor to enhance 'the wealth of nations', and although he fought even more virulently than Smith for the extension of bourgeois rights against such feudal privileges as the Corn Laws and other import controls, Ricardo noticed more pointedly than Smith that the benefits of unimpeded economic growth were not necessarily shared equitably among all classes involved in production. Consequently, he sought to make distribution rather than growth the principal problem of political economy. *On the Principles of Political Economy and Taxation* (1819) deployed the same class model of the economy introduced in 1776 by Smith (proprietors of land, owners of capital, labourers) but went further than *The Wealth of Nations* in so far as it identified and analysed an entirely new category of income – unearned income. This was to provide a crucial influence on both Marx's subsequent developments of economic analysis and also the conservative (marginalist) tradition of enquiry which, half a century later, changed the 'whole focus of political economy'.

Ricardo's achievement was to set up an abstract model of the class structure of the economy and to work through the logical consequences of the expected behaviour of these class groupings. In this way, he formulated a critique of the deleterious consequences of the class of rentiers (mainly landowners) which was simultaneously a defence of capitalist employers. He consistently argued that the high rents accruing to landowners were an impediment to capitalists' profits and therefore to capitalism itself. The analogy between recipients of unearned income (rent, which was a surplus) and earned income (wages, which was a price) began to break down. Different forms of income implied differential involvement in capital accumulation.

These class aspects of capitalist development derive from the parameters of the discipline which Ricardo set out quite boldly in his preface:

> The produce of the earth – all that is derived from its surface by the united application of labour, machinery and capital, is divided among the three classes of the community; namely, the proprietor of the land, the owners of the stock or capital necessary for its cultivation, and the labourers by whose industry it is cultivated.

9

But in different stages of society, the proportions of the whole produce of the earth which will be allotted to each of these classes, under the names of rent, profit, and wages, will be essentially different; depending mainly on the actual fertility of the soil, on the accumulation of capital and population, and on the skill, ingenuity, and instruments employed in agricul- ture. To determine the laws which regulate this distribution, is the principal problem in Political Economy (Ricardo, 1819, p.iii)

In seeking to remedy deficiencies in earlier political economy, especially that of Smith who had 'overlooked many important truths which can only be discovered after the subject of rent is thoroughly understood' (1819, p.iv), Ricardo proposed a simple model of a capitalist economy whereby significant relationships between classes and distribution could be brought into relief – in abstraction from the institutional and historical intrusions which had featured in Smith's *Wealth of Nations*. Ricardo envisaged a capitalist economy but focused primarily on capitalist agriculture. In this system, landlords owned land; capitalists rented the land from the landowners and hired wage-labourers to work the land; and labourers made themselves available to the capitalist employers. The capitalists supplied whatever equipment and raw materials as were required for cultivation; thus, they owned the produce. When it was sold they paid rent to the landowners and wages to the workers; but the sources of income were not equivalent.

In the world of capitalist agriculture, as increasingly less fertile land is brought into cultivation, landowners with the more fertile and productive land are able to demand higher and higher rents. In response to increasing population, production moves to marginal areas. As the costs and difficulties of producing agricultural products in the less attractive circumstances mount, the prices that must be charged consequently increase. This results in more or less windfall profits to the producers in the fertile, low-cost areas because market pressures will keep produce grown under favourable conditions at the same high price as that grown under unfavourable conditions. Hence, landowners are able to charge very high rents for the use of fertile land and there will be a tendency for profits finally received by the capitalist farmers to be equalized throughout the economy. The rents accruing to landowners in this way were seen by Ricardo as 'unearned income' – they derived not from any productive contribution on the part of landowner but accrued merely by virtue of ownership of the land.

CLASSES, ACCUMULATION AND CRISIS

Competition among capitalists for cultivatable land would ensure that their own profits were kept at low (or 'normal') levels and that, as population increased, unearned income (rent) would continue to be received by the owners of land.

Although some simplifying assumptions are needed to sustain this conception of the class shares of income (e.g. subsistence wages paid to the labour employed), Ricardo clearly considered that a basic feature of a capitalist economy had been demonstrated and that these characteristics would pertain even when the assumptions were relaxed and more realistic conceptions were developed.

There is in Ricardo's writings, then, the beginnings of a theory of profits – but it is not an independent theory of profit-determination. The level of profit is set by what remains after rent and wages are deducted from the total product. The importance of this conception of profit for Ricardo was not only its representation of intrinsic conflict between capitalists and landlords, but its suggestion that as more and more marginal land was brought into use the rate of profit throughout the economy (and not only on the marginal 'no-rent' land) would tend to decrease. Provided competition tended to equalize profit rates throughout the economy and provided wages were determined by the costs of subsistence on the marginal land, the rate of profit even in manufacturing industry would be determined by the productivity of production on marginal land. As these costs increased, profits would tend to fall.

Consequently, in so far as Ricardo (with Smith) identified prosperity with capital accumulation and economic growth, and in so far as he believed that diminishing productivity in agriculture would reduce profits (while increasing rent) and therefore pose a limit to economic growth generally, he was able to conclude that industrial capitalists and owners of landed property were always in an antagonistic relation: 'The interest of the landlord is always opposed to the interest of every other class in the community' (Ricardo, 1815, quoted by Dobb, 1973, p.72). To promote capital accumulation, it was necessary to allow cheap grain imports and therefore challenge the power and interests of landowners. The class implications of progress, originally recognized by Smith, were further extended in Ricardian analyses.

It may be said of Ricardo's, just as much as of Smith's, descriptions of the emergence of capitalist market economies that they were anthropologically unsound; but, with Ricardo, the 'edifice of classical economics' became 'the most formidable conceptual instrument of destruction ever directed against an outworn order' (Polanyi, 1944, p.223).

By developing the theory of unearned income, Ricardo necessarily maintained that rent was not a cost of production (Sraffa, 1951, p.lvi). From this flows his 'theory of value' (that is, his explanation of why prices were as they were). He understood that supply-and-demand influences applied only to 'scarce' commodities and not to those which could be readily produced. For this latter category (the majority) of commodities, price was determined by the interaction of wages *and* profits, because the 'durability' or longevity of capital required in a production process would call forth a demand for recompense from the owners of capital for the entire period that these funds were not otherwise available. If not for this circumstance, the long-term exchange value of commodities would vary in proportion to the amount of labour embodied directly and indirectly in their production.

Whereas Smith had allowed that the exchange value of two commodities whose process of production involved the use of capital would not correspond to the amount of labour involved, Ricardo disagreed. Even when tools and equipment are involved, he claimed, exchange will tend to be in accordance with the quantities of labour used unless the proportions of capital in each activity are massively unequal. When the ratio of capital to labour is altered, the exchange values will tend to depart from labour quantities embodied in the products, but not significantly. Ricardo's purpose was not to defend a labour theory of value but to deploy it. He wanted to be able to trace the effects of any imaginable change in wages on price or profit levels. The implication of the labour theory of value for Ricardo was that an increase in wage levels would not increase prices but reduce profits (because exchange values were determined by the quantity, not the cost, of labour). This would be especially so where large amounts of capital were involved in production; less so when labour's proportionate share in production was below the average for the economy. There would therefore be occasions when prices would decrease in response to a rise in wages (Dobb, 1973, pp.80-2). This model of the interdependence between wages and profits rested on abstract reasoning and simplifying assumptions – but it allowed Ricardo a logically coherent way of explaining profits as a residual after the payment of wages. It therefore served a specific analytical purpose whose relevance diminishes once cyclical fluctuations in capitalist development and independent explanations for profits are introduced (Deane, 1978, p.68), or when the given relationships between an economic structure of dominance and distribution were called into question.

That there is a class-specific content in the writings of the classical economists is clear when consideration is given to the changing political function of this advocacy as capitalist economic behaviour became consolidated in the nineteenth century. Joan Robinson has noted this shift in progressive thought:

> Ricardo existed at a particular point when English history was going round a corner so sharply that the progressive and the reactionary positions changed place in a generation. He was just at the corner where the capitalists were about to supersede the old landed aristocracy as the effective ruling class. Ricardo was on the progressive side. His chief preoccupation was to show that landlords were parasites on society. In doing so he was to some extent the champion of the capitalists. They were part of the productive forces as against the parasites. He was pro-capitalist as against the landlords more than he was pro-worker as against capitalists . . . Ricardo was followed by two able and well-trained pupils – Marx and Marshall. Meanwhile English history had gone right round the corner, and landlords were not any longer the question. Now it was capitalists. Marx turned Ricardo's argument round this way: capitalists are very much like landlords. And Marshall turned it round the other way: landlords are very much like capitalists (Robinson, 1935, p.267)

The two consequent streams in political economy (Marxism and orthodoxy) are respectively attempts to defend the class emphasis in economic analysis or to purge it.

Marx and the critique of political economy

Karl Marx (1818–83) had considerable respect for the contributions to political economy of Smith and Ricardo. He also extended much of this respect to capitalism itself. It was a progressive step in a chain of social evolution which, although it created a new class of exploited participants in economic activity, had also, in permitting the further development of skills, techniques and capacities for material wealth, liberated a greater proportion of the population than ever before. This liberty was for the majority, however, only notional. Beneath the formal freedoms of market exchange and free contract there remained a realm of substantive suppression, specific, Marx argued, to capitalist social relations.

For Marx, the classical economists were correct to point out the positive aspects of capitalism; but this was only part of the task of political economy. Marx wanted to 'complete' the project begun by Smith and Ricardo: this is what his 'critique' implied. As Dobb has put it:

> In demonstrating the laws of laissez faire [the classical economists] had provided a critique of previous orders of society; but they had not provided an historical critique of capitalism itself. This latter remained to be done in order to give capitalism its proper place in historical evolution and to provide a key to the forecast of its future (1937, p.55).

Ultimately, the central thrust of Marx's analysis of the dynamics of capitalist development was to demonstrate that however progressive a force it had been and despite its transformative powers, capitalism was in the long term an unsustainable mode of production. Capitalism was not the end point of human and societal development. It was a mode of production which had allowed the unfolding of forces of production to an historically unprecedented extent; but it was a system whose internal structure would ensure that it would, one day, like all previously existing modes of production, be transcended.

In common with his classical precursors, therefore, Marx was concerned with dynamic and long-term questions: growth, accumulation, distribution, crisis, stagnation. Like the classical economists, his analysis relied on a class-based model; moreover, he used the 'power of abstraction' to highlight relationships which would be presumed to remain operative even when the multifarious complexities of the real world were conceded. It is clear, then, that Marx did not set out to develop a theory of class formation or class structure. He used notions of class that were taken from the extant critiques of the French Revolution and from Smith and Ricardo and modified in his own deployment of them. By distinguishing between a social class and its conventional role in production, although his fundamental intention was to analyse the trajectory of capitalist development and not to produce a comprehensive and coherent theory of class, his analysis initiated this account. Once questions concerning the value of different social classes' contributions were raised, critical theory could not be avoided. (We will consider the ambiguities and inadequacies of his class analysis in chapter 2.) For Marx, capital accumulation always implied exploitation of labour. His critique argued that the eventual effect of economic growth itself would be to displace from capital accumulation and material progress the social conditions which allowed a minority of owners exclusive access to the rewards of the historical processes of growth and transformation.

14

Marx's point of departure from the political economy of Smith and Ricardo concerns the problem of 'the origins of profit'. Marx wanted to explore the presumed analogy between rent as a distinctive category of (unearned) income in Ricardo's work and the existence of profit as a distinctive category of income accruing to the owners of capital. Clearly, Marx also regarded profit as a form of unearned income: it accrued to the owners of capital not by virtue of any productive contribution they themselves had made, but by virtue of sheer ownership. Whereas Ricardo had provided a theory of rent which did not regard it as a residual form of income, Marx considered that the origins of profit, also, needed to be explained in unique terms.

The question posed a puzzle because, in a free market economy, exchange took place on the basis of 'equivalent for equivalent' and was voluntary. Marx looked to the social relations in capitalist society, to the class structure, in order to establish the analogy between the existence of a surplus in earlier forms of class society (rent) with the existence of profits in capitalist conditions. He therefore derived the distinction between labour and labour power. Under capitalist social relations, owners of means of production buy labourers' capacities to work (labour power) and non-owners of means of production sell, not themselves, but their labour power. Labour power hence becomes a commodity – but a unique commodity: one which, in use, can create additional value. The exchange value of labour power is less than the value of labour.

This is the origin of Marx's labour theory of value. For Marx, value is what is created when labour is applied to raw materials or means of production. Like Ricardo, Marx believed that only labour could create value. Value is the quality that something acquires when it has had labour applied to it. Resources in their natural state do not have 'value' in this sense; they acquire 'value' only when and in so far as labour has transformed them from idle objects to instruments of social utility. Only when labour works upon things, do they acquire value; value is what labour creates and only labour can create it. Nor is capital inherently productive. Until it is inserted into capitalist social relations, 'capital' is merely tools, means of production, raw materials, etc. For Marx, then, 'value' has a very precise meaning; it is not intended to do more than indicate that a certain qualitative transformation occurs when labour power is used. Consequently, labour becomes considered a highly specific factor in production.

When labour power, in the context of a production process, produces a surplus beyond that necessary to replenish the equipment and raw materials depleted and the value of subsistence for workers, the relations between the owners of the means of production and the owners of the labour power assume a 'value form'. In contrast to earlier forms of society where part of a period's produce was annexed by a lord or master, in capitalist society surplus product when realized in the sale of commodities, takes the form of surplus value. Surplus in capitalist society does not consist of quantities of products but takes on a 'value form' (Dobb, 1937, p.59; Bradley and Howard, 1982, p.4). It is worth noting that Marx did not claim that all prices reflected labour-embodied values, primarily because market competition would tend to equalize profits across the economy and therefore redistribute the surplus value that was produced in individual enterprises. Marx did not claim either that *all* labour produced 'value' or that labour which did not produce value was unnecessary or useless.

With the (admittedly abstract) category of value, Marx proceeded to detail some fundamental relations that would pertain in a capitalist economy if it was to work satisfactorily. In these analyses he went considerably further than Smith or Ricardo in elaborating the economic consequences of the class relations of capitalism as fundamentally asymmetrical.

In the normal course of its operations, capitalism needs to ensure both production and reproduction. Reproduction, in economic terms, involves the replacement of any worn-out machinery and equipment as well as provision for (subsistence) wages for the workforce. Hence, any period's output would necessarily need to include components to cover these two types of production. Marx refers to means of production and raw materials as 'constant capital' and to labour power as 'variable capital'. In addition to these two inputs to production which need to be replenished by eventual revenues, there will normally be a 'surplus' which, once produced is appropriated by capitalists to be used either productively (that is, reinvested) or unproductively (that is, consumed by the capitalist class). Symbolically, therefore, it is possible to refer to the flow of 'production in any period as the sum of these three components of production, 'C + V + S'.

Marx then manipulates these symbols to represent, respectively, the rate of profit $\frac{S}{C+V}$, the rate of surplus value (or rate of exploitation) $\frac{S}{V}$ and the organic composition of capital $\frac{C}{V}$. One of the purposes of this manipulation is to allow Marx to argue that if the organic composition of capital rises, then there is a tendency for the rate of profit to fall.

Marx constructs various models of a capitalist economy: 'simple commodity production'; 'simple reproduction'; and 'expanded reproduction'. His model of simple reproduction envisages a situation in which there is no growth or accumulation. Under these conditions, the system merely reproduces itself without quantitative change from one period to the next. Even under such simplified and abstracted conditions, certain crucial relationships can be demonstrated. If the economy is considered as two interconnected sectors, one producing means of production ('capital' goods) and the other producing means of subsistence ('consumption' goods), it is possible to establish a definite relationship between the two parts of the economy. The intersectoral relations implied by this formulation need to be ensured for conditions of stability to prevail.

Marx's point in this exercise is to suggest that even under conditions of 'simple' reproduction (no growth or accumulation) the conditions are so specific as to be met only by accident. There are no mechanisms in a normal capitalist economy to guarantee that these conditions will be met; therefore, crisis in the form of sectoral imbalance (disproportionality) is likely.

When a more complex (and more realistic) model is used, we can presume that the consequent relationships between the relevant sectors of production will be even more complex and even more unlikely to be secured. Crisis is even more likely. In *Capital II* (1885), Marx sets out the conditions for expanded reproduction in order to show that capital accumulation cannot continue indefinitely without crisis (McFarlane, 1982, pp.153-63).

It is clear that Marx's abstract analysis of the operation of capitalist economies and of their dynamic tendencies pointed only to the formal likelihood of periodic or general crises and did not outline in systematic detail the actual causes or courses of those crises which were likely to develop. This is partially because, as for the normal operation of a capitalist economy in its specific political and institutional setting, the precise form of the economic developments which give rise to actual crises are not knowable in advance; they do not feature in the models Marx uses. What Marx's abstract model does is to indicate that any disruption to the valorization process – by which capital is advanced for commodity production, those commodities are sold, a surplus is realized and the surplus subsequently reinvested – will initiate either a contraction in investment or over-production of commodities which in turn can prefigure crises of a more general nature. We have already seen that the conditions for continued production and reinvestment are so specific as to be capable of being met only under quite extraordinary and unlikely circumstances; we will outline in chapter 9 the reasons why stability in capitalist development requires constant, even increasing, accumulation and growth. However, none of the models which produce these conclusions is able to specify precisely the form, effects, duration, timing or extent of crisis in particular economies. The range of institutional responses is broad enough, the political structures compatible with capitalism are diverse enough and the strength and effectivity of class struggle are emphatic enough to preclude a specifiable general pattern of capitalist crisis. None the less, certain tendencies and potentials resultant upon the class-specific orientation of capitalist investment decisions can be noted.

The theory of economic crisis in Marx's work is somewhat equivocal. Although it is clear that the dynamic tendencies of capitalism as a system of social and economic relationships are affected by the continuing development of the forces of production, it is far from clear whether the resulting dislocations in this development path would produce merely periodic and continuing crises or usher in a final, somewhat apocalyptic, transformation of the capitalist mode of production.

In a much quoted and flamboyant statement of the tendencies he envisaged, Marx seems to suggest that a conjuncture of economic crisis and social upheaval would bring forth, quite dramatically and rapidly, the demise of capitalism. In a short chapter of *Capital I* entitled 'The Historical Tendency of Capitalist Accumulation', the results of capitalist competition are presented in this way:

> Along with the constant decrease in the number of capitalist magnates, who usurp and monopolize all the advantages of this process of transformation, the mass of misery, oppression, slavery, degradation and exploitation grows; but with this there also grows the revolt of the working class, a class constantly increasing in numbers, and trained, united and organized by the very mechanism of the capitalist process of production. The monopoly of capital becomes a fetter upon the mode of production which has flourished alongside and under it. The centralization of the means of production and the socialization of labour reach a point at which they become incompatible with their capitalist integument. This integument is burst asunder. The knell of capitalist private property sounds. The expropriators are expropriated (Marx, 1976, p.929).

As we will argue later, capitalist enterprises are becoming larger and a tendency to automation seems to be producing higher ratios of capital to labour within them. It is even evident that in the long term, without substantial usurpation of the conditions which define an economy as capitalist, the numbers of people more or less permanently unable to secure satisfactory employment could increase. In these circumstances, it would not be unreasonable to claim that the ways in which productive activity under capitalist conditions is carried out would impose constraints on further intensification and development of that productive capacity.

If the social relations of capitalist economic activity were to impede production, then presumably some significant alteration in the structure of those relations would be sought either by organized capital, or organized labour. The conditions of capitalist production could be altered. As we will argue in the final chapter, such transformations are possible – for reasons not entirely at variance with those advanced by Marx. This is, however, a very generous interpretation of the passage and the argument we have produced from Marx. Other commentators, taking Marx's suggestions more literally could well feel entitled to claim that the picture of crisis-led transition from one mode of production to another is both unscientifically formulated and unlikely to eventuate.

There exist the seeds of a more convincing account of transition in Marx's earlier 1859 preface to *A Contribution to the Critique of Political Economy*. The same structural basis for transition exists in this passage, but the process seems to be more considered and less apocryphal:

> At a certain stage of development, the material productive forces of society come into conflict with the existing relations of production or – this merely expresses the same thing in legal terms – with the property relations within the framework of which they have operated hitherto. From forms of development of the productive forces these relations turn into fetters. Then begins an era of social revolution. The changes in the economic foundation lead sooner or later to the transformation of the whole immense superstructure . . .
>
> No social order is ever destroyed before all the productive forces for which it is sufficient have been developed, and new superior relations of production never replace older ones before the material conditions for their existence have matured within the framework of the old society (Marx, 1970a, p.21).

This formulation of the likely process of crisis and transition could almost have been extrapolated from the analyses of the rise of capitalism as presented by the classical economists. Marx's theory derives its strength none the less not from historically informed speculation, but from the logic of the technical apparatus he developed in the volumes of *Capital*. There is, as

19

well, the hypothesis that the processes of maturation of an economic system can nurture social arrangements appropriate to its successor. It is clear that class conflicts would play an important role in such a process.

The implication of this suggestion is that the role of social classes as contributors to production processes and as constituent elements in 'civil society' (those dimensions of everyday social existence not directly related to economic or political matters) will not be fixed but constantly changing. In general, capitalist economies allow a dominant role to capitalists – the bourgeoisie; and an emergent role to the newest class – the proletariat. However, Marx seems to be indicating that these roles will themselves pass through various definable stages as capitalist economic development takes place. In its earlier stages, capitalism was developed under an ideology, if not reality, which promoted wholly market modes of regulation. Later, as crisis tendencies are averted by internal or external interventions, market regulation can be expected to give way to political drive. Consequently, the various instances of capitalist crisis may be purely transitory (cyclical) or their existence may anticipate more dramatic social change. How might structural imbalances and instabilities contribute to any 'final' transformation of capitalism? What scope is there for class mobilization to dramatically affect processes which would unfold in a regime of unimpeded laissez faire?

The possibility, amounting to virtual inevitability, of disproportionality between crucial sectors of a capitalist economy will be bound to multiply as the industrial structure of an economy develops and as the relations which need to be satisfied to ensure stability become increasingly complex. This is demonstrated in Marx's models of expanded reproduction (economic growth) where accumulation from one period to the next produces increasingly complex relations between the relevant sectors of production. Marx's models show that in an uncoordinated market economy, the conditions for steady accumulation are unlikely to be met; crises are inevitable.

The form of crisis is variable, however. Sectoral imbalances may take the form of a decline in profitability. There is sometimes said to be a long-term tendency for the rate of profit to fall. This 'tendency' can have many causes. As a result, it is necessary to distinguish between the forms of crisis and their causes (Hussain, 1977). The ability of political interventions by either capital or labour successfully to institute counter-tendencies in crisis situations will be discussed in our final chapter.

Apart from the sectoral imbalance (disproportionality) there exist other conditions which could tend to lower profits. Marx assumes that capitalists' proclivity to increase the ratio of capital equipment to labour (to increase the organic composition of capital) is such a tendency. With a constant rate of exploitation, any decrease in the proportion of labour (variable capital) will undermine the extent to which labour's work with raw materials and machinery creates value above and beyond that which is needed to replenish stocks of equipment and raw materials used up during the production process. If this surplus value declines, then, in ordinary circumstances so will capitalists' profits, although there is not a fixed relation between surplus value and money profits which finally accrue to capitalists. Profits must inevitably be derived from the difference between the value created by labour and the portion of that value which is used to offset the costs of production. This is an issue which Marx adopted from the classical writers. 'In place of Ricardo's resort to diminishing returns, Marx substituted the effect of technological change in raising the ratio of constant to variable capital' (Dobb, 1973, p.157).

Profits do not necessarily have a long-term tendency to decline as a result of increasing bargaining strength and militancy of labour (Glyn and Sutcliffe, 1972). Wages and profits do not constitute a fixed amount of income in such a way that struggle over them becomes a zero-sum game. In some circumstances both may rise together; in other circumstances both may fall. We will return to a discussion of these circumstances in chapter 9.

There is yet another factor contributing to crisis (and to falling profits) in a capitalist economy. This is the tendency for over-production or 'under-consumption' which also featured in the works of earlier political economists. Marx did not believe that periodically recurrent tendencies towards stagnation would bring about the ultimate demise of capitalism. In fact, the argument that insufficient purchasing power would accrue to consumers to purchase the full volume of production output is a feature of Keynesian rather than Marxian analysis (Bleaney, 1976). In Marx's view, wages would not remain fixed at a level which would permit such a crisis to develop. None the less, as we argue in the final chapter, tendencies towards this type of imbalance and the inconsistent responses by capital or the state to such situations are not without significance for the ongoing accumulation of capital.

It is well known that Marx recognized that any crisis tendency such as those mentioned here could be countered, within the process of private capital accumulation, by either deliberately initiated or automatically generated 'counter-tendencies'. Tendencies which countered crisis could take the form of increases in the rate of exploitation, a cheapening of the elements of constant capital, reorganization of the labour process, state intervention to redress sectoral disproportionality, industry subsidies, capital-saving (as well as further labour-saving) technological innovation or the expansion of markets (Dobb, 1973, p.157). The process of centralization and concentration of capital itself can act in this way by making individual capitalist enterprises less susceptible to the forces which simultaneously create future crisis tendencies for capital as a whole. No particular crisis situation is ever likely to run its full course without the emergence of some of these counter-tendencies to stave off such crisis. Massive crises may well be averted indefinitely – for a century or more. None the less, the analysis which Marx provides of the 'contradictions', or the unlikelihood of stability when investments are controlled privately, remains valid.

The emergence of the modern state as an economic manager – as an agency of regulation – has itself become a contributor to crisis through its ability in some circumstances to implement anti-crisis strategies. Despite its ability to intervene at appropriate moments to avert crisis, the state is ultimately unable to remove all impediments to continuing capital accumulation. There is evidence to suggest that successive waves of crisis-mediating state interventions either make subsequent measures more difficult or themselves displace crisis tendencies to other terrains (Wright, 1978, pp.154-63). The development of capitalism and the changing role of the state do pose strategic political dilemmas, however. In such circumstances, alternative strategies for capital accumulation may be proposed, such as we consider in the final chapter.

None of the available crisis theories seeks to explain every likely development in capitalist economies. It seems that at different stages of capitalist development, different 'impediments' emerge and different 'solutions' may be found. However, each imposed resolution of a crisis tendency, each evocation of a counter-tendency, seems sooner or later to set in train further impediments and further forms of resolution. 'The impediments to accumulation can be considered *contradictions* in accumulation rather than merely obstacles to accumulation. They are contra-dictions because the "solutions" to a particular impediment become themselves impediments to accumulation' (Wright, 1978, p.112). As we will argue later, it is class relations which are influential in the operation of such impediments and solutions.

Classical and Marxian political economy both recognize the value and progressive nature of the epoch of industrial capitalism which appeared concomitantly with the rise of the bourgeoisie and the emergence of the industrial proletariat. As capitalism develops, the bourgeoisie begins to adopt a less progressive role, even retarding its own interests in production to prevent conflicts produced by unchanging 'social relations'. As capitalist forces of production (technique, modes of organization, forms of capital accumulation) begin to outstrip the property and social relations in which they were nurtured, the working class may begin to use the opportunity to take a more assertive, conscious and effectual role in economic life. Perhaps the working class, the class that came into existence with the Industrial Revolution, can be said to be fully functioning as a social class only when the bourgeois conditions which produced capitalist prosperity begin to be dismantled by new conditions these very achievements have created (Schumpeter, 1943; Simpson, 1983).

To a large extent this is implied by the very first sentence of *Capital I*. Marx wanted to examine conditions in societies in which the capitalist mode of production prevailed. There is little reason to expect either the influence of class conflict on the economy or the influence of economic processes on class structure to be the same in societies where the capitalist mode of production prevailed differentially. Successive chapters will explore in some detail the persistence in such societies of a class structure more complex than the one idealized in the models Marx deployed. Even if these more complex structures are not a permanent culmination of class formation, their apparent ossification in contemporary capitalist societies has consequences which warrant investigation. However, neither the evolution of class structure nor the developmental phases of capital accumulation follow predetermined trajectories.

Instability and inequality

It is not only Marxian analysis which suggests that ongoing stable growth of capitalism is unlikely. The resurgence of interest in growth during and after the Second World War produced models which indicated that the conditions postulated as being necessary for steady growth would be, once recognized, unlikely to eventuate. If the rate of growth 'warranted' by producers in view of their capital investment and savings plans exceeds the 'natural' rate of growth allowed by population and technological conditions, then there would be a persistent tendency towards depression and chronic unemployment; if the 'warranted' rate of growth were to fall below the 'natural' rate, then inflationary booms were likely (Dobb, 1973, pp.226-8). If the accumulation plans which entrepreneurs need to ensure their capacity is fully utilized exceed those technically possible, then unemployment and downturn will ensue; if the accumulation plans which suit entrepreneurs fall below the rate needed to keep up with population growth and technological change, inflationary booms caused by shortages and speculation will follow. Any departure from the growth path appropriate to entrepreneurs is highly unstable.

> The economy must continually expand. . . . The economy finds itself in a serious dilemma: if sufficient investment is not forthcoming today, unemployment will be here today. But if enough is invested today, still more will be needed tomorrow. . . . Investment is at the same time a cure for the disease and the cause of even greater ills in the future (Domar, 1957, quoted in Dobb, 1973, p.229).

The upshot of these Keynesian-influenced growth theories was to show that capitalist economies do not tend towards equilibrium and social harmony. For recent growth theorists, equilibrium conditions cannot be met. Hence, instability in capitalist economies is inherent. Investment decisions made in the past establish a pattern of industrial activity which cannot be readily altered. Additionally, this prevents mobility of capital to the extent required for alleged market mechanisms to perform their equilibrating role. At the same time, investment decisions made in the present (on the basis of expectations of future private profitability which may be disappointed) are likely even to enhance immobility. Steady growth is unlikely because, contrary to market principles, there is no neutral starting-point for investment; decisions are always made in the context of past social, economic and technical conditions (Asimakopulos, 1977, p.384). The desire of enterprises to accumulate can always, potentially, produce socially deleterious outcomes. To the extent that harmony is not a normal expectation, political conflict is always incipient. Unemployment is a permanent possibility.

It is conventional in neoclassical economic theory to presume that 'the market' is a neutral mechanism of resource allocation which uses non-prescriptive means (the 'invisible hand') to harmonize competing interests, generate rational prices as the basis for rational decisions and set in motion self-adjusting tendencies towards 'full employment equilibrium'. In this view, distribution of income is in accordance with principles of social optimality: profits are always the fair and just return to the owners of capital because they represent the marginal product of capital; wages are always equal to the marginal contribution made by labour to production. The marginal productivity theory of distribution is anti-classical (neoclassical) in that it eschews the large questions of growth, distribution, accumulation and crisis which preoccupied the classical theorists and ignores the historical, institutional and class determinants of income distribution. Its intention in redefining the problem of economics as the 'science of allocation' was to avoid the moral and political problems of discussing or accounting for the existing state of inequitable affairs. Orthodox theory, as it became known, insisted that the large macro questions were 'too hard' and that a more scientifically respectable orientation would be to consider not why production and distribution are as they are, but rather how decisions should be made in the real world. The matter of production itself and the class relations within the labour process dropped out of the agenda, to be replaced by questions of resource allocation in the context of scarcity and competing demands.

Of course political implications of this reorientation persist. Economies were to be seen as places where relations between inputs and outputs were demonstrated. Labour, along with capital, became a 'factor of production' entitled to market-determined rewards in accordance with marginal (not historical) contributions. This conceptual identification, albeit economistically over-determined, of a factor of production with a social class, was forgotten or repressed. Eventually, it would become the legitimation for the conceptually suborned inequities of class. In time, it seemed as if the repressed category was simply absent rather than opaque. In the marginalist model of distribution, classes do not appear. Production itself is not an issue. Resources are allocated; inputs are transformed; an output appears which, when sold, returns profits to capital and wages to labour.

Criticisms of this basis for legitimating the class distribution of income derive from the classical and Marxian perspectives. These perspectives have never regarded capital as a fixed physical entity or as a fixed sum of money. The amount of capital in existence is a changing quantity subject to fluctuations in economic activity in general and to profit/interest rates in particular. The amount of capital available cannot be determined independently of its productivity. Under these circumstances, it is not reasonable for neoclassical theorists to claim that profits are the reward for the productivity of capital. The concept of capital cannot be used in the way that it needs to be for such a marginal productivity theory to be valid. Capital in use is a collection of factories, machines or money, together with their attendant social relations, in various stages of usefulness and deterioration. Their capitalized value cannot be used as an indicator of the aggregate

25

total of capital in existence. If there is no meaning that can be attached to the value of capital, there is commensurately no meaning that can be given to profits as its marginal productivity, nor to wages as a fair and final reflection of labour's contribution (Robinson, 1954, 1974, 1979; Hunt and Schwartz, 1972; Harcourt and Laing, 1971; Hunt, 1979; Harcourt, 1975, 1977b). The only other possible explanation for income distribution is to regard wages and profits as the outcome of institutional class struggle. As a result of these criticisms it is no longer possible to claim that income distribution can be explained independently of economic institutions, economic history and all the other social and political arrangements which determine the structure of economic activity. Hence, we need to endorse the revival of political economy in the tradition of classical and Marxian analyses, to determine how classes are formed, the effects their formation and action can have on the economy and the effects that economic fluctuations – especially the current recession – can have on collective political behaviour.

There is no corresponding need to regard every classical utterance as the final adjudication on these class issues. In some respects, the founding statements are incomplete and unhelpful; in other respects, there may be contemporary experience which demands the inclusion of new concepts, new analyses, new data and new strategic consequences. However, the reality of class societies as structures of power, rule and domination grounded in economic patterns of action, should not be overlooked. These structures exhibit a complexity irreducible to the classes of classical political economy. For instance, to the extent that national income has definite components of profits and wages and other forms of personal income, variations in the distribution of these will have to be mapped through the political process on to a complex class structure, if anything like the realism of classical political economy is to be integrated into empirically adequate sociological analysis. It was the relation between macro questions of growth, accumulation, distribution and crisis, and the structure of classes inscribed in national income accounts, which signalled the innovations of classical political economy.

Marx may be said to have provided a bridge between classical political economy and modern sociology. His debt to the former is evident in the continuity with which these macro questions are posed in his work. Sociology enters into the picture through the way in which Marx's treatment of the 'two great classes' becomes a landmark in the theorization of class structure. Evident continuities will be found in Weber's analysis of economic domination. A more empirically oriented concern with social structure produces an equally evident discontinuity: the structure of classes, henceforth, cannot be adequately represented in a binary model. From this flows the central analytical and empirical tension of subsequent developments. Analytically, class structure has to be conceptualized in more complex items. Empirically, in political representation, its traces are still visible in parties founded on a simpler model of the 'two great classes'. This tension is one of our overall themes. Its resolution, we would argue, is analytically implicit in the classical tradition of political economy. Empirically, its realization remains a central issue of class politics and the economy.

2 Marx and Engels: class formation, class structure and class struggle

The analysis of class which emerged with the tradition of political economy initiated by Adam Smith and David Ricardo was continued by Karl Marx and Friedrich Engels later in the nineteenth century. Despite the fact that no formal identification of class analysis appeared in the latters' work the project of such an analysis is indissolubly linked with their confident assertion in *The Manifesto of the Communist Party* (1848) that 'the history of all hitherto existing societies is the history of class struggles.' It is from this assertion that much of the subsequent elaboration of class analysis begins. At least three stages of analytical development have been identified in their work. These progressively invoke varying problems with the relationship between classes and their economic context. It must be repeated, however, that Marx's and Engels's primary analytical purpose was not to provide a systematic analysis of social class but to examine the salience of the presumed fact of class structure for the development of dynamic tendencies in a typical capitalist economy.

Simple abstract model

In those youthful writings, published before the early revolutionary expectations of 1848 were disappointed – principally *The Economic and Philosophical Manuscripts* (1844), *The Poverty of Philosophy* (1847), and *The Manifesto of the Communist Party* (1848) – several themes emerged from the discussion of social class. These derive from the central theoretical proposition which Marx and Engels use to illuminate the bourgeois epoch: that 'it has simplified the class antagonisms. Society as a whole is more and more splitting-up into two great classes directly facing each other: bourgeoisie and proletariat' (Marx and Engels, 1969, p.49).

In a subsequent footnote, Engels clarified these key terms:

By 'bourgeoisie' is meant the class of modern capitalists, owners of the means of social production and employers of wage labour. By proletariat, the class of modern wage labourers who, having no means of production of their own, are reduced to selling their labour power in order to live (Marx and Engels, 1969, p.48, fn.1).

It is clear that this dichotomous representation of bourgeoisie and proletariat in terms of the ownership/non-ownership of property is not a literal description of any actually existing capitalist society even in its classical period. It is an abstraction from existing societies. Even in the *Manifesto* there was a recognition of class elements not described: for instance, 'the lower strata of the middle class – the small tradespeople, shopkeepers, and retired tradesmen generally, the handicraftsmen and peasants' (1969, p.56). These strata were expected to 'decay' into the proletariat, along with 'fresh elements of enlightenment and progress' drawn from the ruling class.

This representation was an abstraction in a further sense. Marx and Engels identified a tendency, abstracted and projected into 'the self-conscious, independent movement of the vast majority, in the interests of the immense majority' (1969, p.60). Realization of this tendency is precipitated unwittingly by the bourgeoisie as it undercuts 'the isolation of the labourers, due to competition, by their revolutionary combination, due to association . . . what the bourgeoisie, therefore, produces, above all, is its own gravediggers' (1969, p.61).

Marx and Engels anticipated that the burial could be hastened by the abject misery of the working class, imposed on its members of necessity by the *separation of capital, ground rent, and labour'* (Marx, 1973a, p.65). Labour was able to live only through the sale of its capacity to work, thus *'demand for men necessarily governs the production of men, as of every other commodity.* Should supply greatly exceed demand, a section of the workers sinks into beggary or starvation' (Marx, 1973a, p.65). The forms of income associated with bourgeois forms of property would increasingly skew towards the owners of the means of production, away from the owners of what Marx was later to term 'labour power'. The only exception to this, Marx conceded, would be a society in which wealth is increasing. In the absence of such growth, Marx concluded that misery would be inevitable for the working class, not as its ultimate destiny but certainly as part of its trajectory. The increasing concentration of fewer and fewer capitalists into bigger and bigger consolidated units of production would necessarily facilitate the organization of the working class in its struggle against its conditions of existence: 'this mass is thus already a class as against capital, but not yet for itself. In the struggle . . . this mass becomes united, and constitutes itself as a class for itself. The interests it defends become class interests' (Marx, 1956, p.173). None of this abstract formulation is self-evident.

It was this transformation from a class 'in itself' to a class 'for itself' which Marx saw as heralding the declining power and eventual interment of the bourgeoisie. Despite an expanding division of labour, workers would realize that their misery and alienation, although experienced personally and privately, were in fact common. Other workers, comrades in the concentration of labour in the large factories, were experiencing the same alienation from their selves, their products, their work and their social life. With the common realization of a condition of rightlessness *vis-à-vis* capital, a class would emerge 'for itself' from what was previously a class only in an objective but unaware sense. Marx is suggesting the objective possibility of a working-class-based political economy. This would be one where the proletariat consciously would be able to choose the trajectory of social and economic development. As such, it would be a very different set of choices from those pertaining at any stage prior to the full maturity of capitalism, when the bourgeois class clearly would be expected to retain this dominance. Such a development of working-class politics would hasten the last rites of the bourgeoisie. The grave would be dug by the changing social relations within both the factory and economy at large coming into contradiction with 'the productive powers already acquired'.

The argument suggests that to the extent that workers become 'socialized', to the extent that they begin to acknowledge a common experience, then the 'social relations of production', the established hierarchical organization of labour and capital, would be subject to potential challenge.

Many significant issues were introduced in these early texts which, despite their recognized naivety, provide rich exegetical yields, as Hall (1978) has demonstrated. Amongst these we may note, first, the problem of the middle classes. Although Engels's addendum goes some way to identifying the working class (or proletariat) and the ruling class (or bourgeoisie), it says nothing of other classes – particularly middle strata. Second, there is the question of class organization. In 1844 Marx was pessimistic about the possibilities of working-class organization as compared to that of the bourgeoisie: 'Combination among the capitalists is customary and effective; workers' combination is prohibited and painful in its consequences for them' (Marx, 1973a, p.65). By 1847 and the completion of his critique of the anarchist Proudhon, he was far more alert to the possibility of working-class organization as we can see in the stress that he puts on consciousness with respect to 'class-in-itself' becoming 'class-for-itself'. In 1848, with the ten-point programme of the *Manifesto*, Marx and Engels had produced a programme around which they believed working-class organization could be mobilized (Marx and Engels, 1969, pp.69-70). This raised the issue of the type of programme around which conscious class awareness might be organized. Third, class analysis involved 'objective' and 'subjective' dimensions. An important question arises from the articulation between the problem of the middle classes and the organization of consciousness: what was the relation between the 'objective' class position of the reasonably unequivocal identification, in property terms, of bourgeoisie and proletariat by Engels and the 'subjective' consciousness of the agents who fill these class positions?

Complex descriptive model

Marx's views were further developed in a series of articles written after the defeats of 1848. A less schematic, less assertive view of class and class formation emerged from Marx's examination of these political events in France. In February 1848, in Paris, the regime of Louis Philippe was overthrown and a provisional government proclaimed. In June an armed insurrection of artisans was crushed. Between these two events a complex history was inscribed which, in Marx's view, laid the foundations for the coup d'état of December 1851, by which Bonaparte assumed power. Marx attempted to explain why the confident aspirations expressed in the *Manifesto* seemed so ill-timed. With the spectre of communism that he had hoped would haunt Europe seemingly suppressed, he provided an account and analysis of the defeat in two articles published in 1850 and 1852 respectively as 'The Class Struggles in France' and 'The Eighteenth Brumaire of Louis Bonaparte'.

In these articles Marx argued that the defeats of the insurrectionary movement of 1848 were due to the immaturity of existing class relationships. Sharpened contradictions had not yet produced the two great classes which the *Manifesto* had anticipated. The *Manifesto* was far more certain about the projection and immediate materialization of these tendencies than was its author just three years later. The defeats were the result, he maintained, of 'pre-revolutionary traditional appendages, results of social relationships which had not yet come to the point of sharp class antagonisms' (Marx, 1969b, p.322). Class organization was clearly dependent upon stages of societal development which could not be willed by political fervour alone.

The spectre, it seemed, had more time to wait in the wings, the ceremony taking somewhat longer than anticipated. Marx, of course, was to maintain the latter. 'The development of the industrial proletariat is, in general, conditioned by the development of the industrial bourgeoisie' (Marx, 1969b, pp.331-2). It was not the industrial bourgeoisie that ruled in France in 1848, but the financial section of it: 'bankers, stock-exchange kings, railway kings, owners of coal and iron mines and forests, a part of the landed proprietors that rallied round them – the so-called *finance aristocracy*' (1969b, p.323). Fully developed forces of production could not be forged under such auspices. The industrial bourgeoisie, petty bourgeoisie, the peasantry, their ideological representatives and spokespersons – all were specified by Marx at this time, but their class places and therefore their developmental functions remained to be formally identified. Their political role, however, did appear vital. While the industrial bourgeoisie formed part of the official opposition, the petty bourgeoisie and peasantry were excluded from political power altogether. Although the Parisian labouring class made the February revolution, it lost the republic. It would be wrong, however to conclude that this made the 1848 revolution 'proletarian'; the majority of its protagonists was, as the record of those who died on the barricades demonstrates, not so much industrial and proletarian as artisanal in composition.

The antagonists to whom the republic was lost comprised an alliance between the oppositional faction of the bourgeoisie, the industrialists, and the small peasant proprietors and petty bourgeoisie. Marx claimed that this alliance was cemented because of the predominance of the financial bourgeoisie, which he maintained, was driven by its 'immediate' rather than 'fundamental' interests. Immediately, the allied struggle was against what Marx termed 'capital's secondary modes of exploitation, that of the peasants against the usury in mortgages or of the petty bourgeoisie against the wholesale dealer, banker and manufacturer' (1969b, p.332).

Fundamentally, Marx maintained that the peasants and petty bourgeoisie, 'standing between the proletariat and the bourgeoisie', would, in the as yet unrealized trajectory, be forced to attach themselves to the proletariat as the 'protagonist' of the 'mass of the nation', rather than cement an alliance with the industrial faction of the bourgeoisie against the immediate enemy of the financier. The industrial working class was still in the process of formation.

Returning to the situation before 1848, Marx also identified the relationship between the ruling-class faction, the financial bourgeoisie, and the state. Rather than the state being 'merely the organized power of one class for oppressing another', as the *Manifesto* had maintained, the state was now regarded not simply as oppressive but also, and more especially, as facilitative of the ruling-class faction's economic dominance.

During 1848, the divisions between the different factions of the bourgeoisie intensified. They had already been exacerbated by the preceding two years of commercial, financial and agricultural failures. These failures had in turn intensified the demands being made by the rapidly increasing urban population upon the Parisian bourgeoisie and their state. Confronted with the common enemy of the labouring classes, the divided bourgeoisie, which was also a class still in the making, changed its tactics. It decided to mobilize support from the peasantry so that its resources would be available to pressure the government to crush the Parisian workers.

Paradoxically, given that the history of all societies was presumed to be a history of class struggle, the most significant political dramatis personae after 1848 was not a class, but an unorganized 'vast mass' which became the basis of Bonaparte's political representation:

> The small-holding peasants form a vast mass, the members of which live in similar conditions but without entering into manifold relations with one another. Their mode of production isolates them from one another instead of bringing them into mutual intercourse . . . In so far as millions of families live under economic conditions of existence that separate their mode of life, their interests, and their culture from those of the other classes and put them in hostile opposition to the latter, they form a class. In so far as there is merely a local inter-connection among these small-holding peasants and the identity of their interests begets no community, no national bond, and no political organization among them, they do not form a class. They are consequently incapable of enforcing their class interest in their own name, whether through a parliament or through a convention. They cannot represent themselves, they must be represented (Marx, 1969c, pp.377-8)

History, rather than being written by class struggle, was, in this instance, an effect of struggles between *factions* of classes, notably the bourgeoisie, whose different interests were mobilized through the state. The state, in 1851, became a state seemingly independent of class power through Bonaparte's representation of the 'vast mass' outside of class society. Marx maintained that in the long term this 'mass' would be doomed to extinction within class society, because of the post-Napoleonic division of the land, by inheritance laws, into ever-smaller parcels shared amongst the propriety peasant offspring with an 'inevitable result: progressive deterioration of agriculture, progressive indebtedness of the agriculturalist' (Marx, 1969c, p.380). With the decline of the 'vast mass', Marx argued, the state structure erected upon its back would collapse, and with it the illusion of a classless state. The anticipated collapse would be due, once more, to the inevitable trajectory of capitalist development.

Behind the bourgeoisie's support for Bonaparte, there remained one decisive factor. The development of capitalism in France after 1859 meant the making of a new working class, an industrial proletariat. Marx had argued since 1844 that it was, in a real sense, the embodiment of a negation of the existing order of property relations. It was a class which owned nothing, in distinction from all the other allies. This fact, the spectre of an emergent proletariat, more than anything else, legitimated for the bourgeoisie the pretensions, pomp and vanity of the new Bonaparte. First, they feared the spectre more than they loathed the classless 'illusion'; second, they feared their own representatives' interest in their own careers (and the continuance of the democratically based Constituent Assembly of 1848–51) would lead to concessions to the working class that would prove to be the thin edge of the socialist wedge; and third, they feared the spectre sufficiently to endorse the growth of a strong state apparatus to spy on it, repress it, ideologize to it and contain it (Perez-Diaz, 1978, pp.34-52).

What Marx's writings in this period seem to show is that there are remnants and ruins inherited from the past, which are dying out, becoming of only historical interest. The 'self-sufficiency' of the peasant family, for example, points to the existence of what Giddens (1973) has termed 'transitional classes'. Additionally, there are classes which have not yet reached historical maturity and are still being formed: on the one hand, the French peasantry; on the other, the mid-nineteenth-century French proletariat. Moreover, classes which are already formed, such as the bourgeoisie, may be internally divided around immediate interests on the lines of differing economic factions, in this instance between the industrial and financial elements.

The empirical analysis of these immediate post-1848 writings serve to define further the evident tensions and ambiguities of Marx's earlier schemata. Empirically, classes had formed less around abstractly conceived political programmes, but rather more around individual and factional opportunism. This opportunism served to obscure the clarity with which Marx conceived the structure of classes. Moreover, it demonstrated that politics was not organized around abstract programmes pitting labour against capital, so much as a battle for command and control of the state and its resources, between factions of the bourgeoisie. In other words, the assembly of politics could not be reduced to the 'objective' assembly of classes. The complex play of subjectivities and circumstances rendered opaque the reality that Marx had earlier perceived as transcendent. Class structure could not be mapped on to class consciousness; nor, in reverse, could empirical consciousness be superimposed on to theoretical structure, without considerable ingenuity in the marshalling of *ad hoc*, conjunctual explanation. Such ingenuity calls the earlier theoretical elegance and simplicity into question.

In conclusion to this section, we may note that these immediate post-*Manifesto* writings are far less programmatic than their hastily composed precursor. Moreover, analytical abstractions are gradually abandoned in favour of substantive, complex and historically specific analysis (Marx, 1973b). *Capital* presents a fusion of these two approaches.

Complex abstract model

The fusion which is achieved in *Capital* is one in which 'abstraction' is methodologically dominant. In the 'Author's Preface to the First German Edition' of 1867, it is once again pointed out that 'the power of abstraction' has to be the principal method in the analysis of economic forms:

> The subject of study in the present work is the capitalist method of production, and the relations of production and exchange appropriate to that method. The region where these relations have hitherto assumed their most typical aspects, is England. That is why English conditions have been mainly drawn upon in illustration of my theoretical disquisitions. . . . What we are concerned with primarily is, not the higher or the lower degree of development of the social antagonisms which arise out of the natural laws of capitalist production, but these laws in themselves, the tendencies which work out with an iron necessity towards an inevitable goal (Marx, 1974, p.xiix).

By the time of the second German edition of 1873, Marx responded to critics of the first edition by citing a review from a Russian newspaper with which he clearly concurs. This review stressed that forms of the evolution of social relations 'are not merely independent of the will, the consciousness and the purposes of men, but conversely, determine their will, their consciousness, and their purposes' (Marx, 1974, p.lvii). This affirms the historical materialist position first advanced clearly in Marx's preface of 1859. Analysis through abstraction does not entail as a corollary abstracted analysis – 'there are no such abstract laws . . . every historical period has laws peculiar to itself' (Marx, 1974, p.lviii). The formulation of these laws involved, as Engels's preface to Marx's *Capital* pointed out, 'a revolution in the technical terms of that science [of political economy]'. This new science will concern itself with the 'critical analysis of the actual facts, instead of writing recipes . . . for the cook-shops of the future' (Marx, 1976, p.99).

In *Capital* Marx provides his most complex and abstract representation. Unlike the earlier model this work contains its own *dynamic*: that is, it contains an explanation of the formation and transformation of class society. An explanation such as this was not possible in the earlier works because the necessary concepts for its development had not yet been forged by Marx and were not to develop in their maturity until after 1847 (Althusser, 1969). The crucial concept is the *mode of production*. This is conceptualized as the dynamic beneath the surface of concrete, historical, descriptive detail, that is, as the underlying 'motion' of what historical materialism terms the *social formation*. The former is the analytical category while the latter is the site of its actualization. In the first volume of *Capital* Marx provides an analysis of the capitalist mode of production as it developed in its specificity in the social formation of Britain. It is from this volume, in particular, that the basis for a more dynamic analysis of class emerges. However, it is only in the third volume of *Capital* that the short and incomplete fragment which is specifically on 'classes' is to be found:

> The owners merely of labour-power, owners of capital, and landowners, whose respective sources of income are wages, profit and ground rent, in other words, wage labourers, capitalists and landowners, constitute the three big classes of modern society based upon the capitalist mode of production.
>
> In England, modern society is indisputably most highly and classically developed in economic structure. Nevertheless, even here the stratification of classes does not appear in its pure

form. Middle and intermediate strata even here obliterate lines of demarcation everywhere (although incomparably less in rural districts than in the cities). However, this is immaterial for our analysis. We have seen that the continual tendency and law of development of the capitalist mode of production is more and more to divorce the means of production from labour, and more and more to concentrate the scattered means of production into capital. And to this tendency, on the other hand, corresponds the independent separation of landed property from capital and labour, or the transformation of all landed property into the form of landed property corresponding to the capitalist mode of production (Marx, 1959, p.885).

Marx indicates, however, that difference in *income* cannot be used as the basis of class identification: if this were so, it would lead to an 'infinite fragmentation' of classes. What is crucial is ownership: of labour power and capital (landed property, he notes, increasingly comes to be a form of capital). This is the basis for the transformation of the two great classes of capital and labour, bourgeois and proletarian, ruling class and working class. These classes, based on the ownership/non-ownership of the means of production, do not appear in reality in their pure form, as they do in abstraction in the model of the mode of production. The model, although its workings underlie social reality, is not precisely the equivalent of that reality. It is an analogue of inherent tendencies which will characterize any social formation organized on principles such as those formulated in their pure form in the model of the mode of production.

The primary tendency is seen to be the formation of a dichotomous class structure based on capital and labour. However, even in its 'most highly and classically developed . . . economic structure' it 'does not appear in its pure form'. The purity of the underlying form is made opaque by the existence of 'middle and intermediate strata'.

In *Theories of Surplus Value* (volume 2), Marx (1969a) suggested that these middle strata were constantly growing and that their function was to enlarge the social security and power of 'the upper ten thousand' – the ruling class. He also noted that they pressed 'like a heavy burden' on the working class. In this they would not differ essentially from non-producing and non-owning 'parasite' groups such as those providing ideological, military, religious and personal support to members of ruling groups in any other mode of production. In so far as the role and presumed allegiance of 'middle strata' have since become increasingly complex, then a more sustained analysis than Marx's is clearly required. In view of developments since the nineteenth century in all the advanced industrial capitalist societies, it would seem advisable to develop a theory of class in which the 'middle strata' can be accommodated as an essential rather than vestigial feature of class in a capitalist society. Indeed, as we shall argue, the role of the 'new middle class' or 'new petty bourgeoisie' has become central to most recent debates in social theory and analysis.

Exchange

Marx notes that if an epoch is to be recognizably capitalist, then it would need to be systematically organized around a number of specifically capitalist forms. Chief among these are competitive organizational units of capital, defined by their control of means of production. Competitition is organized through the operations of the market. In pursuit of opportunities for continuous accretion of value (valorization) antagonistic class relations are also necessarily reproduced. Under the conditions posited in the complex model this pursuit of valorization will tend to produce a constantly increasing rate of mechanization of labour and, eventually, a concentration and centralization of capital, with the differential consequences for social classes discussed in the previous chapter.

Marx's abstract model of the capitalist mode of production takes as its starting-point the most apparent feature of this mode: the 'immense collection of commodities' that it has produced. Beyond the most obvious differences between commodities – that they are different things, different objects – Marx argues that they embody an underlying similarity. This is that *all* commodities which exchange for each other on the market embody 'definite quantities of congealed labour-time', conceived as an abstract, socially average amount of labour conventionally required to produce a given commodity. All commodities have a two-fold character: their value as an inherently useful thing, their 'use value' (a functional criterion), and their 'exchange value', what they will trade for in relation to each other on the market (a potentially quantitative criterion). In a society whose products generally assume the commodity form, that is where production is primarily for exchange, rather than use, as occurs at the margins of a simple, subsistence society, exchange values represent the labour inputs of many producers, no one of whom makes the total commodity, but each of whom contributes to only a part of it.

Commodities can be exchanged by their owners and will be accepted for exchange only if owners of other commodities have a use for them and are able to exchange their commodities as well. It is money which mediates exchanges and which enables exchange to take place in a commodity-producing society.

Two types of exchange process may be distinguished. Exchange for the satisfaction of definite needs, such as buying food to eat, may be distinguished from 'buying in order to sell' where 'the end and the beginning are the same, money or exchange value and this very fact makes the movement an endless one' (Marx, 1976, p.252). Thus, the circulation of money becomes not a means to an end such as the gratification of a definite need, but an end in itself, which is ultimately limitless. This is because its ultimate end is the satisfaction of no definite need other than the constant expansion of value, or combining of labour power and means of production and exchange. Marx terms this process the 'valorization' of a given value; it can occur only through 'the constantly renewed movement':

> As the conscious bearer [*träger*] of this movement, the possessor of money becomes a capitalist. His person, or rather his pocket, is the point from which the money starts, and to which it returns . . . the valorization of value . . . is his subjective purpose, and it is only in so far as the appropriation of ever more wealth in the abstract is the sole driving force behind his operations that he functions as a capitalist, i.e., as capital personified and endowed with consciousness and a will. Use-values must therefore never be treated as the immediate aim of the capitalist nor must the profit on any single transaction. His aim is rather the unceasing movement of profit-making. This boundless drive for enrichment, this permanent chase after value, is common to the capitalist and the miser; but while the miser is merely the capitalist gone mad, the capitalist is a rational miser. The ceaseless augmentation of value, which the miser seeks to attain by saving his money from circulation, is achieved by the more acute capitalist by means of throwing his money again and again into circulation (Marx, 1976, pp.254-5).

This is the historically progressive role of the capitalist and of the bourgeois epoch.

Only one commodity 'possesses the peculiar property of being a source of value . . . the capacity for labour [*Arbeitsvermogen*], in other words labour-power [*Arbeitskraft*]' (Marx, 1976, p.270). One could criticize this view by raising objections as to the role of machinery, technology, etc. Marx's answer was to regard these produced means of production simply as a transposition of value from one form into another, being simply the result of previous production, rather than the immediate production from which they have most recently emerged. The only value which can be actually produced in a production process, according to Marx, is that added by new amounts of labour. In the labour process workers must work sufficiently not only to reproduce themselves (and their families) but also to reproduce the capitalists: thus, labourers work beyond the time required to reproduce their life, embodied in the wage form of the exchange value. This surplus time is materialized in commodities which belong to capital, which capital 'realizes' on the market as fresh exchange values. These fresh exchange values thus have to contain a value surplus to that embodied in them by the sum of exchange values (wages, raw material, machinery, running costs, etc.) of which they are composed. Thus can 'rational misers' prosper.

Valorization of capital proceeds through the exploitation of wage-labour by capital. This exploitation occurs in the exchange process between labour and capital. Capital (defined by its appropriated ownership and control of the means of production) hires expropriated labour (defined by its non-ownership and control of the means of production) which is formally alienable on the market. What the worker sells to the capitalist in return for a wage is labour power. Capital uses up this power, which is thereby alienated from the worker, who in return receives a wage. Logically, this cannot be a 'fair' exchange. If it were, the capitalist would quickly have no money left, because if the capitalist did not share in the labour all the money would soon pass to the labourer. Marx maintains that where there existed profit there could not also exist fair exchange.

Marx has therefore constructed two ideal types of economic agents: on the one hand, the rational miser, the owner of money; on the other, the rational freeperson, the owner of labour power, owner of the capacity to labour. These archetypes correspond to the 'two great classes' of the *Manifesto*: the bourgeoisie and proletariat. But these are not naturally existing classes. The relation

> has no basis in natural history, nor does it have a social basis
> common to all periods of human history. It is clearly the result
> of a past historical development, the product of many
> economic revolutions, of the extinction of a whole series of
> older formations of social production (Marx, 1976, p.273).

This development particularly concerned the transition from feudalism to capitalism. It was this evolution which produced those two major economic groupings characterized by Marx as labour and capital in terms of their social relations. The capitalist class differs from previous dominant groups because of its appropriation and ownership of the means of production and the nature of the commodities bought, made and sold. One of these commodities was labour's ability to work. Unlike the feudal lord, the capitalist hired wage-labour bought at the marketplace. Once the wages had been paid, the responsibilities of the capitalist ceased, as did the rights of ownership of the workers to their labour and its fruits. Thus the capitalist had the advantages of ownership without responsibility, as well as the surplus value, the profit, that this labour created. The development of capitalism produced a special kind of worker, unknown before in history. The labourer was formally free from ties with a master, but this freedom contained no rights. Theoretically, the worker could offer services to anyone. Practically, without possession and control of instruments of labour, labour capacity can be offered only to whichever capitalist might wish to deploy it.

Labour capacity, like any other commodity, has two types of value: 'use value' and 'exchange value'. The use value is the materialized effort and time expended as surplus over and above the exchange value received in return, as the wage. This wage, the exchange value, then passes once more into circulation as the workers reproduce themselves on the market. The commodities necessary for sustenance – food, shelter and clothing of workers and their families – can be bought only from capitalists. The exchange value therefore flows from capital to labour to capital as a process of accumulation.

With the commodity labour power, the worker sells an economic capacity which can be measured in money terms, just as any other material product can be. Its costs of production and reproduction can be calculated as can those of any other commodity. The cost of this production and reproduction is the average value around which the exchange value of the wage form will vary. As such, it presupposes a definite structure of economic relations, in which the value of the product is produced by the socially necessary labour-time used to produce it. The latter will,

> in particular . . . depend on the conditions in which, and consequently on the habits and expectations with which, the class of free workers has been formed. In contrast, therefore, with the case of other commodities, the determination of the value of labour-power contains a historical and moral element (Marx, 1976, p.275).

Costs of production and reproduction will include factors such as the costs of rearing the next generation of workers, as well as natural and socially shared needs. Not only must shelter, food and clothing, for instance, be included in the costs of production and replacement of labour but also the acquisition of skill and dexterity necessary to the production of labour power of a developed and specific kind. Capital as capital requires as an *a priori* labour as alienable, formally free and incapable of any recourse other than to offer itself for sale at the market rate. (Hence, the importance of labour not being able to flee into primitive commodity or agricultural subsistence production, as can happen when attempts are made to insert capitalist relations of production into newly targeted colonies. Where exit is an option, alienability becomes problematic, as Marx observes in chapter 33 of *Capital*, 'The Modern Theory of Colonization'.)

Just as the value accruing to labour is reckoned this way, so is the product which the workers in a given social division of labour are engaged in making. Its exchange value, if the capitalist is to stay in business, must be greater than the exchange values of the sum of the labour powers which produced it, plus the costs of the raw materials, machinery, rent, etc., used in making it. In other words, the capitalist receives a far greater use value from the labour hired than the exchange value expended in hiring it. This unpaid labour is the source of surplus value. Whereas under feudalism surplus was appropriated in the concrete form of forced labour or expropriated produce, under the abstract value-producing form of capitalism, it is appropriated in the form of labour, unforced by anything other than alienability according to contract, producing value in an alienated mode.

The exchange of commodities does not in itself delineate a society in which the capitalist mode of production is dominant; but the commodification of labour power and the commodified character of most production does make fundamental class divisions quite stark. Marx's class theory rests very firmly on the consequences of the exchange of commodities.

The labour process

In terms of Marx's method, circulation and exchange of commodities takes place on the surface of social life, but should be analysed in terms of the 'hidden abode of production' – the labour process. In its simple, abstract form, as Marx first presents it, the labour process 'is purposeful activity aimed at the production of use-values' (Marx, 1976, p.290) bereft of specific social relations of production.

The specifically capitalist labour process develops in an evolution from formal to real subordination. Irrespective of the particular stage of capitalist development it exhibits two characteristic phenomena. First, the capitalist controls all the elements of the labour process and

> takes good care that the work is done in a proper manner, and the means of production are applied directly to the purpose, so that raw material is not wasted, and the instruments of labour are spared, i.e. only worn to the extent necessitated by their use in the work. . . . Secondly, the product is the property of the capitalist and not that of the worker, its immediate producer (Marx, 1976, p.292).

The labour process takes place between commodities controlled by capital for a specific purpose: valorization. The capitalist labour process is thus one in which the combination of elements of the labour process takes on a specific class character determined not just by the production of use values but of use values subordinated to the production of self-expanding value: that is, the process of valorization. This entails the production of commodities having not simply a use value but also an exchange value.

Marx mistakenly believed that the character of the labour used mattered little because any 'distinction between higher and simple labour', 'skilled labour' and 'unskilled labour . . . [has] . . . long ceased to be real' (Marx, 1976, p.305). Here lies the source of the somewhat one-directional 'deskilling' thesis of Braverman (1974) and other contemporary Marxist studies of the labour process. As we shall elaborate later, the skill character of the labour process, labour force and labour market is central to an understanding of class. Indeed, Marx prefigures this in the importance that he attaches to the mediating and legislative role of the state, in particular as it had intervened in struggles over the length of the working day through successive Factory Acts.

The English Factory Acts curbed 'capitalists' drive towards a limitless draining-away of labour power by forcibly limiting the working day on the authority of the state' (Marx, 1976, p.348). Although, as Marx noted, this was a 'state ruled by capitalists and landlords' it was one which clearly acted neither unambiguously as their instruments nor in terms of their own conceptions of their interests, to judge by the vociferous opposition to the Acts which Marx records. However,

> the working class's power of attack grew with the number of its allies in those social layers not directly interested in the question. . . . The establishment of a normal working day is

therefore the product of a protracted and more or less concealed civil war between the capitalist class and the working class (Marx, 1976, pp.409, 412-13).

More or less concealed it may have been, but not from the 'state apparatuses' of the day, whose role was as neither neutral arbiter nor as the protagonist of the logic of capital. Not only are individual Factory Inspectors singled out for praise, but also the whole apparatus (Marx, 1976, p.426). The reports themselves, in as much as they recognize 'the broad principles of the rights of labour' which 'requires the strong arm of the law to protect it', are also regarded as a positive, indeed radical, reform (Marx, 1976, pp.414-15). It was moral argument concerning the abuse of children, from Tory radicals and Christian humanists, which advanced the case for the Factory Acts. Marx was cognizant of a further argument, however: Parliament was aware that the long-term future and interests of the property-owning classes in general, required that the workers be less brutally, thoroughly and ruthlessly exploited. Here we may detect an interest in 'reproduction' on behalf of the ruling class and an awareness in practice, irrespective of what might be said in theory for ideological consumption, that labour *was* the source of value. Moreover, property requires able-bodied soldiers to defend it against foreign aggression. From not only the reports of the Factory Inspectors, but also the scandals uncovered by the Health Inspectors of adulterated food, it was not at all clear that the new generation of proletarians could have upheld the traditions of the thin red line protecting British property around the globe, particularly, at home, against the threat of European expansionists. The Factory Acts, as Stephens (1979) has argued, represent a substantial qualification of the capitalist mode of production to the benefit of that class which capitalism had introduced on to the historical stage: the proletariat. Henceforth, capitalism was less pure in its mode of production in this formation due to the weakening of the market principle. The Factory Acts represented, albeit marginally, a restriction on and interference with the 'normal' functioning of what had become the capitalist labour market. A perfectly pure capitalism no longer existed.

The legal limitation of the working day precipitated, then, a major shift in the capitalist mode of production which was to have important effects on the formation and structure of the working class. This shift was from the formal to the real subordination of the labour process by capital. No longer able to extract additional surplus simply by an extensive change –

lengthening the working day – capital had to devise other, more intensive, means of valorization.

The most primitive forms of capitalist labour process simply subordinated labour power and means of production as they are found already existing in a form of co-operation:

> At first, the subjection of labour to capital was only a formal result of the fact that the worker, instead of working for himself, works for, and consequently under, the capitalist. Through the co-operation of numerous wage-labourers, the command of capital develops into a requirement for carrying on the labour process itself, into a real condition of production. That a capitalist should command in the field of production is now as indispensable as that a general should command on the field of battle. . . . The work of direction, superintending and adjusting becomes one of the functions of capital, from the moment that the labour under capital's control becomes co-operative. As a special function of capital, the directing function acquires its own special characteristic. . . . Moreover, the co-operation of wage-labourers is entirely brought about by the capital that employs them. Their unification into one single productive body and the establishment of a connection between their individual functions, lie outside their competence. These things are not their own act, but the act of the capital that brings them together and maintains them in that situation. Hence, the interconnections between their various labours confronts them, in the realm of ideas, as a plan drawn up by the capitalist, and, in practice, as his authority, as the powerful will of a being outside them, who subjects their activity to his purpose (Marx, 1976, pp.448-50).

On the one hand, co-operation produces an increasing mass of wage-labourers while, on the other hand, the need to control these in the interests of valorization leads the individual capitalist to hand over

> the work of direct and constant supervision of the individual worker and groups of workers to a special kind of wage-labourer. An industrial army of workers under the command of a capitalist requires, like a real army, officers (managers) and NCOs (foremen, overseers), who command during the labour process in the name of capital. The work of supervision becomes their established and exclusive function (Marx, 1976, p.450).

It is the transition from formal to real subordination which marks the emergence of the new middle class of supervisory and white-collar workers. It is their task to supervise the

> collective workers, formed out of the combination of a number of individual specialized workers. . . . Since the various functions performed by the collective worker can be simple or complex, high or low, the individual labour-power, his organs, require different values. Manufacture therefore develops a hierarchy of labour-powers, to which there corresponds a scale of wages (Marx, 1976, pp.468, 469).

By the conclusion of the eighteenth century, manufacturing, through its development since the middle of the sixteenth century, had produced the

> skill of the specialized worker by reproducing and systematically driving to an extreme within the workshop the naturally developed differentiation which it found ready to hand in society. . . . If it develops a one-sided speciality to perfection, at the expense of the whole of a man's working capacity, it also begins to make a speciality of the absence of all development. Alongside the gradations of the hierarchy, there appears the simple separation of the workers into skilled and unskilled (Marx, 1976, pp.459, 470).

In stressing this division of labour into degrees of skill, Marx stresses not just productive gains, but also losses:

> The possibility of an intelligent direction of production expands in one direction because it vanishes in many others. What is lost by the specialized workers is concentrated in the capital which confronts them. It is a result of the division of labour in manufacture that the worker is brought face to face with the intellectual potentialities [*geiskige pokenzen*] of the material process of production as the property of another and as a power which rules over him (Marx, 1976, p.482).

This process, begun in simple co-operation and developed in manufacture 'which mutilates the worker' is completed in large-scale industry, where scientific knowledge is brought into production.

Mutilation there may be, but it is never total, for, as Marx goes on to remark, while craft skill remains the foundation of manufacture 'capital is constantly compelled to wrestle with the insubordination of the workers' (Marx, 1976, p.490). This is the barrier which the manufacturing system constantly comes up against in its pursuit of valorization.

It is machines that abolish the role of the handicraftsman as the regulating principle of social production. Thus, on the one hand, the technical reason for the life-long attachment of the worker to a partial function is swept away. On the other hand, the barriers placed in the way of the domination of capital by this same regulating principle now also fall (Marx, 1976, p.491).

The regimes of co-operation and manufacture (up until the dawn of the nineteenth century) are characterized by the exploitation of absolute surplus value. Productivity is achieved by directing more labour and working longer hours. This continues well into the nineteenth until the real subordination of labour is effected by the introduction of the machine as a means of producing surplus value. With the adoption of production by machinery the labour process is no longer subordinated to a more or less skilled, more or less controlled, labourer. Instead, labour itself becomes subordinated to the machine, breaking the resistance of male workers to the 'despotism of capital' by the importation of women and children into the labour process.

With the widespread adoption of machinery in the face of limits to the length of the working day, won by the upsurge of working-class revolt and legislated by Parliament, there was imposed 'on the worker an increased expenditure of labour within a time which remains constant, a heightened tension of labour-power, and a closer filling-up of the pores of the working day' (Marx, 1976, p.534). Machinery introduced by one capital unit to increase productivity makes some workers formerly employed in that unit unemployed. 'Their presence in the labour-market increases the number of labour-powers which are at the disposal of capitalist exploitation' (Marx, 1976, p.578). These unemployed labour powers can find employment only 'through the agency of a new, additional capital which is seeking investment' (Marx, 1976, p.567). The spur to the adoption of machinery provided by the Factory Acts also hastens 'the decline of the small masters, and the concentration of capital' (Marx, 1976, p.607) because of the increasing amount of capital required to compete efficiently in the changing market. Production becomes increasingly tied to capital investment, and increasingly 'revolutionary . . . continually transforming not only the technical basis of production, but also the functions of the worker and the social combinations of the labour process' (Marx, 1976, p.617).

Capitalist production is revolutionary in a further way. 'It is concentration of capitals already formed, destruction of their individual independence, expropriation of capitalist by capitalist, transformation of many small into few large capitalists' (Marx, 1976, p.777). This revolution is also apparent in the increasing centralization of separate units of concentration of capitalist production. Expanded production leads to not only a greater surplus of value but also of labour, as more and more is produced with less and less living labour. Finally, in its creation of one market for capital formation (hence implying class formation), the capitalist market is revolutionary because it breaks all traditional ties between production for known consumer needs in traditional small-scale markets. It is this break between traditional production and consumption in a rough-and-ready local equilibrium, and modern production, which produces the revolutionary crisis in capitalism. Over-production, in terms of the effective demand of the aggregate of consumers on the one market, now becomes a real possibility, as the market is now a dynamic, uncertain aspect of production. No longer known intimately, traditionally and locally, it can all too easily subvert the concentration and centralization of individual capital units by not providing conditions for the consumption of the expanded production of commodities. This gives rise to those crises which, for Marx, would be endemic to modern capitalism.

Marx's class analysis, therefore, is subordinated to a more complex project: the historical and conceptual study of the consequences of the social organization of the developing capitalist mode of production and the capitalist labour process.

What then is the distinctive contribution made by Marx and Engels to class analysis? Perhaps most fundamental is the notion of a social formation as being unequally structured through relations of possession/non-possession of means of production. It is from this basis that class formation, class structure and class struggle in societies dominated by the capitalist mode of production are generated. Additionally, we would point to the importance of realizing that the pure model will never adequately describe the complex reality; correlatively, it would be odd if 'abstract laws' could be read off from the former and be said to have determined the latter, or even its 'tendencies'.

Capital offers to subsequent class analysis insights not afforded by the earlier texts: the dynamic model of capitalism as a system of private property relations upon whose evolution the labour process depends. Crucial to this evolution remains an undertheorized contingency: the role of the state in providing not only the legislative framework within which the rights of capital and labour are abstractly defined, but also the organizational apparatus whereby such rights may be enforced, changed or contested.

Implicitly, the analysis displays its historical context, even while pointing beyond it to the changes which will be sought by capitalist development. However, one observation must be admitted. While Marx may have been right in anticipating the growing concentration and centralization of capital in the economy, the implications he drew for both politics and class are less certain. With universal adult suffrage why should the mass remain tied to a system of economic domination, Marx reasoned, when they had both the political will and the class interest to overthrow it? The failure of history to have produced what Marx considered a reasonable answer to this question invites reflection not so much on history's failures, but on the adequacy of some interpretations of the question put to it. Modern Marxists have been too ready to seek convoluted explanations as to why working classes have not effected political transformation. One part of the answer must include consideration of the transformation of capitalism into a complex structure of capitalist relations which today define not just proletarian and bourgeois roles, but a complex totality which will not readily admit of such limited dramatis personae. Again, we must point to the importance of a vastly expanded middle class employed both in and out of the state, as well as the continuing role of a petty bourgeoisie seemingly inured to the role of historical oblivion. Moreover, the significance of capitalist social relations is not exhausted merely by analysis in terms of the ownership and control of the means of production by particular actors: increasingly, corporate organizational forms obscure 'the physiognomy of our *dramatis personae*' (Marx, 1976, p.280). Owners of money no longer stride forward as capitalists *per se* but fuse into complex, corporate, apparently seamless forms.

Meanwhile, according to much recent debate, the proletariat becomes further entrapped not so much by the scenario envisaged by Marx, but through the material benefits of capitalist development. The trajectory of this development has remained contingent upon the framework negotiated through state forms, forms into which the proletariat has increasingly been admitted. Contemporary 'Marxian' accounts of class formation are thus paradoxical in their focus on factors such as 'dominant ideology', the role of segmented labour markets and the political implications of corporatism, which run counter to the theses of economic rationalization and political mobilization which were expected on the basis of Marx's own emphases.

The failure of the class-rationalizing project, grounded in the economy, does not necessarily render the political project redundant. What it does entail, however, is a realization that

49

class politics does not simply represent interests putatively located in the 'objective' class structure. For one thing, the structure of classes is frequently more complex than the structure of political parties, particularly in those countries characterized by what is an effectively two-party system. Ironically, in such a situation, the political class struggle assumes the apparent form of Marx's structure of 'two great classes', but mapped on to a terrain which does not recognize such a simplification. Consequently, the parameters of class structure and political representation can never be coincident. Single classes are not self-evident or sufficient constituencies for the formation of successful political parties involved in the democratic class struggle.

Class is neither a fetish, capable of illuminating everything, nor is class struggle a *deus ex machina* to which all the descriptive detail of actual politics, ideology, etc., can be reduced. The observation that economically defined classes do not necessarily correspond to representational practices of political community and solidarity is implicit in the analysis of the eighteenth Brumaire. In the next chapter we consider how the reasons for this lack of fit between economic demarcation and social experience may be found in accounts of Max Weber's arguments on 'stratification'. Weber, in positing 'status' and 'party' as different 'dimensions' of stratification, produced an analysis which highlighted alternative aspects of the experience and practical consequences of class. In some respects, Weber's framework is incompatible with that of Marx. In so far, however, as Weber is concerned to produce a more systematic class analysis than Marx was, the multifaceted bases of societal demarcation which he emphasized must be seen as a complementary contribution.

3 Weber: economic class and civil status

Weber's framework for the analysis of capitalism modifies Marx's model of capitalist dynamics. While Marx's analysis is a guide to the development of a capitalist labour process, it says little about the apparatus of bureaucratic control which develops to dominate it, both at the site of production and in the constitutive framework of the state (but see Perez-Diaz, 1978, for a construction of this theoretical 'lapse'). Bureaucracy *is* the inevitable fate of our times, inasmuch as these remain predicated on large-scale productive organizations and centralized nation states (as anti-bureaucratic socialists such as Castoriadis (1982) would be among the first to admit). Opposition to bureaucracy, for Weber, can only be the mark of a certain dilettante illusion. Bureaucracy, both in the state in particular and in organizations in general, becomes the basis for the normal exercise of rule in any large organization or nation (see Clegg and Dunkerley, 1980, chapter 6, for a discussion of empirical verifications of this hypothesis).

Bureaucratic administration, the impersonal rule-bound application of standardized procedures, is the bulwark of the stability of any stable state. The basis of this stability is captured in the definition of the state as the single locus possessing the effective monopoly of the legitimate use of the means of violence within a given territory. Hence, the basis of social order is, rather as Gramsci (1971) saw it, the result of varying mixtures of domination both by organized coercion and organized consent.

Domination by bureaucratic administration emerges out of capitalist development. While in its early stages of evolution industrial capitalism requires ideological conditions of existence – the role of Protestantism's peculiar elective affinity with capitalist rationality – this is no longer the case for economically complex,

51

large-scale bureaucratic organization (Abercrombie, 1980, p.106; Abercrombie *et al.*, 1980, p.174). In such conditions, more mundane motives of dull compulsion and custom will serve. Further, it is Weber's view that if oppositional movements are to develop out of this dulling habituation, then they too will have to be bureaucratically organized in the form of parties.

Stress on bureaucracy is one of the factors which provides Weber's discussion of class concepts with its distinctiveness compared to that of Marx. Unlike Marx, it means that Weber has no faith in the emergence of a class-conscious proletariat as the bearer of a radically new epoch of social organization. For Weber, the proletariat is but a special case of a more general tendency: this is the expropriation of the vast majority of workers, whether proletarian or not, from the means of execution of their various tasks. Officialdom, just as much as the proletariat, is distinguished by its separation from the means of administration. Hence, although there is a degree of formal similarity in the treatment of class by Marx and Weber, there is an immediate divergence in their appreciation of struggle.

Class, status and party

One factor which is apparent in the enormous secondary literature on Weber is that his work, almost as much as Marx's, has been seen to have suffered from 'vulgar' misrepresentation. (One can consult the following statements of this misrepresentation: Korpi, 1978, p.10; Giddens, 1973, pp.41-2; Clegg, 1975, pp.57-9; Cohen *et al.*, 1975; Therborn, 1976, pp.270-315; Wenger, 1980; Omodei, 1982.)

Weber's early formulation of the issue of class occurs under the heading 'The Distribution of Power within the Political Community: Class, Status, Party' (Weber, 1978, pp.926-40). He proceeds from premises which are similar to those of Marx and Engels, in the importance attached to property:

> It is the most elemental economic fact that the way in which
> the disposition over material property is distributed among a
> plurality of people, meeting competitively in the market for the
> purpose of exchange, in itself creates specific life chances
> (Weber, 1978, p.927).

Although this formulation is elaborated in the context of a marginal utility perspective, it shares with Marx the view that 'property' and 'lack of property' are to be regarded as 'the basic categories of all class situations' (Weber, 1978, p.927). It is also proposed that not only is it just the fact of possession/non-possession but also the 'meaning' given to the utilization of property. Attempts to locate Weber's 'principles of stratification' wholly on the 'subjective' axis have to minimize these 'facts' of possession to allow for the stress on their 'meaning' (for example, Barbalet, 1980, p.407). Neither emphasis alone is useful.

The simple differentiation between possession and non-possession of property is made progressively more complicated by introducing a distinction between the 'kinds of property usable for returns' and the 'kind of services that can be offered in the market' (Weber, 1978, p.928). Each of these categories is subject to further internal differentiation of a quite complex kind. However,

> always this is the generic connotation of the concept of class: that the kind of chance in the *market* is the decisive moment which presents a common condition for the individual's fate . . . the factor that creates 'class' is unambiguously economic interest, and indeed, only those interests involved in the existence of the market (Weber, 1978, p.923).

Such interests do not automatically lead to class formation in an organized struggle. Class positions do not determine class interests. Indeed, Weber considers class interest to be an 'ambiguous' concept if one understands by it anything other than the 'average' of individual interests pertaining to people in a common class situation. Implicitly, this places the analytic focus on issues of class mobilization. It is only when differential life chances are experienced by those subject to them to be the result of either a 'given distribution of property' or 'the structure of the concrete economic order' that rational association – that is, class organization – can be expected. For Weber, just as much as for Marx, the most important historical example of struggle against the concrete economic order is that of the modern proletariat (Weber, 1978, p.930).

Class situations of organized struggle can emerge only on the basis of social action. The decisive social action for class organization

> is not basically action among members of the identical class; it is an action among members of different classes. Social actions that directly determine the class situation of the worker and the entrepreneur are: the labour market, the commodities market, and the capitalistic enterprise (Weber, 1978, p.930).

The existence of a capitalistic enterprise presupposes some specific conditions. In particular, it 'presupposes that a very specific kind of social action exists to protect the possession of goods *per se.*' One set of goods, especially, has to be protected. This is the 'power of individuals to dispose, in principle, freely, over the modes of production; a certain kind of legal order' (Weber, 1978, p.930). The less that any other form of reciprocal social action intercedes in this 'power of individuals' the more dominant property 'rights' (guaranteed in law) on the market will be. Historically, Weber sees a trend from class struggles over 'consumption credit towards, first, competitive struggles in the commodity market and then towards wage disputes on the labour market' (Weber, 1978, p.931). Mediating factors in such class struggles, Weber argues, will be the existence of *stände* (status groups) which can 'hinder the strict carrying-through of the sheer market principle' (1978, p.930).

The precise rendition of Weber's concept of *stände* is a matter of some recent contestation (Wenger, 1980; Omodei, 1982). The concept is derived from the notion of a feudal estate, whereby elites within the economically given class structure are able to effect social closure to such a degree that they are able to usurp its purely economic basis through mechanisms of deference, esteem, prestige, respect and honour. It is this latter set of mechanisms which, in their positive moment, are referred to as a 'status situation'. Within such a situation is encompassed 'every typical component of the life of men that is determined by a specific, positive or negative, social estimation of *honor*' (Weber, 1978, p.932). Inasmuch as further discussion of the concept focuses on the positive aspects of *stände*, then the common emphasis on them as volitional phenomena is justified, together with the equally customary emphasis on status honour as achieved through 'usurpationary' strategies (Parkin, 1979). As Weber (1947, p.188) puts it, 'the development of status is essentially a question of stratification resting upon usurpation. Such usurpation is the normal origin of all status honor.' This aspect of *stände* clearly indexes the elite aspects of class structure and is appropriate to the analysis of the ruling class which, in feudal terms, is appropriately contained within the appellation 'estate'.

Stände rest on a ruling moral, conventional, and legal order with its conceptions of honour. These 'honours' typically are interknit with the class structure, while being derived from phenomena such as a shared way of life, based on some positively evaluated attribute of civil society. At their most prescribed there is the existence of ethnic segregation and castes, which are capable of directly inhibiting the rational functioning of the market and the class principle of stratification.

Weber (1978) argues that in feudal society, the process of

social closure of collectivities, of *stände* out of classes, is most likely to develop in conditions of social stability. He is referring to the probability of an especially honoured stratum developing at the apex of the class structure. On this account, the concept of *stände* may have more general rather than purely historic application in its 'positive' moment. Under conditions of social stability in other than feudal formations we may expect to be able to observe processes of *stände* formation in practice. For instance, we will argue that the corporate ruling class of contemporary capitalism offers this sort of stability as analysts such as Domhoff (1967, 1971) and Baltzell (1958, 1967) have suggested. A self-conscious elite stratum within a ruling class, enjoying a special culture and the concomitant usurpation of 'status honour', buttressed by a class-specific legal order, is not merely an historial curiosity.

At the other end of the class structure, the 'negatively evaluated social antithesis of the precipitating *stände* (i.e. non elites) are excluded by the actions of an already powerful elite, not by their own activities, as in a class/market situation' (Wenger, 1980, p.366). In a developed class society, there will be *stände* volitionally formed not only by usurpationary strategies amongst the upper echelons of the class structure. There will also be *stände* formed by the negative evaluations of others which will objectively exist quite apart from the volitions of the *stände* thus formed. These negative evaluations will be imposed upon the *stände* thus defined by differential access to positions within the class structure that particular 'types' of individuals may have. Hence, negative *stände* formation may not be volitional or even conscious on the part of the *stände* thus formed: indeed, the characteristic form will often be disorganization rather than organization of any putative unitary class interest. It is as likely to be signified by the absence of mechanisms for achieving such consciousness as by any guarantee of their existence. (In this respect Weber was consciously arguing against the Lukács of *History and Class Consciousness* (1971).)

These earlier formulations were later developed into the notes on 'status groups and classes' which form chapter 4 of *Economy and Society*. Typically, Weber begins with a series of definitions which refine the earlier and more discursive exegesis:

'Class situation' means the typical probability of:
1. procuring goods,
2. gaining a position in life, and
3. finding inner satisfactions,
a probability which derives from the relative control over

goods and skills and from their income-producing uses within a given economic order (Weber, 1978, p.302).

One possible interpretation of this definition lends to it a certain continuity with Marx's stress on property relations. While for Marx the basis of class formation was the ownership/non-ownership and control of property, Weber relativizes 'control' by making it a variable. Additionally, while Marx focuses on control of the *means* of production Weber also insists that we consider differential control of the *methods* of production, in terms of 'skill'. Thus, class formation may be based not only on the degree of control of the means of production (and their non-control), but also on the basis of the degree of control over the labour process available to individuals due to the different degree of skill vested in them as workers. Further, the vesting of 'skills' is something which occurs within a 'given economic order'. In a capitalist society, this will be one dominated by the rational calculations of economic agents competing on the market. Before proceeding further with Weber's discussion of class, it is useful to examine in more detail his conception of the 'given economic order' of capitalism, the investigation of which comprises his discussion of the 'sociological categories of economic action' in the second chapter of *Economy and Society* (1978, pp.63-211).

Classes are economically determined. That is, they are a phenomenon of economic action, defined as 'any peaceful exercise of an actor's control over resources which is in its main impulse oriented towards economic ends' (Weber, 1978, p.63). When instrumental means–end rationality, exemplified in deliberate planning, is found, we have *rational* economic action. Rational economic action pertains to the cost and potential usefulness of using various means to achieve given ends and is 'primarily oriented to the problem of choosing the *end* to which a thing shall be applied' (Weber, 1978, p.67). This is in contrast to technical rationality, which is concerned purely with means. Weber argues that, historically, technical rationality is determined by economic rationality:

> the main emphasis at all times, and especially the present, has lain in the economic determination of technological development. Had not rational calculation formed the basis of economic activity, had there not been certain very particular conditions in its economic background, rational technology could never have come into existence (1978, p.67).

This is a significant and important argument. It bears directly on contemporary arguments about the role of 'strategic choice'

(Child, 1972) and the economic rationality which determines technological developments which 'deskill' or 'degrade' labour, and change the bases of class formation in terms of the distribution of skills (Braverman, 1974; Marglin, 1974; Fox, 1974; Clegg and Dunkerley, 1980).

The essence of economic action is in the 'deliberate planned acquisition of powers of control and disposal' and is thus 'the principal source of the relation of economic action to the law' (Weber, 1978, p.67). Weber's conception of the analytical importance of this fact brings him to a conclusion which is consistent with the view that economic action, vested in formal organizations, entails the organization and control of the labour process (Clegg and Dunkerley, 1980; Clegg, 1981). This interpretation relies on Weber's noting that any type of organization of economic activities must involve some type of *de jure* or *de facto* distribution of powers of control and disposal, in order to

be able to count on having some kind of control over the necessary services of labour and of the means of production. It is possible to obscure this fact by verbal devices, but it cannot be interpreted out of existence. For purposes of definition it is a matter of indifference in what way this control is guaranteed; whether by convention or by law, or whether it does not even enjoy the protection of any external sanctions at all, but its security rests only on actual expectations in terms of custom or self-interest. These possibilities must be taken into account, however essential legal compulsion may be for the modern economic order (1978, pp.67-8).

Control over the labour process is the essential basis of the organization of economic action. This control may be secured either in law or in convention or in terms of the expectations of the parties to the action. In a further clarification Weber makes the Marxian point explicitly: 'the concept of powers of control and disposal will here be taken to include the possibility of control over the actor's own labour power, whether this is in some way enforced or merely exists in fact' (1978, p.68).

Organization and control of a labour process may occur either in a household, where the principle of calculation is budgetary (exchange of money for purposes of consumption by the members of the household), or in an enterprise, where the principle of calculation is capitalist accounting (exchange for profit). It is in the latter type of organization, the enterprise, that the proper terrain of social classes is to be located. For Weber, class is simply the generic term for all persons in the same class situation: when we are dealing with 'the totality of those class situations within which individual and generational mobility is easy and typical' (1978, p.302) then we have identified a social class. There are four of these, according to Weber: the working class, the petty bourgeoisie, the propertyless intelligentsia and specialists (the 'new middle class'), and the classes privileged through property and education (1978, p.305). For the present, we will consider only the 'two great classes' identified by Marx and Engels, those of capital and labour, in order to point out continuities between Marx's and Weber's treatment of them.

Weber defines capital in an analogous manner to Marx and Engels, but with a more concise definition of the mechanisms of capitalist reproduction based on 'business calculation':

> What is meant when we speak of the 'power of capital'? We mean that the possessors of control over the means of production and over economic advantages which can be used as capital *goods* in a profit-making enterprise, enjoy, by virtue of this control and of the orientation of economic action to the principles of capitalistic business calculation, a specific position of power in relation to others (1978, p.95).

The power of capital is vested in economic enterprises constituted by 'autonomous action capable of orientation to capital accounting' (Weber, 1978, p.91). Capital accounting is the rational orientation of opportunities for calculating profit and loss. Where there is rational calculation it 'is oriented to expectations of prices and their changes as they are determined by the conflicts of interests in bargaining and competition and the resolution of these conflicts' (1978, p.92). In its most rational shape, says Weber, capital accounting 'presupposes *the battle of man with man*' (1978, p.93).

This is not only struggle between enterprises on the market or between enterprises and other power constellations, which are expressed in the prices of various commodities, including labour. It is also associated with struggle within the enterprise. 'Strict capital accounting is further associated with the social phenomena of "shop discipline" and appropriation of the means of production, and that means: with the existence of a "system of domination" ' (Weber, 1978, p.108; also Clegg, 1975, pp.55-66). A system of domination demands that there can be some 'others' who are dominated. Domination may appear to be formally voluntary yet still be domination.

> This is true wherever the unequal distribution of wealth, and particularly of capital goods, forces the non-owning group to comply with the authority of others in order to obtain any

return at all for the utilities they can offer on the market . . . in a purely capitalistic organization of production, this is the fate of the entire working class (Weber, 1978, p.110).

The working class is defined by its distinction from managerial labour: that is, it is 'oriented to the instructions of a managerial agency' (Weber, 1978, p.114). Its orientation to these instructions is facilitated by a number of structural factors which serve to 'concentrate' the workers' motivation. These will be a strong self-interest, direct, or indirect, compulsion:

> The latter is particularly important in relation to work which executes the disposition of others. This compulsion may consist in the immediate threat of physical force or other undesirable consequences, or in the probability that unsatisfactory performance will have an adverse effect on earnings (Weber, 1978, p.150).

Weber agrees with Marx that piece-rates represent a 'higher' degree of formal rationality than non-performance-related payment systems. This rationality presupposes that

> the expropriation of the workers from the means of production by owners is protected by force. As compared with direct compulsion to work, this system involves the transferral, in addition to the responsibility for reproduction (in the family), of part of the worries about selection according to aptitude to the workers themselves. Further, both the need for capital and the capital risks are, as compared with the use of unfree labour, lessened and made more calculable. Finally, through the payment of money wages on a large scale, the market for goods which are objects of mass consumption is broadened (Weber, 1978, p.151).

Weber constantly stresses that the major sources of the motivation to work are the absence of an alternative source of income, leading to a fear of dismissal, the opportunities for high piece-rate earnings, and the possibility that workers may 'value economically productive work as a mode of life' (Weber, 1978, pp.110, 151). The latter point is developed in *The Protestant Ethic and the Spirit of Capitalism* (Weber, 1976).

As with Marx, the class situation of these objects of more or less dull compulsion is viewed within the context of 'the development towards capitalism', in which a number of stages are identified (Weber, 1978, pp.147-8). These are quite compatible with any Marxian account of class formation, whose conclusion is familiar: 'All material means of production become fixed or working capital; all workers become "hands".'

Part, at least, of Weber's account of the development towards capitalism is well known. We refer to the essay concerning the elective affinity between certain aspects of Protestantism and capitalism (Weber, 1976). In this essay certain material factors are specified as contributing to the rise of capitalism, which are themselves taken to be the unanticipated consequence of quite other social actions (Clegg and Dunkerley, 1980, pp.33-5). There is also another and more extended discussion of such developments in Weber's (1923) *General Economic History*, the importance of which is its sociological contribution to the general analysis of capitalist development (Collins, 1980). Part of this contribution is made in *Economy and Society* where Weber adds what may be regarded as a further footnote to Marx's comments on joint stock companies: 'As a result of the transformation of enterprises into associations of stock holders, the manager himself becomes expropriated and assumes the formal status of an "official". Even the owner becomes effectively a trustee of the suppliers of credit, the banks' (Weber, 1978, p.148).

Apart from an account couched in terms of economic history, Weber also identifies more specifically sociological determinants of the expropriation of workers from the means of production. A number of technical conditions facilitate the increased economic rationality of capitalist enterprise, in terms of capitalist calculation. They include the following:

(i)   where the means of production require the successive or simultaneous employment of many workers;

(ii)   where the rational exploitation of sources of power requires simultaneous employment of many workers for many similar tasks under a unified control;

(iii)   where many complementary processes can be combined under continuous common supervision;

(iv)   where special technical training is given for the management of a large-scale co-ordinated labour process;

(v)   where unified control over the labour process enables the subjection of labour to a stringent regime of discipline in order to control effort and quality (Weber, 1978, p.137).

Additionally, there are a number of economic factors which bear especially on the rational and calculable capitalistic deployment of clerical and technical staff. For Weber, their expropriation from possession of the means of production depends upon

(i)   the absence of any type of worker's control or participation;

(ii)   the absence of any established rights of workers on management, the unrestricted control by management of the goods and equipment which underlie its borrowings;

(iii) the extension of the market to its furthest limits (1978, pp.137-8).

With the extension of the market and the constitution of economic calculation in 'rational' terms (whether as a result of the market's 'superior' and 'indispensable' form of calculation or as a result of structures of power relationships) other factors which favour expropriation come into play. The following characteristics of an enterprise fully oriented to market calculation also serve to favour the expropriation of workers in general:

(i)   the premium placed on rational capital acounting;

(ii) the premium placed on the purely commercial qualities of managers – their responsibility for the 'bottom line';

(iii) speculative business policy;

(iv) the sheer bargaining superiority that is granted to any kind of property ownership *vis-à-vis* the workers;

(v)   the extension of commodity markets where an enterprise is working with capital acounting, owned capital equipment and borrowed funds, compared to enterprises operating at 'lower' levels of rationality;

(vi) the existence of free labourers and the complete appropriation of the means of production which create the most favourable conditions for discipline (Weber, 1978, p.138).

In contrast to the meaning applied to it by Marx, expropriation thus becomes a general concept for understanding the development of rational calculation in all spheres. Weber argues that an enterprise structure which is objectively most polarized in terms of the economic determination of social classes, with a complete expropriation of workers from all property and means of production, is the most formally rational type of organization structure for capitalist enterprises. However, he agrees with Marx that the formal rationality of capital accumulation is also the source of substantive irrationality: 'the fact that the maximum of *formal* rationality in capital accounting is possible only where the workers are subjected to domination by entrepreneurs, is a further element of *substantive* irrationality in the modern economic order' (Weber, 1978, p.138).

The appropriation of all rights of control to the holders of property entails as a possibility the effective separation of capital as property ownership from capital as a relation of discipline, control and domination within the enterprise. At one level this is formally rational. The 'separation of managerial functions from appropriated ownership . . . through . . . appropriation of the enterprise as expressed by shares of the nominal capital' leads to the rational selection of persons for managerial posts who are most efficient at the economic calculation of profitability (Weber,

1978, p.139). However, at another level, it may open the way for a further development of 'substantive irrationality' in the form of 'outside interests'.

These 'outside interests' may not be rationally calculable enterprises. They may be wealthy household units whose only interest is in a high rate of income, at the expense of rational planning of longer-term economic calculation. Alternatively, control may pass into speculative outside interests whose major concern is less with the enterprise as a calculative functioning unit than with the enterprise as a bundle of inflatable shares. Finally, ownership may pass to outside interests who, through their control over markets or credit (finance capital), may pursue their own, often contrary, interests, rather than those of the enterprise. What distinguishes 'outside interests' for Weber is that they are 'not primarily oriented to the long-run profitability of the enterprise' (1978, p.139). It is precisely this increased possibility of orientation to shorter-term speculative profit which leads to a further element of substantive irrationality:

> The fact that such 'outside' interests can affect the mode of control over managerial positions, even and especially when the highest degree of *formal* rationality in their selection is attained, constitutes a further element of *substantive* irrationality specific to the modern economic order. These might be entirely private 'wealth' interests, or business interests which are oriented to ends having no connection whatsoever with the organization, or finally, pure gambling interest.
>
> By gaining control of shares, all of these can control the appointment of the managing personnel and, more important, the business policies imposed on the management. The influence exercised by speculative interest outside the producing organizations themselves on the market situation, especially that for capital goods, and thus on the orientation of the production of goods, is *one* of the sources of the phenomenon known as the 'crisis' of the modern market economy (Weber, 1978, p.140).

The most evident difference between Weber's understanding of class and Marx's analyses is a reluctance in the former work to view the labour/capital cleavage and struggle as the essential and unifying centre of advanced capitalist formations. The concept of status illuminates cleavages and conflicts which can be said to be differentially located to those of class, although it is an empirical matter as to whether or not they serve to reinforce or weaken the class cleavage. In the section which follows, we will consider some of the bases of this status group formation.

For Weber, neither the existence of classes nor of status groups automatically guarantees their development of political action. Only the existence of freely associated people joined together in a party oriented to the achievement of power in order to further the advantages of its members will provide any guarantee of political action. To be effective in the modern world, it is argued, these must be mass, bureaucratically regulated, parties. Such parties may be the elected affiliates of classes and status groups. One consequence of the relative autonomy of parties is that liberal democracy may take many forms in spite of the 'constancy' of the mode of production as capitalistic. Similarly, status group formation may lead to radically different class structures: for instance, the respective heritage of black slavery in the United States and a 'White Australia' policy in Australia contribute to the development of very different proletariats.

Class structure, status groups and civil society

Within the structure of classes it is clear that for Weber life chances distributed in and through the structure of the markets for capital and labour, as well as their relative degrees of differential status organization and closure, are decisive. Members of the same status group are constituted as such by the phenomenology of civil society. In other words, their status in common is achieved through the common ascriptions and estimations, negatively or positively defined, which are widely current within that civil society. Collectively, these comprise distinct stratifying practices of discrimination.

Such estimates as obtain are socially organized in and through particular practices. Among the more important of these are the degree of access and closure that people *qua* status group membership enjoy *vis-à-vis* differential positions of control in the labour process. This access is socially organized on the basis of status desiderata reproduced within the wider civil society. Consequently, the basis of status group formation may not be the consciousness of the members of the group thus defined. On the contrary, they may well be disorganizedly unaware. Instead, one would look to the practices that structure objective labour and capital markets, in which distinct statuses may be organized. Historically, such statuses become of general interest as contingent properties of personal identity in Europe only with the dissolution of the bonds of feudal society.

Civil society, as a concept, registers this dissolution. It emerges in Hobbes's (1962) *Leviathan* as a contrast to the fictional 'uncivil' society, the state of nature (Macpherson, 1977). With

Hegel's (1967) *Philosophy of Right* it begins to be conceptualized less by fictional contrast and more by empirical reflection as the 'order of difference' which the modern world inserts between the ascriptions of familial status (in an order of estates) and the achievement of the status of citizen.

This conception of the importance of the concept of civil society as one in opposition to the state recurs in all thought influenced by Hegel, notably in varieties of Marxism. (Perez-Diaz, 1978, has a useful discussion of Marx and Hegel on 'the state, bureaucracy and civil society'.) What this stream of thought adds, of course, is the idea of the functional centrality of the economy in terms of the patterns of determination of state and civil society and the subordination of the latter to the former.

Even on the basis of the Marxian conception of state and civil society, there is a need to recognize the independent and non-determined nature of the statuses inscribed in civil society. These can be differentiated from class positions, determined by the relations of production, and those rights and obligations determined by citizenship in a given national state. Social classes, inasmuch as they are bases for organization and representation, can be mobilized only on the pre-existing terrain of human subjectivity constituted by the practices of civil society.

In Weber's terms, these practices would seem to constitute typical *stände*, or what may still be termed status groups. What these status groups have in common in a non-feudal concept of *stände* is their constitution by practices of subject formation and identification. The locus of these practices is civil society.

What is at stake in civil society is the problem of identity. Civil society is composed of an aggregate of biologically similar but socially diverse men and women, engaged in a myriad of discursive practices in and as their 'private lives'. It is in and through these private lives that 'self-identification' takes place. Self-identification concerns cognition of oneself as a member of gender, family, territorial and other groups, It entails the construction, maintenance and identification of the shifting boundaries of social significance. Boundedness is fought over and maintained through social relationships which simultaneously establish pressures and controls on identity (Perez-Diaz, 1978, p.58). This struggle for the construction of self is an element of the quotidian round of everyday work and life, although it achieves its most dramatic expression in the sphere of social movements committed to the inviolability of particular identities. These usually operate with a more or less articulate ideology of difference.

The degree of determination by status in civil society, and the degree of encroachment upon it through either the state or economy, is the historical terrain of class and popular struggles. Historically, the private sphere of civil society has been extended to the labour market, capital accumulation, the formation of the nuclear family and a whole range of public expression of modes of individualism (Therborn, 1978, pp.66 et seq.).

Subsequent development of capitalist society has substantially affected the statuses nurtured in civil society. On the one hand, they have become increasingly subordinated to the state, in large part as an effect of successful working-class and popular pressure, succeeding in winning legal definitions of equality in substantive spheres such as those of sexual and racial status, the growth of state direction of policies concerning incomes, health and safety issues at work and the length of the working day. On the other hand, status privatization is encouraged precisely by trends in its classical locus, the sphere of consumption. Here we may refer to tendencies such as the growth of the suburban environment (Game and Pringle, 1979) and its centrality as a zone of consumption focused on the nuclear family in the postwar boom.

The forms of status structuration are various. Different forms will predominate at different places and times and we may simply note those which are most important with respect to the field of class practices.

First, what is being constructed are classes constituted by the historicaly developed patterns of capital accumulation and the relations of production they entail. Second, the pattern is one of interpellation that occurs through the process of subjectification and qualification of persons who present themselves for employment, as bearers of specific types of status, indicated by particular occupations and skills (Allen, 1975, pp.214-16, 1977, pp.640-7). Third, skills are acquired non-randomly by people of a specific gender, age, ethnicity and race, regional and national interpellation within civil society (Urry, 1981, p.66). Fourth, classes are inscribed within state formations composed of a system of apparatuses distinguished by their legitimate monopoly of 'coercive defence, political governance (by supreme rule-making), administrative management (by rule-application), and judicial regulation of a given social formation' (Therborn, 1978, p.37). Hence, class formation is both nationally and personally structured and experienced.

Perhaps the most pervasive form of personal structuration of class by status is that associated with gender. This is not always clear in empirical studies of class which are often based on samples in which gender is not an explicit dimension. Consequently, extrapolation of findings is limited when a sample proves to be overwhelmingly or entirely male.

Gender interpellations constitute distinct status groups with a dual relationship to the class structure, mediated by relationships of dependency of women on men and their often assumed sole responsibilty for domestic labour and childcare (Garnsey, 1978). Such dependencies are not always manifestly apparent. Primarily for reasons of tax inheritance, women have an almost equal share in the ownership of wealth: 'they owned about 40 per cent of all private wealth in 1970' (in Britain) as Wainwright (1978, p.163) remarks. This ownership of capital is pre-eminently more nominal than real. It is family property invested by the husband. Households will be the major site of struggles by women seeking to escape subordination by attempting to opt out, and join another subordinate grouping, that of wage-labourers (Barrett, 1980, pp.187-226; Urry, 1981, pp.78-9), on the principle that it is easier to change employers than husbands. This has a direct bearing on the wives of ruling-class males, because to the extent that they have neither real ownership of capital nor employment of their own, their own position in the class structure as relatively privileged is maintained through a highly dependent state which is not usually sustainable outside of the marriage contract. Hence, divorce transforms not only their civil status but also often their class position in a way which does not affect men.

Access to ruling-class positions on a non-property basis occurs through the possibilities of entering the highly discontinuous status orders of modern organizations at a point of entry which allows the possibility of either a career with control, or access to positions enjoying professional closure, as Weber suggested. To be able to do this, a person must have credentials. Contemporary empirical inspection suggests that, whatever else may be useful, being male presents a headstart in gaining them (Martin, 1980).

Retrospect and prospect

The conceptualization of status formation which is offered here is clearly not couched in orthodox 'Weberian' terms. It owes more to Gramscian-influenced formulations by authors such as Urry (1981) and Perez-Diaz (1978). We would maintain, however, that in view of recent discussions of Weber on status, notably by Omodei (1982) and Wenger (1980), that this initially unorthodox, seemingly un-Weberian conception, may not be as erroneous a characterization as it might seem. Moreover, it is capable of illuminating the discussion of class formation in particular circumstances which might otherwise be resistant to an analysis, if not a description, in class terms.

This chapter began by discussing Weber's conception of class concepts. It proposed that these were in many respects not too dissimilar to those of Marx. A number of analytical points have also been made. Weber's model of class formation is more complex than the capital/labour model used by Marx, but shares many, if not all, of the same assumptions. Discussion of status in the context of civil society leads to the clear realization that class positions can never be occupied by pre-social subjects. Consequently, there can be neither an 'essential' class interest nor a 'necessary' class struggle. There can be only possible bases of, and resources for, mobilization. These will depend upon the particular practices of status formation and the struggles to which they give rise. Classes develop as the result of struggles, rather than the converse.

Whether or not the terrain of civil society, where multifariously constituted individuals develop social statuses and practices, is the only site of class formation and class struggle is not only an empirically contingent matter. Only under certain conditions does the class principle overtly and unambiguously prevail, but social science is entitled to abstract from these observable and experiential criteria if there is reason to suspect, as both Weber and Marx did, that the less contingent demarcation of ownership and non-ownership is still more fundamental and still capable of exerting some real class effectivity.

We will argue that the determination of property relations is still pervasive, albeit never unmediated. Not only is it mediated through the terrain of civil society and the state, but also, as we will argue, by the characteristic phases of the economy. For instance, at all stages of the non-linear phases of capital accumulation there will continue to be patterned changes in class distribution of income, predictable consequences of shifts in the proportion of national revenues allocated to investment and consumption respectively, and cyclical fluctuations in production, incomes, employment and living standards. These structural aspects of any market-based economic order are not necessarily appreciated by or accessible to the social participants most immediately affected. Class struggles, such as occur over wages or for political control of investment, for example, are not necessarily perceived as such by the protagonists. Struggle is something engaged in by collectivities of individuals inscribed within the statuses of civil society, but whether or not these people struggle primarily against capital cannot be determined by their relations of production alone. As Aronowitz puts it:

historical subjects are *themselves* an effect of struggles about class formation, whose discontinuity is determined by phases of capitalist development which are in turn the outcome of the relatively autonomous economic, political and ideological relations within the totality of social relations (1981, p.74).

We have now developed a framework, derived from a synthesis of aspects of Marx and Weber, for the analysis of class structure and its organization. Subsequent chapters are based on the principal classes, categorized as the petty bourgeoisie, the corporate ruling class, the new middle class and the working class. These classes form the organizational basis not only for opposing interests in the industrial sphere but also for the organization of political parties in the state. Rarely do parties correspond either to the membership or the representation of interests of these principal classes, as Weber suggested.

Major points of significance for politics premised on an explicitly class model emerge from this investigation of class structure. First, the petty bourgeoisie will be seen to play a more important ideological role than their potential as an aggregative source of votes would suggest. Second, the corporate ruling class *per se*, is a small segment of the population, rarely comprising more than 1–5 per cent of voters. Thus, it is not clear why the preferences of capitalists should prevail in open and democratic electoral contests. That they often do so means either that these interests are capable of garnering wider support or that they may be reproduced other than through formal politics. We will endorse both of these suggestions. Third, the new middle classes are the sector of the class structure from which mass parties must gain support for their platforms, over and above any core of bourgeois or labour constituencies, if those platforms are to be attractive to a broad electoral aggregate. Fourth, implementation does not simply depend on aggregation. Politics have to be fought through and in state forms which do not organize either parties or other interest associations in a disinterested and equally liberal mode. The state is a structure of complex organization in which different interests come into play with variable effectivity.

Analysis of the class structure begins with the petty bourgeoisie. Rather than being condemned to wither on the vine of advanced capitalism, this class, in its highly variable composition, has important and symbiotic relationships with the core of concentrated and centralized capital. Despite its internal heterogeneity this class embodies a crucial ideological role: it articulates what are by now quite archaic but none the less core values of the capitalist ethos. Just how archaic becomes apparent when one contrasts the political economy of late capitalism, articulated around the core corporate ruling class, with the anti-organization and aggressively individualistic ethos of the petty bourgeoisie. This individualism finds little resonance in the organizational structures of this class of modern property. In contemporary terms, analysis of the ruling class must entail the analysis of mechanisms of complex organizational structures, rather than simply key personnnel. The petty bourgeoisie to the extent that its enterprises remain small, rarely concerns itself with the complexities of structural design. And, as we shall see, this is a contributory factor to both the high formation and mortality rates of this class.

4 The concentration of capital and the petty bourgeoisie

Marx and Engels hypothesized that with the continuing development of the capitalist mode of production there would be an increasing concentration of capital investment opportunities, i.e. of the ruling class. The process is defined in terms of the

> concentration of capitals already formed, destruction of their individual independence, expropriation of capitalist by capitalist, transformation of many small into few large capitals. . . . Capital grows to a huge mass in a single hand in one place, because it has been lost by many in another place (Marx, 1976, p.777).

The notion of ownership vested in a 'single hand' is one that has become increasingly irrelevant, but, none the less, we can conceptualize concentration as the way in which competitive units of capital are reorganized through 'the expansion of ownership over a process of valorization' (Aglietta, 1979, p.216). As we will argue, this expansion of ownership takes on an increasingly institutionally rather than personally or family-controlled character as property.

The demarcation of the petty bourgeoisie

To demarcate a ruling class we need to adopt more parsimonious criteria for identification than simple ownership and control of the means of production. It may well be the case in a purely abstract model that all ownership of a valorization process defines capital, but as Scherer (1970) notes, economic returns to capital vary greatly across organizations and across industries, with the major variable being an individual business's market power and the degree of concentration in an industry. It seems reasonable, therefore, to express reservations about the proposition that ownership of any enterprise defines an aspect of ruling-class control.

The effects of workforce size on differentiation within the abstract category of ownership are significant. It has been estimated that only 1 or 2 per cent of the economically active population constitute the capitalist class proper, because only this group has effective ownership of large corporations (Wright, 1976). There are two aspects to the expansion of ownership. The first aspect is the tendency to centralization, which is the focus of this chapter, while the second aspect is the identification of the nature of linkages that constitute this centralization: the property relations characteristic of advanced capitalist economies and the ruling class they define, which we turn to in the following chapter.

The strength of the historical tendency towards concentration is quite marked. In Britain, for instance, before the First World War about 2,000 large corporations produced half of all manufacturing output. The subsequent reduction in the number of dominant enterprises, on this criterion, is quite dramatic. By the end of the 1960s the figure was less than 150 (Prais, 1976). By the mid-1970s

> the top 100 companies accounted for 62 per cent of turnover, 64 per cent of capital employed and earned 69 per cent of profits; the top fifty companies accounted for 48 per cent of turnover, 49 per cent of capital employed, and earned 56 per cent of profits (Scott, 1979, p.15).

Furthermore, of the 1,000 largest companies, 1 per cent had 24 per cent of the total turnover. Similar concentrations are also found in the financial sector (i.e. banks, insurance companies). Neither is this concentration parochially British, as Prais (1976, p.157) reminds us: 'the development of large enterprises has followed a more or less similar evolutionary process and, if some countries lag behind others, the time lag cannot be said to be enormous.' Thus, for instance, in the EEC in the mid-1970s over half of the total industrial sales were accounted for by just 300 companies, while 100 companies controlled almost a third of industrial sales (EEC Commission, 1976). Various estimates have it that we will shortly find that the capitalist economies are dominated by approximately 300–400 companies, controlling up to two-thirds of world industrial output and three-quarters of world manufacturing assets (Holland, 1980; Barber, 1970). Their size and dominance is such that 'they exert a major impact on macro-economic aggregates such as employment, output, trade,

the 151 largest accounted for almost half the income of all manufacturing companies; in mining, the ten largest accounted for four-fifths of all mining companies' income; in retailing, the sixteen largest accounted for over two-fifths; in banking and hire purchase, the largest thirty-one companies accounted for four-fifths; and in insurance, the top twenty took almost three quarters of the income of all insurance companies (Wheelwright, 1974, p.117).

Of the 900 largest corporations, 296 accounted for roughly four-fifths of total assets, employing one in five of the workforce. The correlation between revenue and assets has often been noted.

The overall and sectoral picture has been brought up to date in a volume edited by Crough, Wheelwright and Wilshire (1980). In particular, Wheelwright (1980) demonstrates that on a comparative basis the penetration of the Australian corporate sector by foreign capital is second only to that of Canada while Nankivell presents detailed factual information on the structure, ownership and control of three primary industries central to the Australian economy, which demonstrates that the 'private agribusiness sector in Australia is characterized by a high degree of concentration and centralization of ownership, particularly by trans-national corporations' (1980, p.167). The general picture is completed for the major sectors by Crough (1980a, 1980b).

In view of this more recent information we would concur with Connell (1967, pp.46-7) that although family ownership is not insignificant, the result of foreign penetration together with the concentrated levels of shareholding would suggest that the Australian corporate economy has been characterized by family control slowly eroding into a situation of minority control with some key families retaining possession.

The extent of concentration in Europe is, on the whole, less than in Britain or the USA (Prais, 1976). In France, Germany and Sweden, the dominance of economically concentrated large firms is about half the British or US rate, in Italy about a third or quarter, while in Switzerland and the Benelux countries the degree of concentration is similar to that in Britain.

Within the European corporations, Scott (1979, p.72) indicates that 'the extent of direct family control is greater than in the USA though the extent varies considerably from country to country.' In France, Belgium and Germany (Bléton, 1966; Morin, 1974; De Vroey, 1973, 1975; Krejci, 1976) family control, while still important, has declined as family fortunes have been dispersed in a wider range of shareholdings. Half of the largest French industrial corporations were still family-controlled, although as firms grew in size the proportion of family holdings declined. Finance capital is predominant as the form of non-family control in both Belgium and France. In German, forty-seven out of 115 top industrial companies were controlled by family interests, while in fifty-one of them, three banks were dominant minority interests. Sweden and Norway have the most marked family control. In Sweden, there are fifteen families and two corporations with a majority ownership in 200 large industrial companies, employing half of those working in private industry (Tomasson, 1970). Gustavsen (1976) reports very high degrees of share-holding concentration in the top 282 companies, the top twenty shareholders holding between 41 and 86 per cent of the stock. Personal ownership is most dominant in Norway (Higley et al., 1976, pp.131-2). There, almost all companies in primary industries and shipping are personally owned, while over 80 per cent of companies in manufacturing and services are personally owned. For corporations, in 1963, 85 per cent had at least 50 per cent of the stock owned by the twenty largest shareholders, two-thirds of whom could be identified as personal controllers.

In the major Asian economy, Japan, the same pattern of declining family control and the evolution of more impersonal control is evident. The early period of pre-industrial commerce that characterized the Tokugawa period (1600–1867) was organizationally based on multi-functional family units. The period of rapid modernization that developed from the Meiji Restoration of 1868–1912 (Allen, 1965) saw the erosion of family control through two key innovations. One was the practice of direct state investment in and operation of key enterprises which were considered to be militarily or economically strategic to the modernization of Japan into a major power (Smith, 1955). As a further part of this state-sponsored modernization, private enterprise on Western lines was encouraged by the state-aided development of legally incorporated enterprises formed on joint stock principles (Westney, 1980). From these modernizing institutions emerged a new principle of capital organization – the *zaibatsu*.

Zaibatsu were large conglomerate holding companies. Four of these, Mitsui, Mitsubishi, Sumitomo and Yasuda, were dominant in the economy. All four were family-owned and controlled, despite the important state equity which was built up as part of modernization. During the 1920s and 1930s the *zaibatsu* become consolidated around bank holdings, with family control declining in importance in formal terms. However, the founding families retained minority control, relaxing majority control in order to

75

incorporate external credit.

Even after the defeat of Japan and the American occupation's attempted dismantling of the *zaibatsu*, in 1946 the four major combines still held 25 per cent of all capital, closely followed by a slightly larger number of slightly smaller combines holding a further 16 per cent. The dominance of a small number of concentrated capitals persists to the present. Halliday (1975) found that of the top 170 enterprises, 75 per cent of sales was accounted for by the thirteen largest. This concentration is no longer centred on family control, however, but on banks which appear to be less tightly coupled in their interlinks than was the case in the interwar period (Scott, 1979, pp.203).

To a considerable extent it appears that Marx's (1976) 'capital-logic' view of economic concentration becoming greater and greater has been confirmed for the major economies of the advanced capitalist world. In the largest of these corporations the concentration has tended to erode personal control through ownership, however. The thesis of a 'single hand' is not sustainable. Nor, as we will argue, has this entailed a polarization into two great contending classes. Rather, the class structure of advanced economies in its descriptive detail corresponds more closely to Weber's outline of it than it does to Marx's. This can be established through an investigation of some of the corollaries of concentration. The other side of concentration is manifest in the many dispersed firms which form the fragments of unconcentrated capital.

The extent of economic concentration would suggest that it is important to make a distinction in terms of the amount of economic resources controlled by capitalists, particularly the number of workers employed. For instance, in the most developed capitalist economy, that of the USA, 90 per cent of all business establishments employ less than 100 people, and the majority of all establishments employ less than 10 people (Aldrich, 1979, Table 2.3, p.41). Of all business establishments in the USA, only 1.7 per cent accounted for million-dollar-surplus receipts. However, this tiny percentage accounted for 76.3 per cent of all receipts. In 1973, the 93 per cent of all corporations with assets of less than a quarter of a million dollars accounted for only 7 per cent of all corporate assets (Aldrich, 1979, pp.41-2). It would be a mistake to assume that there is no qualitative difference between the two quantitative extremes.

Differentiation by workforce size has been seen as important to the analysis of capitalism in several studies. Aldrich and Weiss (1981), for example, argue against the notion that firms which have 'no employees' are those which are petty bourgeois rather than capitalist enterprises. Any small business employing labour would be assigned as capitalist on this basis. The gap between firms with and without employees may not be an empirically significant dimension. One consideration is that even when a business appears not to have any employees it may still be the case that exploitation occurs. Often, petty bourgeois businesses use, if not formally employ, substantial amounts of family labour, particularly of spouses and children. The critical distinction would seem to hinge on the differentiation of organizations on the basis of organizational scale, the environments in which they operate, and their control of varying amounts of capital investments. Large, central firms are distinguished from small peripheral establishments. The former tend to be clustered in key manufacturing industries while the latter abound in more competitive marginal industries. It is the largeness of the firms in the central economy which defines them as such. As we would expect, from Pugh and Hickson (1976), largeness gives rise to organizations which are more complex, differentiated and technically sophisticated, as well as more diversified, more extensively planned, heterogeneously skilled, management-controlled and financially sourced.

The size of organizations cross-cuts an industrial hierarchy in which there are key versus marginal industries within manufacturing. Key industries are the leading edge: they diffuse technological innovations, produce capital stock for industrial production, lead in research and development and in wage-fixing, have input and output linkages with other industries, control their own longevity and fuel economic growth. Large organizations increasingly tend to straddle more than one key industry and are interlocked into a network of firms. The relevant cut-off point between the small number of significant, large employing organizations and the large number of individually insignificant small organizations is an empirical matter (see Aldrich and Weiss, 1981, for instance). Broadly speaking, we would not ordinarily expect firms of less than ten employees to be anything other than petty bourgeois. The ruling class on this criterion would comprise, at the minimum, those capitalists combining real economic ownership with control over a labour and valorization process which is organized in large-scale units (where 'large-scale' becomes an empirically pragmatic judgment).

In demarcating the ruling class from the petty bourgeoisie the most distinctive axis of differentiation is the relative size of the organization of production, as Averitt (1968) as argued. His depiction of industry hierarchy is of a set of distinctive organization–environment interaction and interorganizational relations. In particular environments intricate organizational dependencies are the rule. These firms may obtain power by occupying an important niche, thus constituting strategic resource dependencies that hold other firms captive in networks dominated by the central organizations. The form of organizational goals, activity systems and boundary definitions that emerge do so in response to the resource constraints of the niche the organization occupies. This process has resulted in the emergence of what has been termed a 'dualistic' economy, characterized by the dichotomous differentiation of scale. Dualism of this order has been discussed in the context of specific industries in Britain (Friedman, 1977; Watts, 1980) and in the USA (Averitt, 1968).

Variations within the petty bourgeoisie

The predicted relationship between environment and form is not immutable, however. Variation within the dichotomous forms exists, as well as ambiguity between them (Barron and Bielby, 1983). With respect to variation, a number of sub-types may be suggested. An understanding of these, particularly with respect to the smaller firms, is important in differentiating types of capital. The sub-types suggested here derive from the work of Taylor and Thrift (1980).

Leader small firms

These are usually young, innovative enterprises, built on 'personal innovation and invention in terms of a new product or process, a new market or a new service' (Taylor and Thrift, 1980, p.36). Their strategies of development will be 'offensive' or 'opportunist' *vis-à-vis* the existing market structure, as they search for gaps in the market. Consequently, they will have both high birth and morbidity rates, because they operate in highly unstable and competitive environments.

Leader firms which begin as petty bourgeois enterprises, have the potential to develop into large business enterprises. This potential is rarely achieved. First, there may be shortages of finance. 'Offensive' and innovative firms will be keen to secure orders, but if these appear at an incrementally unmanageable rate, as is likely when sudden and substantial orders require a rapid expansion in business capacity, then 'the smaller the small firm the larger are likely to be the financial requirements in proportion to net assets' (Taylor and Thrift, 1980, p.36). Given the fixed costs of a share issue, then these will be proportionately more expensive for a small firm compared to a larger one (Davis and Yeoman, 1974), which will create a greater dependence of small capital upon external loan finance. This is available, however, either from major financial institutions, usually not characterized by their propensity to risk (Johns *et al.*, 1978; Johnson, 1978; Binks, 1979), or from extremely high-interest sources. A further reason why leader small firms rarely develop into large business organizations is that they are extremely susceptible to takeover by larger firms. In this way, large organizations can purchase innovative capacity whose risky development has been undertaken elsewhere. Innovations tend to be researched and 'broken-through' in small firms, but then are often developed into production in the large business organizations that take them over (Blair, 1972; Kay, 1979). Consequently, one can suggest a general pattern. Small leader firms which successfully research a niche in the marketplace tend to be taken over; if they are not successful innovators, they tend to fail in their highly competitive market environment.

There are further reasons why small firms often fail. It is much more difficult for them to survive a credit squeeze or cyclical recession. Frequently, they are linked to one innovatory idea. It is because of this that they are highly susceptible to the market for that product or substitutes for it. Despite high flexibility in developing the innovatory idea, putting it into development may mean over-stretching all resources for just one product, thus becoming highly inflexible and highly vulnerable.

For these reasons, owners of leader small firms are likely to stay petty bourgeois for only limited periods and to 'enjoy' a circulation through the class structure, most probably into either managerial or scientific middle-class positions in the large organizations that absorb the small firms, or more rarely into ruling-class positions in these organizations (Bland *et al.*, 1978, discuss the social mobility of the petty bourgeoisie). Fidler (1981), found that the latter case was rare: only 13 per cent of his sample of elite businessmen could be said to have followed such a route. Bankruptcy is always a risk for the leader petty bourgeois, of course, given the uncertainty of the environment, because their diminutive capital does not suffice for the scale on which modern industry is conducted, and partly because they may be swamped in competition with the large capitalists.

Intermediate small firms

These consist of either 'satellites' or 'loyal opposition', to use Averitt's (1968) terms. These firms are usually relatively older than leader firms because they have survived in a niche of the market which is protected by either the large business organizations' indifference or goodwill.

The 'loyal opposition' consists of single-product or single-market firms that follow one or other of two strategies. A 'traditional' (Freeman, 1974) strategy is either where product and market are rarely changed, or alternatively where firms move into a niche in the market for something no one else offers. They will remain unchallenged by large business organizations for the following reasons. The large organizations' 'enacted' environment (Weick, 1969) does not attend to them; such organizations may be fixing all their attention on issues elsewhere, or they may be complacent because of high profitability. Finally, large firms may not be legally allowed to direct their attention to a specific area of the market because of anti-monopoly legislation (Averitt, 1968). 'Satellites' are sub-contractors or franchisees of large business organizations. Sub-contracting is common in many industries in the construction sector, for instance, but can involve the use of long-term contracts and technical agreements between firms. For instance, British Leyland had sub-contracting relations with 400 firms (Friedman, 1977) while in Italy, in 1971, Fiat was estimated to have over 15,000 job contracts (Cervi, 1971).

Depending on the degree of permanency of the sub-contracted relationship and the size of the sub-contracted firm, we would expect sub-contractors with more or less permanent contracts to a few contracting large organizations to have the most potential for growth out of the petty bourgeoisie. Correlatively, the small firm sub-contracting on an independent basis to several or many other organizations, without any relationship with the contractors other than the job contracted, (i.e. no credit advance, material supplied, etc.), is more likely to remain petty bourgeois. Sub-contracting thus offers two routes: either a small but precarious independence or a larger, more certain but more dependent situation.

The existence of an almost permanent petty bourgeois sphere of operations is particularly subject to the prevailing economic winds. Sub-contracting satellites absorb much of the uncertainty of the business environment for large business organizations. This occurs in several ways. Small sub-contractors are less likely to be union shops than large business organizations. They are more readily able to lay off labour. This is particularly important in industries, such as construction, which are acutely sensitive to economic fluctuations. If some part of a larger contract is sub-contracted, and the contracting organization has a tight cash-flow or liquidity situation, it can ease it by stalling settlement with a sub-contractor: should this satellite then be bankrupted in consequence, it scarcely matters to the contractor, because the nature of the sub-contracting market is competitive and other firms will be available to take its place. This strategy is merely an extension of the 'centre–periphery relationship' that ordinarily occurs between large business organizations and competitive sub-contractors. As a risk-spreading device, large business organizations, particularly in the auto and engineering industries, will usually have several sub-contractors each producing a percentage of their demand for a given component. Should supply be jeopardized in any one sub-contractor (through strikes, bankruptcy, machine failure, etc.) then the others can fill the gap by increases in their production. Also, each competing sub-contractor is able to be competitively played off, one against the other, to minimize the costs to the central large business organization. There are clear economic advantages for larger firms in maintaining a network of small firms around them. Particularly where, as Berger (1981a, p.77) suggests, the product displays a highly non-routine degree of variability in its demand schedule, which cannot be predicted, or where the labour content is high.

Franchise satellites

These are found primarily in the retail sector. Franchisees are classic petty bourgeoisie. They have no possibility of autonomy from the centre, operate in strictly regulated and competitive markets, and are major employers of unskilled, low-wage, non-union, casual labour, which is quite ruthlessly exploited, often with their own families as the source of profit in the business.

Laggard small firms

These are ranged across manufacturing, retailing, distribution and services. They start small and remain small. These firms are also classic sites of the petty bourgeoisie. 'Satisfied' firms have been kept purposely small by their proprietors, either to retain personal or family control, or to resist bureaucratization (Smith, 1967; Fletcher, 1973; Stanworth and Curran, 1976). These firms rarely out-live their proprietor unless they pass through the family as an inheritance.

Laggard small firms are operated by craftspeople who purvey manual skills which might otherwise be for sale as wage-labour. They are founded by skilled members of the working class on small amounts of capital, often requiring little more than tools of the trade, transport, and a telephone with a domestic labourer (usually a wife) to answer it and organize the business. Such petty bourgeois operations are unlikely to lead their proprietors anywhere other than back into the proletariat if chance should disrupt the steady flow of jobs.

The ideological significance of the petty bourgeoisie

The small-business sector has a key symbolic role to play in the maintenance and reproduction of a capitalist society. As an economic role it is relatively easily acquired with small amounts of capital. Socially, it is a niche in which 'failed' sons and daughters of the middle classes who did not achieve the credentials for a 'new-middle-class' career in a bureaucratic structure can easily settle without too much status incongruity. On the other hand, it is an 'escape' from the alienation of life at the bottom of these bureaucracies for those members of the working class for whom collectivist or solidaristic strategies are anathema. This is particularly the case for the retail sector.

Many petty proprietors enjoy their role as small business-people. 'Autonomy', however illusory it may really be, is cherished. Pecuniary losses, such as fraud and pilferage, are feared as a consequence of hiring employees whom they do not trust. Research suggests this lack of trust is both well founded (Ditton, 1977) and well established (Scase and Goffee, 1980). The vast majority of small shopkeepers appear to live their lives through the values and ideology of an 'economic traditionalism' as well as being in an economically traditional area of activity. Three key elements define this ideology. First, a deeply held belief in the advantages of 'independence'. Second, a distrust of what may be regarded as the 'rational legal' elements of large complex organization, seasoned with a distaste for involvement in it. Finally, this articulates with a dislike of change and a reverence for stability and continuity and the traditional ways of doing things (Bechhofer et al., 1974, p.114).

Elements of this ideology of economic traditionalism resonate with beliefs which stress the value of a passionately held, rugged, competitive individualism founded on the belief in the moral goodness of hard work and individual achievement. In turn, this extends to a belief in what have recently been lauded as 'Victorian values' by Margaret Thatcher, particularly the commitment to a laissez-faire conception of the economy. In such an imagined reality, it is maintained that if only the state, big business and big unions would allow, such individualistic hard work would find its just and rich rewards. And where petty bourgeois success occurs, it reinforces values central to the liberal market ideology of capitalism – whether for a proletariat envious of the presumed mastery of the shopkeeper (Bechhofer et al.,

1974, p.126) or for the new middle classes fuelled by an example of buccaneering entrepreneurism and 'bootstraps capital accumulation' (Gerry and Birkbeck, 1981, p.130).

Although the small-business sector is often viewed by the employed bourgeois or proletarian as an independent and autonomous sphere, it is, of course, highly dependent on factors in the local and national economic environment, such that the life expectancy of most new entrants to the self-employed ranks is often very low indeed. Within two years a large percentage of new small businesses fail, partly because it is a highly competitive sector, and hence highly uncertain, partly because the competence of new entrants is often low. This lack of competence is not simply in financial and market knowledge, but frequently concerns the 'lack' of 'skills necessary for the supervision of labour' (Scase, 1982, p.159). Only those who were previously employed as managers will typically have these skills and many of these people may well have 'escaped' into small business as an exit from the 'constraints of the capitalist employment relationship'. This is especially likely when, in times of severe structural change, displaced skilled employers are re-engaged as self-employed sub-contractors.

If the leading-edge and intermediate small firms are one 'fuzzy' perimeter of the capitalist/petty bourgeois continuum, the small shopkeepers are at the other end of the continuum between petty bourgeois and proletarian. Between the well-paid, skilled manual worker and the petty bourgeois perhaps the only axes of privilege differentiating them are a certain independence and property. Outside of these factors there is little else. The hours are longer, the working conditions frequently as unpleasant and the responsibilities cannot be 'clocked on' and 'clocked off'. Nor are the economic returns usually at all substantial. Frequently, they amount to little more than simple reproduction. Rarely do they give rise to substantial capital accumulation. The shopkeeper is typically a very small bourgeois indeed, and quite the most marginal component of the traditional bourgeoisie, as Scase and Goffee (1982) suggest, together with the small employer, 'old laggard' firm.

Some elements of the petty bourgeoisie, particularly the small industrial and manufacturing firms, have frequently been singled out for special attention, by way of reports and commissions, even through state intervention on their behalf, as has occurred in Italy (Berger, 1981a). This focus is concentrated by state interest in the employment-generating or employment-absorbing capacity of small business. There is evidence from societies such as Japan, France and Italy (Berger, 1981a, pp.84-6) that in recession the traditional petty bourgeois sector, particularly of sub-contractors, expands. (However, alongside this must be placed the overwhelming comparative evidence of the *formal* decline of small business. This is to suggest that the growth that may have occurred will be formally unrecognized. Much petty bourgeois activity is highly *informal*, taking place in the 'hidden economy' outside the gaze of the state.) This expansion occurs both as a result of initiatives by capital-intensive industry, to reduce rigidities of labour control and supply, and of initiatives by those made unemployed. For large capitalist enterprises, the growth of sub-contracting and domestic 'out-working' is a mechanism for minimizing state and union control over their labour process, and of maintaining a core of reliable, dependent and more trusted long-term employees. However, particularly where the growth of employment is primarily the effect of a growth in 'out-working' by independent petty commodity producers, it might be analytically more correct to speak of this as a form of disguised wage-working where self-employment is entirely subordinated to the market relationships imposed and controlled by the sub-contracting capitalist organization. Whatever the situation that prevails, the relationship between petty bourgeois and large capitalist organizations is always interdependent, with varying degrees of domination of the former by the latter. The petty bourgeoisie is not simply a remnant, a decaying residue, of an earlier epoch, but a stratum with a particular, if somewhat equivocal and contradictory, ideology.

One factor is common to the petty bourgeoisie, despite its differential experience, and that is its common market situation of ownership. Ownership serves not only to differentiate these entrepreneurs from the propertyless proletariat, but from other elements of the class structure as well. On the one hand, they differ from the impersonally propertied bourgeoisie precisely in the personal meaning of their property, often expressed in the fusion of 'property for use' and 'property for power', that is captured in the phrase 'living above the shop'. But it is not just the small shopkeepers, so well documented by Bechhofer and his colleagues (1971, 1974, 1976), who have this personal meaning vested in their property. It applies particularly to the young, entrepreneurially active leader firms developed from a personal innovation, as well as to the more traditional petty bourgeois 'satellite' or 'laggard' firms.

The fusion of property in its more personal mode is most explicit when the form of that property is not so much something either acquired or accumulated on the market, but *inherited* in the family. It is the matter of inheritance which for Newby *et al.*

(1981) distinguishes the agrarian petty bourgeois from their urban compatriots, particularly shopkeepers and other more traditional members of the stratum. Because of the high cost barriers to entry in farming in most, if not all, of the advanced societies, few farmers establish themselves by the ideologically time-honoured ways of saving and hard work. As Newby *et al.* (1981) point out, with respect to their English East Anglian sample, most are farmers because their forebears were farmers. They were born into farming, were socialized into farming and, most importantly, they inherited farms. In this respect, the agrarian petty bourgeoisie is an example of an occupational *and* property-owning community with strong intergenerational local ties and commitments, with relatively little exposure to the labour market as a seller of labour (Newby *et al.*, 1981, pp.48-51). Where traditional rural social relations persist, members of the community will also tend to be 'deferential' in their respect for larger landowners.

What small, property-owning farms and other members of the petty bourgeoisie tend to share, irrespective of the intensity of their personal relationship to their property as one of guardianship or stewardship, at the agrarian extreme, shading into more calculative relationships, is an opposition to large, impersonal organizations. This frequently manifests itself in a populist opposition not only to trade unions, but to large organizations of capital and to the state as well. Indeed, Conway (1981) in his discussion of the rise and fall of the agrarian petty bourgeois in Canada, characterizes the political ideology of the petty bourgeois as being, typically, in Lenin's (1963) terms, that of 'populism'. Hence, the characteristically remarked opposition of the traditional petty bourgeois to big labour *and* big capital is a response to both as manifestations of industrial capitalism's development. As Conway (1981, p.5) succinctly puts it: 'Such modernization is a threat because of the unavoidable consequences of unfettered capitalist development for all small producers: either they enlarge themselves at the expense of others or they go out of business and join the ranks of wage-labour.'

Petty bourgeois commodity producers tend, on the one hand, to have a more intense personal involvement with their property. On the other hand, this leads them to be critical and hostile towards those manifestations of capitalist development which threaten them with a highly uncertain and a dependent future. Typically, their response to the progressive development of capitalism is regressive: a response which evokes an earlier, mythologized independence, security and certainty, against a future which they grasp only inasmuch as it seems to hold only highly restricted places for them. The regression desired, the myth held in retrospect, is of a 'moral economy' (the term so aptly borrowed from Thompson (1971) by Bechhofer and Elliot (1981), in which capitalism would once more be in a free, healthy infancy, unsullied by cancers of state, labour or corporate power and intervention, setting a stage on which they might proudly and fearlessly parade their leading roles. Such 'retrospects', as Bechhofer and Elliot (1981, p.193) stress, signify deeply resonant existential crises, as well as economic crises, in the advanced societies, which can and have been orchestrated into politically popular refrains by right-wing parties. However, the programmes promoted by these parties have to face the *realpolitik* of the state and its baroque institutions, in a complex economy and society dominated by highly concentrated and centralized capital.

The 'fate of our times', Max Weber predicted, was to be bureaucracy. More recently, it has been discovered that bureaucracy is a necessary concomitant of bigness (Pugh and Hickson, 1976). The depersonalization of rule and property has come to define a minuscule ruling class proper, although ownership more generally defines a larger petty bourgeoisie. However, the ruling class of ownership is surrounded by vast layers of a far more complex corporate structure than that defined by simple 'men of property'. Ruling in this sense refers to the strategic planning of the major goals, activities and decisions of the corporate economy, state and civil society, to which we shall now turn. It is, we will see, a far distance from the mythology of the petty bourgeoisie.

5 The organization and structure of the corporate ruling class

Ownership of the means of production is increasingly not actually vested in an individual. This has been the case since at least the development of the joint stock company in the latter half of the nineteenth century. With the development of joint stock companies, a form of organization is constituted which is 'a distinct legal entity comprising members who provide the share capital for its activities and officers who act in its name' (Scott, 1982, p.229). Where a group of such corporations is held together by either a complete or majority ownership of shares by some other corporation it is conventional, as Scott suggests, to refer to this group as an 'enterprise' or 'concern'.

Ownership

The stock company is an institutional mechanism for organizing capital provided by a multitude of private owners. The development of the stock exchange to its present significance was contingent upon the advent of limited-liability legislation (from 1856 onwards) in consequence of which the owners of an enterprise were no longer directly responsible for ensuring its viability. Prior to the development of such legislation in Britain, owners were responsible for any debts incurred by the enterprise. One consequence of this had been to limit the size of the company and to maximize the amount of involvement of the owner/entrepreneur whose personal fortune was at risk if the enterprise failed. Henceforward, there were no such impediments to the growth of capitalist organizations. Joint stock legislation and the extension of credit raised the possibility of capital and personal assets being wholly separate. The owner/entrepreneur was thus free to risk not personal assets but those of others. The existence of this freely available credit enabled organizations to achieve a growth unlimited except by their capacity to raise capital on the market and to manage the increased scale of operations.

The existence of financial resources meant that organizations could grow through an increasingly concentrated organization of what had hitherto been small, independent firms. As these organizations grew, the membership increased and the workload of the original owner/entrepreneur would come to exceed any individual's powers of conception and execution. In these instances, the usual step was to appoint an executive group, whose task it was to carry on the organizing activity as deputy to, and on behalf of, the owner(s). Within a profit-making corporation the executive comprises a board of directors elected by the shareholders. This elected executive then selects an employed executive of managerial and salaried workers, who in turn employ wage-labour. The private owners of capital execute their mandate either personally or by proxy at the shareholders' meetings provided for by company law and statute (Abrahamsson, 1977; Abrahamsson and Broström, 1980). As we shall argue in a subsequent chapter, intervention by non-executive shareholders in the running of companies is an extraordinary occurrence.

Stockholders' capital is invested in shares in the form of stocks or other securities, which function as separate units of 'ownership' on the capital market. These shares of accumulated capital define 'capital' in an abstract and broad sense. The additive accumulation of a discrete bundle of ownership rights in the form of shares invested in a stock company represents a particular and a generalizable interest at one and the same time. Particular, because it engages a part of the capital employing men and women in particular tasks at a particular place and time. Generalizable, because the possessors of the shares invest them with only one general interest in mind: valorization. That this takes place through a particular firm is immaterial: the capital market is simply an exchange for mobilizing fluid investments at the return best calculated to serve the general interest in valorization. Hence, no specificity attaches to the particularity of any investment. It may just as easily be made elsewhere by selling one set of shares and buying another, giving rise to the profits and losses associated with investment in shares as fluid or 'liquid' assets.

There is, however, one very particular consequence of this mobilization of a multitude of discrete units of capital. As a form of property it has an important organizational significance. This is because materialization in a share of stock represents an individual's power not only to 'risk' private capital, but also, and more importantly, *all it entails*. The ownership of a share in capital entails a very important and most powerful right of ownership. This is one which by itself defines the various other kinds of ownership that can be enjoyed. These may include physical control over objects, the right to use these objects as one chooses, the right to transfer ownership, and the right to income from the lending of objects (Honoré, 1961; Abrahamsson and Broström, 1980, p.23). All of these rights are contingent upon the right to destroy, consume or dispose of the object(s) over which these rights are claimed. As Becker (1977, p.20) put it: 'One who has all the rights on the list but lacks the right to capital may possibly own the object in a derived sense, but one who has the right to capital owns it "essentially".' Thus, the right to capital represents an 'essential' ownership.

Derived ownership would consist in the 'right a person has to a job, for instance, working on objects with all the powers delegated to an incumbent of that particular position, except the right to destroy, consume or dispose of the objects upon which such individuals expend their labour. This right, as well as the delegated right to labour, depends on the prior disposition of capital in the form of shares of stock. These are invested subject to calculation (and frequent miscalculation) in anticipation of a better-than-average return in a particular organization. Such an organization thus becomes contingent upon those particular shares. Capital, in the form of investments, may be withdrawn from particular organizations, all rights therein being liquidated, and then reinvested with similar rights elsewhere. In so doing, however, the particular derived rights of specific people to labour at their jobs at their place of employment is ineradicably withdrawn. Hence, the very real dependency of labour on capital in a formal as well as a substantive sense.

The dependency of labour and the power of capital is not only formal, but substantively secured through the legal system. It is the importance of legal definitions of ownership which leads Abrahamsson and Broström (1980), citing Hedenius (1975), to distinguish between two dimensions of ownership rights. The first is contingent on the substantive system of law and is referred to as 'protection of possession'. This is the protection that an owner has in terms of the legal system from being involuntarily dispossessed of a thing to which ownership is 'rightfully' claimed. It protects an owner's access to something owned. A further dimension of ownership is 'freedom of disposition', which is the right to do with that which is owned as one will, including the right to let others work for one 'in' that which is owned. It is this

89

right of disposition which enables capital to have what is an inherent capacity for control over people, because of the control over the means of production and hence the 'life chances' of employed persons. However, due to the pervasiveness of abstracted individualism, this appears under law simply as a set of dependencies between individual legal subjects. Capitalist enterprises are constituted by the state as an individual legal subject (one who can sue and be sued). Hence, the formal equality of abstracted individualism appears to constitute not only concrete individuals, rendering them all as equal citizens, but also to treat equally all forms of an incorporated company, masking enormous differences in social relations, contingent upon the increasing concentration of capital.

Phases in the economic concentration of the corporate ruling class

The process of concentration of capital appears not to have been marked by regular attrition of autonomous individual corporations as by discontinuous moments of mergers, consolidation, bankruptcies, etc. These processes are always evident in some area of the economy. Characteristically, however, they display heightened peaks of activity, particularly with respect to mergers. Typically, accentuated merger activity 'occurs in waves, with a precise location in the overall movement of capital formation' (Aglietta, 1979, p.219). The process of capital accumulation, which is also a process of class formation or consolidation, has always been an uneven one. Cyclical movements in growth rates, profit levels, class distributions of income and the political and institutional strength of classes can be seen to be related to the more fundamental movements in the rate of capital accumulation.

The form and intensity of what can be seen as class struggle alters at different stages of this cycle. At the end of the 'ascendant phase', or upswing, the rate of surplus appropriation and redeployment begins to slow down and the rate of new investment consequently declines. At this point, with obsolescence of equipment and under-capitalization potentially weakening corporate responses, mergers typically occur. They are also liable to occur at the end of the downswing because of the under-capitalization that exists in this phase of a recession. In this conjuncture, centralization is achieved by being one of those units of valorization that have survived the 'massive destructions of capital'. New class relations are then formed by the destruction of former organizational conditions. The elimination of inefficient businesses and the centralization of economic activity establishes new competitive relations and possibilities of valorization (Aglietta, 1979, p.219).

Specific structural forms emerge to organize this centralization of capital. A single centre of disposal and control can in this way accumulate quite distinct cycles of valorization, in terms of the production and realization of commodities. Chief amongst these forms of enterprise are the giant multinational corporations and financial centres controlling differentiated divisional profit centres, adding a new centre for each new cycle of valorization.

Over the last century it has been established that there have been three major phases of capital centralization: in the late 1890s; in the late 1920s; and in the late 1960s (Aglietta, 1979, pp.222-3). Concurrently, independently and to some extent in parallel with these phases have developed distinctive successive organizational forms: the bureaucratic structure, the divisional structure, and what might be characterized as a cultural structure.

There is some debate in the literature as to whether or not these phases can be regarded as 'long waves' of capitalist development. The notion that capitalist development is punctuated by long waves was introduced by Kondratief (1979), who concluded that capitalist development displays a characteristically long-wave cycle, an analysis which has been taken up by other investigators, notably Schumpeter (1939), Rostow (1978) and Mandel (1975). (Recent bibliographical guides are Hill, 1980, and Barr, 1979.) The central question-mark about the long-wave approach must be to what extent these periodic movements can be generalized, with regional variations, to the world economy, given the evident differences between countries in resources, population growth levels, stages of development, technologies and levels of interdependence. The USA has had a hegemonic role in international capital formation in the twentieth century, and hence a generative role in the development of international phases which have been complementary primarily to the dominant US economy. Models of corporate organization have been characteristically innovated, initially in the USA, during these discontinuous phases which have achieved widespread adoption. Changing phases of capitalist development are thus connected with associated strategic decisions on corporate policy, which have had the effect of producing forms of organization characteristic of each phase.

There are two sets of circumstances which are conducive to heightened merger activity at particular phases of capitalist development. The end of the downward phase, when inefficient units have been eliminated, new markets explored and the reallocation of productive capacity has taken place according to the calculation of different potentialities of growth, and also the end of a long phase of increased capital formation, when the rate of growth begins to dip or decline (e.g. 1926 and 1967) as a result of the fall in the overall rate of return on productive capital (Aglietta, 1979, p.224). Stronger, more efficient corporations can attempt to profit from high rates of return to extend their own space for valorization. Thus, a wage of mergers follows, in the appropriate financial conditions. These are, first, that there is an upswing of financial circulation and/or, second, the existence of a cash-flow surplus to the requirements of the corporation. However the mergers are financed, what is effected are *transfers of ownership*, a qualitative transformation in property relations.

Organizational development and management structure

The merger wave of the end of the nineteenth century consisted of horizontal mergers (diversification) and vertical mergers (incorporation of suppliers, marketing outlets, etc.). These produced an organizational form in which several distinct establishments were constituted under a unified ownership as a single process of valorization. It was during the period of the 'Great Depression' (1873–96) that a great many petty bourgeois artisanal industries disappeared. Initially, the subordination of distinct plants to a central organization was more formal than real. Within these plants previous owners frequently continued to control the labour process, but now as more or less independent managers, directing, evaluating and disciplining work (Edwards, 1979, p.18). Their methods of doing this were much as they had been throughout the century, combining elements of patriarchal family autocracy and paternalism (Hobsbawm, 1976, p.216) with detailed technical knowledge of the labour process derived from 'greater mastery of the rules and greater ability, knowledge, and experience in production' (Offe, 1976, p.25) than subordinates, due to the still essentially task-continuous status organization of the labour process, where each level of the task hierarchy presupposed a mastery of all lower levels. This was the traditional type of organization structure which had developed from the guild form of organization. In these organizations, position in the status hierarchy was co-terminous with position in the skill structure. The higher the level of skills mastered, the higher the status. Under these circumstances the property and control relations were apparent. They were reinforced by the relatively tight discipline of a product market in which there was a large number of small competitive firms and by a largely unorganized labour market, outside of the craft unions.

A single entrepreneur, usually flanked by a small coterie of foremen and managers, ruled the firm. These bosses exercised power personally, intervening in the labour process often to exhort workers, bully and threaten them, reward good performance, hire and fire on the spot, favour loyal workers, and generally act as despots, benevolent or otherwise. They had a direct stake in translating labour power into labour, and they combined both incentives and sanctions in an idiosyncratic and unsystematic mix. There was little structure to the way power was exercised, and workers were often treated arbitrarily. Since workforces were small and the boss was both close and powerful, workers had limited success when they tried to oppose his rule (Edwards, 1979, pp.18-19).

These methods of control were of much less value once enterprises began to develop into large-scale organizations, such as was occurring in railways, mines and steel mills. This was particularly the case in the latter, as formerly independent sites of small labour processes, which had been previously linked through the market, were brought under the discipline of a single hierarchical centre as a result of economic concentration. The 'continuity' of the status hierarchy and the task organization no longer held. Organizational structures were becoming increasingly 'task-discontinuous' (Offe, 1976), in which simple, direct, personal owner-control no longer had any technical basis. It was in this situation that inside contracting developed as the predominant regime of discipline and control (Clawson, 1980; Littler, 1980).

Inside contracting, as Clawson (1980) calls it, or internal contracting, to use Littler's (1980) term, was well established in both US and British industry in the nineteenth century. In Britain it was particularly developed in textiles, mining and ironworks and it was in the metal-working industry in the USA that it became particularly well entrenched. Essentially, the system comprised an employer and owner of capital hiring a number of internal sub-contractors. Some similarities existed between inside contractors and independent sub-contractors. The major exception was that, unlike the latter, the former were employees of the company, working inside the company buildings, using the company's machines, materials and equipment to produce commodities for sale only to the company. The inside contractor hired and fired employees, set wage rates, methods of production and exercised discipline over the workers. The contracting system was the continuation of task-continuous status organization under changed conditions of valorization. Inside contracting could mediate between one centre of valorization and many labour processes, where these were now combined through hierarchy where once they had been combined through the market (the distinction between market and hierarchy as differing principles of control is developed in Lindblom, 1977). One centre of valorization could employ as many inside contractors as it subordinated labour processes. Even though diverse labour processes were subordinated under a single centre of valorization, this subordination was achieved through pre-bureaucratic, direct and personal control. Clawson (1980) suggests that much of this personal control was self-imposed and monitored by workers in the application of craft skills. This may well be true, but would certainly seem to be over-stated. Other accounts stress that notions of craft control are not only romantic, but indeed 'could often be a cloak concealing ugly relations of exploitation and ill-treatment' (Littler, 1980, p.157). Doubtless in some situations pride in the application of hard-earned and jealously protected skills was an essential element of control of this labour process. But it should not be assumed that this was the widespread rule.

Internal contracting solved by default the problem of surveillance and control of an increasing scale of operations which capitalists geared up to where greater financial leverage was available. By default, we mean that it was simply an extension of pre-existing forms of direct, personal control which incorporated within a larger organizational form the petty capitalist basis of prior, smaller production. It instituted the profit motive in a lower order of quasi-entrepreneurs whose calculation concerned only the labour power utilization of the sub-contractees. Now, as Clawson (1980) suggests, this did not necessarily entail naked exploitation: craft control could cloak it or it might even be subsumed entirely by co-operative forms of sub-contracting such as Schloss (1898, cited in Littler, 1980, p.160) reports.

Internal contracting had a number of attractions from the capitalists' point of view. It was flexible in terms of demand fluctuations and their impact on employment. No risk was entailed to the capitalist by defects or variety in the raw material characteristics as only finished products were accepted. (By the same token, however, it was wide open to pilferage and fraud.) As a fixed payment was made for the finished product, the employer was saved the risk of capital accounting and actual costs getting out of line. Capital risks could be determined easily. For the workers, it 'provided financial incentives, and a path of upward mobility, for key groups of workers'; and managerially, for the contractor, 'it was the agency of effort stabilization and task allocation' (Littler, 1980, p.161).

In both Britain and the USA internal contracting began to decline during the last quarter of the nineteenth century (in Japan, it declined in the period 1910–20). In both countries the decline was linked to the Great Depression, although the response was quite dissimilar. In the USA a situation of declining demand, saturated existing markets, increasing costs of production and massive growth in trade unionism led to the fairly widespread adoption of piece-rates, a high-profits, high-wages policy in leading-edge industries premised on more or less 'bastardized' forms of Taylorism (see Clegg and Dunkerley, 1980, pp.84-6 for more extended discussion). In Britain internal contracting developed under an intensification of effort into a more direct employment relationship, in which the contractor gradually became a foreman, or else became submerged into a directly employed work group as either an ordinary worker or perhaps a chargehand. However, as Littler (1980, p.167) notes, pressures were under way which served to undermine the foreman's role almost as soon as it had emerged. These consisted of the sub-division of the foreman's role with the appearance of a number of white-collar technical operations, prefigurative of a more systematic management, and the development of a centralized wages department to administer payment systems designed by new white-collar workers. Not only did this remove discretion from workers, it also removed it from foremen. From this development dates the antipathy that, in the late 1920s and 1930s, foremen and supervisors were to articulate towards the rationalization of Taylorism – opposition which, however, was necessarily weakened by the depression.

Class struggles between 1860 and 1920 established the limits and frontiers of organizational control (Goodrich, 1975; Clegg and Dunkerley, 1980; Clawson, 1980; Clegg, 1981). Bureaucratic forms of control, as we know them today, developed from this era, earlier in the USA, Italy and France, later in Britain, when capital attempted to establish its control over labour, particularly skilled craft labour. Essentially, this took the shape of smashing craft unionism, introducing piece-work (and, subsequently, scientific management) and developing the apparatus of management structures, functional departments and control associated with it. Workers lost craft control to the extent that they became less skilled and their jobs became less demanding of skill, and they lost the capacity for collective action as they became more isolated from each other and the craft tradition.

Control passed from a direct, extensive, personal basis to a bureaucratic structure of planners, technicians, time-and-motion experts and foremen, buttressed by a rapidly burgeoning female, clerical, 'white-collar' labour force. These developments, particularly the introduction of scientific management and change in the organization of work, amounted to a strategy of expanding capital's control in the pursuit of efficient capital accumulation, particularly as this could be achieved by technical innovations that could be introduced as craft controls were eroded.

It is important not to assume too much of a 'capital-logic' in the process however. Under the same general imperatives of capital accumulation, but on quite distinct terrains of civil society (and, one might add, state formation), a similar structure of internal contracting was quite differently articulated.

In Japan, particularly in the engineering and metal-working industries, up until the early 1920s, internal contracting on the *oyakata* system was prevalent. *Oyakata* were independent labour contractors who provided sub-contracted labour, *kokata*, for a lump-sum contract. However, the internal social relationships between *oyakata* and *kokata* were neither purely exploitative nor mediated only by a craft consciousness. They were influenced also by a highly traditional social solidarity founded on norms of patriarchal authority for the *oyakata* and loyal submission and devotion, by the *kokata*, regulated by a strict status hierarchy determined by length of service.

What undermined this determination of production relationships by the status desiderata of the Japanese civil society was the development of the productive forces themselves. By the 1920s the *zaibatsu*, as we observed in the previous chapter, had become widely established. The scale of plants and rates of technological change were increasing markedly. A proletarian class and consciousness were forming. New relations of production in a booming economy were creating high labour turnover and other, more explicitly vocal, forms of class struggle. The strategy that developed amongst Japanese capitalists to cope with this conjuncture was to tighten their recruitment screening, to move from sub-contracted labour to direct employment. The response by the *oyakata* leadership, predictably, was to resist this undercutting of their own power, and, given the civil relations, this resistance was founded on solidarity between *oyakata* and *kokata*.

The response by Japanese capital to this threat was one of eventual incorporation. Strategically, it was the best course of action open to them given the highly task-discontinuous nature of Japanese corporations. The *oyakata* had a virtual monopoly of technical expertise; most company officials were university graduates lacking practical shop experience, a situation very different from that in Britain (Littler, 1980, p.177). In the face of continued resistance, solidarity, and task-discontinuity, Japanese capital could hardly practise stand-off tactics. The appropriate strategy appeared to be one of acknowledging the success of the *oyakata* struggle and to incorporate them into the future of the corporation rather than attempt any exclusionary tactics: 'Employers offered the *oyakata* guarantees of lifelong employment, regular salaries, and even management-led recognition of *oyakata*-led unions' (Littler, 1980, p.177). One could say that the foundations of Japanese welfare-paternalistic capitalism were laid on the success of the *oyakata* class struggle. From this incorporation developed the characteristic dualism of the overall Japanese economy between the paternalist, protective core corporations with their highly age- and seniority-stratified internal labour markets, and the periphery of highly competitive, unstable, small, sub-contracting firms. (See Littler, 1980, and more especially, Dore, 1973.)

Real subordination of the labour process was only achieved with the subsumption of forms of internal contracting. More especially, in the larger corporations, it was achieved more satisfactorily with the creation of a unitary centralized functional structure. Three principles govern this centralized functional structure. The first of these was the creation of separate *functional departments* for vertically integrated labour processes. Each major managerial function reached from a centralized head office in a chain of command into the different departments, which became organized on functional lines. Each category of commodity thus developed a production department. Second, the *separation of production and marketing* as distinct functions emerged in order to handle in an efficient and economic manner the problem of sales and realization of value. Differentiated functional units, defined not by a completed commodity but by a function in an integrated process, cannot, however, be the organizational unit from which a rational sales policy could emanate. A centralized sales unit developed, which, within parameters defined by the production units, marketed the enterprise's commodities. Finally, a *head office* was created whose task was to co-ordinate the functionally differentiated whole. The logic is impeccably Spencerian and its result – the consistent correlation between the size of organization and the degree of bureaucratization of its formal procedures – is well established (Pugh and Hickson, 1976).

This structural form was related to the development of parti-cular industrial sectors. In the USA it was connected to the dominance of the railroads industry at the turn of the century.

97

Hence, it was centred on the iron and steel, metallurgical indus-tries, spreading into automobile manufacturing as it developed.

The growth of unitary structures, particularly as a result of mergers, produced organizations with increasingly cumbersome hierarchies. As firms were merged, previously autonomous directors, often of what had been family firms, were co-opted on to the new board as part of the merger deal. Consequently, this frequently produced conflicting channels of communication and control between the not yet wholly subsumed structure and that which was created by co-optation. Moreover, even where these conflicts between a founding/managing family and a more anonymous capital did not exist

> Excessive staff and managerial slack at each level of the
> hierarchy will induce imitative consequences among lower-level
> staff and the presence of functional heads in strategic decision-
> making will introduce biases and inefficiency given that their
> position will be at least partly dictated by their own empire-
> building objectives (Cowling, 1982, p.83).

The next major innovation in structural form was connected with the growth sectors of the interwar and postwar periods, particularly in the petrochemical and pharmaceutical industries, and became widely touted as a means of overcoming some of the above-mentioned problems.

This innovation was that of *divisionalization*, which occured as a result of the intensified conditions of accumulation of the second great wave of this century, the downturn phase of which was the 1920s and 1930s, punctuated and defined by the Wall Street Crash of 1929 and the worldwide depression of the ensuing decade. Divisionalization was initially prompted in the USA by the process of diversification which developed in the down-phase of accumulation (i.e. during the late 1920s and 1930s). This diversification of production maximized the chances of economic survival of enterprises in these competitively difficult years. Hitherto, the typical enterprise had been organized around a single product line on the basis of large-scale production, with product lines related by technology and with one major market. The shift was to a diversification of product lines, but inasmuch as these differentiated products were produced, and marketed in widely different circumstances, the central strategic objective of valorization became increasingly difficult to control, as the centralized structure was increasingly remote from the fields of operation. Consequently, it operated under conditions of increas-ing uncertainty with respect to strategic areas such as sales, costs, production norms, investments, technologies, sources of capital, etc. Such uncertainty was open to self-interested exploitation by local management seeking its own self-aggrandizement, material comfort and security. At the level of each functional department it was easier to cope with these problems, although there remained no effective mechanism for integrating the different departments in the interest of overall valorization.

The organizational solution consisted of the development of a multidivisional product structure, headed by functional managers, in which the commodity rather than the function became the basis of the organization, with each division acting as a profit centre, under highly autonomous operational management. At the same time, highly centralized policy units were introduced such that the head office became the locus of the overall strategic functions of finance, planning, co-ordination, research and development. Subordinate, divisional profit centres thus became highly accountable in terms of their contribution to overall profitability – they could be axed, developed or bifurcated as overall organization strategy dictated. Control could be much tighter than under the unitary structure.

Modern divisionalized business organizations became corporations organized around profit centres and composed of a number of constituent companies, spread across a number of plants or sites. The corporation develops as a global system of centralized informational control. There exists a central co-ordinating and planning apparatus which processes all information which converges on it. Telephonic and electronic communications were essential to this.

It would be mistaken to assume that the 'modern' divisional form emerged universally and naturalistically out of the 1930s merger and restructuring of production. No unilinear evolution can be assumed

> from the loose but centralized control of the owner–manager to a highly formal hierarchical structure in which operational policy is delegated to specialized divisions and performance is monitored by the representatives of the owners in a manner remote from the geographical and social location of operations (Loveridge, 1982, p.26).

While this may have been the preferred US form, captured so vividly in Chandler's (1962) case-studies, which by a combination of mimesis (Meyer and Rowan, 1977) and natural selection (Aldrich, 1979), has become the embodiment of modernity on an international scale, there is substantial evidence demonstrating that increasing concentration of capital and scale of activities may not entail anything like as formally rational and 'real' subordination of distinct managerial labour processes. On the contrary, merger and acquisition may not produce rational reconstruction on divisional lines, so much as 'federations of separate authority structures based on disparate cultural systems and mode of operation' (Loveridge, 1982, p.33). This is particularly characteristic of the British engineering and metal-working industry. Here, concentration has produced a loosely coupled holding company in which subsidiary profit centres 'have retained an apparent autonomy in marketing, commodity buying, and employee relations for nearly a hundred years' (Loveridge, 1982, p.33). As other observers of the British industrial scene (e.g. Child and Francis, 1977) have noted, the same pattern has remained characteristic even for many enterprises which only emerged out of the 1960s merger wave. What develops is a less strongly divisionalized and decentralized firm. Instead, the enterprise which co-ordinates the federally structured profit centres functions as a strong market base for raising liquidity at the lower interest rates that obtains for prime borrowers. This capital then was able to be spread through the individual firms to minimize risk, or increasingly be used to acquire new assets abroad as well as in the UK. Capital limits were the main device of central control and cost accounting the main mechanism of surveillance of the individual profit centres (Loveridge, 1982, p.32). As with the example of Japanese paternalism, the federal form owed its structure as much to the forms of resistance and response from those below as from a rational strategy designed from above:

> The federal structure of control permits the assertion of the
> localized system of values and beliefs incorporated in the
> structure and technology of long-established small enterprises.
> It recognizes the importance of sectionalism in union organiza-
> tion and of the utilitarian individualist beliefs . . . underlying
> union policy in Britain over the last century. The system of
> employment from which these beliefs arose is therefore
> sustained as much by the expressed preferences of labour as
> those of management (Loveridge, 1982, p.50).

It would be mistaken to conclude, however, that the strength of federalism, where one might, on the basis of US-inspired models, have expected divisionalization, is simply another instance of the shopfloor power of British industry entrenching 'irrationalism'. It is doubtful if it would have succeeded for so long if it did not also offer corporate rulers very tangible results. Most notable of these was the opportunity it offered for isolating and fragmenting the corporate workforce and operational management. With increasing state intervention into this fragmented structure through agencies such as the Industrial Reorganization Commission in areas such as the machine-tool and motor industries, there have been attempts to exert a more centralized, long-term discipline on the local profit centres' short-term calculations, primarily through central office specialists attached to local firms. A consequence of this attempt at increasing formalization is both greater workforce–management conflict at the local level, and greater conflict between local management and strategic management as discipline tightens. One consequence of tightening discipline has been divestment of profit centres that fail to meet target contributions to profit. Given the federal structure, and the way that it has maintained intact the local culture and identity, a frequent response to this strategy of liquidation has been the development of 'sit-ins' leading to worker co-operatives, as at Triumph Meriden motorcycle works (Fleet, 1976). Management as well as workers have been involved in these. Once more the attributes of civil society can be seen to be resistant to the logic of both capital and state. Class formation always occurs on civil terrains whose distinctness can produce quite diverse effects from seemingly identical capital-logic requirements.

One consequence of both the aggrandized unitary and holding companies was that they maintained a much larger managerial stratum than the 'lean and hungry' divisionalized forms. The development of the latter was 'an adaptive response by top-level, equity-holding management to the growing encroachment on profits of discretionary behaviour by lower-level management,' as Cowling (1982, p.90) observes. This analysis suggests that the adoption of the multidivisional form is a result of politically strategic choices and resistance to them. During the early years of the merger wave, in the 1930s in the USA, in the 1960s wave in Britain, the over-run of costs due to the exertion of operational management's discretion, led strategic management to impose a new structure as a mechanism for tightening control. As part of this increased control it is likely that different company divisions within the divisionalized corporation will become specialized on a particular stage in product or market development. What is also likely is that, in doing so, the range of consumer choice becomes narrowed. It is not just that mergers produce market concentration, but that they have been entered into largely to eliminate competition and thus increase market dominance. Newbould (1970) discovered that these considerations, rather than economies of scale, were behind merger activity. Thus, it is not surprising that merger activity has led in part to an internationalization of capital.

With the rapid development of large business organization in the post-Second World War period, a new internationalization of productive capital has developed in the form of the transnational corporation (TNC). This is not to argue that in earlier periods the internationalization of capital had not occurred. It had done so, originally in terms of the international commodity trade between different national producers in national markets, organized through trading companies such as the East India Companies of Holland and Britain or the Hudson Bay Trading Company of Canada. A second phase of internationalization occurred with the development of finance capital associated with the wave of centralization that centred on the late 1890s in the USA and continental Europe. This saw the development of nationally based financiers investing in bonds (and occasionally stock) in other countries' productive units. The contemporary phase of internationalization matured in the postwar period with the development of large divisionalized business organizations with their operations divided on a global scale. This process of the internationalization of capital has been the subject of many recent contributions to the literature (e.g. Magdoff, 1969; Vernon, 1971; Murray, 1971; Rowthorn, 1980; Emmanuel, 1972; Barnett and Muller, 1974; Poulantzas, 1975; Hymer, 1976; Radice, 1975).

The internationalization of capital represents an intensification of the basic tendency, which Marx (1976) recognized, towards the concentration and centralization of capital. First, capital has become concentrated such that its operation is no longer consistent with the sovereignty of a purely national territory. Second, the centralization of economic power in a single centre of strategic calculation and control over a diversified, conglomerate and oligopoly market, internalizes diverse markets within the structure of a single TNC. This has created a relative immunity to the macro-economic policies of the state, which now have a restricted ability to control national economic markets. This is not so much because of industrial market concentration in any one sector but because of the increase in conglomeration and diversification across sectors (Blair, 1972, pp. 41-83; Blumberg, 1975, pp.16-81). Strategic control becomes possible over a far broader business environment for any particular firm, to the extent that the modern conglomerate creates an 'internal market' which behaves quite differently from traditional oligopolistic markets and responds in a different fashion to policy prescriptions (Hawley and Noble, 1980, pp.7-8).

This strategic control is further enhanced by the TNCs' ability to administer their prices in situations quite unresponsive to market forces, because of calculation and operations in a global arena. Such calculation is able to include factors such as tax and/or tariff minimization and transfer pricing, or strategies of recording low or negative profitability for subsidiaries during wage-bargaining, control of raw material and product markets, manipulation of final demand, etc. (Hawley and Noble, 1980, p.8). Pricing becomes rather more a matter of political than purely economic calculation, although one should not over-state these capacities.

One consequence of political calculation is that the world market has become specialized, allowing different mixes of leading, intermediate and laggard companies to be found in different regions of the world economy (Fröbel et al., 1978). This is clearly a decisive factor in the formation of classes on a world scale. It may well be the case that leader companies will in future be set up mainly in developed regions, if only because of the reluctance of their managers to live elsewhere or because of the unavailability of skilled labour. Similarly, laggard companies may in future be the ones that are established in less developed regions, thus exacerbating the problems of low wages, unskilled labour and consequent instabilities and low rates of capital formation. Those firms may have only a short-run duration in their new locations because they may well be nearing the end of their product or market cycle, and so in highly competitive but non-developing situations will be looking only for plentiful or cheap labour for which the next logical move is over the border to the next cheap-labour haven. As a managerial strategy, this depends upon the degree of organization of the labour movement on either a national scale, or in particular regions of the world economy. One central factor affecting the corporate profile within any given region will be the policy of the state in enticing capital to the region and its attractiveness in terms of labour-force requirements, access to capital and so on.

During the 1970s there is evidence that the divisional form is itself being superseded among firms at the leading edge, such as Hewlett Packard (Peters and Waterman, 1982; Deal and Kennedy, 1982). With the development of access to computer power from decentralized terminals, the functional necessity of a convergent centre disappears. And this is in fact what appears to be happening in leading corporations in areas such as California's Silicon Valley. However, this is not simply a devolution of centres and their reconstitution in what were previously peripheral divisions. Instead, what we have is an attempt to decentre organization entirely. This is especially the case in the new high-technology industries that have sprung out of the micro-chip industry, at the product design and implementation level. (The chip assembly itself takes place in Asian factories under quite different circumstances.) With easy computer access, decision-making data are no longer necessarily centralized. The tendency is to try and create group, informal and consensual decision-making and responsibility without formal centres and hierarchy, premised on common managerial access to information, collective discussion, and control of the agenda through the parameters modelled in the data and their analysis. These parameters are placed there in terms of the dominant values of the corporation, often embodied in the mythological and ideological functioning of the chief executive officer. This person becomes lionized as the bearer of the 'corporate culture' in an elaborate iconography of values created, maintained, proselytized, mythologized and ideologized as the 'soul' or 'essence' of the firm that 'plays together', or whatever. Consensus, achieved through a 'common culture' (hence a certain facile fascination with Japanese practice) becomes the hallmark of management as *corporate*, rather than functional or divisional. The assumption is that cultural corporate-ness can overcome tendencies to interest maximization through strategic contingency. Consequently, control shifts to a highly internalized and group-reinforced mode, where a premium is put on collective creativity by a management team, often remuner-ated in part by profit-sharing. Management gurus at Graduate Schools of Business who are also tightly coupled with networks of international consulting firms tout this as the 'wave of the future'. How generalizable it will actually be, given its development in primarily non-unionized and high-technology industries, is not clear at the present. With sufficient state support through anti-labour policies, it may find a more general acceptance.

Two points stand out clearly from this historical overview. The first is that control which began as personal, direct surveillance and supervision rapidly became far more complex, impersonal and embedded in the organizational apparatus itself, with the development of new organizational forms contingent upon successive concentrations of capital. This concentration, as we have argued, was characterized by discontinuous merger waves at distinct moments in phases of capitalist accumulation. A second point concerns the controllers themselves. With the effective separation of ownership from control, the growth of control mechanisms has meant until quite recently the contingent growth of new-middle-class employees in the managerial stratum of modern organizations. With this growth, particularly in those organizations which did not become divisionalized, a conflict of interest between the capital owners and the employed middle classes becomes apparent. Divisionalization and corporate culture thus become capital strategies whose main target is precisely the limiting of managerial prerogatives. Consequently, as we will argue in the next chapter, no necessary unity of interest can be said to cohere in management–capital relations, any more than in the relations of either of these groups with labour.

Property relations and the demarcation of the corporate ruling class

We will now consider the implications of changes at the level of property relations. While the characteristic form of nineteenth-century capitalist property relations was the family-owned and managed firm, in which capital could be personified (Hobsbawm, 1975), this is not as characteristic of capitalist property relations in the late twentieth century. Marx anticipated this development when he wrote:

> Stock companies in general – developed with the credit system – have an increasing tendency to separate . . . management as a function from the ownership of capital, be it self-owned or borrowed. . . . The mere manager who has no title whatever to the capital, whether through borrowing it or otherwise, performs all the real functions pertaining to the functioning capitalist as such, only the functionary remains and the capitalist disappears as superfluous from the production process (Marx, 1959, pp.387-8).

Problems arise for any identification of the ruling class on the basis of the social relations of property ownership, because a simple personification of ownership and control fused in a single person or family may no longer be empirically correct. As a consequence, many writers since Marx have proposed a 'managerial revolution' thesis which claims that the dispersal of ownership and its separation from control indicates that new organizational imperatives have undermined the classical model of capitalism. The economic system itself is said to have been transformed into a post-capitalist form. Theorists of the 'managerial revolution' (Burnham, 1962), have argued that, given the 'decomposition of capital' attendant upon the separation of ownership and control, power no longer resides in ownership, but in management. The idea of the separation of ownership and control in large corporations is widely accepted among economists, and is generally held to be derived from Berle's and Means's (1932) classic *The Modern Corporation and Private Property*. This book was the first attempt to make an empirical investigation of data concerning stock ownership in the context of assumptions that shareholders were becoming less influential in the conduct of corporate affairs and that, as a consequence of this, the control function of ownership was being superseded by that of management.

Berle and Means (1932) propose that a number of significant institutional changes have attended the early-twentieth-century transmutation of capitalism. First, they observe what all observers agree on, that there has been a significant concentration of capital. As a corollary, they propose that the assets that comprise the concentrated capital come under the control of managers who do not own a significant share of these assets. Under managerial control they suggest that the external discipline of the capital market becomes a considerably weakened constraint on managerial action. Finally, it is proposed that profit maximization ceases to be the most salient goal of managerial action (Wildsmith, 1973).

While the first proposition, as we have agreed, is accepted by everyone, the proposition of management versus owner control has generated an enormous, if increasingly historic, debate. Recent investigations, such as those of Mizruchi (1982), suggest that a certain historically limited credence can be attached to the 'managerial revolution' thesis, as is suggested by our previous discussion of divisionalization. Given that Berle and Means published in the early 1930s, they described a 'revolution' in terms of the decline of personal dominance from the peak of the late nineteenth century. It was then that a number of key individuals controlled the commanding heights of the US economy, as a result of the merger wave of the end of the century. By the 1930s this individual dominance based on personal ownership appeared to have become far less significant.

There is overwhelming evidence that at the turn of the century the corporate landscape was dominated by a handful of individual capitalists (Mizruchi, 1982). J.P. Morgan, John D. Rockefeller, George F. Baker and James Stillman, for example, were at the centre of extensive intercorporate networks, sustained through holding multiple and interlocking directorships. These personal empires were consolidated out of the merger wave at the end of the nineteenth century. However, by the 1930s, when Berle and Means were writing, these people were either dead or retired. Although in some instances they were succeeded by almost equally flamboyant individuals, such as J. Pierrepoint Morgan, Jnr, on the whole they were not.

The decline was in part due to changes in the institutional framework (such as the Clayton Act of 1914, which made corporate interlocks between competing firms illegal), and in part due to the death or retirement of the founding fathers of the US corporate landscape and their replacement with more institutionalized successors. Control became less fused with a few dominant individuals.

The control function of ownership derived from what Berle and Means identified as 'the traditional logic of property'. With the emergence of the joint stock legal form of organization, property rights became dissolved into a form of *nominal* ownership with revenue rights attached, through share ownership, and into the *effective* ownership of exclusive private property rights, through the actual control of the property and social relations constituted by the nominal share ownership. Possession of the latter

> consists less of their ownership of some part of the corporation's physical plant and stock of materials and products than of their rights to a revenue from the ability of the corporation to manoeuvre profitably in a very imperfect market (Macpherson, 1973, p.131).

The corporation is the legal entity charged with ownership of the assets. These assets are, however, controlled by what Carchedi (1977) refers to as 'real' ownership. This 'real' ownership is the capacity to organize labour power in concert with raw materials, plant, tools, etc., and to set the rate and intensity of work. Real ownership pertains to the organization and control of this labour process as a process of valorization.

What is suggested by Macpherson (1973) is that just as modern property rights emerged quite explicitly to facilitate bourgeois forms of legal possession, so has the continuing evolution of the conditions of production, reproduction and capital accumulation involved a transformation in the ways that ownership or strategic control of the processes of valorization are effected. Legal ownership still grants a right to revenue from the possession and disposition of shareholdings, but this is not necessarily equivalent to real ownership. The latter refers to the relations of production, not just the possession and disposition of shares defined by legal ownership.

Theoretically, real and legal ownership may be located on a continuum ranging from total coincidence to total non-coincidence. Interestingly, two distinct theses and sets of problems attach to identification of empirical situations towards either pole. First, identification of a high degree of non-coincidence with the thesis that contemporary capitalism is characterized by a high degree of separation of ownership and control in modern corporations.

107

Second, a high degree of coincidence is associated with radical critics of this thesis, such as Poulantzas (1975), who suggests that a few large shareholders may in fact possess effective real ownership. Crucial to the identification of this issue is the extent to which owners of shares are involved in decision-making in an effective way. Ownership of shares, as we have noted, entails a legal, but not necessarily social, relationship. These do not necessarily occur in parallel:

> For example, one may conceive of a corporation whose main stockholder is a family holding 10 per cent of the total stock, with the remaining stock widely dispersed among small holders. If this family is active in management, the case exhibits a high degree of stock dispersion but no separation of ownership and management (De Vroey, 1975, p.4).

From this we may draw the conclusion that where legal and real ownership are fused, depending on the degree of their fusion, there is a capacity for effective control and possession. Only where there exists real ownership (what Scott, 1979, terms 'effective possession') is there a capacity for actual control of corporate assets.

The actual control of corporate assets is usually referred to as strategic control, to distinguish it from operational control. Each deals with a different type of decision. *Strategic decisions* involve the *capacity* to constitute the parameters within which organizational activity occurs, while *operational decisions* involve the *exercise* of power oriented towards the achievement of goals formulated within and through these parameters. Thus, strategic decision-making relates to long-term planning, while operational decisions relate to medium-term implementation. Chandler's (1962, p.13) definition of strategy captures this distinction nicely; it is, he suggests, 'the determination of the basic long-term goals and objectives of an enterprise, and adoption of courses of action and the allocation of resources necessary for carrying out these goals.' Operational decision-making is vested in the structure of the organization's management, in a design devised so that its structure follows the logic implicit in the corporate strategy. The distinction between the two spheres is represented in Table 5.1. Strategic decisions thus involve

> major decisions in the transformation of the conditions of production and change, designed to shift the constraints of competition significantly rather than merely to adapt to them – decisions liable to determine far-reaching changes in the

TABLE 5.1 *Strategic and operational decisions*

The two types of decision-making	
Strategic	*Operational*
planning of: investment finance mergers liquidation combination sale of assets change in voting rules executive recruitment legal structure of corporation	planning of: plant management marketing personnel wages suppliers hiring firing industrial relations production management

relative contributions that the different divisions make to the firm's overall profit (Aglietta, 1979, p.263).

Operational decisions, the sphere of management's control procedures, are more in the way of monitoring, feeding back information, observation and recording of functional performances, corrective intervention and control, within the overall parameters of strategic planning.

Strategic decision-making thus refers to the 'strategic choices' open to organizations in their attempts 'to influence the conditions prevailing within environments where they are already operating' and the 'degree of environmental manipulation' open to the organization (Child, 1972, p.4).

This distinction between strategic and operational decision-making has been rightly criticized as overly rationalistic (e.g. Wood, 1980) – as if all that was necessary for a board was to plan a strategy, design a structure and sit back and watch it unproblematically unfold. Strategic planning will always be multi-dimensional and processual. Organization and control of differential processes can engender potential rivalries between functional departments. Their necessary role in formulating a plan of action and implementing, monitoring and revising a plan, can threaten the cohesion of the valorization process as a whole in intraorganizational power conflicts. Moreover, organizations do have a high degree of inert conservatism inscribed within their sedimented structure of tried-and-tested ways of doing things. Given this 'garbage can' (Cohen *et al.*, 1972) aspect of organizational life, then, as Wood (1980, p.62) suggests, 'the relationship between strategy and structure' may not be 'so much causal as symbiotic. The firm's goals and missions may not be . . . independent of its existing resources.' Moreover, it may be fallacious to assume that a strategy will be devised for some of the most uncertain areas of a firm's operations. More likely a number of distinct but less planned scenarios may be countenanced.

As a final caveat concerning strategy, we may also recall the earlier discussion of the subordination of internal contracting in Japan and resistance to divisionalization in Britain. In the former, the resistance from the combined *oyakata* and *kokata* directly influenced the strategy formulation and the structure of Japanese organizations. This resistance developed some of the most distinctive features of Japanese organizations. Lifetime employment, wages based on length of service and age, developed from the normatively quasi-familial patriarchy which the *oyakata* enjoyed *vis-à-vis* the *kokata* (Littler, 1980, p.177). The process by which the work group was incorporated also saw the adoption of the civil aspects of the production relationships. Wages were scaled from the *oyakata* downwards which, together with the practice of paying the newest recruits the least income, ensured a high degree of labour-force stability. To buffer this incorporated and inflexible cost-accounting core, the system of temporary *rinji-ko* workers developed. Hence, an organizationally specific dual labour market developed as a result of worker resistance rather than purposive strategy. Additionally, even in more familiar British enterprises, workers' and managers' resistance to corporate strategies could substantially change them, as both our earlier discussion as well as examples ranging from 'work-ins' to 'alternative corporate plans' demonstrate. As Wood (1980, p.63) suggests:

> Since organizations do not have given goals, or a monolithic management which is charged with co-ordinating activity to realize them, we must admit of competing corporate strategies and that different groups may be attempting to assert particular strategies or resist others.

At the level of long-term capital accumulation and calculation, there may be an apparent 'capital-logic', as we argued earlier. But, as we stressed, it will always be a 'logic' whose actual unfolding takes place in and through diverse civil societies.

Hence, it is only at the most macroscopic levels of economic concentration that a logic appears to be at work. Elsewhere, as we move from the longer-term changes in capital accumulation, and the long-term strategic planning of them, to the actual shorter-term processes of implementation and control, then we necessarily become more aware of how the best-planned strategies or the most apparent logics actually unfold.

The importance of personal control in the study of economic concentration is that it represents the ideal of total, or least-dispersed, control. In an ideal typical sense, control would be most concentrated where actual possession, real disposal, and legal entitlement to assets were fused in the unitary form of a single person. However, the ideal conditions for this control are those which Offe (1976) designates as task-continuous status organization. In the modern world we will find this type of control to be characteristic of only small, petty bourgeois, technologically simple, low-capital organizations where real ownership and effective possession of means of production may well be co-terminous with legal ownership. In the world of the large corporations some strategic control must necessarily be dispersed because of the complexity of the organizational structure. The extent to which dispersed strategic control and dispersed shareholding, and hence effective possession, overlap is an empirical question of considerable importance:

> with nominal ownership passing to the corporation itself, the question of who is able to control corporate strategy becomes all important. It is possible that the stockholders, or a portion of them, will continue to exercise strategic control – since the 'separation' is one in law, not one of fact – but it is also possible that those who are employed as operational managers will exercise strategic control (Scott, 1979, p.37).

Control is embedded in the complex structure of social relations in and of production, which constitute organization. It is not that there is 'control', as a superstructure erected on the controlled labour process base, conception being raised up high over execution. Control is constituted, in the whole complex of sedimented structure, in organization, with different principles of control becoming specific to different levels of the organization structure (Clegg, 1981). Not only can we identify different underlying principles of control, we can also observe different aspects of what it is that is being controlled.

One could conceptualize the organization as being composed of a complex of boundaries whose definition is always more or less salient and more or less contested, in terms of the people

111

within and about the organization. For instance, as we will discuss in chapter 7, there is, on the one hand, the ownership and control of methods of production in the labour process itself, the internal work organization. On the other hand, there is the ownership and control of the means of production, the shifting definition of who owns and to what extent controls the enterprise through being able effectively to define its strategic choices.

Control of strategic choices involves not only actual control of what Wright (1976) termed 'money capital'. It also entails determination of the structural limits within which any discretion can be exercised. Where one can control the rules within which the exercise of power occurs, then that power can be safely left to subordinate discretion, as Clegg (1975) argues. Within this control of these structural limits, then, varying levels of control can be identified, using a framework which stresses the time-span of discretion (Jacques, 1956; Fox, 1974). The structure is hierarchical. At the top of the hierarchy is control of the key resources of capital for investment and resource-allocation purposes. The control of these resources is over-arching because they involve the greatest commitment of capital, over the longest time perspective and with the most irreversible effects. The next two levels are equivalent to control of the physical means of production, while the last three are concerned with control over the actual productive labour process (which, of course, presupposes the higher levels) (Figure 5.1).

A new set of questions is raised by these concerns. The extent to which legal *ownership* (which, as an entitlement rather than a social relationship, may be more nominal than real) defines a ruling class becomes problematic, as does the extent to which it may be defined by effective possession and control (which may be quite separate from legal ownership).

Problems arise, maintain commentators such as Parsons, because of the demise of Marx's paradigm of the two-class family firm:

> With the growth of scale of operations, of advanced technology, and other factors, however, the two-class firm has given way to a quite different type of organization. The corporate legal form has facilitated the differentiation of the functions of ownership from those of management, so that the active managerial components no longer have been directly pursuing their personal financial self-interest in striving to maximize the profit of the firm. They have been operating in an occupational role, based on a form of employment which has certain structural resemblances to that of workers (Parsons, 1970, p.111).

```
                    ┌─────────────────────────┐
                    │   distribution of profits│
                    │      investments         │
                    │   financing, budgeting   │
              ┌─────┴─ ── ── ── ── ── ── ──┴─────┐
              │         choice of products       │
              │         quality of products      │
              │         quantity of products     │
        ┌─────┴── ── ── ── ── ── ── ── ── ──┴─────┐
        │              technology                 │
        │              organization               │
        │              planning                   │
        │           administrative routines       │
    ┌───┴── ── ── ── ── ── ── ── ── ── ── ──┴───┐
    │                    hiring                   │
    │                    firing                   │
    │            distribution of work tasks       │
  ┌─┴── ── ── ── ── ── ── ── ── ── ── ── ── ──┴─┐
  │        individual level decisions such as     │
  │     work speed, work methods, choice of       │
  │        tools, ordering of tasks, etc.         │
┌─┴── ── ── ── ── ── ── ── ── ── ── ── ── ── ──┴─┐
│       work and annual leave schedules,           │
│       administration of welfare services         │
│       general collective decisions only          │
│       marginally relating to work                │
└──────────────────────────────────────────────────┘
```

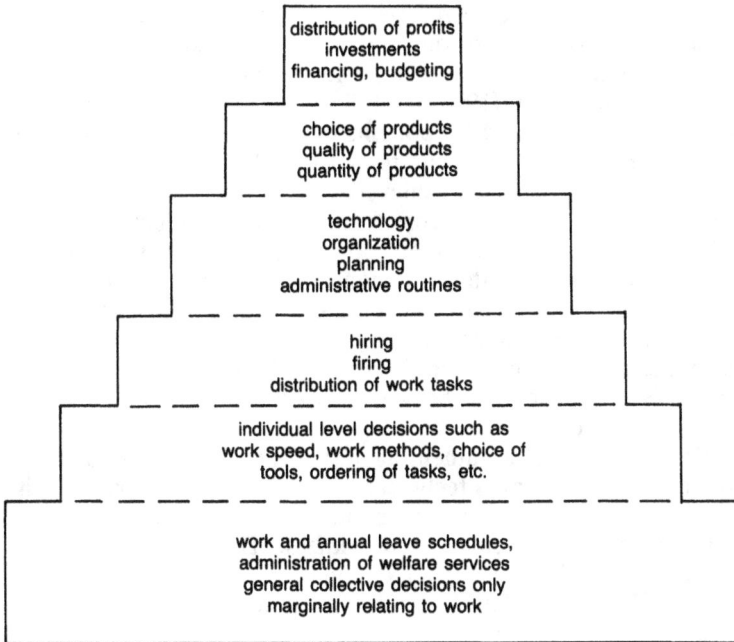

FIGURE 5.1   *Levels of control*
Source: adapted from Stephens, 1979, p.24

It no longer makes sense, Parsons maintains, to speak of a ruling class, defined by property ownership. Instead, new occupational groupings of managers and professionals have garnered power to themselves. This power, it is argued, derives from the technical, strategically contingent, expertise of the new class of managers. Here, the argument joins forces with one of the most frequent of 'post-industrial' theses (Bell, 1974, pp.294-5; Galbraith, 1967, pp.74-84; Hickson *et al.*, 1971; Hinings *et al.*, 1974). As Galbraith (1967), who is perhaps the most notable proponent of this view, has put it, the decisive power has passed from capital to organization, from the individual capitalist to the industrial bureaucrats who comprise the 'technostructure'.

It has been suggested, on the assumption of the veracity of the thesis of a 'managerial revolution' separating ownership from control, that one consequence of this has been a major transformation in the goals of private capitalist, large-scale organizations. Managers, allegedly unlike buccaneering entre-preneurs, are less oriented to profit maximization and rather

113

more oriented to long-term survival and stability. Risk-taking, it is argued, will decline in favour of steady-growth strategies securing highly remunerated managerial positions and careers. Economists such as Samuelson (1973) and Schumpeter (1943) have been advocates of this view. Proponents of this thesis agree that profit still retains significance, but tend to stress that once a certain minimum profit has been achieved at a 'satisficing' (Simon, 1976) level, the management is free to pursue goals oriented towards others besides the shareholders, so as to incorporate stakeholders such as employees or the local community. Paralleling this view, it has been suggested by commentators such as Galbraith (1967) that, because management acts as the vital gatekeeper of corporate information, then this technical knowledge can become the basis of real control, because any other agencies would have to rely on it for effective control.

There is a strong argument against this last view. The fact that modern management is technically complex is not a source of its systematic power (although it might explain lower-level strategic contingency), so much as its weakness. The sphere of competence of specialists is strictly defined by specific and particular skills as Blackburn (1972, p.178) has noted. These are not the basis of a general power.

The empirical investigations which have been conducted into aspects of the 'managerial revolution' thesis tend to disconfirm its core hypotheses. Early studies into the comparative profitability of owner-controlled and management-controlled firms have produced mixed results (see, for example, Monsen et al., 1968; Larner, 1960). Recent research by Zeitlin (1974, 1976) has also undermined the thesis both empirically and theoretically. First, it was not established that managers do in fact control most large organizations (Zeitlin, 1974, pp.1084-9). Second, the theory of managerialism is at bottom a motivational theory rather than a structural theory. It assumes that managers not only have different motivations, expressed in orientations to differing goal-priorities, but that these motivations produce different effects. Against this, Zeitlin (1976, p.902) notes that motivations may well be irrelevant if the structure of economic life has a real and over-riding determination on what it is that managers are able to do, irrespective of what they might profess to want to do. Hence, the question of the relative decline in family control of corporate capital does not necessarily entail the answer that the institutional structure must change because its membership has changed. Once a corporate organization is established, it may endure with a set of systemic rather than personal characteristics.

Research reported by James and Soref (1981) investigated the rate at which executives were fired. Their hypothesis was that this would be a more likely occurrence in firms which failed to perform adequately in terms of profits. This proved to be the case, irrespective of whether or not that firm was managerially or owner-controlled. Irrespective of whether or not corporations are managerially or privately controlled, they are effectively governed by the structural imperatives of capitalist production, notably the rate of profit. Failure to achieve the standards of profitability by which executive performance is judged adequate will lead to executive dismissal.

These findings on US firms confirm the research into British enterprises by Pahl and Winkler (1974, p.115), who concluded that 'the profitable allocation of capital is the key functional requirement of the structure as a whole.'

In their response to the adequacy of this planning, larger shareholders will have a disproportionate interest in policy and consequently exercise a greater constraint. In fact, it is not so much that large shareholders *do* exercise this constraint that is important, as that they have the capacity to do so. Because of this capacity management is effectively constrained even when, as in the majority of instances, direct control by the major shareholders does not occur (Gordon, 1945; Westergaard and Resler, 1976; Scott, 1979). In the normal course of affairs, major shareholders will be better informed, have better access to management and be in a better position to make their views known, particularly where they are acting through the inter-mediary of investment professionals (Scott, 1979). However, the theory of power and organization suggests the normal situation is one in which major shareholders do not intervene, not because they are disinterestedly passive, but because the routine manage-ment serves their interests sufficiently to make intervention a non-issue (Clegg, 1975, 1979; Bachrach and Baratz, 1962; Lukes, 1974). Intervention is a sign of crisis, an extraordinary rather than normal state of affairs, particularly where the firm has run into serious financial or legal difficulties. Intervention usually will mean that the composition of the board will change to represent more adequately those interests which have effective possession, by virtue of consolidated legal ownership, of the corporation. Only when issues arise which are strategic to the profitability of these active shareholders will they exercise, or attempt to exercise, power over the board (Zald, 1969). As Scott (1979, p.45) emphasizes, intervention is rarely a dramatic proxy fight, but rather more a 'gradual but firm imposition of the interests of the controlling group over the company's manage-ment', whether this controlling group be a minority or some coalition or constellation of interests.

Intervention in the control of the corporation will probably be in a form which disguises its real nature. Changes will be wrought under the auspices of financial exigency or technical reordering of priorities. Imperatives other than those of managerial ineptitude are likely to be involved. Changes in control as Aldrich (1979, p.298) stresses, may also occur through some other credit mechanism than shareholding (for instance, bank overdrafts). All these mechanisms of effective possession can limit managerial control.

In view of the empirical evidence which the literature has offered on the actual overlap of management positions and control interests, it is hardly surprising that top managers have an overwhelming interest in profitability. We can cite further data in support of this proposition, again from the US. In 1962 top executives of the ninety-four largest firms owned on the average $650,000-worth of their own corporation's stock. This meant that 40 per cent of their income derived from dividends, to which must be added the increase in stock appreciation on a yearly basis (Pryor, 1973, p.121). As Stephens (1979, p.36) argued:

> The practice of offering stock options ensures that most top level managers will also have large property holdings. This not only contributes to the inter-generational continuity of the capitalist class, it also minimizes the purported effects of the separation of ownership and control on the behaviour of corporations. The direct financial benefits of firm performance to managers in terms of revenue income, dividends, stock options and stock appreciation is quite substantial.

In relation to discussions of workforce size, a clear correlation has been repeatedly observed between higher levels of managerial compensation and the size and performance of the employing firm (McGuire et al., 1962; Lewellyn and Huntsman, 1970; McEachern, 1977). Research evidence has suggested that performance is primarily due to differences in market environments, rather than to differences in management (Lieberson and O'Connor, 1972). Because of this relationship a number of writers (e.g. Lenski, 1966; Perrow, 1979) argue that the relationship between management remuneration and corporate size/performance is one in which, as Allen (1981, p.1114) states, 'larger firm size and greater profits merely provide larger surpluses within these organizations which managers can allocate, at least in part, to their own compensation.' In other words, large managerial salaries are an effect of managers' power. This is supported by research which has found that, where firms are family-controlled, the management generally receives less compensation, particularly with respect to chief executives who were not family members (McEachern, 1977). However, we should note that this study has been criticized by Allen (1981, p.1115) because of its limited sample size, and a failure to differentiate between family-controlled firms with a chief executive who is the principal stockholder and firms in which there are other principal stockholders on the directing board.

When such considerations as whether or not a chief executive officer is also the principal stockholder are taken into consideration, a hierarchy of control configurations can be constructed (see Figure 5.2).

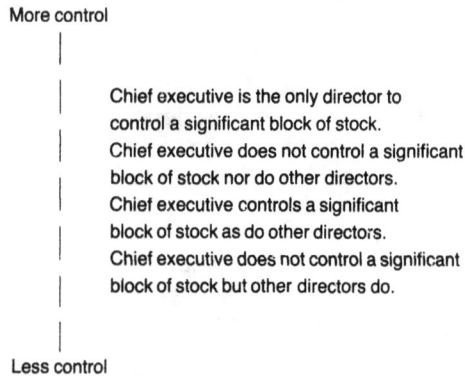

More control

Chief executive is the only director to
control a significant block of stock.
Chief executive does not control a significant
block of stock nor do other directors.
Chief executive controls a significant
block of stock as do other directors.
Chief executive does not control a significant
block of stock but other directors do.

Less control

FIGURE 5.2   *Control of chief executive*

On the basis of the type of distinctions represented in Figure 5.2 Allen (1981) investigated the relationship between chief executive control and compensation in 218 of the largest US corporations. The sample was controlled on corporate size and performance measures. Chief executive officers who are in corporations which have no principal stockholders as directors are generally over-compensated relative to the other chief executives, in terms of both direct remuneration (i.e. salary, bonus, deferred payments) and total remuneration (which also includes capital gains on stock options). Where there are one or more principal stockholders as directors, then chief executives tend to be relatively under-compensated, more so if they are not themselves principal stockholders. Where the chief executive is the only principal stockholder among the directors, relative under-compensation exists in terms of aggregate income. Allen adds that this would be a rational strategy for minimizing the risk of any potential proxy contests or shareholder squabbles about managerial compensation.

This analysis in terms of the single control of the chief executive is useful in differentiating degrees of control and the powerful consequences of these for the aggregate income of the corporate chiefs of the ruling class. It underscores once again the importance of workforce size as well as underlining Child's (1972) 'strategic choice' thesis. The ability to be able to reward one's self disproportionately is a major indicator of strategic control and power over corporate resources.

The previous discussion of the chief executive's control considered a variable range of situations in which there may be a greater or lesser fusion of proprietary and strategic control. The category of proprietary control contains a number of forms through which legal ownership can be translated into strategic control. Berle and Means (1932, p.70) identified the following situations: first, where legal ownership is by virtue of almost complete share-ownerships; second, where a clearly discernible majority of shares held by either an individual or a group can be identified, and third, where there is majority ownership through a legal device, such as a pyramid of holding companies. Situations of non-proprietary control, where legal ownership and real ownership are still fused, would be situations where there is a high degree of fragmentation of shareholdings. In such a situation, even a small co-ordinated shareholding which is less than a majority but more than any other fragments, can provide working control. Originally, 20 per cent control was thought to be the minimum for minority control (Berle and Means, 1932) but later writers have suggested that minority control can be achieved with as little as 5 per cent (Scott, 1979; Scott and Hughes, 1976). Zeitlin (1974) has suggested that minority control is the typical pattern in contemporary capitalism.

The argument put forward by Berle and Means regarded minority control as an interim stage of development on the way to management control, which, it will be recalled, was proposed to be increasingly the dominant form of capital. Managerial control, it was hypothesized, developed because of the fragmentation of shareholdings, and the emergence of shareholders as people who simply receive a dividend. In such a situation, there is no effective legal or proprietary control and, it is argued, the interests of ownership and management diverge. Because effective control becomes lodged in management, it is maintained that management interests will ordinarily prevail, except in unusual circumstances where fragile, shifting, unstable minority coalitions are able to mobilize against the management line.

These and other corporate developments have contributed to a point of view which Nicholls (1969) has termed 'managerialism'. The thesis of a separation of ownership and control has been seen in the context of increasingly selective recruitment of managers (Stanworth and Giddens, 1974) and the emergence of a 'managerial ideology' and its institutional organization (Child, 1969) as a clear indication that Burnham's (1962) 'managerial revolution' has been completed. There is substantial evidence from England suggesting that such a view has become widespread, although this is not just specifically a managerial, but a more general business ideology (Fidler, 1981, pp.262-6, particularly). This is characterized by its pragmatic, technically rational complexion; its opposition to any form of socialism; and, more especially, its espousal of 'managerial' elements which stressed an 'ethos of balancing interests' of the various stakeholders in the enterprise.

Berle's and Means's (1932) thesis was partly correct in other respects, as Mizruchi (1982) argues. In so far as the first third of the century saw a decline in the personal power of 'robber barons', such as Morgan and Rockefeller, there was an undoubted decline in personal control. However, this does not necessarily entail a 'decomposition of capital' into separated, fragmented and non-owning, managerially organized, small shareholder capital. Since 1935, the degree of interconnectedness of corporate interlocking networks has increased in the USA.

This increase in interconnectedness was signalled quite early in the debate. In 1940 the US Temporary National Economic Committee (TNEC) reported. It had been commissoned by President Roosevelt's government to investigate the ownership of the 200 largest industrial firms. Its findings demonstrated that

Out of a total of 7 million shares with voting rights at that time, an average of some 35,000 shares for each company, the average distribution took the following form: 20 very large shareholders held 32% of the voting rights, 980 major shareholders held 18% and 34,000 small shareholders divided the remaining 50% between them. This degree of inequality in the composition of ownership disclosed the existence of controlling groups, which in certain circumstances can become antagonistic, and of alliance and splits as financial groups restructure their investments in industry, seeking to reconcile controlling power and immediate requirements of profitability. The conclusions of the TNEC study showed that eight financial groups played a dominant role in controlling the 200 leading industrial corporations (Aglietta, 1979, p.267).

There are a number of methodologically critical points that one can make against Berle's and Means's argument. First, they did not check on the form of ownership of corporations which controlled other corporations through a 'legal device'. When these holding arrangements are investigated further – and they composed 21 per cent of the sample – it would seem that they should be categorized as some form of proprietary control, either private, majority or minority ownership, as has been suggested by Larner (1966), Zeitlin (1974) and Scott (1979, pp. 50-1). Further, both Zeitlin (1974) and De Vroey (1975) criticize the amount of data, relative to the amount of guestimation, which was involved in assigning over half of the 44 per cent of the sample said to be management-controlled. This criticism is sustained by Burch's (1972) reanalysis of their data, which substantially reduces the estimate of management-controlled firms as against the number of minority-controlled, family-owned firms. The extent of management control of large corporations in the 1930s in the USA had been over-estimated while the extent of majority ownership and family control had been under-estimated.

Subsequent research, reported in detail in Scott (1979, pp.54 *et seq.* and in Mizruchi, 1982), confirms that we should remain sceptical about this 'managerial' trend for the period from the 1930s to the present. Further, it has been noted by Perlo (1958, pp.29-30) that the twenty largest investors in the original sample increased the proportion of the stock they held between 1937 and 1954, and that the period saw a marked rise in financial holdings (from 8 per cent to 33 per cent). In the 1950s, Kolko (1962) demonstrated that the situation had remained quite similar over the ensuing twenty years since the findings of the TNEC. Further evidence in 1961 shows that a small number of majority shareholders were in control in about 40 per cent of the cases, where at least 20 per cent of the stock was held by the ten largest shareholders. This was in those corporations with more than 5,000 shareholders, while in those with fewer than 1,000, over 50 per cent had more than half of their stock held by the major interests.

Against these interpretations there stands the well-known confirmation of the Berle and Means thesis by Larner (1966), which found that 84 per cent of the top 200 corporations were controlled by management. This study, based as it is on Berle's and Means's methods, has been criticized on similar grounds, and, as Scott observes, Burch's (1972) and Palmer's (1972) reanalyses both show that Larner's case is over-stated. The conclusion that Scott (1979, p.59) draws from this, and other evidence, is 'that the period from the 1930s to 1965 saw a diminution in the extent of family majority ownership and a concomitant increase in the extent of minority and management control', while 'the predominant trend may have been towards control through a constellation of interests, with many families remaining on the board only because the effective possessors permit them to do so.' Family control has declined about 10 per cent, management control was increasing about 3 to 5 per cent per decade, while the new leviathans of the corporate landscape were the financial institutions.

The term 'financial institutions' is somewhat amorphous, for there are several different types of organization that could be subsumed under this category. Not all of them have increased in centrality. For instance, according to Mizruchi's (1982, pp.122-3) data, the centrality of insurance companies declined between 1904 and 1912 (probably as a result of the Armstrong Investigation of 1905, which obliged insurance companies to divest themselves of a number of holdings in other companies). After 1919 their degree of centrality slowly increased to a peak in 1969, but not so that they were a 'dominant' sector of financial institutions. The largest insurance companies are regularly involved in loan consortia, specializing in long-term loans and leaving shorter-term lending to banks. However, these banks are not as important today as the investment banks with which Morgan and his compatriots wielded such power in the early 1900s. Investment and commercial banking were legally separated in the USA in 1933, making the investment banks dependent upon commercial banks for loan financing. Hence, the latter have become the centre of the US corporate system, becoming particularly central at times of crises in accumulation such as the 1930s, the depression era, or the merger wave of the late 1960s. At these times, banks became absolutely central to the reconstruction of more profitable centres of valorization through merger and conglomeration.

Family ownership is one of several ways in which there may exist a homogeneous controlling group, enjoying a majority in shareholders' meetings. Another form of majority control is where a

> financial group that holds control of the enterprise does not
> have a major presence on the board of directors; in this case it
> favours the perpetuation of a homogeneous directing group
> that buys up shares in favourable conditions by way of option
> schemes. A close and almost unbreakable alliance is formed
> between the financial group which is the true owner of the

corporation and the group of directors who are internal to the firm. This alliance forms a solid controlling group dominated by the financial group (Aglietta, 1979, p.270).

While this was the mechanism used by the Rockefeller family to maintain its oil empire, even after it had withdrawn from the boards of the oil companies concerned, more conventional family ownership is to be seen in giant US concerns such as E.I. Du Pont de Nemours or the Mellon group. The former is directly controlled by the Du Pont family, while the latter has mediate control of Alcoa through placing several top administrators of the Mellon bank in Alcoa's top positions.

Where these forms of majority control do not exist, there is characteristically a situation which corresponds to a coalition of interests. This generally arises after an original owning group liquidates its investments. Reorganization of the company is subsequently usually undertaken by a coalition of banks and other financial agencies, which carefully composes a board reflecting the commercial, financial and political connections which it is calculated that the company requires (Aglietta, 1979, pp.270-1).

The general trend of economic concentration is from family ownership and control to control and ownership by institutionalized intercorporate relations. It is a process which has developed since the 1930s when Berle and Means (1932) wrote and, while it has consisted of a routinization of individual, personal control, it is not correct to say that this has effected a 'managerial revolution'. What has emerged out of this process of the institutionalization of intercorporate relations is a coalition of interests primarily between financial agencies and industrial firms. The central role of transport companies (that is, the railroads) at the turn of the century has been replaced by a more variegated collection of industrial firms, with the rise of the automobile age and concomitant decline of the train. These industrial firms, in turn, are interconnected with financial institutions which are themselves heavily interconnected (Scott, 1979, pp.79-80; Mizruchi, 1982). It appears that this complex interconnection of interests is not confined to US corporate capitalism but also characterizes France, Britain and Belgium at least, as Scott (1979, pp.77-80) established in his survey of the field. The mechanism of this complex interconnection of interests is the 'interlocking directorship'.

The corporate ruling class and interlocking directorships

Many lay observers, particularly among the ranks of corporate spokespeople and conservative politicians, have pointed to the existence of the large number of individual shareholders in the modern corporation as evidence of the decline, or at least 'democratization', of capitalism. The existence of the phenomenon known as an 'interlocking directorship' undermines the force of this claim. Interlocking directorships are the chief mechanism of corporate interconnectedness. Ordinarily, the less interlocked a firm is the greater we would anticipate the propensity for that corporation to be competitive.

An interlocking directorate exists when one person simultaneously sits on the board of directors of two or more corporations. It is these corporate interlocks which have been posited as the mechanism securing and reproducing corporate interconnectedness between financial and industrial interests.

Corporate interconnectedness through the mechanism of interlocking directorships is one of the significant features of an advanced capitalist economy because it reduces and centralizes the legal and formal responsibility for the operation of a firm and the protection of owner interests. The extent of multiple directorships vested in one person is significant. For instance, in 1969 in the USA, only 8,632 individuals served as directors of the 797 largest financial and non-financial corporate organizations. Of this number, 1,572 were interlocking directorships, where the same person held simultaneous seats on the boards of two or more companies. This is almost a fifth of all directorships (Mariolis, 1975, p.433).

The issue has even achieved Congressional recognition in the USA, as Useem (1979, p.556) reports. In 1965 the US Congress House Committee on the Judiciary Antitrust Subcommittee, expressed an anxiety that interlocking might be leading to a situation in which 'inordinate control over the major part of US commerce' could become the preserve of an 'inner group'. Not surprisingly, from Mills's (1959) seminal work to the present, there has been a healthy interest in the issue.

A number of approaches within the rapidly growing literature on corporate interlocks may be identified (for overviews of the literature, see Mizruchi, 1982; Pennings, 1980; Sonquist and Koenig, 1976). Following Palmer (1983), we will characterize the field in terms of an 'interorganizational' and an 'intraclass' paradigm, locating hypotheses pertaining to management control and environmental control and reciprocity under the former, and hypotheses pertaining to financial control and class hegemony under the latter.

The interorganizational paradigm focuses on the network of linkages between organizations. Interorganizational relationships are conceptualized in terms of networks of exchanges. Organizations have interests and resources. In order to further their interests they have to exchange resources, thus creating dependencies with other organizations. One of the ways that they do this is through establishing interlocking directorates. The people who fill the positions of director are thus agents and resources of the organization involved in coalition-building (Cyert and March, 1963), in bargaining and influence systems (Abell, 1975), in environmental management (Allen, 1974; Burt, 1979; Dooley, 1969; Pfeffer and Salancik, 1978) and in the reduction of organizational uncertainty to a level of organization adequate to the complex nature of the particular aspects of the environment in which it operates (Pfeffer, 1972). Much of this literature has a 'cognitivist' complexion: organizations seek to reduce uncertainty, resolve equivocality, exchange information, and so on. Interlocks are entered into by organizations

> primarily to facilitate co-operation for mutual benefit. They enable the limitation of potentially disruptive influences or interference from other organizations with whom scarce resources must be shared. . . . Interlocks provide the links through which arrangements for swapping of goods and services and through which quasi-legal co-ordination of policy can take place (Sonquist and Koenig, 1976, p.56).

In the interorganizational perspective, interlocks are regarded as either 'co-optive devices' or as 'control devices'. The former regards interlocks as means whereby legitimate organizational ends of environmental adaptation and management are pursued. Studies in this perspective tend to link dependence to interlocking and interlocking to organizational effectiveness (Allen, 1974; Burt, 1980a, 1980b; Burt et al., 1980; Pennings, 1980; Pfeffer, 1972; Pfeffer and Salancik, 1978). The 'control' perspective suggests that this effectiveness can be further facilitated by direct intermediation of centres of corporate control (Thompson and McEwan, 1958; Evan, 1966; Thompson, 1967). Interlocks are thus 'control devices', and empirical manifestations of a less cognitivist and more concrete nature will be emphasized, such as anti-competitive behaviour. Networks of control can be shown to have sociographic centres. Research has demonstrated that these are frequently banks (Allen, 1974; Burt, 1970b; Levine, 1972; Mariolis, 1975). The bases for this centrality are generally regarded to be the leverage afforded banks by their role (among some other financial institutions) in the circuit of commercial capital in the overall process of valorization (Ingham, 1982; Harvey, 1982; Thompson, 1977; Aglietta, 1979).

This role entails the capacity to advance credit, to vary interest rates, to possess stock and voting rights, to transmit advice, information and specialist services (Patman Report, 1968). Key positions in this role tend to be the most highly intraclass reproductive, where the mechanisms of reproduction are those of an elite status group formed in the civil society of privilege (Ingham, 1982).

The intraclass paradigm views organizations as resources of ruling-class actors, defined in the usual way, who use the organization's resources in order to pursue their class interest in accumulation. This leads them to establish relationships with other people in effective possession and control of other organizations. The centrality of financial institutions to interlocks fits in with one version of this paradigm, which stresses the capitalist functions of accumulation and valorization. Interests of directors are thus identified with the organizations of which they are members. Where these organizations are centres of control of the process of valorization, their most strategic and generalizable resource will be capital. Hence the dependence of most corporations on large financial institutions which, because they control the supply of capital, are strategically contingent to corporate organizations. Hence, such organizations have to enter into interlocks with financial institutions in order to maintain access to their strategic resource. This sets up a resource dependency with financial institutions, which are able to 'take advantage of this to arrange reciprocity agreements between clients and to attempt to manoeuvre firms into profitable (for the bank) long-term, large-scale borrowing and dependence' (Sonquist and Koenig, 1976, p.57).

This version of the intraclass paradigm is usually called the 'finance capital' thesis. It stresses the dominance of banking interests in corporate interlocks and was originally associated with Hilferding (1981). Contemporary research into interlocks demonstrates that financial institutions do stand at the centre of both regional networks and national networks. For instance, in the USA, Sonquist and Koenig (1976) found that in 1969 there were thirty-two regional networks of identifiable interlocks of from three to fifteen corporations, organized around a financial centre, with an industrial periphery. They noted overlapping of regional networks by a large New York group. Over half the central financial institutions were banks, and in many of them a single bank was central. Additional research by Bearden et al. (1975) demonstrates the stability of the financial core over time, even though the corporations comprising the industrial periphery vary over time. This finding is given further support by Mizruchi (1982).

Over 80 per cent of 167 corporations which were heavily interlocked by the multiple directorships of single figures such as J.P. Morgan, in the early 1900s, remained heavily interlocked by less personal mechanisms in 1974. Financial institutions clearly control the most strategic of capitalist resources, hence their centrality in networks. This holds elsewhere than in the USA. For instance, one can consult Whitley (1973, 1974), Stanworth and Giddens (1974) and Johnson and Apps (1979), for the UK; for Japan there is a useful picture in Halliday (1975); Australia has a detailed guide from the studies by Rolfe (1967), Encel's (1970) overview, Hall (1982) and Stening and Wai (1984); for Canada one can consult Carroll *et al.* (1982), Ornstein (1976) and Clement (1975); while New Zealand has been reported in Fogelberg and Laurent (1973). Additional data for Germany and the Netherlands are given by Scott (1979).

The extent of financial centrality to interlocks suggests that the identification by directors of their interest in valorization, seen by them as growth, reinvestment and enhanced corporate strength, leads to extensive relations with financial institutions, although not necessarily a situation of dependent financial control (O'Connor, 1974).

There is another version of the intraclass paradigm which stresses less the immediate interests of valorization and accumulation, and more the long-term reproduction of the capitalist system. This is the 'class hegemony model' (Sonquist and Koenig, 1976; Koenig and Gogel, 1980). From this perspective the most important aspect of ruling-class interlocks is the long-term promotion of a broad-based cohesion, self-consciousness and consensus on general issues, achieved by the communication of techniques, values and beliefs between directors.

Holding interlocking directorships is regarded less as a means to an end (i.e. control of the environment in order to reduce uncertainty) and more as an end in itself,

> as expressive as well as instrumental behaviour. A consequence of multiple participation is the maintenance of well-oiled communication channels through which business deals of a wide variety can be furthered when need be. Cut-throat competition can be effectively discouraged, and though the intention is not necessarily explicit, the long range position of the small percentage of the population who hold the bulk of the corporate stock can be insured (Sonquist and Koenig, 1976, p.59).

An obvious indicator of business prominence and potential power would be the number of board seats held (Useem, 1978, 1979;

Zeitlin *et al*., 1974). This is referred to as 'inner group centrality', which it has been hypothesized will be highly correlated with 'finance capitalist' status – the possession of a bank board seat (Useem, 1979; Radcliff, 1980).

When moving from a simple head-count, such as the number of board seats held by an individual, to the characteristics of the networks constituted by the interconnectedness between individual board members, some methodological issues have to be taken into consideration. Mizruchi (1982, pp.55-81) discusses these. First, certain firms, with larger boards, will necessarily have a greater propensity to interlock than those with smaller boards. High network centrality could thus be an effect of board size if it is not taken into calculation. Second, interlocks are not necessarily of equal value. An interlock with a firm which is otherwise relatively isolated in terms of corporate interconnectedness will be of far less potential value than one with an organization which is itself already highly interconnected. The significance of any particular position in a network can be viewed as an effect of three criteria: the number of links to other points; the 'intensity' of the links; and the centrality of those with whom one is linked (Mizruchi, 1982, p.56). Additionally, the 'ties' that constitute corporate interconnectedness may be said to be directional: one corporation may be said to 'send' a director to another one which receives it. (Further distinctions involve 'weak' and 'strong' ties, not to be discussed here: see Mizruchi, 1982, pp. 58-61).)

Research on interlocks from an interorganizational framework stresses the intentional nature of the actually existing interlocks. They are not merely contingent but purposeful. Similarly, the 'finance capital' version of the intraclass paradigm also stresses the intentional role of self-interested bankers. The class-hegemony framework is more structural and less intentional, emphasizing not the role of particular agents and their intentions, so much as the structural role which interlocks fulfil. One way of empirically testing the extent of the intentionality of interlocks as against a class-hegemonic view, is to research what happens when an interlock is broken accidentally – that is, when its elimination is not planned by the firm it links. This is to research not strategic but wholly contingent events, in order indirectly and empirically to determine strategy.

It has been hypothesized by Koenig *et al.* (1979) that if interlock ties are accidentally broken – for instance, by the death of the actor linking the corporations – then if the tie has connective and directional continuity because it fulfils a specific, intentional purpose, it will be reconstituted with the same direction. From any corporation previously tied to the other corporation(s) there will be 'sent' a new tie from the previously focal organization to the previously recipient organization.

Following this procedure enables one to establish to what extent ties do function as a means of exerting influence or power. Ties which are vehicles of such relationships will not be allowed to lapse. Continuity would be maintained if they were accidentally altered or broken. Although not all ties which are continued will be such vehicles, the continuity of the tie, by providing the mechanism of transmission, will be a necessary if not sufficient condition of the existence of any such strategic continuity (Palmer, 1983).

The study by Koenig et al. (1979) disconfirms intentionalist hypotheses. In only 6 per cent of the 102 cases of broken ties that were studied were the ties re-established. Further research on a sample of 238 altered ties, from a sample of 1,131 of the largest US corporations between 1964 and 1966, confirms the general picture that the vast majority of ties (in this case, 85 per cent) were not vehicles of explicit, intentional co-ordination (Palmer, 1983). Further, this research found that where ties were reconstituted they were frequently done so in a different direction to the broken tie. This is clearly important with respect to both the co-optative and control variants of the interorganizational paradigm. For either of these to be not disconfirmed, we would expect continuity of direction (i.e. that where the dominant organization is the 'sending' firm then there is a relationship of control; where the dominant organization is the 'receiving' firm then there is a co-optational relationship). The lack of continuity in this respect suggests as a possible explanation that what is at stake is not the directional (control or co-optative) aspects of co-ordination but the representational aspects, stressing that interlocks represent the prominence and power of hegemonic individuals in the capitalist class, based on criteria of class cohesiveness rather than co-optative or control effectiveness.

Evidence from other, diverse sources, tends to confirm this view. Both Mace (1971) and Chandler (1975) suggest that non-executive interlocked directors tend not to be interventionist, while from Britain, there is similar evidence from Fidler's (1981, p.140) research which found that

> many executives interviewed in the study . . . insisted that their non-executives were playing a valuable role on the board . . . [w]hat . . . the value of the role almost always consisted of was their experience, or the helpful advice they could give

particularly in specialist skills brought from other fields. Non-executives are not regarded by full-time executives as the controllers of British industry.

Directors involved in interlocks are there more as prominent, prestigious and influential members of the capitalist class than as agents of co-optation or control. They are also, it seems, there to learn. One executive pithily regarded the value of being a non-executive director in these terms: 'If you want to just bottom-line it, it's a hell of a tool for top management education' (Useem, 1982, p.210). Consequently, companies use non-executive directorships as a grooming device for aspiring top executives in their own organization. The most prominent, prestigious, influential and permanent directors involved in interlocks are associated with financial institutions, which are the most central corporations. Bank ties, being most valuable, are most sought after. The overall network is such that little conscious capacity to achieve specific intended effects can be inferred. Interlocks function more as systems for the transmission of expressive behaviour, as communication channels, as loci of class hegemony rather than as specific channels of corporate dominance. It is the centrality of financial institutions as sources of loan capital and thus their strategic role in the flow of corporate information which produces the centrality of banks to contemporary interlocks, rather than their being the intended effect of the cunning of controllers of finance capital.

Further support has been added to the 'class hegemony' hypothesis by recent research conducted into the composition of the British business elite (Useem and McCormack, 1981). This elite was defined in essentially the same way that we have defined the ruling class, in terms of ownership and strategic control. The study investigated the directors of approximately 1,000 of the largest and most dominant, in terms of indices of economic activity, of British companies. As a result of their research into this business elite, Useem and McCormack (1981, p.382) suggest that there exists a 'dominant segment' which 'has acquired the capacity to serve as a leading organizer of the capitalist class as a whole.' The mechanism linking the individuals in this 'dominant segment' is that of interlocking directorships. The mechanism which creates 'the capacity to serve as a leading organizer of the capitalist class as a whole' (i.e. the capacity for reproducing class hegemony) is the representation of this dominant segment on the boards of major government advisory organizations and non-profit organizations. They are appointed in large part through their visibility in major peak organizations such as the Confederation of British Industry (CBI).

Interlocking directorships display two decisive properties which are at the basis of this dominant segment's formation. First, the structure of interlocks is highly inclusive of large companies, as a result of the increased concentration already documented (see also the time-series data of Giddens and Stanworth, 1978, and Johnson and Apps, 1979). Second, the interlocks are highly diffuse, rather than highly specific, exchanges, partly because, as Bacon and Brown (1977, p.93) found, interlocks are often constituted with persons from companies and institutions not doing business with the focal organization. Other reasons which have been adduced to explain diffuseness include the suggestion that it is the result of class strategies for controlling large corporations (Koenig *et al.*, 1979), of managerial strategies for enhancing individual careers (Palmer, 1983), as well as a result of company strategies for reducing the uncertainty of other companies' practices (Useem, 1980). Probably all of these are more or less marginal factors of variable influence in different situations. The outcome of these strategies of diffuse interlocking is clear. It is that large corporations become interlinked in a manner which does not so much facilitate specific market exchanges between them as provide a communication grid through which flows 'highly generalizable information about the problems and practices of nearly all major companies' (Useem and McCormack, 1981, p.384).

The formal linkages are further reinforced by a series of informal networks centred on a small number of major exclusive gentlemen's clubs. Gender is clearly an explicit variable in ruling-class structuration. These clubs

> can be viewed as nodes in which the informal social networks of the corporate elite concentrate. Initiation of a corporate director into a 'club' signifies a measure of network acceptance, an acceptance further extended by the opportunities for additional contacts within the rounds of club activities (Useem and McCormack, 1981, p.395).

The exposure to the problems, issues (and non-issues) of the general business environment is, it has been argued, greatly facilitated by the club atmosphere of social cohesion, which reinforces the executive perspective of 'class hegemony' developing into an interlock situation where multiple directorships are held across divergent types of corporation and markets. This club society, it is further maintained, enables these directors to develop a broad view, based on experiences in different sectors, with different interests, and in interaction with other directors in similar but also different interlocks. However, some empirical evidence seems to counter this view. The research conducted by Fidler (1981, p.113) found that of the eighty-seven top executives for whom he had documentary evidence, only forty-one of them were members of 'exclusive London clubs'. They were by no means concentrated but were spread thinly through twenty different clubs which, as he notes, 'would seem a poor way of co-ordinating the activities of the business elite who could probably have far more contact through interlocking directorships or the CBI.' Moreover, he argues, such clubs can hardly facilitate co-ordination with top civil servants as so few of them are members (Chapman, 1970; Fidler, 1981, pp.234-5), nor with Labour governments, for the same reason. More generally, on the basis of his detailed interviews with executives, Fidler (1981, p.247) concludes 'that sociologists have tended to exaggerate the importance of shared class background, and of personal connec-tions of shared education, interlocking directorships and shared social clubs amongst elite groups.'

The corporate ruling class and the state

Class hegemony within the ruling class may be reproduced by the role of interlocking directorships. Some researchers would extend this argument to reproduction within the state.

Interlocking directorships may be arranged in a continuum of 'inner group centrality' (Zeitlin et al., 1974; Useem 1979, p.555), ranging from an outer axis of one directorship to the other axis of four or more directorships. This inner group, the more so that it holds more directorships, has a distinctive political role to play in advanced industrial societies such as Britain or the USA (Useem and McCormack, 1981; Useem, 1979). It is well established that the directors and executives of the largest corporations are over-represented in the state apparatus (Mills, 1959; Miliband, 1969; Domhoff, 1971; Freitag, 1975; Dye, 1976; Clegg and Dunkerley, 1980). What is established by Useem (1979) is that this representation is skewed towards a disproportionate number of inner-group members in the USA (also see Zeitlin et al., 1974, for Chile; Useem and McCormack, 1981, for Britain; as well as Useem, 1982).

Class hegemony may thus also be reproduced by the high incidence of representation of multiple directors in governmental (and non-profit) organizations of all kinds. Multiple directors in Britain are between three and six times more likely to have served in some capacity in governmental or quasi-autonomous non-governmental organizations (quangos). A similar ratio is apparent with respect to non-profit organizations such as universities, arts establishment organizations and research bodies. In part, it is argued, this over-representation will be a result of sponsorship by members of the corporate ruling class, proposing those people considered most able to serve as representatives.

One of the most important forums in which ability can be realistically judged is in the context of peak organizations such as the CBI, as Useem and McCormack's research demonstrates (1981, p.392). Positions of leadership in such organizations are frequently an opening into positions, in an advisory capacity, on various boards formally constituted by the government. There is a far greater probability of achieving a position of rank in such organizations where the person already holds multiple director-ships and such positions of rank give the person a far greater probability of membership on a governmental or public board. Such multiple directors, have 'a relatively distinct location in the social process of production' (Zeitlin et al., 1976, p.1009) which gives them a distinct political role to perform as a dominant segment of the ruling class: 'Uniquely positioned to transcend, however imperfectly, the narrowness of political vision imposed on most company directors, this fraction has assumed a political role on behalf of the class that the class as a whole is incapable of playing' (Useem and McCormack, 1981, p.399). This role is that of articulating and reproducing class hegemony in the leading organizations of the state, economy and civil society. As such, the general interest may not be that of particular interests, but that of the broad view, developed by those uniquely qualified to have such a view. Intercorporate rationality, maintains Useem (1982), is a class-wide rationality founded on the rationality of the dominant segment of the contemporary corporate ruling class. As he proposes:

> The participants in this network are prone to favour govern-ment programs coincident with the common and longer range concerns of most large corporations. The advocacy of classwide politics is sure to be opposed by many if not most corporate managers when these policies adversely affect their own firms, but the classwide principle asserts that there will be a segment of the corporate elite with at least a nascent capacity to promote the broader needs of big business, to act as political leadership for the entire corporate elite (Useem, 1982, p.202).

In earlier work Useem presented data on 'inner group centrality' in 797 of the largest US corporations of 1969, and found that the participation rates of multiple directors in non-profit private organizations, as advisors to local, state and national government agencies, as members of major business policy lobbies and associations, was twice that of single directors, with double and triple directors exhibiting intermediate rates (1979, p.567). The reasons for this greater involvement lend further support to the 'class hegemonic' or 'class-wide rationality' thesis. It was hypothesized that multiple directors were over-represented because

> of their greater capacity to mobilize corporate resources and because of the greater likelihood that they would be more involved in a national transcorporate social network of corporate directors. It was anticipated that these factors would result in inner group members being more often promoted for institutional governance positions by other members of the business elite, and in inner group members being more desirable business representatives from the standpoint of the recipient institutions (Useem, 1979, p.567).

While representation and participation may not be translated into the actual exercise of power they do represent the necessary capacity to be able to exercise power at all. These results lend weight to general theoretical points which we shall elaborate, concerning class organization, in chapter 8. Both the US and British corporate elites possess a central inner group whose role is crucial in the wider organization of the capitalist class. In Britain it has developed largely as a response to 'the socialist challenge' of the Labour party (see Holland, 1975), while in the USA the 'enemy' is far more likely to be 'big' and 'interfering' government regulation (Useem, 1982). This group is uniquely qualified to represent capital-as-a-whole in the organization of the state, rather than simply their particular interests of capital. Thus, the representation of capital in the higher levels of the state, although not intentionally designed to overcome the divisions between capitals, does tend to minimize them. These interlocks are also supported by the diversification of family holdings and the increase in institutional shares; the integrative role of commercial banks, professional law firms, and brokers (Szymanski, 1975); as well as kinship and acquaintances which span the lives of intercorporate elites (Whitley, 1973).

The conclusion to be drawn from these studies is that those capitalists who most often represent business to the state 'already represent a degree of reconciliation of the conflicting and contradictory interests dividing the capitalist class. The corporate community itself, then, appears at least partially capable of identifying its classwide interests' (Useem, 1979, p.570).

The 'classwide interests' are not simply represented to the state but become embodied in the routines of the state's administrative functioning as 'vested interests'. This is empirically ascertainable by reference to the detailed documentary investigation which Roy (1981a, 1981b, 1981c) has made of the process of bureaucratization of the US State Department which occurred in the late nineteenth and early twentieth centuries. With the transition from a political mode of placing incumbents in office through patronage to a bureaucratic mode of formally rational organization (Weber, 1978), the nature of interest representation shifted from policy outcomes which were primarily *reactive* to the representation of interests to the State Department (overwhelmingly those of the financial–industrial class segment of US capitalism (Roy, 1981b)), to policies which were primarily *proactive*, whereby interests became routinely embedded in the normal way of doing things.

What is important is that the routines which became embedded in the organizational functioning of the agency developed out of the earlier reactions to specific *ad hoc* requests. Thus the constitution of routine did not occur in a neutral field, but in one already prestructured by specific interests. They became sedimented in the routine functioning of the bureaucracy.

Two avenues of empirical enquiry into the class structure of the state apparatuses have been suggested here. One concerns the representatives of the interests of capital that capitalists themselves propose. The evidence suggests that these are more likely to be people who are in a position to have a view of the interests of capital as a whole by virtue of their interlocking directorships. Second, we have touched on the vesting of interests in the state apparatuses themselves, in the routine functioning and enactment of environments and issues.

Interlocks may be considered to be one aspect of the 'reproduction rules' (Clegg and Dunkerley, 1980; Clegg, 1981) of late capitalism in general rather than of specific interests in particular. They are one of the mechanisms through which ruling-class hegemony is reproduced. Multiple directorships provide a community of identity and non-identity, conditions of ethical valuation and conditions which contribute to the selective limitation of shared beliefs about social and economic issues and overall goals.

There is in all the advanced capitalist societies a relatively small ruling class, ranging from 1 to 5 per cent of the population, which is defined by a very restrictive range of ownership in legal terms and in terms of effective possession of the process of valorization and the labour process it entails. Members of this class tend to more likely to live together, work together, play together, be educated together and to marry each other than they are likely to do any of these things with 'outsiders' (Mills, 1959; Miliband, 1969; Stanworth and Giddens, 1974; Domhoff, 1967, 1971, 1974; Clement, 1975; Connell, 1977; Baltzel, 1958, 1967). We have yet to establish the extent to which this economic power is passed from generation to generation and the mechanisms through which this generational cohort will be augmented by the co-optation of talented members of other social classes. As we will argue, capitalist reproduction does not reproduce the ruling class *per se*. The reproduction of the ruling class is a dynamic process, both in its capacity to co-opt and to exclude, particularly through practices of 'credentialism'.

Ruling class reproduction in civil society

The evidence that we have reviewed demonstrates quite clearly that a ruling class, constituted through family control of capital which is transmitted intergenerationally, has weakened during the twentieth century. The reasons advanced for this have been primarily in terms of structural changes associated with the greater concentration of capital and its complex interconnectedness. However, other factors play an important role as well. Among these must be counted the twin uncertainties which the capitalist market and genetic inheritance pose for class reproduction. With respect to the latter, it is not so much the genetic deficiencies of a ruling class which are at issue, but the degree, admittedly low, of intergenerational mobility into elite strata that these uncontrollable contingencies allow. Consequently, practices of ruling-class closure achieved through predominantly intraclass recruitment remain imperfect at the level of specific holdings of capital. With respect to the dynamic aspects of the market it may be noted that

> Property in an expanding and commercially energetic society is too volatile to serve as a reliable safeguard against either class demotion of bourgeois offspring or the steady infiltration of parvenus . . . landed, industrial, commercial and finance property each tend to have a different social foundation, so making it difficult for any group based on one type of property to prevent the rise of new groups based upon a different type (Parkin, 1979, pp.60-1).

Hitherto, we have conceptualized capital primarily in terms of property relationships. In considering strategies of closure we must understand how a ruling class (defined in terms of its control of the means of production) is able to ensure a sufficient

135

degree of monopolization of access to privileged social positions, such that a relatively stable structure of class relations is reproduced over time. This need not entail that there exists social immobility – such would necessitate an absolutely static occupational structure. This is not the case. Occupational structures change markedly over time, as well as existing independently of the persons filling the positions.

Earlier we suggested that being someone or other is what is at stake in civil society. If some recent research is representative, class identity, in terms of being a member of a given class, is hardly problematic for most ruling-class members (Fidler, 1981). However, there were exceptions and these exceptions are instructive in revealing what Garfinkel (1967, p.116) has referred to as the exertion of 'close controls' over persons in transit from one identity to another, 'the transfers of persons from one status to another'. As he makes clear in his account of one particular accomplishment of the phenomenon of 'passing', these transfers consist in part in the individual having to manage, in a reflexive manner, the relationship between routine, trust and rational performance in diverse locales and times.

For the majority of members of the corporate elite the suggestion that identity might be problematic or precarious would be ludicrous, for the simple reason that in Britain (and Britain is not unique amongst the advanced capitalist societies in this) 'children from privileged backgrounds have substantial, indeed grotesque, advantages in the competition for elite positions,' as Heath (1981, p.76) summarizes the position. The extent to which this judgment is warranted can be seen in the statement that it

> would probably be correct if we were to say that a man from a working-class home has about one chance in fifteen hundred of getting into *Who's Who*; the man from a white-collar background has perhaps one chance in five hundred; the man from the higher professional and managerial home has one chance in two hundred; but the man from the elite home has a one-in-five chance (Heath, 1981, p.77).

What such rough orders of magnitude indicate is that amongst any representataive sample of what we have termed the corporate ruling class, there will be a large identifiable group of men with an experience of quite similar locales, notably elite public (i.e. private) schools (and, of course, it is not only Britain that has such a private-school system: in the US, for instance, Baltzell (1958) and Domhoff (1967) noted the centrality of such schools in producing this class in what is nominally the least archaic capitalist democracy). The cultural capital acquired, rehearsed, reinforced, inculcated and stylized there (and in complementary locales) clearly sets the scene for what is tacit knowledge of normalcy, routine and rationality in the corporate peaks, in terms of dress, speech, attitudes and general demeanour. For these people, the corporate locale poses no particular problem of identity. This would not be the case for the rare female executive and upwardly mobile manager for whom cultural knowledge must be acquired on the job and cannot necessarily be taken for granted.

Locales (Giddens, 1979, 1981; Thrift, 1983) are settings for interaction. Whether or not the trajectories of particular types of individuals interact in these locales is the stuff of social mobility studies. Taking what we have termed the corporate locale as the physically, geographically separated centre of control and calculation of valorization (archetypally, the boardroom), then we know, for Britain at least, that here a particularly cohesive core of individuals do share similar life-paths. These locales, together with the accompanying, tightly coupled core of collateral life-paths through elite schools, have quite decisive effects on 'other people's life paths through the constraints they place on a person's ability to interact with other people, engaged in activities within them,' as Thrift (1983, p.40) suggests. Certainly, Fidler's (1981) research endorses this view when we consider those of his respondents who testified to the effects of their having been upwardly mobile. These people clearly recognized, as one representative put it, that there are 'groups in society who identify with each other very clearly' with whom 'it's very difficult . . . to have sensible conversation . . . because their philosophy and ethos is different' (Fidler, 1981, p.201). Or, as another upwardly mobile respondent suggested, 'it would be very difficult for someone who went to a secondary modern or the D-stream of a comprehensive to change rapidly enough to end up at the top of this company.' Naturally, what is at stake in this remark is not so much ability as demeanour. The explanation is explicitly one of cultural deficit, defined in core terms: 'Whatever we say about it, there is a barrier; if your voice doesn't sound right, or if you go drinking in the evening instead of playing golf – it does make a difference. And it pulls the wife with him as well, and it's much more difficult for her' (Fidler, 1981, p.201). Hence, these locales, although not entirely closed, apparently relax their closures on terms which imply acceptance of the core status group's value formation. We might, adapting Giddens (1981) slightly, regard this as a tendency to cultural sequestration in its demoting of certain apparent aspects of identity and its privileging of a certain set of terms for successfully 'passing' as a member of good standing. These terms may be conceptualized as 'cultural capital' or 'cultural asset'. This suggests a more elaborate notion of capital than merely material assets.

Following Bourdieu and his colleagues (Bourdieu and Passeron, 1977; Bourdieu, 1973; Bourdieu *et al.*, 1973) we can consider the following significant forms of capital assets: economic assets in the form of money and fixed capital; social assets in the form of networks of contacts and social skills; and cultural assets in the form of educational qualifications and the more ethereal *culture générale*. There are three major forms of social capital. First, there are kinship ties and connections which one can expect to be mobilized on one's behalf to obtain positions and exert influence. These may not only be familial ties (with the role of marriage being particularly important) but also the networks of personal contacts formed through common educational class background, particularly ties formed in and through recreational activities. Second, there are the relative degrees of opacity or transparency of perceptions of how educational and occupational structures are related and positions allocated within them. This type of knowledge is highly structured in an unequal manner in its distribution in any given society. The collective social knowledge of one's family and kin networks is crucial. The greater the extent to which these networks straddle positions, then the less opaque the structure of educational and occupational opportunities will appear to be. Finally, there is the existence of those 'gestures which reveal quintessences', as Anderson (1965, p.63) so perfectly put it. These are those skills obtained via family upbringing and schooling revealed not so much in particular faculties as in 'particular modes of speech, dress and bodily movements' (Marceau *et al.*, 1978, p.137).

These forms of social capital, or social assets, are not only associated with economic assets but 'also play an important role on their own as means of coordinating and concentrating economic capital, centralising information and influence and ensuring continued reproduction of elite personnel' (Marceau *et al.*, 1978, p.137). Together with cultural assets such as educational qualifications, which facilitate access, and the general air of cultivation (*culture générale*), these help to define the selection limits of ruling-class reproduction in very tangible ways. It has been argued by Halsey *et al.* (1980) that these notions of cultural capital have their most influential effects on the selection of children for schooling in elite schools. However, other evidence points to their pervasiveness beyond the school career. Indeed, those mechanisms operate more explicitly at the level of selection procedures generally (Clegg and Dunkerley, 1980, pp.429-31;

Salaman and Thompson, 1978; Silverman and Jones, 1976), particularly as capital becomes more concentrated and centralized into larger and more impersonally organized units of valorization, and family control of capital declines in importance. Particular types of credential (Collins, 1979), particularly those obtained from elite business schools, become of greater importance for access to positions of strategic control. Holders and heirs of existing forms of cultural, social and economic assets will try to convert these into the new currency, by effectively securing for themselves access to credential assets. With the growth of non-family and impersonal forms of ownership of more concentrated and centralized processes of valorization, the development of management education, particularly of a generalist kind, becomes a crucial provider of new forms of cultural assets which can in principle facilitate reconversion strategies. In practice, argue Marceau et al. (1978), it has been the case that the development of management education has provided the gloss of a dominant ideology sufficient to subject and qualify individuals for successful business careers in functions of strategic control. These are positions in finance, consulting, marketing and corporate planning, in particular. Initially on graduation, these are more likely to be in large, frequently US or multinational corporations, but later in their career will be likely to be in smaller firms. At point of entry into the business schools these graduates are much more likely to be from the most prestigious social origins. In France, students attending *Institut Européen d'Administration des Affaires* (INSEAD), the top European business school, are heavily concentrated in family backgrounds in which the father was an owner of either an industrial or commercial enterprise, often in a declining branch of capital such as textiles.

This is important for it means on the one hand that the fathers of the persons concerned (virtually all men) can no longer place all their offspring with their economic capital alone (especially as there tend to be several sons to place). In order, therefore, to maintain or improve the socio-economic position held by their families of origin some at least of the sons are thrown on to the 'public' labour market and therefore have to rely more on their cultural capital, principally, that is on the educational diplomas they hold (Marceau et al., 1978, pp.140-1).

A similar background of privilege, with a much greater probability of being born into the homes of company directors and senior managers, of being educated in the elite public schools and universities, also attached to the British sample. Under the

139

auspices of state control and sponsorship, the business schools have become the major loci of the 'reproduction rules' whereby reconversion strategies may be pursued by declining elements of capital. Increasingly, possession of a business school credential is the appropriate cultural asset into which the sons of the elite can convert other types of asset. The evidence seems to indicate a higher degree of success in achieving this. The fact that opportunities for positions of strategic control in areas like finance and marketing 'do not appear to be available to the small proportion of sons of clerical and manual workers among business school students' serves only to reinforce the ideological role of the business schools, supported by the state, in 'maintaining the invisibility of the true criteria used by business in recruitment to controlling positions and facilitate[s] the production and continued credibility of new legitimating ideology' (Marceau *et al.*, 1978, pp.146-8). Credentials may be necessary, but not sufficient, criteria for career advancement. They remain embedded in a context defined by social and cultural assets as well as economic property. Similarly, cultural and social assets are in themselves necessary, but not sufficient, criteria. The different assets are linked tightly together and continually reinforce each other, but do not do so perfectly.

The transition in the organization of the ruling class, which we have discussed in this chapter, may be connected to the vertical division of labour and the limitations placed on cognitive development by modern extended institutionalized systems of education (Bernstein, 1975; Dahlström, 1979; Apple, 1979; Wexler, 1982). These embed and embody within society those 'taken-for-granteds' about what credentials mean which frame the actions that can be taken rationally in modern, complex organizations. This applies particularly to those persons who are vested with the tasks of selecting and training people for positions in the organization structure. In this regard, it has been noted that there is little evidence to suggest that variations in the level of formal education are matched by variations in the quality of the work performed (Berg, 1973). The function of selection seems to be that of simplifying and legitimating the exclusionary process, through legitimating certain types of knowledge as extant and authoritative and defining certain categories of person as legitimate bearers of legitimate knowledge (Meyer, 1977). In so doing, education produces and reproduces both elites and citizens, both rulers and ruled and both ruling positions and ruled positions. Education as a legitimating and allocative institution expands the authoritative culture and the specialized positions entailed and entitled by this knowledge-culture. Irrespective of

the efficacy of particular knowledges, they constitute authoritative new discourses and canons of rationality which come to be
incorporated in particular positions in society. As Meyer (1977,
p.69) puts it:

> institutionalized education does more than simply allocate
> some to success and others to failure. The educated learn to
> claim specialized functions of others. The less educated learn
> that they are part of a social world of rights and duties
> elaborated far beyond the traditional community. This is one
> of the core meanings of the modern social status *citizen*.

Formal qualifications are increasingly necessary for positions of
control. To the extent that cultural assets can be insinuated into
the defining characteristics of specialized, superordinate positions, then the possession of the appropriate credential can
become a device for attempting to secure that privilege (in a non-
property form) can be passed intergenerationally.

On all these grounds it is necessary to regard credentialism as a
form of exclusionary social closure comparable in its importance for class formation to the institution of property. Both
entail the use of exclusionary rules that confer benefits and
privileges on the few through denying access to the many, rules
that are enshrined in law and upheld by the coercive authority
of the state. It follows from this that the dominant class under
modern capitalism can be thought of as comprising those who
possess or control productive capital and those who possess a
legal monopoly of professional services. These groups represent the core body of the dominant or exploiting class by virtue
of their exclusionary powers which necessarily have the effect
of creating a reciprocal class of social inferiors and subordinates (Parkin, 1979, p.58).

We have suggested that credentialling will consist of more than
simply formal qualifications. It also entails the équipage of
'cultural capital'. Indirect evidence of the importance of such
linguistic skills, education and personal contacts in the reproduction of the ruling class may be gleaned from research into the
images of experience of society that elite businessmen have. Such
research has been conducted on a sample of 130 top executives
drawn from a representative selection of British capitalists
(Fidler, 1981). The findings of this research revealed, for
instance, that only 9 of the 130 men had fathers with manual
occupations. Overall, their personal experience of social mobility
was low. Most of them had been born into families in which their
fathers had class positions very close to their own present

position. The majority of them had attended the most elite public schools. Thus, their personal experience of linguistic styles other than their own, or of people being educated in a diversity of educational settings, was low. Civil society was highly restricted in terms of their direct experience.

This discussion of reproduction through interlocks and credentials has served to emphasize that the upper echelons of the class structure – the corporate ruling class – exist in a greater or lesser degree of determination, complementarity, competition and conflict with ideological interpellations other than those characterized as purely bourgeois, with gender clearly having a particular salience, in that most controllers of industry are males. As a whole, this system of relationships is decisive as it is formed and reproduced within the practices of civil society, rather than through any functional or property interest in particular.

In spite of the general tenor of these remarks, we should emphasize that the extent of conflicting and contradictory interest running through the ruling class has, none the less, been represented through a series of structural forms which embody, in their routine practices, a broad degree of reconciliation. We have argued that these practices are structured through a dynamic of reproduction which exhibits a capacity to co-opt or exclude, particularly through forms of credentialism. Thus, we may conclude from the foregoing analysis that the ruling class needs to be seen as both a property and a control relationship, articulated through the vertical division of labour and the institutionalized systems of selection, education and certification for positions in the organizational echelon of the structure of society.

The processes which we have described display in comparative perspective a simultaneous degree both of 'capital-logic' and civil indetermination, reflecting in turn the confluence of the economic, state and civil forces which collectively structure the terrain of struggles whose outcome is the organization or reorganization of class positions. There are several aspects of these processes which require further elaboration. It is important to note, for example, that analysis cannot be limited only to those who occupy positions within the system of production. Socially available surplus labour power also exists outside the ambit of productive employment. Hence, class analysis of itself poses only a partial perspective. The forms of social organization of surplus labour, both within and without production relations, are nevertheless linked directly to the process of class struggle.

The descriptive material and argument which we have set out in this chapter clearly demonstrate that the identification of a ruling class based on property relations of effective possession and control necessitates detailed and complex analysis. However, this should by no means lead us to assume that positions not so identified necessarily fall within the working class. Not only must we identify and account for the role of the petty bourgeoisie, which has been discussed in chapter 4, but it is also important to locate the historically emergent and complex middle strata of contemporary capitalism.

The state and intensity of class struggle structures the degree of clarity or fuzziness surrounding class boundaries at any particular historical moment. The parameters within which such struggles occur are ultimately constituted by the social relations of production. In emphasizing production, it is not our intention here to imply that social relations of exchange – of market capacity – are unimportant, but rather that their theoretical relevance is itself contingent upon production relations. This point of emphasis of Marxist analysis, which has been elaborated in previous chapters, serves to underscore the dynamic process through which the structure of class relations determines the contours and directions in which political struggle and social change proceed. It is in precisely this context that those positions generally characterized as the 'new middle class' assume a critical focus in shaping the political allegiances and axes about which social and economic conflicts are formulated and fought. In the chapter which follows, we shall consider the implication of these positions for the organizational transformation of the political bases of class struggle.

6 The new middle class: organization, division and incorporation

At the highest level of abstraction – that of the pure capitalist mode of production – only two classes need to be considered: the capitalist class and the working class. In concrete analysis, as Marx's writings of the early 1850s make clear, the emergence of intervening locations between polarized classes becomes evident. These intervening locations are not filled simply by statistically average wage-earners. Patterns of distribution of income, of education and of occupational status have led to definitions of the middle class as those groups occupying intervening levels of such categories; but such definitions leave much to be explained. In the material which follows, we shall argue that there is an analytical coherence between what Wright (1976) terms 'contradictory locations within class relations' and many of the positions which are commonly referred to as middle class. These positions draw their identity from production relations which, Poulantzas's objections (1976, p.204) notwithstanding, is to distinguish them from what might be termed the old middle classes, those more traditional members of the petty bourgeoisie whom we have discussed in an earlier chapter.

Conceptions of the new middle class

An analysis of class positions is required which is not limited simply to determination based solely on position in the mode of production. These positions are not static. Necessarily they are subject to the dynamics contingent upon the development of the forces of production. Characteristically, these transformations are themselves an effect of the trajectory of a capitalist system of production and its rationale. Consequently, we may suggest that the rise of a new middle class be analysed as a process which emerges from within a given structure of social relations of production. Emphasis is placed on structural contradictions in social relations of production which are consequent upon each historical cycle of expansion and contraction in the realization of surplus value and the accumulation of capital. In expressing this argument we follow the formulation of Aglietta who notes that

[t]here exist historical phases in which the conditions for expanded reproduction of the capitalist relations of production are not fulfilled. The balance of forces which makes the law of capital accumulation a general movement of value expansion is then broken. The cohesion of the structural forms whose overall operation canalizes and fragments the class struggle, displacing the points at which tensions arise in such a way as to reduce them by financial flows, is undermined. Such a situation is a *crisis*. It is clear that a crisis of this type is always social in character, in the sense that it is born out of the relations of a class society. But it can have differing effects on the forms in which these relations exist (1979, p.351).

As barriers to accumulation are overcome through structural transformation of capitalist production, our analysis must focus on the rationalization of the labour process and its supervision, change and control. Requirements of co-ordination are inherent in the development of the technical division of labour. Increasingly elaborate mechanisms of control have become necessary for the appropriation and realization of surplus value on a large scale. These have generated controlling but capital-subordinate and propertyless occupational positions for some highly skilled workers. For others the development has been into more routinized and proletarian 'skills', with little or no control. This process of transformation parallels the development of new managerial positions of control in both public administration and private capitalism (Mandel, 1975, pp.261-9; Hill, 1981).

A focus on the new middle class necessitates analysis of the ways in which specific relations of production structure the forms of the division of labour. Technological and organizational innovation, it has been argued, involves a process of 'deskilling' certain occupational categories and 'upgrading' a limited number of other positions, thus bringing about the development of an intermediate level of occupations. The role of these occupations is what has been termed 'the global function of capital' (Carchedi, 1977; also see Braverman, 1974; Edwards, 1979). We shall argue that, while the implications of skill requirements reflect the relative capacity of opposing occupational groups to defend or extend their command over specialized domains of technical expertise or knowledge, the fundamental parameters within which bargaining and closure take place can best be explained as the structurally determined outcome of the struggle among classes for social and economic advantage (Johnson, 1977; Johnson and Rattansi, 1981). Technological change can be situated within a broader context of social forces. It has no necessary neutrality.

The most important regulator of the forms of class conflict and the structures which arise from them is the state. The increasing scale of state intervention has a number of effects. It acts as a guarantor of monopolies of expertise and knowledge through the process of credentialism (Collins, 1979). It can support exclusionary strategies of some, and not other, occupational groups through legal frameworks. Moreover, state regulation tends to produce a framework which organizationally separates economic from political struggles. Trade unions become organizations separate from political parties and the organization of classes assumes a representative form (Przeworski, 1977, p.373). The particular form of organization of political struggle which is inherent in capitalist democracy allows capitalists to appear as bearers of a universal interest, because profit is the necessary condition of expansion in capitalist societies. As Przeworski notes, capitalists

continually 'vote' for allocation of societal resources as they decide to invest or not, employ or fire labour, purchase or sell state obligations, export or import, *ad infinitum*. Moreover, they exert a direct influence over the state, since the state is dependent upon their private, economic actions (1977, p.375).

These alternatives, inscribed in civil society, will be further discussed in chapter 8.

Workers, on the other hand, under 'normal' conditions, must pursue their claims to a much greater, and often almost exclusive, degree through the electoral process, rather than through broader forms of political pressure. The agenda which determines the validity or legitimacy of such normal claims is shaped by the negotiated representation of interests which is currently explicit. Ordinarily it is through these that the profits which capitalists appropriate can come to be seen as the sole determinant of the capacity of the entire society to improve the future conditions of material life (Przeworski, 1977, p.376; Gramsci, 1971).

The growth of the new middle class is both a consequence of the conflict between opposing classes and an expression of the developmental tendencies which are a product of capital–labour antagonisms. Significant elements of the new middle class are dependent for their growth and power on the emergence of political forces within state apparatuses. In the past it has been argued that these people were involved in advancing institutional reforms which were compatible with the long-term stability of capital accumulation (Burris, 1980, p.28). In this context we shall note the mechanisms of conflict transformation inherent in the administraton of corporatist strategies. These endow state managers with a structural position which enables them to transcend sectional interests in pursuit of a broader rationality of development of the accumulation process. There seems to be a scope for managerial autonomy which liberalism has frequently accorded.

As we point out in our discussion of the state in chapter 8, some theorists have suggested that a democratic state must ordinarily try to act to reproduce legitimacy within civil society, at the same time as it encourages a sufficient level of economic activity in order to ensure the maintenance of conditions favourable to accumulation. Typically, responses involve the expansion of the state's role in the regulation of the economy and particularly in the provision and manipulation of the social policies of the welfare state. These have an important role in system stability as well as in rationalizing the accumulation process. In so doing, they have contributed to a significant expansion of new-middle-class positions within the state apparatus.

In elaborating this material in the following pages we must therefore endeavour to explain the increasing scale of state intervention in the economy and in civil society. We will do this by analysing the structural tendencies and contradictions of capitalist development and the integral role of the state in relation to them. These must be seen in the context of the dynamics of class formation and the class and popular struggles to which they give rise.

A review of the literature indicates that there are three broad categories of theoretical work which endeavour to account for the structural determinants of the formation of new-middle-class positions in contemporary capitalism (see e.g. Wright, 1980a, pp.327ff.; Burris, 1980, pp.18ff.).

The first category of theoretical work is associated with the label 'new working class', a term coined by Serge Mallet (1975a). In very broad terms this work locates a distinct stratum of workers whose positions are upgraded by technological innovations and who occupy a vanguard role with respect to working-class attitudes and actions. In effect, Mallet retains a modified polarization model of the class structure of advanced capitalism through incorporation of the new occupational stratum within a specifically working-class categorization.

The second approach places those occupational strata whose position in the mode of production is indeterminate not within the working class but as a new class in its own right which has consolidated its position with respect to both capitalists and the working class (Ehrenreich and Ehrenreich, 1979; Larson, 1977). This so-called 'professional–managerial class' is defined in terms of its specific functions in the reproduction of class relations.

The third approach argues that there exist what are termed 'contradictory locations within class relations' (Wright, 1976, 1978, 1980a; Carchedi, 1975a, 1975b; Poulantzas, 1975, 1977). In this problematic, new-middle-class positions are said to share common characteristics with the working class. This commonality exists within the social division of labour in which some proportion of the labour power of each is sold to an employing organization. (However, as the next chapter will demonstrate, this sale can occur through quite segmented markets for labour.) Moreover, neither class shares in the ownership of the means of production. On the other hand, 'middle' positions typically involve some degree of control over production and over the labour process in which they are located. This is what makes them 'contradictory'.

The new working class

During the 1950s and 1960s, for many social theorists working during the prolonged economic upswing of the postwar era, orthodox Marxist accounts of the development of capitalist societies and the role of the working class as the motive force behind class struggle and social change, seemed quite unrealistic. In the context of unprecedented developments in the economic well-being of the working class, a significant diminution in the reserve army of the unemployed, and new evidence of a changed working-class consciousness amounting to 'embourgeoisement' (Roberts *et al.*, 1977, pp.37-65), there appeared to be pressing grounds for a fundamental re-examination of the structural forces influencing working-class action in capitalist society. A sociological consensus began to emerge. This stressed that important sectors of the working class had achieved a level of economic security which enabled them to adopt the social attitudes and images, if not the material lifestyle, of the bourgeoisie. The studies of Lockwood (1966), Mackenzie and Silver (1968) and Goldthorpe *et al.* (1969) identify individualism, consumerism and instrumentalism as social images held by the working class which were linked with political quiescence and incorporation (Dunkerley, 1980, p.170). Heavy emphasis was placed on integrative forces. The idea of a more or less cohesive future society provided an interpretative framework in which working-class attitudes or ideologies could be located and analysed as a sign of the further integration of the working class into the institutional framework of the new, stable 'post-industrial' society (Bell, 1974; Touraine, 1971).

A crucial development in the analysis of the erosion of working-class consciousness and class struggle came from the realization of the profound implications for capitalist industrial development of what became known as the 'second industrial revolution' (Crompton and Gubbay, 1977, pp.163-4). The evolution of capitalist production technology founded on highly automated information technology and electronic data processing came to be viewed as a critical structural element in the development of class boundaries and class consciousness. For Touraine (1971), the multiplication of middle-level technical categories of occupations and the increasing complexity of the channels of influence produced a dislocation of the social hierarchy. More importantly,

the analysis of social classes no longer offers a general framework for the understanding of industrial societies. . . . Economic growth and social change are governed by a more or less unified network of decision-making and organizational structures. In opposition to these structures, resistance or revolt appear, as well as a desire for the democratic control of the instruments and results of growth and change. 'Real' classes are formed to the degree that social domination is no longer concentrated and that the dominated groups are conscious enough of their own interests to defend a counter-model of development instead of simply opposing social interests to economic pressures (Touraine, 1971, p.82).

Political processes, in so far as they can exist in such a model, involve little more than 'the political expression of more or less diversified and articulated social demands' (Touraine, 1971, p.78).

This position, adumbrated by Touraine in the 1960s, proposed that a critical fragmentation had occurred in the working class, reflecting the emergence of a new category of occupations embodying a distinctive attitude to management and its structural location in the capitalist system. For Touraine, traditional working-class organizations and politics were of little contemporary relevance. His analysis develops the notion of a new subordinate middle stratum as the vanguard of groups for whom the new grounds of cohesion and integration are yet to be established. The implications of contemporary production technologies were held to be such that the determination of class boundaries based on ownership of the means of production were diluted by potentially contradictory divisions in social relations. The consequence of this was that a diversity of loosely connected interest groups sought to mobilize power within structures of authority whose legitimacy was being constantly eroded.

The previously emergent orthodoxy had developed from studies which stressed the role of technological innovations in production as factors leading to the social integration of workers within the existing structure of the capitalist enterprise. As a result of Touraine's work, an alternative theoretical problematic began to gain support, which, although it had theoretical antecedents in Touraine's ideas, also displayed significant differences. Workers centrally located in the new technological processes of production who were equipped with knowledge, and therefore a degree of control over production, are most likely to be engaged in new forms of conflict according to this analysis. These conflicts, according to Mallet (1975a, pp.28-9), will rise out of the contradictions inherent in a system of production in which the short-term profit of the owners inhibits the development of non-hierarchical production relations based on knowledge and skill, the egalitarian norms of the 'open society' ideology of the science in which they were trained (Wilson, 1977). These views gained support from the struggles of May 1968, in France. André Gorz, in an initial assessment of these events, placed much emphasis on the strategic role of these new categories of workers:

> Engineers and technicians were the driving force behind the contestation of management's authority, of the hierarchical division of labour, of differences in income, of the logic of capitalist profits. A fact which can hardly surprise since those who hold professional skill and intellectual autonomy are the first to become aware of the limitations which the pursuit of financial profit imposes on research, technical improvements and the full utilization of human creativeness (Gorz, 1970, p.261).

The final link in this theoretical account of the role of new occupational categories contingent upon technological processes of production was the argument that such workers might well lead or radicalize the rest of the working class in social and economic struggle. The most fully developed version of this thesis posits a revolutionary alliance between technicians, certain operational managers and manual workers (Mallet, 1975a,

1975b). Mallet contends that solidarity, fostered by 'high trust relations' (Fox, 1974) between these groups, moulds unified action in a struggle for control against the owners and managers of the means of production.

What is the theoretical coherence of Mallet's argument and to what degree does the empirical evidence from contemporary studies of capitalist production relations support it?

In general terms, Mallet's work draws on and parallels that of Touraine. However, there are fundamental points of divergence. For Touraine, 'post-industrial' conflict is generated by a vanguard segment of the educated new middle stratum of scientific–technological occupations. Contrary to Mallet, Touraine places this group not in the vanguard of working-class struggles but sees it as an entirely new and differently structured subordinate class (Ross, 1978, p.185). In effect, Touraine's broader interpretation of contemporary class structure withdrew any qualification for revolutionary capacity from manual worker groups. 'The mantle of the "historic subject" fell upon strata unhampered by an outmoded consciousness' (Rose, 1979, p.84). In contrast, Mallet suggests that the new locations for class conflict within capitalist production have created a true collective worker transcending the traditional manual/non-manual dividing line and blurring productive/non-productive labour distinctions (see Mann, 1973a, p.57). It is these workers that Mallet perceives as the new working class.

Mallet's theoretical contribution was initially constituted as a polemic against the Marxist orthodoxy of the French Communist Party in the 1960s. The conventions of this view held that the vanguard of working-class struggle was drawn from a homogeneous category typified by semi-skilled factory operatives (Ross, 1978, p.183). In Mallet's view the thrust for social change would be diverted by division between traditional industrial workers and new categories of scientific–technological workers. What was required was 'a renewal of Marx's theory . . . which would take into account the effect of the evolution of the technology of work on the nature of the relations of production' (Gallie, 1978, p.16).

At the centre of Mallet's conception of the new working class is an historical model. This is based on Touraine's hypothesis of the three periods of development of the capitalist labour process. Furthermore, Mallett (1975a, p.35) notes 'within the working class and in each period, the existence of a *structural kernel* around which concepts, forms of organization and action of the labour movement are organized.'

Mallet traces the transformation of the quality of work deriving from the changing framework of production and particularly the increasing division of labour. He emphasizes the erosion of workers' own identities as producers and the consequent shift of emphasis in workers' consciousness from work to spheres of consumption (Mallet, 1975a, pp.35-83). The development of the manufacturing division of labour constitutes the first phase of Mallet's analysis. Here, for the first time, 'the labourer is brought face to face with the intellectual potencies of the material process of production, as the property of another, and as a ruling power' (Marx, 1974, p.341). In this phase 'anarcho-syndicalism . . . became the dominant ideological current of the "polyvalent skilled worker".' The growing union movement is regarded as a reflection of desires to dispossess the capitalist of control and to return to craft autonomy (Mallet, 1975b, pp.25-9).

The second phase of development corresponded to the final decomposition of the manufacturing process through the application of machinery and mass production techniques. This period marked a significant degradation of labour as workers became mere adjuncts of machinery. It also corresponds with the ascendancy of the semi-skilled worker. Because of the structural location of such workers, it also witnessed the emergence of bureaucratized forms of working-class action. As Mallet argues, 'the insecure status of the semi-skilled workers made the organization of movements in the factory very difficult. . . . What the semi-skilled worker was incapable of obtaining as a producer, he sought to gain as a consumer' (1975b, p.36).

The critical turning-point, in Mallet's view, came with the third phase in the transformation of the technology of work through automated electronic processing:

> Automation, a truly dialectical negation of the fragmentation of work, developed at full speed in the advanced industries, those whose object was the treatment of new materials: oil and petrochemicals, synthetic chemistry, electrical energy, tele-communications (Mallet, 1975b, p.38).

Not only the technical relations of production, but, more importantly, the social relations of production are profoundly altered. Automated industry

> brings the progressive elimination of the distinction between manual and intellectual labour . . . between the operator . . . and the engineer or higher level technician who supervises him, there is no longer a difference in kind, simply a difference in hierarchical situation . . . as modern industry tends to 'technicise' the entire working class (Mallet, 1975b, p.41).

In this period, technicians and engineers who would thus constitute the main labour force begin to regain an overall perspective on the labour process which had been progressively eroded since the assumption of control by capitalists in the first stages of co-operation and machine production. Such a transformation of organizational relations occurs, according to Mallet, because these workers are situated hierarchically above the automated productive apparatus which 'destroys the fragmentation of work and recreates the synthetic vision of a complex task at the level of the team or even of the whole workforce' (Mallet, 1975a, p.67).

An important corollary of these changes is the development of a relationship of mutual indispensability between workers and the specific enterprise in which they are located. Workers' economic security becomes much more closely linked with the performance of a particular enterprise, as their economic rewards are determined primarily by the overall economic situation of the enterprise and by the success of its commercial strategy. Their fate becomes dependent on organizationally internal labour markets. These complex integrative forces, bound up with an identification of career with the enterprise and its performance, are considered to heighten the responsibility and involvement of workers in the enterprise. These forces for integration are not simply employers' strategies dictated by a need to retain expertise and capacities specific to the firm and to build up a fluid organization (Rose, 1979, p.86). Instead, they are considered to involve the development of high-trust relationships between operating managers and the new occupational categories as a consequence of reciprocal needs (Fox, 1974, p.346).

Mallet attributes to the new class of workers forms of organization and action which constitute a radical departure from past union practices. The objective integration of workers into enterprise, he argues,

> facilitates the passage from 'trade unionist' consciousness to the consciousness of the managing class – the will to acquire control of the enterprise by and for the workers – and thus to a new political awareness, as this demand develops at the level of the large national sectors and against the policy put into effect by the State (Mallet, 1975b, p.105).

Thus, the contradiction between the technical rationality of the new class and the logic of capitalist accumulation, in the context of which such workers must operate, has become the target of their struggle. The focus of such struggle is control over the relations of production, from the technical organization of the immediate work process to the determination of critical investment decisions. Moreover, as Mallet noted in the foregoing quote, the struggle for control of economic decision-making in key sectors necessitates an increasing awareness of the need to exert political control over global economic policy at the level of the entire society. The concern with issues of control at the level of the enterprise invokes a revolutionary prospect for Mallet. This prospect is premised on the need fundamentally to reconstitute existing social relations within the organization, producing a revolution from below rather than one predicated on the seizure of state power at the highest levels.

Finally, the goals achieved through the struggle of the new class will provide a model for the development of a broader class action which will initiate a process of social change encompassing critical implications for the entire working class. Drawing on the experience of May 1968 in France, Mallet asserts that

> demands for control of the organization of production, for the guarantee of security of employment, against bureaucratic methods of running the economy, have now become generalized in the same way as they emerged in the advanced sectors of industry. . . . By drawing into the united movement, despite misgivings and resistance, at least nine or ten million workers, the advanced sectors of manufacturing and servicing industries showed that it was possible, at least in terms of action, to get the working masses in the traditional industries to go beyond the narrowly defensive and corporatist vision of their own interest (1975a, pp.30-1).

The events of May 1968 assume a crucial role. They display the possibility of a transformation of 'trade union consciousness' in Mallet's interpretation. From the workers' responses a strategy emerges focusing on slowing down the rate of exploitation and raising the level of political consciousness. The goal of this consciousness is the abolition of the mode of production and its political system. However, this is not to suggest that Mallet under-estimates the internal antagonisms of the working class. The approach of the union organizations representing the new working classes, which is described by Mallet as 'neo anarcho-syndicalism', certainly produces a political consciousness 'but it does so through a theoretical schemata which is "pure" and abstract: new working class neo-capitalism. And in so doing, it isolates itself in relation to the real social formation' (1975b, p.213). It is in the latter that a homogeneity of conditions leading to a class consciousness has yet to be developed. It is at this level that Mallet stresses the conventional Leninist role of the political revolutionary party.

Mallet's work explicitly re-emphasizes the materialist dialectic in Marxist theory through a redeployment of Marx's thesis on the central contradiction of capitalism – the increasing disjuncture between an inefficient system of individual relations of production based on private ownership and the increasingly collective character of the forces of production (Gallie, 1978, p.19; Mann, 1973a, p.59). It refocuses attention on working-class struggle and its role as a critical force for societal redevelopment, particularly as this occurs over issues of control. At the same time, it suggests a conjunction of the interests of both manual and non-manual workers against capitalist forces of production. Finally, it points to the emergence of a new consciousness from within, and as a direct consequence of, the developing capitalist technical process of production and the new social relations of production thus generated.

We have devoted the foregoing section to an exposition of Mallet's work because it represents one of the first of a number of recent attempts to locate an analysis of class struggle within the perspective of Marxist political economy. It focuses on developmental tendencies within the capitalist mode of production and emphasizes the class forces emerging from contradictions within social relations of production. But if these are the strengths of Mallet's work, it is precisely in these areas that its fundamental weaknesses are also located. Mallet argues that these technological and organizational innovations which characterize capitalist production have produced fundamental changes in the power of occupational categories and in the development of class forces. However, he fails to situate these changes within the broader context of social forces from which they are derived. Consequently, his argument is somewhat 'technicist' in the primacy it gives to determination by technology. We shall examine these technicist assumptions in more detail shortly. First, however, there are several other important criticisms which must also be considered.

One of the criticisms most frequently levelled at Mallet's work is the near-complete lack of methodological rigour in the organization of data to support his thesis. Mallet's commitment to proselytize his theory determined a selective, even credulous, use of data for illustrative purposes rather than as an empirical validation of his thesis (Rose, 1979, pp.87-9). The results of more recent studies of workers' attitudes have been at best equivocal on Mallet's claims (Mann, 1973a, 1973b, pp.59-67; Goldthorpe *et al.*, 1969, p.187; Garaudy, 1970; Gallie, 1978, pp. 295-318). For

155

instance, Mallet's evidence in support of one of the major themes of his argument that the new working class will reject quantitative (i.e. salary) demands in favour of qualitative (i.e. control) demands receives somewhat cursory and haphazard treatment. There is certainly little evidence from more recent studies that salaries will be relegated from a position of importance as a focus of dispute in modern process industries (Gallie, 1978, chapter 3). Other weaknesses may be identified in Mallet's work. The theory of the new working class is developed upon an implicit acceptance of the view that technological or organizational innovations introduced by management significantly enlarge the discretionary element in certain categories of occupations. This position asserts that the so-called 'post-industrial' era will involve increased opportunities for greater discretion in work tasks, especially for traditional working-class jobs. It has come to be associated with the work of social theorists such as Bell (1974), Touraine (1971) and Blauner (1964), whose work is located in a much more traditional theoretical domain than that of Mallet. The tendency of post-industrialism, as Goldthorpe et al. argue, would be that 'social inequalities . . . would be modified and structured in such a way that the society of the future will be an overwhelmingly middle class society within which the divisions of the past would no longer be recognizable' (1969, p.6).

Counterposed to those theories which foresee an 'upgrading' of the working class is the tradition of work whose most influential representative is Harry Braverman. Braverman (1974) has persuasively argued that technological innovation has resulted in an increasing division of labour and in increasingly specific work roles. The problem of co-ordination that this poses for management promotes tighter mechanisms of control and a reduction of the discretion available to workers. The twin processes of deskilling and increased control developed through technological innovation led Braverman to forecast a further proletarianization of formerly skilled working-class positions. Thus, the capitalist labour process withdraws the last vestiges of skill and control over work from the working class.

The relative paucity of data, especially longitudinal, makes any clear-cut resolution of the debate surrounding the sets of theories concerning upgrading or deskilling somewhat problematic. Nevertheless, our examination of such 'evidence' as there is from a broad range of recent studies (Carchedi, 1977, p.124, on Italy; Allen, 1977, p.73, on Britain; Poulantzas, 1975, p.243, and Rose, 1979, p.90, on France; Gallie, 1978, 1983, and Mann, 1973a, on Britain and France) suggests, in line with Dunkerley's (1980, p.176) conclusion, that 'the balance of argument seems increasingly to be weighted in favour of the deskilling thesis.'

As Salaman (1979) has pointed out, the design of highly differentiated routinized work cannot be explained simply in terms of the exigencies of modern production technologies. It must be seen in the context of the power wielded by some groups over others in terms of the basic class structures of the societies in which such work is performed (Salaman, 1979, pp. 95, 97). An important corollary of this process is pointed out by Braverman (1974, p.82) in terms of the development of complex expertise and high discretionary roles amongst those who oversee the systems of organizational control. Situations will increasingly be encountered in which small numbers of technical workers who may have formerly engaged mainly in production now supervise, organize and control groups of deskilled production workers (Clegg and Dunkerley, 1980; Salaman, 1979). By concentrating on this group and its emergence within the framework of the upgrading thesis, Mallet has perpetrated a significant misunderstanding about the sociology of the new middle class (Gorz, 1976, pp.167-174).

Mallet's error is compounded in that the assumptions on which his work is founded overlook 'the possibility that technical design and production engineering obey a social no less than a technical logic, that they embody actual or implicit organizational choices which sectionalize the plant workforce' (Rose, 1979, p.88). Mallet does not take into account what is a dual process both of upgrading and of deskilling of labour within capitalist production. His failure is that he assumed an inherent and self-sufficient technological process independent of capitalist relations of production (Poulantzas, 1975, p.243). This technicist conception, which posits an inexorable decline in the working class as a consequence of technical and scientific 'progress' developing independently of the relations of production, fails adequately to theorize the transformations that characterize the present phase of monopoly capitalism. In order to comprehend these processes fully, it is necessary, as Poulantzas (1975) argues, to divorce them from the influence of some intrinsic and self-sufficient technical progress and to locate them in the domain of exploitation and a shift in dominance towards the extensive dequalification of labour (Poulantzas, 1975, p.245). This process may only be fully effected through an increase in the number of technicians whose primary role is that of control.

It is likely that these circumstances provide a more cogent theoretical explanation for the increasing activism of the majority of other professional and technical workers whose tasks are becoming increasingly proletarianized (Boreham, 1983). Furthermore, as Carchedi (1977) suggests, the proletarianization of the new middle class, of which increased white-collar union militancy may be an effect, may be explained not only in terms of devaluation of labour power. It may also be considered in terms of the tendency of the global function of capital, which their positions had represented, to have been made redundant through a technical dequalification of the skill content of the positions which they occupied (Carchedi, 1977, p.208). We would suggest that it is precisely these conditions which provide the framework for the new middle class to form defensive coalitions with highly unionized working-class groups who are already engaged in industrial struggle and thus provide a reference-point for the new working class (Rose, 1979, p.89; Carchedi, 1977, p.124).

Our final point is that in all of his work, Mallet fails adequately to account for the role of the state. Indeed, he is generally silent on the role of the state in class struggle. State power exercised through institutional intervention in industrial relations and the production of organizational reforms, has a decisive role in the outcome of such struggles. Or was Mallet of the view that his 'sanitized revolution', as Rose (1979, p.169) has expressed it, might guarantee a smooth transition to socialism without any resistance from the economic and political forces which comprise the state? In general we are led to emphasize the paradoxical conclusion derived by Rose (1979, p.97) that Mallet's theory invokes a 'Marxist' sociology of labour which largely accepts the propositions of recent capitalist political economy.

The professional–managerial class

An alternative thesis to that of Mallet also had its origins in a search for what one might term 'left praxis'. It stands as an important contribution to a series of debates surrounding opposi- tional strategies within the new left and the minuscule new communist movement in the USA, in particular the inability of such groups to enlist significant working-class support. Concur- rently with these accounts, difficulties were encountered by certain contemporary Marxist accounts of class structure. The difficulties concerned the lacunae and the obstacles in developing an adequate analysis of the growing numerical strength and combativeness of certain middle-level occupational groups in a climate characterized by the relative quiescence of traditional working-class struggle.

An important development came with the work of Barbara and John Ehrenreich in the late 1970s. This put forward the concept of a distinct professional–managerial class as a formation specific

to the monopoly stage of capitalism. The Ehrenreichs characterize this new and separate middle class as a class of 'salaried
mental workers who do not own the means of production and
whose major function in the social division of labour may be
described broadly as the reproduction of capitalist culture and
capitalist class relations' (1979, p.12). Such a distinct class of
'technical workers, managerial workers, "culture" producers,
etc.' (1979, p.9) is able to be sustained by two developments.
First, the growth of the social surplus beyond the requirements of
the bourgeoisie, and second, as the Ehrenreichs assert, because
'the proletariat has developed to the point that a class specializing
in the reproduction of capitalist class relationships becomes a
necessity to the capitalist class' (1979, p.14).

In this account the main function of the professional–managerial
class seems to be to provide the major elements of social control
under monopoly capitalism. This is effected in two ways. First,
through the agency of its members in the (scientific) management
of production, and second, through consequent technological,
organizational and cultural developments. Through these developments, it is argued, skills and cultural resources formerly
located in the hands of the working class were expropriated to
become concentrated in the knowledge of specialists and
managers. The extent to which this process adequately accounts
for changes in the technical and social relations of production is
problematic. Complex social processes such as this may need to
be theorized with considerably more attention to concrete
empirical evidence than has yet been undertaken. Despite this
absence of empirical data, it may reasonably be asserted that,
given the putative goal of a professional–managerial class as the
production of a rational reproducible social order, this goal
places the new class in an objectively antagonistic relationship to
the working class.

In order to account for the existence of the professional–
managerial class as a distinctive formation, the Ehrenreichs had
to establish a necessary opposition between it and the capitalist
class. In this they followed the same path as the new-working-
class thesis, and with little more theoretical precision. In a
passage highly reminiscent of the work of Mallet, they argue that
for the professional–managerial class, 'the very ideals of "objectivity", "rationality", etc., which justified their role to the
capitalists inevitably led them into *conflict* with the capitalists'
(1979, p.22).

The Ehrenreichs suggest that the conflict between the professional–managerial class and the capitalist class is focused upon
the independent status of the goals of accumulation and values of

159

efficiency, order and rationality. It is these which characterize the dominant ideological thrust of the professional–managerial class in asserting and defending its advantaged position in production. The locus of the dispute involves critical issues of occupational control. The role of the professional–managerial class in scientific/ technical innovation and social mediation requires a high degree of autonomy, it is argued, if legitimation is to be generally accorded to these activities. Claims to objectivity and rational decision-making cannot be pursued from a plausibly objective position if it is one which is specified as that of servility to capital. The Ehrenreichs argue that the aspirations of the professional– managerial class, and the ideological determinations which are seen to be necessary to legitimize those aspirations, are exemplified in the characteristic form of self-organization of large segments of the professional–managerial class (henceforth referred to as PMC) – that of the professions.

The major specifications of professional codes and charters include the requirement of a high level of generalized and systematic knowledge accessible only through formal qualifications and generally involving the provision of a credential guaranteed by the state; a set of occupational aims directed towards general community or cultural benefit rather than to individual or group self-interest; and a large measure of autonomy and control vested within the professional association, correlated with barriers restricting interference in occupational practice from bodies external to the profession. The Ehrenreichs consider that these claims of professionalism are 'most commonly directed at the capitalist employing class' (1979, p.26) and, furthermore, that specialized knowledge 'ensures that the PMC can control its own reproduction as a class' (1979, p.26) through lengthy education and socialization processes. Espousing the promise of efficient management and objective scientific–technological development, major segments of the PMC could thus promote, in the name of service to society at large, the interests of capital while pursuing a strategy for their own class advancement.

Without offering any more precise theorization of the 'fundamental antagonism' between the interests of the capitalist class and those of the PMC, the Ehrenreichs assert that this dynamic 'has turned the PMC into an enduring reservoir of radicalism' (1979, p.42). They observe the historical association in the USA of an 'ambiguous mixture of elitism and anti-capitalist militancy' in the PMC's class consciousness. It was this characteristic which

> continued to be a major theme of 'the movement' throughout the sixties. Expressions of it can be found in the 'New Left', the

anti-war movement, the ecology movement, the women's liberation movement – all of which defied 'the system', but often with moralistic contempt for the working class (1979, p.33).

At this point, one might observe that in order to strengthen their thesis the Ehrenreichs also need to insert into their analysis the provision that the PMC may be distinguished by its increasing social and cultural coherence despite that elsewhere they have insisted on its heterogeneity.

The Ehrenreichs conclude their account by suggesting a dissolution of 'the tensions at the PMC/working class interface' (1979, p.44). It is asserted that the historical and present commonalities in both working-class and PMC roles will reassert themselves so as to re-emphasize the development of a dichotomous class model. The systematic critique of capitalism (which is a complementary feature of the relationship between the PMC and the working class) is dominated intellectualy by the PMC, thus allowing the Ehrenreichs to conclude that a mass movement seeking to alter society in its totality depends on the coming together of working-class experience and militancy with the tradition of socialist thinking kept alive by middle-class intellectuals. As with Mallet, a covert Leninism emerges in their analysis.

The Ehrenreichs are concerned with the significant growth of a stratum of professional and managerial workers exhibiting an uncertain structural allegiance either to capital or to the working class. They have highlighted the important questions which are posed for theorists concerned with developmental tendencies within capitalist societies and the role of class struggle in those developments. They share our critical stance towards the proponents of a thesis of a new working class, rejecting the work of such writers in favour of a separate middle class, the PMC, which may be defined in terms of its relationships both to the working class and to the capitalist class and by its role in the process of reproduction of capitalist relations and culture. The rise of the PMC in the twentieth century is regarded by them largely as a consequence of the growth of state apparatuses, and the developing 'rationality' of capitalist production is seen to reflect the evolution of ruling-class–working-class relations under monopoly capitalism. Such a perspective is both deterministic and incapable of yielding the comparative variation that research such as Ferraresi's (1983) provides. In an analysis of recent state theory, Ferraresi demonstrates with empirical reference to the modern Italian state, that rather than a technical, functional 'new class' rationality characterizing the expanded state employees, they are rather more a disaggregated, traditionally particularistic stratum far closer to the old middle classes than to being a new class themselves. The class is hardly professional or even a class, albeit that it occupies a middle stratum in an advanced capitalist economy characterized by a high degree of monopoly capitalism. The PMC thesis may well be an example of an extrapolation from a particular interpretation of local conditions to a global diagnosis. Finally, we can note that whilst on the one hand the Ehrenreichs decisively reject the new-working-class theory they are prepared to extend what they see as the radical leanings of the PMC into a potential anti-capitalist alliance with the working class.

As Wright (1979, p.198) reminds us, the central difficulty with this position is that it extends into an analysis of class, understood at the level of production relations, one which is derived from an analysis based on social relations of exchange. While it is no doubt correct to argue, following Weber, that intellectual skills provide their holders with a special market capacity, this does not allow us to assert that they necessarily have any control over the use of those skills in production. In order satisfactorily to link these alternative accounts it would be necessary to study the specific forms of the labour process in which intellectual workers are engaged to specify the extent to which objective autonomy is granted in intellectual production. In essence, the Ehrenreichs have neglected adequately to distinguish the symbols of autonomy, which are of critical ideological import, from its material conditions (Aronowitz, 1979, p.221).

The most important question posed by the Ehrenreichs' analysis is whether, within the problematic they have established, the PMC may, in fact, be constituted as a class. A critical examination of their work reveals two arguments in support of this proposition. First, they suggest that the PMC is 'characterized by a coherent social and cultural existence' (1979, p.11). Clearly, whilst this may be a necessary requirement of class action it is quite spurious to argue that the various occupational categories included under the PMC label have an internal unity, the logic of which is to identify this stratum of occupations as a class. It is only if a further argument can be maintained that they can be considered a class. This is the Ehrenreichs' second argument, that the PMC is 'characterized by a common relationship to the economic foundations of society – the means of production and the socially organized patterns of distribution and consumption' (1979, p.11).

The clarity of this latter concept of class is seriously diluted through its identification in the Ehrenreichs' analysis with a common *function* in the division of labour. The centrality to their analysis of this functional division – 'a class concerned with the reproduction of capitalist culture and class relationships' (1979, p.14) – raises many more questions than it answers. Such a functionalist conception of the PMC is also a distortion of the notion of reproduction, which for them represents only one aspect of the term as it is generally applied in Marxist discourse – that of reinforcement. As Noble reminds us

> reproduction and production are but two aspects of the same single process of social production . . . the process of production itself . . . is the primary means of reproducing capitalist social relations . . . capitalist production and reproduction are not separate tasks to be assigned to different specialists; they are one and the same task assigned to all (1979, p.131).

Functions within a society, especially the function of reproducing class relations, are perhaps better not introduced into the analysis as categories or positions, as the Ehrenreichs have suggested, but rather need to be understood as dimensions of social relations (Wright, 1979, p.201), which may have more salience for the exertions of some actors rather than others.

To argue as we have done above is not to deny that certain positions are closely associated with the functions of reproduction (an argument which has been advanced by Clegg (1981) with respect to the 'organic intellectuals' of the bourgeoisie). However, there is nothing in the Ehrenreichs' analysis to guide us in allocating certain categories of occupations to particular class locations based on the proportion or importance of functions which are allocated to reproductive rather than productive activities. Moreover, we would suggest that such a determination would contribute little to an explication of class relations under contemporary capitalism. As Wright (1979, p.201) correctly notes, engineers are not only involved in managerial activities, but are clearly engaged in productive functions such as the design of bridges. The Ehrenreichs nowhere offer an adequate theorization of these difficulties, only emphasizing the centrality of the functional requirement which, as we have already suggested, may be inadequate.

Even if these difficulties were surmountable the Ehrenreichs would still be left with a notion of class based upon distributional considerations, thus qualifying it as more of a descriptive than a prescriptive concept. In defining the PMC as a set of positions within capitalist society, rather than in terms of its dialectical relationships with opposing classes, the Ehrenreichs cannot adequately theorize its place in class struggle. We are provided with a highly idealized still photograph of the current stage of evolution of a particular capitalist society. This is scarcely a sufficient model from which to render judgment about the forces for social change in capitalist society in general.

These arguments lead us to a further and more fundamental critique of the Ehrenreichs' analysis. Following Aronowitz's contention (1979, p.231), we would suggest that the Ehrenreichs have failed to explicate the notion of class power. They provide little evidence to suggest that the PMC concerns itself with political power or that it seeks to represent its relation to the social and political order through the development of ideologies. Such forms of representation may include direct trade union action, electoral participation through political parties, or alternative forms of struggle. To some degree the PMC may seek to represent its relation to the political and economic reality ideologically, and indeed the Ehrenreichs suggest a form of technocratic consciousness as the main thrust of such ideological development. However, in thus giving ideological form to its social practice the PMC seems much less concerned with antagonistic relations to any major section of the capitalist class than with an ideological justification for the limited discretionary function which its members are accorded. While the working class may be defined through its objective antagonism to capital, the PMC has a distinctively local basis for any such antagonism: 'They do not challenge the economic hegemony of capital, only its political and ideological strategies for rule' (Aronowitz, 1979, p.232).

Whereas the ideology of the PMC developed along lines which were clearly in accordance with the self-advancement of this class, it could be maintained that these, nevertheless, complemented and fortified some of the aims usually associated with capital. For example, ideologies of rational technological control could scarcely be painted as oppositional ideologies to the dominant corporate ruling-class ethos. This is precisely because these involve a search for technological and organizational interventions in the production process in order to place it further under the domination of capital valorization. Thus, as Aronowitz stresses,

> even those ideologies that purport to oppose the rule of a
> technologically integrated capitalism find difficulty in escaping
> from the vision of total administration . . . the hegemony of
> capital expresses itself as an idea of rationality whose inner logic
> appears seamless (1979, p.222).

Espousing a doctrine of economic growth and efficient management, dominant fractions of the PMC found themselves promoting the interests of capital through the rhetoric of reform. Nevertheless, as Larson (1977, p.147) suggests, their ideological convergence around the goals of rationalization and economic expansion was structurally based, indicating that professionals and managerial specialists with a cosmopolitan outlook were asserting themselves in intimate connection with the central institutions of the capitalist order. Senior advisors and experts within the rapidly growing public sector were at the locus of the ideological expression of the central role of arbitration and social cohesion which was to become important for significant elements of the state apparatus through the developing needs of corporate capitalism. The bureaucratization or the organization of scientific and professional occupations, both in the public and in the private, corporate sectors, provided the typical pattern of middle-class mobility. Thus, the major context of occupational practice and ideological assertion became closely linked with authoritative support for the new institutions of the capitalist state (Larson, 1977, p.148). It was through these very institutions that an ill-defined reciprocity in terms of support and recognition through credentialling emerged.

The problems which beset any analysis of the power of a professional and managerial 'class' in this context may be located squarely in the ambiguities of the power relationships in which they develop. As forms of technological and organizational control are extended towards the upper echelons of bureaucratic hierarchies, those whose functions are in the realms of technological and organizational control are themselves victims of these very developments. On the one hand, as Aronowitz (1979, p.229) notes, they espouse ideologies of professional 'service' – high discretion roles in which occupational autonomy free of political and ideological constraint is accorded – whilst, on the other, they find their own occupational tasks rationalized and subject to deliberate technological forces – the logic of which is to withdraw the control over professional work to a limited number of external agents (Boreham, 1983). Under these conditions, professionals who perceive the threat of proletarianization may well pursue trade union strategies in order to defend their threatened autonomy. The logic of this analysis is that professionals and managers are largely dependent and reliant upon institutions of capital for any vestiges of control which may be retained by their occupations. We would suggest that this creates insurmountable problems for any theoretical determination concerning their class formation. Thus, we are drawn to the appropriateness of

Aronowitz's conclusion (1979, p.224) that, empirically, professionals and managers are unlikely to evidence a sufficient basis for conflict with the capitalist class for them to constitute other than a more or less influential stratum within the logic of capitalist society, linked together by particular professions or by the forms of capital.

The experience of formations at the centre of the world system of capital illustrates the possibilities for the development of a middle stratum under the most propitious economic circumstances. The development of a small proportion of transnational corporations, global in operation but controlled at the centre of the world system, has involved a high level of integration of capital. One consequence of these developments, as Holland (1980) argues, and as was discussed in the previous chapter, is that a highly integrated meso-economic stratum has superimposed a level of planning and rationality upon the international capitalist system which was previously believed to be unachievable. Further consequences flow from this. One is the expansion of a segment of the workforce whose main preoccupation is planning and rationalizaton. This should be viewed together with the existence of an unequal international division of labour between the centre and the periphery as a significant determinant of the concentration in the centre of the system of a PMC (Amin, 1979, p.15). The size of such formations in countries such as the USA (Noble, 1979, p.124, claims that the PMC constitutes nearly one-quarter of the US population – almost 50 million people) has focused the attention of many social theorists, while at the same time narrowing their perspective on the international system of capital. In these circumstances, it is not difficult to understand the tendency of social theorists located in the USA to maintain the importance of the increasing PMC as a third force between capital and labour. Such a view is supported by the high level of visibility of this new stratum in the USA. 'Radical' movements based on conditions, 'personalized' problems, lifestyle, environmentalism – the 'small is beautiful' trend – may, as has been suggested, be clearly distinguished from the majority of issues confronting the traditional working class (Szymanski, 1979, p.58; Goldthorpe, 1982, p.183; Amin, 1979, p.15). They are largely single-issue movements or forms of protest which avoid direct involvement in questions of class struggle either in production or in distribution.

Research findings from Britain suggest that, for most of its members, the experience of being middle class is conceptualized in terms of a 'middle mass [of] individuals, who regard themselves as enjoying similar privileges and life-styles' (Roberts *et al.*, 1977, p.138). This status imagery, in its amorphousness, is, as we will observe, not as characteristic of the working class. It may well be that this far more fluid imagery is a characteristic of the relatively recent and rapid expansion of the ranks of administrative, professional and technical employees. Incumbents of these ranks appear to be there primarily on the basis of educational qualifications, whatever the social processes underlying access to such qualifications (Blau and Duncan, 1967; Heath, 1981; Halsey *et al.*, 1980; Goldthorpe, *et al.*, 1980). Credentials have the greatest impact on mobility in those locales which are most formally rational in a bureaucratic sense, notably the civil service and industrial organizations, but have the least impact on the boardrooms of the City (Heath, 1981). As a result of this relatively fluid mobility, quite disparate life-paths can, will and do intersect in the widely divergent range of locales in which the new middle class is situated.

Although there are pointers such as Fletcher's (1973) account of 'lumpen' and 'nouveau' managers, ideas men, old guard and hatchet men, and of Kanter's (1977) US case-study of *Men and Women of the Corporation*, there are few studies of the effects of contradictory class locations on the identities (and vice versa) of the salaried new-middle-class careers (Sofer, 1970; Pahl and Pahl, 1971), nor on the images of 'men in the middle'. In particular, the end of the 'age of growth' and its implications for those careers dependent on it, becomes important in class terms (Hearn, 1977). To what extent did the 'latent social role' of 'cosmopolitan' versus 'local', identified by Gouldner (1957, 1958), depend upon economic growth for the organization-switching strategy? While organizations generally were growing it was possible to succeed on terms which were low on loyalty to the employing organization, high on commitment to specialized role skills, and more likely to refer to an occupational/professional reference group outside the organization, as cosmopolitans were defined. In an age of growth an occupational career strategy made a certain sense, as one could switch employers as their interests might conflict with one's own. It may well be the case that, today, once classically middle-class positions and their associated cosmopolitan roles are becoming increasingly localized under the constraints of withering organizational growth and decline. Consequently, exit strategies become more difficult to effect and either vocal interest representation or silent acquiescence in the erosion of one's identity may well become of increasing salience.

Part of what makes being in a middle-class position as contradictory and ambiguous as the positions frequently are themselves, is that such positions are structured in a bewilderingly diverse range of locales in which quite heterogeneous lifepaths interact and in which a wide range of group interests are represented. Offe, writing of the representation of primarily middle-class issues in the growth of new social movements, has observed that

> to a large extent, all of them share two characteristics. First, their projects and demands are based not on a collective contractual position on either goods or labour markets, as was the case, for instance, with traditional class parties and movements. Instead, their common denominator of organisation and action is some sense of collective identity (often underlined by ascriptive and 'naturalistic' conceptions of the collective 'self' in terms of age, gender and 'nation'). Closely connected with this is a second characteristic: they do not demand representation (by which their market status could be improved or protected) but autonomy. In short, the underlying logic of these movements is the struggle for the defence of a physical and/or moral 'territory', the integrity and identity of which is fundamentally non-negotiable to the activists of these movements (1983, p.59).

With Offe, we would consider it realistic to regard these new movements not as the new vanguard of the working class, but as far more probably undermining of the class principle *per se*. To the extent that classes have provided the organizational basis for the representation of interests through class-conscious political parties, then the growth of these new movements weakens the terrain of these parties precisely by posing as problematic issues which cannot be resolved within the framework of the traditional competitive party system.

This general conclusion is supported in an important recent paper by Goldthorpe (1982) which questions the view that professional and managerial employees (whom he refers to as the 'service class') can come to see their interests being served by political programmes seeking egalitarian outcomes, such as those which would presumably be pursued by the working class:

> The expectation must rather be – unless powerful countervailing influences can be identified – that these employees will in the main act in the way that is characteristic of members of privileged strata: that is that they will seek to use the superior resources that they possess in order to *preserve* their positions of relative social power and advantage, for themselves and for their children (Goldthorpe, 1982, p.180).

We would argue that, in so far as its interests are processable in conventional terms, the new middle class has a clear interest in preserving the status quo, for these workers enjoy conditions of employment to which generally accrue a degree of autonomy and discretion considerably beyond that of most working-class positions. While an interest may well exist within the new middle classes in enlarging their areas of autonomy and discretion or in reducing the degree of external control exercised over their occupational practice, it is important to recognize, as Goldthorpe argues, that 'any kind of generalized workplace democracy which would give greater decision-making and regulatory power to the rank-and-file could only be threatening to service class employees in implying a greater degree of control "from below" ' (1982, p.182).

Imbued as they are with ideological notions of professional autonomy or managerial prerogatives, it should be expected that the politics of the PMC will always be deployed against developments which may lead towards more egalitarian relations in production. As we have previously argued, the PMC depends for its discretion in occupational practice on the credentials which are granted to it through complex processes involving the reciprocal support of the capitalist state. We would suggest that this stratum of workers is structurally oriented far more towards dependence on the capitalist class than to any collaboration with the working class.

With the extensive growth of capitalist planning, administrative and ideological positions have proliferated at the centre of the capitalist world system. The politics of the new middle stratum which these positions comprise has critical implications for both representative politics and for class struggle. In Europe the labour movement risks political irrelevance unless effective strategies are implemented for an alliance with the new middle stratum, given the declining population of the 'traditional' working class in the class structure. It is therefore of the utmost importance that the questions raised for classical Marxist class theory by such alliances must be clearly formulated and analysed. It is precisely in this context that the work of Mallet was located. The Ehrenreichs, on the other hand, have provided an unsatisfactory blend of strategy and theorization which neglects or glosses over the insights of a substantial body of theoretical work which we shall examine in the section which follows.

The concept of contradictory class locations may be a somewhat more appropriate response than the concepts proposed by the Ehrenreichs for analysing the significance of the development of those contradictory aspects of the PMC's position and function in the division of labour which prevents them from entering an unambiguously antagonistic relationship to the working class (Aronowitz, 1979, p.228). As Wright (1979, p.203) notes, there is a strong tradition within Marxist theory of assuming that all positions within the social division of labour must necessarily fall into one or other class. It is critical at this point to reassert the position we sought to establish at the beginning of this chapter: namely, that classes are to be understood only in the context of struggle – as social relations, not positions. In such a problematic there is no significant problem in asserting that certain positions have a contradictory character within those social relations (Wright, 1979, p.203). We see no theoretical ambivalence in stressing that, sharing both the functions and characteristics of the bourgeoisie and of the working class, the professional–managerial stratum, instead of forming a distinctive class with a collective coherence and political force, falls within a contradictory location within class relations. This is not to suggest, however, that such a formulation does not require further development and clarification.

Contradictory locations or the new petty bourgeoisie

It is not without significance that the debate about the identification of social classes within the socialist movements of Western Europe and the USA has currently assumed a dominant position in establishing the political programmes of those movements. Whilst the outcomes of these debates have an importance for social theory, their political implications and their consequences for political practice may be of paramount concern. The locus of political relevance of what might otherwise be viewed as a somewhat arcane and sterile terminological dispute, lies, in their authors' view, in the justification of socialist political strategies which seek to integrate within working-class political priorities the interests of other classes or strata.

In the material which follows, we shall endeavour to locate three theoretical accounts dealing with the class determination of propertyless, non-manual workers within the parameters of both theoretical and political development. These works, completed during the last decade by Nicos Poulantzas, Erik Olin Wright and Guglielmo Carchedi, exhibit points of fundamental theoretical divergence in their construction of factors determining class placement, although they each focus on the 'objective' interest of such positions in the maintenance or destruction of capitalist relations. Each of these works is expressly concerned with the problems and possibilities surrounding the development of a political alliance between these groups and the working class.

Poulantzas's theoretical work on the salaried middle classes, which he refers to as the 'new petty bourgeoisie', draws its inspiration from a refutation of the French Communist Party's (PCF) espousal of the economism of the Third International. In the view of the PCF, only two real classes may exist within state monopoly capitalism – the bourgeoisie and the proletariat. Social groups who are unable to be placed in either of these classes fall under the umbrella of what are termed 'intermediate strata'. The thrust of the PCF's analysis is that groups not included in the bourgeoisie or the proletariat must be involved in an historical process of evolution towards one or the other of these classes, which is the argument of the *Manifesto* of 1848. Most importantly, transformation of the economic structures of late capitalism are generally viewed by the PCF as productive of tendencies which draw the 'intermediate strata' into a more empathetic relationship with the working class. The expanding categories of new professional and technical occupations are likely to find themselves in an organizational context in which occupational activities formerly characterized by autonomy and high status are increasingly intensified and 'proletarianized'. A complex division of labour is instituted which, according to the PCF, superimposes itself in prior structural categorizations determining class allegiances. The main thrust of the PCF's theoretical understanding leads the party to assert that the blurring of boundaries between productive and non-productive labour and between manual and intellectual workers tends to swell the category of collective labour and to enhance the prospect of working-class potentiality Thus, there exists not a middle class at all, but simply a panoply of intermediate categories for whom changes in the capitalist mode of production have created a specific reorganization of occupational roles which place their objective interests closer to those of the working class.

Integral to this analysis must be a clear assessment of the ways in which changes of allegiance of the intermediate strata are effected through the evolution of economic structures. The assessment by the PCF provides a theoretical rationale for the embrace of a broad spectrum of intermediate groups in a strategy of political alliance. Yet, such an alliance may compromise the strategy of working-class revolutionary change, in order to court the more moderate, reformist elements within the intermediate strata. As Ross (1978) suggests, 'such alliance construction rests on a complicated, and quite precarious, political calculus.' If the theory is too optimistic in its judgment of the progressive leanings of intermediate strata, the consequences may be to propel the movement of working-class struggle into a form of social democratic politics which, from the PCF's perspective, will provide an institutional impediment to both the expression and practice of revolutionary change. The latter is regarded as somewhat instinctual, if repressed. It is precisely such questions which have initiated much of the critical debate on the new middle class, not only from the point of view of theoretical clarification, but as a critique of the practice of what is seen as an opportunistic embrace of such groups as allies of the proletariat and of the social democratic orientation which this has provoked.

Poulantzas's critique thus hinges on an elaborate theorization of social classes which is then to be applied within the totality of the social division of labour of a specific social formation. Throughout this analysis, which is developed in highly abstract terms, the importance of ideological and political dimensions is emphasized. Classes which are defined in and through class struggle are formed in a conjunction of economic, political and ideological levels. Social classes may thus be said to be conceptualized as the effects of the structure of social relations and social practices in the relations of production and in political and ideological domination (Poulantzas, 1975, p.14). However, despite the insistence on struggle, the focus turns out to be on 'objective determination'. The locus of this analysis lies in the importance of separating 'class determination' from 'class position'. Poulantzas is resolute in asserting that reducing 'the structural determination of class to class position would be tantamount to abandoning the objective determination of the places of social classes for a "relational" ideology of "social movements" ' (1975, p.16). The logical development of this formulation is that a social class or a fraction or stratum of a class may assume a class position that is disconnected from its objective interests, which are themselves determined by structural forces that set the parameters of class struggle. The implications of these arguments for analysis of the middle class is that while certain intermediate strata may adopt working-class positions – even, at times, 'leading' the working class in political and industrial struggle – it cannot be asserted that this is indicative of a movement of such strata towards the working class. Their structural class determination is not reducible to their class position.

In order to pursue Poulantzas's argument, it is essential to indicate the importance which he places on the political and ideological practices which characterize the social division of labour. Thus, the constitutive role of political and ideological relations in the structural determination of social classes is expressed in the proposition that

> relations of production and the relationships which comprise
> them (economic ownership/possession) are expressed in the
> form of powers which derive from them, in other words class
> powers; these powers are constitutively tied to the political and
> ideological relations which sanction and legitimize them
> (Poulantzas, 1975, p.21).

This construction seems to suggest that class powers may be
conceived as relations of domination. Hence, in his critique of
Poulantzas, Hirst (1977, p.137) characterizes his conception of
the workplace as one in which domination is exercised by capital
over the working class. 'Agents of domination' play a critical role
in this politicized conception of the relations of production and it
is these categories which are utilized by Poulantzas in his
differentiation of sections of the new petty bourgeoisie from the
working class.

It is in the context of this argument that Poulantzas asserts the
primary importance of the new petty bourgeoisie's position in the
technical division of labour. His argument is that while its
objective position cannot be said to be equated with class
determination, and primary importance is not placed on its
position in the realm of production; rather, its importance is
attributed to its ideological and political status. As Poulantzas
elaborates this contention, occupants of new petty bourgeois
positions perform the

> work of direction and supervision through being endowed
> with specific functions in relation to knowledge. Their mental
> labour, separated from manual labour, represents the exercise
> of political relations in the despotism of the factory, legitimized
> by, and articulated to, the monopolization and secrecy of
> knowledge, i.e. the reproduction of the ideological relations of
> domination and subordination. . . . Politics are in fact always
> legitimized and encased by the dominant ideology. . . . This is
> more than ever the case today, in so far as the basis of
> legitimization of powers within the factory is shifting away
> from the 'natural knowledge' of the boss endowed with divine
> right and towards a technical one (1975, p.240).

That the occupants of these positions are not members of the
working class may be determined because the place they occupy
serves to maintain political and ideological relations of subordination of the working class to capital.

Hunt (1977a, p.91) points to the weaknesses inherent in the
concept of productive labour on which Poulantzas seeks to rest

his identification of the working class. Poulantzas's version of the concept of productive labour is reduced to that which creates surplus value through the production of material commodities. Poulantzas's location of the middle strata rests on an analysis which must therefore largely hinge on the ideological level, at which level mental labour coincides with the 'direct reproduction within the process of production itself of the political relations between the capitalist class and the working class' (1975, pp.227-8). A great deal of Poulantzas's argument is allotted to the class determination of non-productive labour – a group excluded by definition from the working class, but equally unable to be located outside of the class structure because of the logic of the critique which Poulantzas has mounted against the position of the PCF. His resolution of this tension is to locate the 'new' and 'traditional' petty bourgeoisie within the same class alignment. This conjunction is possible, it is asserted, because their economic positions have basically similar effects at the political and ideological level.

The new petty bourgeoisie thus plays a critical role in mediating capitalist legitimacy through the manipulation of knowledge-based occupational activities which are the obverse of those of a deskilled working class. They form part of contemporary capitalism's hierarchy of domination – a hierarchy divided into fractions differentiated with respect to the degree that they are subjected to the reproduction of the mental/manual labour division within mental labour itself. Poulantzas thus stresses the role of transformations within the non-productive wage-earning sector as a whole, which accentuates the fragmentation and polarization of the new petty bourgeoisie as these transformations push particular fractions of the latter towards the boundaries of mental and manual labour that lie between them and the working class (1975, p.257). It is specifically in this context that Poulantzas asserts that, while such groups may encounter an objective conflict between productive and non-productive characteristics, it is the latter which will remain dominant.

Poulantzas contends that the petty bourgeoisie, old or new, can have no long-term, autonomous class position. In the short term, its political position is constituted by a refraction of the ideological positions of both major classes through the common structural location of its members (Ross, 1978, p.174). Poulantzas summarizes this argument by suggesting that the ideological make-up of the new petty bourgeoisie is constituted within an arena of struggle between bourgeois and working-class ideologies. At any specific conjuncture, such a refraction of dominant ideologies through the structural position of the new petty bourgeoisie in itself creates a set of ideological aspects which may be characterized as specific to this particular stratum. It is specifically these features which the capitalist class must come to accommodate. The role of the capitalist state in contending with these ideologies provides the final segment of Poulantzas's account: 'Afraid of proletarianization below, attracted to the bourgeoisie above, the new petty bourgeoisie often aspire to . . . "upward social mobility" . . . by way of "individual" transfer' (1975, p.292). The new petty bourgeoisie is thus forced into an over-reliance on the educational apparatus as a corridor of accession to the bourgeois state or, more particularly, to the upper levels of the hierarchies of intellectual labour through the acquisition of professional and technical qualifications. As Poulantzas observes, the elitist conception of society articulated through notions of meritocracy is determined by the new petty bourgeoisie's aspirations for equal opportunity for its social advancement and the concomitant political programmes which suggest that a society can be constructed around notions embodying social justice, democracy and equal opportunity. As Poulantzas puts it, 'this attitude of the petty bourgeoisie can be summed up by saying that it does not want to break the ladders by which it can climb' (1975, p.292). The conclusion towards which this analysis inexorably leads is that the new petty bourgeoisie regards the state as potentially its own instrument and as a reflection of the general interest which is, indeed, also peculiarly that of the petty bourgeoisie.

A comprehensive critique of Poulantzas's work has developed which repudiates much of the thrust of his analysis. Useful contributions to this critique appear in Hunt (1977b), Parkin, (1979), Wright (1976, 1978), Mackenzie (1982) and Johnson (1977) and will not be elaborated here. The essence of these criticisms is that Poulantzas's analysis ('formalistic and mechanical to the point of aridity', as Mackenzie (1982, p.70), puts it), fails adequately to apprehend changes in the labour process through which intellectual labour is drawn into that process. The division of labour which has been imposed on intellectual work itself has profound implications for the concepts of productive and unproductive labour on which Poulantzas rests his identification of the working class. In abstracting his theoretical development from the actual processess of occupational differentiation within those areas of activity which are the preserve of the new petty bourgeoisie, Poulantzas establishes the basis for a misinterpretation. The imputation of political/ideological relations as criteria of class determination certainly allows Poulantzas to restrict the concept of working class to a definite, pre-existent social category – industrial manual workers – but in so doing reveals the illogicality of such a determination (Hirst, 1977, p.150). This is also the thrust of Wright's critique of Poulantzas, an argument to which we shall return in the following paragraphs.

Whatever status may be attributed to the critique of Poulantzas's work, it is nevertheless clear that his warning that the goals of new petty bourgeois political struggle may not be necessarily coincident with those of the working class is one that would be well heeded by any working-class parties contemplating a strategy of courting intermediate strata. As Hirsch (1981) observes, Poulantzas considered the new petty bourgeoisie to be, at best, a possible ally of the working class but hardly its vanguard. In the context of Mallet's argument, their demand for self-management may also be more of a petty bourgeois rather than radical act. In certain conjunctures, the left may look to a potential opposition within the dominant classes to technocratic solutions which place intolerable strains on democratic institutions. It is in this context that a democratic alliance with fractions of the new petty bourgeoisie in conflict with the dominant class may lead to democratic, structural and radical reforms that challenge the logic of capitalist power (Hirsch, 1971, pp.188-9).

As we have noted above, one of the more serious general criticisms of Poulantzas's work has centred on his exclusion from the proletariat of positions which deviated from any of the dimensions of working-class criteria which he elaborates. His analysis implicitly rejects the notion that positions within the social division of labour can be objectively contradictory with respect to their class location. In contrast to this conclusion, Wright's recent works (1976, 1978, 1979, 1980a, 1980b, 1980c) provide an important set of analyses which focus specifically on whether certain positions can indeed be regarded as occupying objectively contradictory locations within class relations. The main thrust of Wright's work constitutes a specific endeavour to illuminate 'the contradictory character of [these positions'] relationship to the class struggle' (Wright, 1979, p.211).

Deriving its impetus from a critique of Poulantzas's conceptualization of class boundaries, Wright's analysis proceeds through the formulation of three interconnected elements of social relations of domination and subordination within capitalist production. These relations may be so characterized because each defines those positions which have the 'capacity to control' the particular resource and, conversely, those excluded from such control (1980a, pp.328-9). The dimensions identified by Wright, encompass:

(i)   control over capital allocation, involving the determination of investment in production and the overall dimensions of accumulation;
(ii)   control over the physical means of production and the uses to which the means of production are put;
(iii)   control over the labouring activity of the direct producers, in particular, the relations of authority and control to which labour power is subject.
Wright emphasizes the interdependence of these characteristics. He also indicates that they exist within a hierarchy of determination. Thus, for example, control of capital allocation may well set the parameters of social relations.

For Wright, other class positions enter the analysis when, in specific capitalist formations, there is a skewed development of each of the dimensions of social relations of production. Of course, it is precisely the case that the evolution of capitalism has produced specific forces of concentration and control of capital, the logic of which has been to develop a systematic non-correspondence which generates what he terms 'contradictory locations within class relations'. These contradictory locations may be so termed, because

they simultaneously share the relational characteristics of two distinct classes . . . they share class interests with two different classes but have interests identical to neither. It is in this sense that they can be viewed as being objectively torn between class locations (Wright, 1980a, 331).

Wright also argues that the contradictory characteristic of class locations is itself a variable quality. Certain positions are held to occupy contradictory locations in proximity to the boundary of the working class – for example, that of a foreman, whose exercise of control over labour power may be not so much discretionary as formal, as a channel of communication (Dunkerley, 1975). Where a bureaucratic structure of 'rational' rules replaces direct, personal command, it may be appropriate to view the bearers of those rules at certain hierarchical levels as themselves elements of capitalist control. The extension of this analysis to middle-level management and professional occupations which may exhibit much higher levels of discretion leaves Wright in the rather ambiguous position of declaring that 'the contradictory quality of their class location is much more intense' (1976, p.35). Interestingly, he reverts to a reliance on the important role of political and ideological forces in determining the class location of individuals occupying these positions.

On the basis of data from a 1969 survey of working conditions in the USA, Wright estimates that between a quarter and a third of the US labour forces falls into contradictory locations near the boundary of the working class. In Wright's view, these locations represent social positions which 'have a real interest in socialism, yet simultaneously gain certain privileges from capitalist social relations of production' (1976, p.41). The notion of 'real interest', as we shall subsequently discuss in chapter 8, preserves a certain essentialism, perhaps as an habitual reflex. We remain sceptical about putative 'real interests'. Wright's work attempts to chart a map of the class structure – one which is intended to represent 'the multiple possible outcomes of the process of class formation'. This schema is proposed in order to illuminate the form and degree of attachment of certain positions within the social division of labour to working-class political strategies. The important theoretical development formulated by Wright in the works under discussion is the provision of a framework on which to locate the broad constraints which encompass class formation. However, it is largely *within* these parameters that political organization and class struggle are realized. Any adequate theorization of the forms and directions which class struggle may assume, therefore, must involve an analysis of the actual practices of collectivities-in-struggle for the realization of their putative structurally determined interests within specific historical formations (Przeworski, 1977). This is necessary because the potential for the realization of working-class political strategies in advanced capitalist societies depends in large measure on the capacity of this class to recast the political and ideological relations which structure the potential for alliances with contradictory locations (Wright, 1976, p.41).

Wright's analysis of contradictory locations advanced the formulation of the major phenomena involved in class structuration. However, his interpretation is incomplete in four key areas. First, the theorization of political control, vested in the role of supervisory labour with respect to the labour process, may be deficient. Wright tends to conflate the elements of supervision which pertain to much productive labour with those elements of political control over the production process which exist under conditions of class struggle. In the context of an analysis of class structuration which provides for the existence of social classes only in and through class struggle, the contradictory nature of positions in which political control over production is vested may be less clear than Wright suggests. The second point concerns the extent to which the relevance of the labour market is downplayed in Wright's analysis. As Giddens (1980, p.304) has pointed out, several aspects of the 'market capacity' of white-collar workers in particular have been of continuing relevance to class conflict and class structuration. Factors influencing market capacity – such as certain educational qualifications, age and ethnic characteristics of certain status groups – in part determine the level of job security and the availability of a structured career path via formal promotion. Whilst the value of such capacities has been somewhat eroded (see Kumar, 1977; Berg, 1973), they have certainly played an important historical role with respect to class formation.

A third factor, following on from these considerations, is the sexual division of labour and the differentiation of the labour market into what has been termed a primary sector, including relatively well-paid and secure jobs, and a secondary sector which contains lower-paid and more insecure employment. As many people have observed, there is a coincidence between women workers and the secondary labour market. Women workers appear to form a negatively privileged status group in terms of the operation of the labour market. It is clear that circumstances prevail in capitalist industrial societies in which there is a marked tendency towards segmentation in labour markets which structurally disadvantages women workers. A high proportion of positions which have been deskilled through technological change has come to be occupied by women. Giddens refers to a female 'underclass of white-collar labour' in this context and argues that 'the fact that the proletarianization of lower-level white-collar labour has at the same time involved its feminization has probably consolidated rather than dissolved pre-existing divisions between the working and new middle classes' (1980, p.305). The critical issue here is that the relationship between the exploitation of the sexual division of labour and class location does not receive adequate analysis in Wright's formulation of contradictory locations. We adopt the view that these connnections may be apprehended through a more detailed analysis of labour-market segmentation and the cross-cutting of status group and class formation – a theme which we shall pursue at greater length in the following chapter.

The final point to be raised in connection with Wright's work concerns his focus on class analysis exclusively within the boundaries of a specific social formation. His attempt to map the class structure of the USA leads to the discovery of contradictory locations occupying 25–33 per cent of positions in the US labour force. However, as Poulantzas correctly points out (1977, p.119), the labour force that is subject to US capitalist relations resides not only in the USA. It is probable, if strategically unfortunate for the agenda of national labour movements, that a more adequate theorization would need to concentrate on the imperialist context in which transnational capital is able to exploit its position in the world economy (Block, 1978).

Whilst we have briefly summarized the points which differentiate the formulations of Wright and Poulantzas it is equally important to emphasize the significant points of convergence. Both accounts locate forces operating to transform contemporary capitalism which, at the same time, lead to a relocation of important fractions of the new middle classes towards the boundaries of the working class. The necessary conditions are being created which allow for a political alliance between the working class and these fractions. Most importantly, the formation of such coalitions in which the middle strata adopt the class position of the working class is dependent upon a conceptualization of the same political and ideological elements which underlie the polarization of the middle strata in the first place. We should now consider the work of Carchedi (1975a, 1975b, 1977) which further illuminates this understanding.

Carchedi's analysis is centred on an attempt, first, to identify and define class relations on the level of what he terms the 'pure capitalist mode of production'. His formulation derives from a partial definition of class forces in their relation to the economic structure. This is not to de-emphasize the importance of political and ideological levels but to abstract the analysis to a particular level to which other levels are said to correspond. More importantly, it is the changes undergone by the capitalist economic structure in the course of its stages of development towards which Carchedi's analysis is directed.

At the 'highest level of abstraction', Carchedi (1975a, pp.10-13) identified four fundamental dichotomies which characterize relations of production: the producer/non-producer – thus determining the relationship between producers of surplus value and those who appropriate it (what is essential in their relationship is the element of exploitation); the non-owner/owner of the means of production, focusing on 'real ownership' and its concomitant control of the means of production and the appropriation of surplus value; the labourer/non-labourer, focusing on the social division of labour within the production process and identifying the producer as labourer; distribution relations which encompass the share of social wealth going to a class, the mode of acquiring it, and its origin, which separate those agents whose income is determined by the value of their labour power and those whose income is derived from surplus value.

The coincidence of each of the first elements of these dichotomies defines for Carchedi the working class on the level of 'the pure capitalist structure', while the coincidence of the second set of elements depicts the capitalist class. Carchedi's analysis derives its impetus from an endeavour to incorporate into these dimensions of class relations the historical transformations within capitalist production. He identifies three stages of capitalist development in which capitalist production relations have assumed specific forms. The account of the first two stages is similar to that in *Capital* and bears a resemblance also to Mallet's evolutionary schema. Moving from an initial phase in which Carchedi identifies the formal subordination of labour to the individual capitalist in an assemblage characterized by an under-developed technical division of labour, the labour process is increasingly seen to assume a 'co-operative nature'. Thus, the intermediate phase involves the development of a complex division of labour in which workers' control of the labour process is eroded and production is carried out by the *collective labourer* rather than as a function of individual activity. Thus, to 'perform the function of the collective worker means to take part in the complex, scientifically organized collective labour power, to produce collectively use values in order to produce surplus value' (Carchedi, 1975a, p.27).

In the final phase of monopoly capitalism, the role of the capitalist undergoes an analogous transformation to that of the collective labourer, through which there is a collectivization of the function of capital in a differentiated managerial structure of control. This is what Carchedi terms the 'global functions of capital'. The stage of monopoly capitalism also ushers in profound changes in the capitalist mode of production with the further development of the joint stock company. Such changes, which we have explored in earlier chapters, involve the dissociation of legal, juridical ownership in the hands of shareholders and real, economic ownership. Economic owner-ship, which involves control over the means of production and over labour power, is fragmented in that it does not belong to an individual capitalist but resides in the hands of a small number of top managers (Carchedi, 1975a, p.30). A critical extension of Carchedi's argument is that the function of capital is performed not only by those top managers who control the enterprise but

> has become the task of a complex, hierarchically organized ensemble of people who collectively perform what used to be the function of an individual capitalist. That is, the work of supervision and management in its double sense, is not only separated from the legal ownership of the means of production but is carried out collectively by a hierarchically organized bureaucratic structure (1975a, p.31).

Thus, any number of people may be required to undertake elements of control and surveillance whilst remaining divorced from both the legal and 'real' ownership of the means of production. In this process, 'the function of capital becomes the task of a structure, not of an individual, that is, transformed into the global function of capital' (1975a, p.31).

Carchedi's formulation leads to an identification of social classes in monopoly capitalism in which the working class occupies locations which involve the functions of the collective labourer, including the work of what Carchedi calls co-ordination and unity in the capitalist production process (that is, those aspects of collective activity which are part of the labour process itself necessary to produce use values). The capitalist class comprises those locations carrying out the global functions of capital, specifically control and surveillance. For Carchedi, the 'middle classes . . . are only identifiable in terms of contradiction' (1975b, 369).

Under monopoly capitalism the production process includes a hierarchal framework of positions which perform both the function of the collective worker and the function of exploitation and oppression which is the role of the global function of capital. This complex hierarchy includes, on the one hand, positions in which the function of the collective worker is of no or minimal importance, and, on the other hand, positions in which the function of the collective worker is predominant and the global function of capital is minimized. Thus, the function of capital is performed not only by the capitalist class, but by what Carchedi terms 'the new middle class'. This class exhibits the following characteristics:

(i)   it does not own either legally or economically the means of production;
(ii)   it performs both the global function of capital and the function of the collective worker;
(iii)   is therefore both the labourer (productive or unproductive) and the non-labourer;
(iv)   is both exploiter (or oppressor) and exploited (or oppressed) (Carchedi, 1975a, p.51).

Thus, the fundamental theoretical specification of the new middle class is that it performs the function of capital whilst excluded from the ownership of the means of production, and this function is performed in conjunction with the function of the collective worker.

Carchedi employs this schema to analyse the forces acting on new-middle-class political strategies. These forces hinge on the processes of proletarianization which involve two separate dimensions for the new middle class. In the first instance, the devaluation of labour power involved in the function of the collective worker proceeds via changes in the technical division of labour. The second dimension involves the fact that it is only through the function of the collective worker that capital can appropriate surplus value. (Whatever money is paid to the supervisor is unavailable for capital accumulation.) There is a pressure, therefore, for capital to decrease the area of human activity devoted to the global function of capital and to increase that devoted to the function of the collective worker. Thus, Carchedi concludes that the process of devaluation of the labour power of the new middle class proceeds at the same time as there is a constant erosion of the time required for control and suveillance:

> This class is subjected to an attack on a double front. As far as the function of the collective worker is concerned, the devaluation of this class's labour power reduces the wage component. As far as the global function of capital is concerned, its constant and tendential reduction reduces the revenue component (1975a, p.64).

The limit of this process of devaluation of new-middle-class labour power, coupled with the elimination of the performance of the global function of capital, defines for Carchedi the concept of proletarianization. However, he makes it clear that the concept is tied exclusively to the economic sphere – political and ideological conditions are required before any conclusions may be drawn concerning the integration of groups or strata whose functions are being proletarianized into the working class. It is in this respect that the major shortcoming of Carchedi's analysis becomes evident. Whilst Poulantzas's work has effectively demonstrated the need to extend the analysis of the functions of capital to those political and ideological processes of reproduction, Carchedi draws back to the economic domain. Indeed, the locus of his argument is on the specific level of control and surveillance of the labour process. Any formulation of political and ideological factors is excluded by the prior assumptions of Carchedi's framework. As Johnson correctly notes,

> while Poulantzas' work suggests that monopoly capitalism is characterized by a shift in the weight of bourgeois domination from direct economic exploitation to the management of those ideological and political processes involved in the reproduction of capitalist relations, Carchedi is unable to extend the functions of capital into this 'dominant' sphere at all (1977, p.206).

Carchedi's analysis leads to the conclusion that it is certainly probable that an internal stratification will be intensified within the new middle class. Moreover, the implications of this analysis for working-class political struggle are critical. Large sections of what have been termed middle-class locations may already have been proletarianized within certain formations. The issue of political strategy then becomes one of forging an alliance among sectors of the working class, rather than one of an alliance between the working class and the new middle class or the new petty bourgeoisie. It is clear that only an analysis which includes an adequate theorization of the political and ideological levels can illuminate the appropriate strategies. It is to these issues which we shall turn in the concluding section of this chapter.

The general theoretical orientation which has been developed here leads us to argue that an understanding of class struggle requires a shift from an aggregational to a relational emphasis. In order to explicate such relations further, such analysis needs to be accompanied by a narrowing of the level of abstraction at which it is to be conducted. One of the major difficulties encountered with the types of aggregational class analysis examined in previous sections of this chapter is that they have, more often than not, specifically excluded from consideration those elements through which classes are constituted by other than economic (production) relations. The adoption of highly abstract levels of analysis, which assume an over-determination of the economic level in a pure capitalist structure (Carchedi, 1975a), or which involve formulations of reproduction in general (Poulantzas, 1975), tends to obfuscate the internal dynamics of capitalist social formations by fusing quite distinct institutional structures of power. In a similar vein, it is important to avoid the further tendency, almost inevitably encouraged by such analysis, to characterize the social aggregates thus identified with the characteristics of a purposive actor. None the less, as we have stressed in the introductory comments to this chapter, an understanding of the behaviour of social classes can only be meaningful to the extent that it is guided by a structural analysis. Thus, classes, if they are to enter scientific analysis as entities capable of enhancing the study of crucial social processes, must be constituted as deriving their existence through antagonistic and dependent relations. It is precisely this mode of analysis which must also be applied to the relations *within* classes. The capacity for class organization and the expression of class interests at the political and ideological levels is a property of the degree and form of connectedness characterizing a class and the institutional mechanisms which influence the maintenance or disintegration of these forms of sociopolitical cohesion.

The work of Poulantzas and Carchedi has signposted important differences between the social positions occupied by those fractions of the new middle class which have been approximately incorporated into the processes of production and reproduction, and those fractions which have been incorporated into administrative and other superstructural positions concerned with the realization of surplus value. We have outlined our reservations about the proposition that such distinctions are determined by the extent to which the material existence of one group is derived from the creation of surplus value as opposed to those who, alternatively, draw their incomes from surplus value once created. There is little doubt, however, that the ramifications of these distinctions exert a strong, if not determining, influence over the social interest of each specific section of the classes thus affected. We are inclined, however, to place much greater emphasis on the structural effects which the specific position of each specialized group in the sphere of production, reproduction or realization has on the formation of its consciousness (Mandel, 1975, pp.265-73; Johnson, 1977, pp.216ff.).

In order to begin to develop the alternative analysis implied in these remarks we need to examine carefully distinct moments of the production, realization and reproduction processes. First, the specific processes of capital generate a basic differentiation which is itself interdependent with the class positions located within that sphere. The major analytical device upon which this discussion hinges is the assumption that processes of reproduction may be separated from production processes. Further, forms of differentiation involve a dynamic through which the role of economic, political and ideological relations may be determined. Following Johnson (1977, p.214), we would argue that the differentiated institutional structures so generated are themselves repositories of power *within which autonomies may be generated*. This is a useful formation as it immediately illuminates the boundaries around which *fractions of capital* may be in conflict.

Rationalization and control within production

A particularly pertinent example of the struggle for control within direct production, which enables us to elucidate Carchedi's focus on the surveillance and control aspects of the global function of capital, is the conflict and alliances associated with the project of the scientific managers, and their contemporary occupational representation, the industrial engineers.

Scientific management, and the broader processes of rationalization which proceeded to dominate the development of industrial organization during the first half of the twentieth century, largely succeeded in appropriating to bureaucratic structures of control those supervisory functions which formerly rested with craftworkers. However, despite F.W. Taylor's 1903 injunction that 'all possible brain work should be removed from the shop floor and centred in the planning or laying out department' (Taylor, 1967, pp.98-9), the results were to create more fundamental divisions. The more limited achievement of the reorganizations which followed the initial intervention of scientific management was to establish the conditions for a separation of what has been termed 'mental' and 'manual labour'. It should be emphasized that this ideological partition within the social relations of production has never coincided with a simple dichotomous class structure, as new forms of 'mental labour' have emerged whose characteristics and consciousness were those of neither capital nor labour.

This is not to imply that the newly created management positions represented a distillation of the conceptual aspects of labour with which they were then able to establish autonomy over the conception of their work. On the contrary, from the first introduction of scientific-management techniques, the industrial engineers were forced to compromise their autonomy (Stark, 1980, pp.116-18). Capitalists were able to select from a wide range of management systems and practitioners all broadly informed by Taylorist principles. As Larson correctly notes:

> the corporate business leadership, while it was sympathetic to Taylor's rationalization and strict control of labour, was not about to share control of the enterprise with an independent group, no matter how expert and how scientific in its orientations (1977, p.141).

At best, the knowledge of the engineers gave them a lever to further their claims to autonomy and authority. Thus, an ideology of technical expertise was expounded through the broader institutional sphere of the various engineering occupations which sought to organize as a profession. More than anything else, these claims to professional status served as a device to legitimize both their privileged position with respect to the working class and also to defend their autonomy with respect to the capitalist class.

The reformulation of occupational ideology which accompanied the transition to monopoly capitalism's dominance corresponded to structural changes in the capitalist enterprise. Large-scale production in bureaucratically organized factories was characterized by high ratios of fixed capital to labour. The required expansion of planning and administration was to draw on the expert decision-making of engineers. It is clear in this context that scientific knowledge and technical skill in professonal practice functioned as important components of capitalist control. But what of the occupational positions which perform these functions? Engineers increasingly adopted the positions formerly reserved for capitalists. They assumed the global function of capital. They were, therefore, socially distinct from other technical workers and, in Poulantzas's terms, would have the *potential* for antagonistic class relations with them.

The rise of scientific management and the professional engineer heralded two closely related events which had profound consequences for the hegemony of the industrial ruling class. First, the deference applied by both workers and employers to the rationality of 'scientific' decision-making critically undermined the old justifications based on the absolute rights of 'men of property'. This new ideology served the purposes of capital well during the period of its introduction, in which economic crises had unveiled social antagonisms which posed a real threat to the legitimation of employers' prerogatives (Boreham, 1980, pp.21-9). In the longer term, however, the phasing-out of a moral for a pragmatic defence of capitalism places the capitalist class in a position in which it is vulnerable to the economic crises of its own making (Connell and Irving, 1978, p.38). This is because those rational decision-makers are faced with an economic environment whose 'rationality' may not be apprehended by contemporary 'scientific' paradigms, which themselves largely reflect the 'objectivity', if not the ambiguity, of capitalist interests. But this is another matter which is dealt with further in our concluding chapter.

The second consequence of the emerging ideologies of rationality and professionalism was the view, most forcefully adumbrated by Burnham (1941) and later by Galbraith (1967), that the corporate identity of monopoly capitalism and the consequent depersonalization and obfuscation of capitalist ownership amounted to a 'managerial revolution'. Such a revolution, it was argued, would overturn the primacy of class interests in corporate decision-making. The managers would become a new class wielding power on the basis of their technical superiority. In arguing that scientific management was an expression of the legitimating ideology of advanced capitalism, Larson points out that society was to witness, in its appeal to science,

the overall cognitive and normative legitimation for the use of the manager and the rise of the expert: ideologically, the 'carriers of embodied science' – that is to say, trained and credentialled experts – are assigned a crucial and directive role, while the ideology also emancipates them from class allegiances and class interests (1977, p.142).

And the ideology appeared to work. Thus it was asserted, even by commentators as insightful as Veblen, that the production engineers would assume the entrepreneurial role which had previously been the sole province of capitalists:

It is essential that the corps of technological specialists who by training, insight and interest make up the general staff of industry, must have a free hand in the disposal of its available resources, in materials, equipment and man power, regardless of any national pretensions or any vested interests (Veblen, 1921, p.54).

The infrastructural developments which reflected and supported the rise of monopoly capitalism and the success of the industrial engineers were focused in the growth of bureaucratic organization. These complex organizations provided the milieu in which two important social processes were to develop. First, the scale and form of rational organization itself extended the formation in which the power of capital was embedded. Second, the organizations were believed to have been insulated from class interests as the institutions themselves, as represented by the new social stratum of 'the general staff of industry', invoked a transmutation of power into authority by importuning the legitimacy of expertise. 'Mediated by organization, the class structure of monopoly capitalism ultimately . . . [came to be] . . . legitimized as a functional emanation of the social division of labor, and therefore, as the mirror of differential abilities and motivations' (Larson, 1977, p.145).

The authority of the engineer derived from scientific knowledge. Technocracy finds its most appropriate expression in this form (Wilson, 1983). However, the extent of the legitimate area of application of this knowledge was indeterminate, relying, as has been pointed out elsewhere (Jamous and Peloille, 1970; Boreham, 1983), on a complex interplay of forces exerted in part through the state, the professional associations and the capitalist interests who were their major employers. In reality, the engineers and scientific managers could never have attained the position of control which observers had incorrectly accorded to them. The evidence for this may be observed in both the success and failure of the so-called 'professional project'. The campaign to organize the diverse engineering occupations into a profession determining its own affairs was thwarted from its conception by the ability of capitalist business interests to control the engineering societies linked to the specific industries upon which their power was based. Furthermore, the well-documented divisions between 'local' career patterns, which saw engineers assuming managerial positions, and broader 'cosmopolitan' orientations towards more general scientific values, provided an inevitable source of tension within the profession. The move towards professionalization could scarcely provide the groundwork for a separate occupational identity, much less that of the core element of a 'new middle class'.

The industrial engineers and managers emerged with the development of monopoly capitalism and their employment has reflected the structure of that system. Their labour has been sold in markets constituted as an adjunct to the employing capital. None the less, ideologies surrounding professional practice have constituted an important mechanism in the conflicts over the limited occupational autonomy of these positions. These claims to a special status were mediated through the state, but were ultimately directed at the controllers of capitalist industry within which they were located – controllers who, in fulfilling their own ends, were prepared to grant the necessary autonomy.

This analysis suggests that the 'professional project' could never have provided a foundation for an interposed new middle class. Control of the discretionary areas which have been entrusted to the profession does not presently pose a threat to the capitalist institution in which those areas are located. Members of the so-called new-middle-class occupations are sometimes allocated high-discretion roles simply because the principles and practices imbued through professional socialization ensure that they may be trusted to behave reliably and responsibly. It would not be an exaggerated claim to suggest, as Salaman does, that the professions 'are using their autonomy, and their skills and expertise, with considerable and well rewarded "responsibility" ' (1979, p.139).

Research evidence has suggested that it is precisely the control function which engineers find most satisfying in their work (Perrucci and Gerstl, 1969; Glover, 1973). Correlatively, it is the absence of control which is most frustrating (Finniston, 1980; Ritti, 1971). There has been an increasing degree of unionization among engineers in both the USA (Oppenheimer, 1973; McGee, 1978) and Britain (IDS, 1981), as Child (1982) has observed. However, although this tendency to unionization occurs where engineers perceive themselves as having a conflict of interest with management, recourse to unionism appears to have had more to do with anxiety about pay and status than any proletarian solidarism. Similarly, it has been suggested that such anxieties about control as are documented may 'be a problem of organizational design as much as the manifestation of a fundamental tension between professional and managerial principles' (Child, 1982, p.227). No strong evidence for the tension exists with respect to engineers.

In summary, we are arguing that the structural changes associated with the development of capitalism placed the industrial engineers in a position in which they clearly shared the broad interests of management. Ironically, however, it required that they were forever subordinate to the systems of organizational control. At the same time, their self-isolation from working-class organization and solidarity left them unprotected from capitalist exploitation. The professional project, based on an appeal to the state, the outcome of which is largely reflected in the credentialling process, has left them as unequal participants in the determination of their occupational status. We would argue, with respect to those occupational categories which represent management within production, that they are *not* structurally located *between* capital and labour. Rather, their struggle with capital represents a conflict over status and occupational authority: a conflict which must be resolved, ultimately, by the power exerted by capital with respect to the proletarianization of lower-level technical positions and the determination, partly through agencies of the state, of an accrual of power in specific areas by upper-level positions in what must be viewed as a segmented labour market for mental labour (Boreham, 1983, p.713). Depending upon the functions performed by professional employees, we would anticipate their having a differential probability for inherent conflicts of interest. These conflicts are likely to be contained within distinct vertical segments that discriminate between, for example, engineers in management involved in production design and those engineers who execute the plant layout drawings, or between scientists who decide what drugs to put into production while others simply do routine testing in laboratories (Child, 1982, p.234).

The preceding discussion has concentrated on the engineering professions. However, we consider that our major conclusions apply equally to the other major occupations – notably management, accountancy and industrial relations – centred on direct production. We have sought to demonstrate that an analysis of the new middle class must be located at the level of those positions which encompass the middle-to-senior executives of the professional associations and the directors or partners in the smaller professional firms. Somewhat paradoxically, the functions of these positions lie outside of direct appropriation and are principally located in the domain of realization and reproduction. In the section of this chapter which follows, we shall seek further to elucidate the processes of control which apply at these levels.

The new middle class: control, realization and reproduction

With the development to a dominant position of the enterprises characteristic of monopoly capitalism in the advanced Western industrial economies, it has been argued (Johnson, 1977, p.216) that a new dimension is introduced for analysis. In seeking to gain a measure of control over all phases of production, capital was required to extend its sphere of institutional activity in order to encompass not only the direct functions of supervision and control required for appropriation, but also those institutional mechanisms whose sole purpose is the realization of surplus value. Whether these functions fall within the ambit of agencies of the state, or whether they are performed by the institutions of private capital, they are largely carried out by complex bureaucracies whose development parallels production, but takes place autonomously from production. Further, as Braverman has pointed out (1974, p.257ff.), this phase is marked by the complexity of vertical and horizontal integration as corporations formerly focused on industrial production are now integrated with institutions whose functions are concerned more with the distribution and enlargement of capital. We discussed this process extensively in the previous chapter.

Yet each of these sub-divisions is transformed into a labour process 'producing nothing but increasingly elaborate mechanisms of control associated with realisation of capital and its enlargement' (Johnson, 1977, p.217), wherein the function of control is located not just in the person of a manger, but in an organization of workers under the control of an hierarchical arrangement of managers, deputy managers, officers in charge, and so forth. Thus, 'the relations of purchase and sale of labour power and hence of alienated labour have become part of the management apparatus itself' (Braverman, 1974, p.267). Control is subsumed and, in many respects, obfuscated under the functions of an administrative apparatus within the superstructural institutions themselves. The labour processes which result are therefore subordinated to capital not through their role in appropriation, but separately through the organization of their realization functions. Certain specific personnel perform these functions. Specificity derives from their role as 'professional' through their ability to be able to define the criteria of their own performance. Hence, they are partially autonomous of the state and the capital organizations they service.

The interface of these institutional mechanisms and the occupational system is manifested in decisive interorganizational relationships. These are between, on the one hand, firms at the forefront of international accounting practice and private legal representation, together with those represented by national and international banking capital and stock market organizations (including the fiscal and monetary policy agencies of the state), and, on the other hand, the professions of accountancy, law and management, which constitute the specialized labour market from which their personnel are drawn. The paradox of this relationship is correctly located by Johnson when he points out that, 'while such agents occupy positions which are integral to capital realisation, that is implicated in the functions of capital, they are at the same time engaged in a labour process and dispossessed of the "powers" of capital both in its appropriation and realisation functions' (1977, p.218). These professional occupations, which are said to be the major constitutional element of the new middle class, are themselves part of an increasingly routinized division of labour which penetrates the profession and provides the framework for class divisions within the professional occupations themselves. Thus, at the lower levels of professional hierarchies and, despite the assertion of an homogeneity of competence, there are inexorable pressures towards proletarianization. By proletarianization we are referring to the process through which the work activities of those occupying professional and specialist positions at the lower level of professional hierarchies within large legal and accounting offices, for example, are increasingly fragmented and routinized, especially through the development of 'control systems' and data-processing technologies.

In making these claims we would wish to distance our analysis from other aspects of the arguments about proletarianization which appear to be somewhat misconstrued. For example, scepticism should accompany the claims that certain categories of office workers have been proletarianized through technological changes in the design of clerical work (Crompton, 1976). It is by no means clear that the workers under discussion were not already proletarians, albeit with white blouses or collars (Heritage, 1980). On the other hand, it has been argued that the recourse of some middle-class employees to collective action and trade union membership cannot be taken as having the meaning that such action might bear for traditional proletarians. On the contrary, as Goldthorpe (1982, p.181) has suggested, certain types of middle-class trade unionism may 'be far better seen as an attempt to prevent proletarianisation and to maintain favourable class differentials in pay and conditions and in life chances generally'. Some additional support for this thesis may be drawn from an examination of the motivations behind the general strike of professional workers in Sweden in the mid-1970s, the major goal of which was to restore traditional pay differentials with manual workers (Szymanski, 1979, p.58).

At the other end of the scale from those professional and middle-class employees whose positions have been routinized, are the senior partners in the legal, accounting and stockbroking firms who determine the ideological impetus for the operationalization of capitalist relations. In this context, the penetration of national economies by the major transnational accountancy firms has been an essential prerequisite to the growth of the transnational corporation (see Stevens, 1981). The 'big eight' accounting firms are Arthur Anderson, Coopers and Lybrand, Ernst and Ernst, Haskins and Sells, Peat Marwick and Mitchell, Price Waterhouse, Touch Ross, and Arthur Young. Each of these firms, which maintain offices in most of the major cities of the world, has several hundred partners (a 'corporate ruling class'), and between 4,000 and 8,000 employees.

It is clear that certain professional occupations have considerable discretionary powers over the political and ideological determination of the bases for class struggle. However, it is important to note that this discretion is structurally subsumed by the economic relations of capital and is also limited to the particular institutional sphere which is accepted to be their professional domain. One final observation, with respect to those who occupy the upper echelon of the major institutions in which professional practice is applied, is to note the important linking function they fulfil at the intersection of the profession and the work organization. There is ample evidence from both the legal and accounting professions that these same individuals occupy a majority of the executive positions on the professional associations (Carlin, 1966; Montagna, 1973). The significance of this arrangement with respect to accountancy is indicated by Johnson who argues that

> partners in the large firms also dominate the 'professional' hierarchy, enabl[ing] them to control the recruitment, training and work activities (through codes and etiquette) of their colleague–subordinates thus facilitating the fragmentation and

devaluation of certain grades of accountancy work within the labour process. As a result the professional association can be viewed as having important political functions in relation to the organisation of work (1977, p.220).

If, as we propose, Johnson's (1977) analysis is correct, then we are led to two important conclusions concerning the new middle class. First, the notion of a professional managerial class is fundamentally misconceived. The relations between different levels within these occupations are constituted by the same mechanisms of control which surround capitalist relations of production. The marketplace for mental labour is stratified on gender, ethnic and sociocultural relations through the same structural forces which segment markets for manual labour (Epstein, 1975; Perrucci, 1973; Carlin, 1966). Moreover, the degree of closure within particular segments of the market has more overt protection through recruitment, educational socialization and specialist qualification requirements than is generally the case with manual labour (Elliott, 1972; Berlant, 1975; Boreham *et al.*, 1976; Anderson *et al.*, 1978). The following comment from an Australian Court of Appeal judge in a recent submission to the New South Wales Law Reform Commission attests to the processes involved:

> the present situation [of the legal profession] which is disquieting has been brought about by the flooding of the profession by persons who without either professional family association or inadequate indoctrination [sic] have acquired the often dangerous skills put in the hands of lawyers . . . If the maintenance of professional standards, particularly of integrity, which need to be above those of the general community is of fundamental importance, and if it is desired to greatly increase the number of lawyers and to draw the increase from at present largely unrepresented classes, an elaborate course of indoctrination will be necessary (*National Times*, 1978).

The second point is that the *process* of realization has tended to become an institutionally discrete element of reproduction with the development of monopoly capital. However, the political and ideological relations which it encompasses are structurally restricted to the organizational domain in which they are practised – notably those of professional practice. As Johnson puts it:

> the professional association of accountancy is not an expression of 'class powers' of capitalist relations of domination and subordination-in-general. It is able to play a relatively indepen-

dent part in structuring a limited sector of the labour process –
as a system of domination and subordination – because within
the differentiated process of realization it incorporates these
specific powers within a peculiar organizational form – the
professional association (1977, p.221).

We are drawn towards the conclusion that ideological and
political relations may so modify economic determinants in
specific institutional contexts that no conclusions can be reached
about the general class locations of such positions. In the context
of this argument we may note that our analysis follows that of
Poulantzas on several major points. The transformations within
the 'non-productive' wage-earning sector, reflecting economic
circumstances which accentuate the fragmentation and polarization of the new middle class are, as Poulantzas (1975, p.257)
argues, 'accentuating the reproduction of the mental/manual
labour division within mental labour. . . . [Such] . . . transformations bring certain fractions of the new petty bourgeoisie close to
the barrier that separates them from manual labour and from the
working class.' However, Poulantzas reasserts his conclusion
that,

> this mental/manual labour division, which is reproduced in a
> specific form within the ranks of mental labour itself, also
> marks lines of internal cleavage within the new petty
> bourgeoisie, which are in this sense hierarchical cleavages
> rather than cleavages of domination; these are the result of the
> fragmentation of knowledge and the standardization of the
> tasks of mental labour that affect certain sectors and levels
> subjected to capitalist 'rationalization', i.e. to the process of
> qualification and disqualification internal to mental labour
> (1975, p.270).

And yet, this 'hierarchy' reflects a new petty bourgeoisie which is
perpetually in conflict and transformation. Transformation, which
in reflecting broader economic circumstances, can never lead to a
stable new middle class.

As Mandel (1975) reminds us, the era of dominance of
monopoly capitalism witnessed the attempted extension of
capitalist control over many more phases of production and
reproduction, whether effected through the state or through the
dominant institutions of 'private initiative'. The state and the
major capitalist institutions are thus, it is proposed, 'trying to get
an "organisational grip" on the process of the subsumption of
intellectual labour under capital' (Mandel, 1975, pp. 263-4). This
is a direct consequence of the fact that the increasing demand for

intellectually qualified labour is by no means confined to the needs of the production process alone. In directing our attention towards the reproduction of labour power it is necessary adequately to account for the control mechanisms which apply to these processes. The control of reproduction rests at the locus of state and professional association relationships. The formal occupational socialization mechanisms which lie outside of the ambit of individual capitals are subsumed within the variable formal authority of the state broadly to determine the content of the curricula of the professional schools and to circumscribe the manner and setting of professional practice. This can be undertaken through legislative or regulatory mechanisms. For example, in the establishment of specific criteria for unemployment benefits, workers' compensation claims and invalidity pensions, the role of the social work and medical professions is formally routinized. Alternatively, control can be achieved through what are often implicit pressures directed towards the professional schools as they are exerted through funding of research and educational programmes at tertiary institutions (Mandel, 1975, pp.265-6). It is in this way that occupational definitions of, for example, normal and deviant behaviour, health and illness, and the differential enforcement of 'criminal' activities may sometimes be subordinated to official definition.

The focus of theoretical attention must be enlarged in order to encompass not only those occupational activities involved with realization and reproduction, but also the important processes which emerge from state–profession interpenetration in the content and practice of those occupations. It is precisely in such areas as welfare, health, education, law, urban planning and scientific and technological utilization – all important realms of professional practice – that the major reproductive forces are generated. As Johnson concludes, it is in the context of

> the formalization and centralization of such ideological processes of reproduction, [that] elements of the state apparatus may arise to impose such definitions upon an emergent occupation, as is the case with social work, or 'recognize' existing occupational definitions, as with medicine in the context of the national health service in Britain (1977, p.229).

Johnson draws the distinction between practice which is determined through occupational definitions and standards and that which is simply an application of standards and definitions which are a product of state direction of, or intervention in, occupational practice. Johnson suggests that the predominance of state rather than occupational determinations about professional practice is indicative of the class locations of the occupants of occupational positions. Relatively full autonomy from state control indicated the success that certain occupational groups had in acquiring a monopoly over a particular function in an era prior to the dominance of the state. Where state agencies have assumed this role – for example in teaching, where the content of curricula is largely determined by state agencies, or in the welfare professions, where conditions for eligibility are determined by legislative and regulatory requirements – professionals are part of a labour process in which those definitions are routinely applied. Where an occupation retains discretion over occupational practice, on the other hand, the determinations through which these processes are officially sanctioned hinge on the extent to which these occupations *independently* carry out the function of capital in the process of reproduction. Johnson thus concludes that the ideological symbols of which professionalism is the major component, are largely tokens gaining the status of currency in transactions between professions and the state – a currency which obscures an important condition of the transaction – which is the requirement that the occupation fulfils the global function of capital. And it is in precisely this context that the burden of proof of the indeterminate status of 'occupational knowledge' is placed on the profession.

The power and autonomy from organizational control which may thus accrue to the upper levels of internally stratified professional occupations derive from the ability of these occupational groups to maintain the inaccessibility of what has been termed 'tacit knowledge' as distinct from explicit and testable experience. The professions' emphasis on indetermination supports the assertion of the uniqueness of individual practice (Boreham, 1983). It is therefore possible to assert that such practice is unable to be subject to external surveillance and control and that 'trust' based on internalized standards and norms of behaviour ought to be accorded to individual practitioners. It is also in this respect, as Larson notes (1977, p.206), that the essential individualism of professional ideology is manifest. In effect, the regulatory norms of the work process are themselves translated as central elements of claims for power and status. In particular, conceptions of companies of equals democratically exerting mutual supervision over internalized common standards serve to ensure that 'the demonstrability of individual talent in the central elements of the work role is at a minimum' (Offe, 1976, p.76). In conjunction with other ideological components of professional socialization, these conceptions serve to support the role and status of the governing strata of professional associations

197

which depend on ideology for their legitimacy – a legitimacy which nevertheless can be granted only by elements external to the professions themselves. It is through this dynamic that professional elites depend for their more tangible means of power on negotiated positions of authority within bureaucratic organizations. Conversely, it is precisely the negotiation of this legitimacy through the demonstration of identification with appropriate, recognized norms and values in the context of the capitalist organization of the labour process that control is exerted over high-discretion roles in task-discontinuous organizations. Pursuit of this line of reasoning needs to take account of the likelihood that trust in normative orientations, as opposed to technical rules, can be productive of tension and instability in organizational power relationships. The maintenance of loyalty to broader organizational goals, through expectations of obedience to approved norms and values, while broadly determined by socialization processes is, nevertheless, open to reflexive alteration and modification. Instability deriving from imperfections in self-control (which, it has been argued, predominates in high-discretion roles), is the major factor underlying the ability of professional occupations to exploit indetermination. Offe (1976, p.34) argues that reciprocal expectations are therefore of critical importance:

> Only to the extent that both the set of reciprocal expectations within a set of reference groups *and* the self-interpretation and self-understanding of the role partners remain constant can any long-term maintenance of the norms be assumed, and these norms now have to control in an *ad hoc* fashion the area of discretion that is no longer covered by formal rules.

And, furthermore: 'it is clear that the wider social structure determines what rules are followed at work, and that any attempt to evaluate performance in individualistic terms must end up disguising the social origins of the rules themselves.'

It is necessary, at this point, to enquire where the rules originate. Primarily, and with cultural variation, they derive from the more or less negotiated order of economic relationships, development and calculation. The hegemony of capitalist domination in this order is, as Palloix (1976) argues, exercised not only through control of the production of commodities and the reproduction of commodity relations at the point of production, but also through the integration of new occupational strata into alliances with the bourgeois class. This is accomplished by broadening those strata in society which can be brought to function ideologically within the ruling 'historical bloc'. It is in such positions that the professions are predominant. That is, they are the dominating elements in the reproduction of the hegemonic strata of the bourgeoisie. Their imputed function, it is suggested, is 'to disguise the contradictions that develop at the level of production and of the organization of the labour process of mass production' (Palloix, 1976, p.61).

We would conclude, *contra* Johnson, that it is not the ratio of state–professional control which is indicative of the class position of members of the professions, but rather, that it is the extent to which the penetration of professional discretion has allowed for the development of a proletarianized labour process within each profession. It is the boundaries beyond which discretion is accorded to particular members of the profession about which a critical intraclass struggle is waged.

It is possible, on this basis, to differentiate between the *established* and *marginal* components of the new-middle-class structure. The basis of the established salaried middle classes, depends on maintaining the inaccessibility of tacit knowledge through 'professional' rather than state regulation of the credentialling process, for which the prototype is the medical profession. The marginal middle classes include the various routine, lower-professional, supervisory and technical workers, all of whom occupy essentially 'blocked' careers because of the credentialled basis of task-discontinuity. It is amongst these workers that it is proposed that a process of 'proletarianization' of their work process is occurring (Roslender, 1981; also see Crompton, 1979, 1980, and Heritage, 1980, for the original point of departure for his comments). Between these marginal, 'proletarianizing' middle classes and the established professions, stand those credentialled members of the new middle class whose certification is regulated rather more by the state and rather less by the profession. This 'determination' should not be regarded as unqualified. In view of research which demonstrates the importance of analysing individuals' 'work histories' (e.g. Brown, 1982; Goldthorpe *et al.*, 1980) it is worth issuing a caution. Certainly, barriers may exist objectively, but the meaning they have for the people who occupy those class positions is highly variable, in terms of civil status. The young articled clerk whose position is subjectively defined merely as a status passage *en route* to a credentialled position, is a different type of 'proletarianized' worker from one who has had, and still expects to have, a lifetime in the lower-status position.

It is a major irony of the credentialling process that the very means through which certain professional occupations have gained exclusive rights to specific practices have also provided the condition to effect state control over increasing segments of that practice. The tensions inherent in the locus of relationships between the professions and the state are subject to significant pressures deriving not only from the economic environment, but also the specific history of state formation. The degree of professional autonomy is an emergent feature of the process of state formation itself, as examination of the credentialling process suggests (and as Johnson (1982) latterly argues). The unity of each sphere as a zone of monopoly is in part dependent upon the other. The extent to which indirect occupational control, in the form of professionalism, can be maintained in the face of 'proletarianization' reflects directly on the class-heterogeneous nature of individual professions. It would seem to be necessary to consider the specific forces accounting for the twin dichotomies of professionalism–proletarianization and state–occupational control over professional practice in specific institutional settings. Not only is it necessary to analyse the functions performed by the occupation with respect to the realization of value and the reproduction of labour power, but also the elements of discretion retained by the occupation in determining its functions. The structural ambiguity of class situations involved in realization/ reproduction cannot be resolved either by reference to one dichotomy alone or by introducing totalizing concepts such as 'reproduction in general'.

We may only conclude that the structurally ambiguous complex of heterogeneous class location at the political and ideological level simply lacks sufficient specificity to allow it to be constituted as a class. Such locations contain elements of both collective worker and global capital. They are characterized by a range of differentiated market and status positions for which there can be no common ground for class identification on the basis of interests.

The analysis of the 'new middle class', then, becomes one which focuses on the structural forces which apply to those positions engaged in maintaining economic relations. These must be perceived not in a general sense, but in specific institutional locations concerned with the reinforcement of capitalist economic relations between factions of capital, the state and capital, the state and working class, and capital and the working class. In general, we may conclude that the 'middle class' is a product of the relations of possession and exclusion which arise in specific forms generated by the differentiated functions of production, realization and reproduction. It is at the interface of these processes that middle-class locations emerge and are reabsorbed into the working class in an environment characterized by constantly changing tension and conflict.

The likely outcome of this configuration of tensions and forces relies on the forms of interest intermediation which it is possible to utilize or develop in the light of historical development of the institutions of political power in particular societies. The strength of differing class and popular organization becomes most salient in those neo-corporatist forms of policy formulation which are dominated by highly centralized union councils and employer bodies under the aegis of specialized agencies of the state. It seems likely that the direction of reform of social and economic policy in the forthcoming decades will be contingent upon the extent to which the policy agenda is articulated in such terms as are able to provide the basis for lasting alliances between one or other of the principal classes of capital and labour and the political organizations and forces which seek to articulate the interests of the new middle class.

The tensions surrounding such alliances are such as to place formidable barriers in the way of their long-term coherence, for, as we have indicated in this chapter, the new middle class nurtures the seeds of its own division and incorporation within the interests of the corporate ruling class in its upper echelons. None the less, the dominating position of significant elements of the new middle class in the reproduction of capitalist relations makes its acquiescence in the vocabulary and motives of the capitalist class a critical target for attention. It is important to emphasize in this context that the increasingly proletarianized stratum of middle-class technical and professional labour power has a highly ambivalent relationship with both capital and the state, in a manner which further clouds the resolution of political allegiances.

We must take care not to give credence to any theoretical assertion of a natural alliance of manual workers and non-manual, new-middle-class workers against a common exploitation by capital. It is certainly true, as Goldthorpe (1982) suggests, that a workforce largely engaged in work in the bureaucratic organizations of the modern state has no necessary class allegiance with the interests which overwhelmingly structure the goals and practices of such organizations. Changes in the class basis of such interest representation might also be paralleled by a realignment of the existing division of labour in a manner which might entail real costs to those who are compensated by the existing inegalitarian arrangements. Even though disaffection on the part of the 'lower orders' of the new middle class is the most likely manifestation of the effect of those economic policies of the new right which seek to enhance specifically capitalist incentives and disciplines, at the expense of public expenditure and welfare state institutions, there is no basis on which to argue that such disaffection will necessarily be channelled into support for working-class strategies. The problem is not only the absence of an agenda which includes a satisfactory programme of transition (Edwards, 1979, pp.200-16). More importantly, as long as the design of jobs and the allocative mechanisms for entering particular occupational domains appear to favour reproduction of the new middle class through forms of mediation with capital, then there is a compelling incentive to preserve those arrangements which are exemplified by their privileged position in the existing social division of labour (Gagliani, 1981).

Even though these are important grounds for rejecting an automatic alliance between the working class and the new middle class, there are some reasons to argue that, if certain elements of the new middle class were to exhibit an increasing degree of stability or coherence, then these would not be seriously disadvantaged by the implementation of an alternative social and economic programme to that of the corporate ruling class. Within such forms, distributional processes would become subject to greater democratic political control and the outcomes would in part reflect the degree to which collective interests were able to be organized and represented politically (Goldthorpe, 1982). There are reasonable grounds for arguing that the new middle class would not be seriously encumbered in such an organized representation of its political interests.

The final issue which this presupposes concerns 'the level at which the agenda of politics and the relative priority of issues and solutions is determined and the durability of alliances and compromises is conditioned' (Offe, 1983, pp.60-1). These factors are contingent upon the matrix through which social classes, status groups, and other social categories are able to exert influence in moulding and remoulding the political agenda and closing that agenda to inputs which are not part of the socially 'agreed' vocabulary of what is acceptable and what is possible. An element upon which this matrix is aligned is the highly unequal distribution of control over, and therefore access to, the means of communication and information which collectively structure the environment of political and economic policy formulation at the societal level. The means of communication are themselves responsive to the ability of particular collectivities to articulate an effective representation of their political interests in terms of 'the general interest'. This ability depends, in part, on conjunctural variations which enhance or qualify the forms through which such collectivities exploit their specific social power in particular periods. In the chapter which follows we shall examine the extent to which the working class is capable of representing its interests in a class-oriented political strategy which will engender the support of significant segments of the new middle class. In order to do so, we shall argue that the present locus of class struggle within the labour process is facilitative only of partial working-class strategies which lead ultimately to division and contradiction.

7 The working class: structure, segmentation and control

Class structure and class consciousness

A spectre haunts the analysis of the working class: the spectre of its 'making' under the uncompromising gaze of E.P. Thompson, whose magisterial work *The Making of the English Working Class* (1968) has had such an enormous impact. Its reception has been limited not only to Britain. One notes, for instance the evocation of this work in contemporary US (Gutman, 1976) and Australian (Connell and Irving, 1980) accounts of class formation. To write of a spectre in this way is to identify the influence of Thompson as in some way baneful. At one level, as we shall argue, such an interpretation is singularly apposite. This level would be that at which class *analysis* has been subsumed by the enormous undertaking of providing *accounts* of national class formation, in which the categorical imperative has been yielded to the rich panorama of densely textured narrative peopled with fragments of the relived experiences of men and women of the times.

Process is emphasized vividly in Thompson's stress on the *making* of class: 'The working class made itself as much as it was made' (1968, p.213). One danger with this approach, as has been pointed out by Connell and Irving (1980, pp.10-12), is that concentration on the *narrative* aspects of class formation – the actual people, places, times and events involved in the process – may lead us to lose sight of class as a structural, enduring order of relationships which link the disparate situations of one's lived experience as a coherent whole. Such an undertaking, in Thompson and others, may indeed provide a rich sense of document and narrative, but one in which argument as a structural device for generating concepts and categories, capable of redeployment on a terrain peopled elsewhere, by other histories, may be limited in generalizability through the specificities of the conjunctures in which it is located.

Such problems are not peculiar to Thompson. Any analysis which bases itself on the criterion of 'common experience' or 'consciousness', as Anderson (1980, p.31) terms it, is irrevocably committed to the peculiarities of time and place. Its implicit criterion of meaning is based on an analytical process of contextual *verstehende*, or a coming-to-accounts-with culturally specific meaning. The problems this can generate for rational understanding have been most thoroughly debated in the responses (Wilson, 1977) to Peter Winch's (1958) extreme statement of the theme, but they can never be far from a perspective in which 'Class is defined by men as they live their own history, and, in the end, this is its only definition' (Thompson, 1968, p.11).

The Making of the English Working Class centres on the necessity of making the reality of class dependent upon its cognition as such by, and through, the experience of particular collectivities. Thus, to argue, as does Thompson, that classes exist because men and women 'feel and articulate' the identity of their antagonistic interests and come to 'struggle, think and value in class ways' (Thompson, 1968, p.9; 1978, p.299) is to concentrate one's attention on class consciousness as the very hallmark of class formation. It seems to us that the ultimate conclusion of such a voluntarist and subjectivist definition will be that class may only be apprehended through scientific analysis in so far as the analytical subjects so constitute themselves. We are thus confronted with a situation in which, while there may be no problem in discussing class in an epoch of heightened class consciousness, there is every problem in extending this discussion to epochs in which ordinary people constitute their lived experience in a key more mundane and resistant to articulation, or in which collective experience and existence are affected by objective factors in respect of which people are unaware.

Thompson's account is narrowly focused on subjective experience or culture, which, for him, identifies class, rather more than on the relations of production within which the consciousness of class is shaped by the forces through which emerged a supply of free and rightless proletarians – a class of alienable wage-labourers dependent upon the capitalist class for a livelihood, initially through the wage contract and finally in the real dependence of their integration into mechanized production.

One's lived experience links the disparate situations and locales of life not only internally, in terms of one's identity, but also relates one to broader collective identities. It does this through the key institutions within which the power differentials of social life are organized. With respect to class, the basis for these remains grounded in economic domination.

Class analysis is necessarily structural analysis if it is to be of either categorical or generative use. For, *contra* Connell (1977, pp.4-7), these are not mutually exclusive or contradictory but necessarily interwoven aspects of an adequate class analysis. Basic categories of existence which persist and endure, *despite* whatever one may think of them as a conscious subject in one's lived experiences, are the generative structure of the densely populated terrain whose topography is mediated by, and through, lived experience. These basic categories of existence are, as we have determined earlier, 'established by nothing but . . . objective place in the network of ownership relations', as Cohen (1979, p.73) has put it. Consciousness, experience and meaning do not enter into this objective placement at all: one does not become a boss or a capitalist by thinking, acting or living like one unless one already *is* one. One's being is specified in terms of the objective co-ordinates of one's activity rather than such activity being the objective effect of the co-ordinates of one's reflection.

There can be no doubt that there has been a general decline of class consciousness since its initial surge during the intensification of immiseration perpetrated in the period leading up to the Industrial Revolution. Given that this is the case, Thompson's (1968) analysis leaves little room for the contemporary relevance of anything like the same degree of the class principle. In his essay 'The Peculiarities of the English' (1976), Thompson admits as much in sketching a general evolutionary model of working-class formation which is, in fact, quite similar to that proposed by Bergier (1973). Briefly, the evolution follows this logic: the industrial proletariat develops as a mass from its artisanal background, and matures to a conscious and combative class with its own identity, and later, its own political and trade organiza-tions, which subsume the earlier 'climacteric moment' to more limited and more rewarding reformism. These earlier climacteric moments have been seen by certain sociologists, including Bendix (1956) and Smelser (1959), as conflicts produced by the working class's inability to achieve political redress under early capitalism, because of its exclusion from, and non-incorporation into, the institutional frameworks of this society. In Giddens's (1973, pp.115, 202) terms, it is only early capitalism as it comes into contradiction with elements of extant feudalism, which is characterized by 'revolutionary class consciousness'. Such a consciousness involves a belief in the possibility that social relations can be radically reconstructed through concerted class action around class principles of the working class.

More mature conjunctures may be said to be characterized by a 'conflict-consciousness' in which 'perception of class unity is linked to a recognition of opposition of interest with another class or classes' (Giddens, 1973, p.112), but this conflict-consciousness has no necessary relationship to revolutionary consciousness. The former is an inherent part of 'the outlook of the worker in capitalist society' while the latter is not (Giddens, 1973, p.202). The latter arises as a result of the contradiction between agrarian feudalism and industrial capitalism, as it is experienced by those most exposed to, and least incorporated in, the vanguard mode of production, and most committed to the existing mode, and where this transition takes place within a framework in which the bourgeois political revolution to liberal democracy has not been achieved (Giddens, 1973, pp.113, 147-8). The full scenario has been sketched most economically by Anderson (1980, p.49):

> The working class is rebellious in its youth because it has not yet accepted the irreversible advent of industrialism, unwillingly adjusts to the reality of the capitalist order in middleage, and becomes reconciled to it through new levels of consumption towards retirement – before passing away altogether in post-industrial society.

There have been many pronouncements of the end of class (summarized in Connell and Goot, 1979) in the twentieth century, notwithstanding that the diagnoses have been mistaken and the obituaries somewhat premature. Pervasive inequalities of opportunity persist despite the changes which have undoubtedly occurred in the structure of the labour market and labour process. To be sure, this pervasiveness does not give rise to a 'revolutionary' class consciousness. Nor, incidentally, is it masked by hegemonic incorporation, as many theorists have suggested. The case is less pessimistic than that allowed by the 'dominant ideology thesis' (Abercrombie et al., 1980). The nature of conscious involvement in work does have a non-reproductive (if not 'revolutionary') potential under certain circumstances, circumstances which suggest the irrelevance of the reform/revolution distinction which is implicit in the dichotomy of conflict versus revolutionary consciousness.

We will first consider some recent analyses and accounts of the contours of the contemporary working class, in a general way; and will then examine the major types of status differentiation governing access to variable skilled positions in the labour process, notably those of ethnicity and gender. These do not invalidate the picture of a working class, but they do qualify it.

In its broad outlines the structure of the working class is clear, even if an acrimonious dispute exists as to its boundaries. It consists of the mass of workers who have nothing to sell but their labour power as the basis for their entry into social relations of production. This mass is, of course, not undifferentiated, but its constituents do share certain characteristics.

The basis of the first common characteristic is that there are many individual sellers of labour power on the market relative to the number of purchasers. Hence, the balance of power lies with the buyers. These buyers or employers are usually organized into large complex organizations, which, within limits established by the history of class and national struggles, may choose and discriminate between sellers. Moreover, if they consider it more rational to do so they can dispense entirely with this labour power by technological substitution for specific functions, or manipulate and dilute the skill content of a specific labour power in relation to other sellers or in relation to machines (Allen, 1977, p.65).

Not all sellers will be equally inferior. To the extent that labour power is obtained for its skill content, then wide qualitative variations in its individual provision enter into the equation. The greater the specificity of skill, the less dependent the person who provides it is in relation to an employer, all things being equal. Major countervailing variables will include, amongst other things, the capacity of an employer to be able to 'dilute special skills by mechanizing them in part or total', as Allen (1977, p.66) puts it. Total mechanization of skills means that people whose particular capacity as labour power was formed by these skills will find their market position undercut. In other words, their labour power would have been cheapened to the point of substitutability. They would become redundant, unable to sell their skill on the market at its previous exchange value, irrespective of the fact that the skill is the same, with the same use value. If such skills are no longer required, it is because the tasks and work they contributed to the labour process would have been reorganized. Reorganization occurs when skills can be provided at a higher rate of exploitation or at a lower cost through technological substitution. All workers who lose their jobs in this way become redundant inasmuch as all their energies and capacities have been specialized for the market by the acquisition and development of skill.

A further characteristic common to labour power is that its bearers are compelled to hawk their skills around in varying forms when confronted by unemployment, irrespective of their income level and status when formerly in employment. Sellers of labour power share a common situation of 'inferiority, helplessness, subordination, [and] subjugation to varying extents' (Allen,

1977, p.66) when in the labour market, even though the conditions of its exercise, once sold, may be quite variable, and the registers which statistically calculate it, in and out of employment, quite distinct.

Labour power, once sold, is engaged as part of a more or less complex organization of the labour process. For the working class in this labour process existence is primarily under the planned discipline and calculated control and surveillance of some element of that new middle class which we have already considered. Such control is complex: in part, it is external to the worker and coercive; in part, it is constituted by the worker in the nature of the involvement that individuals have with their work situation; in part, it is constituted through the objective structuration of labour markets and labour processes, particularly as they display elements, respectively, of labour-market segmentation and work discipline constituted in the 'technical rules' of the labour process (Clegg, 1981). Thus, members of the working class – such as skilled or unskilled manual workers, service workers, shop assistants or lower-level clerks – will operate in qualitatively different labour markets. However, in terms of the controls under which they labour, they will have much in common. This will be so, not only in the way they sell their labour power, but also in the objective, external constraints which control their exercise of such labour power once it has been sold.

The picture varies with each national formation, as constituted by its specific legal, administrative, macro-economic and other policies, because state formation, on the one hand, and the structure of economic relations, on the other, traverse the terrain of civil society. However, there are characteristic patterns which will not vary in their relational aspects even though the qualitative picture will. In reconstructuring these relational characteristics we will be primarily drawing from British examples because they are the most extensively documented. While we recognize the uniqueness of the British case as the first industrial capitalist state, we will concentrate on the more generalizable aspects of relational class structure. For we are advancing an essentially theoretical account of why empirically descriptive detail should be as it is, not in its particulars but in its internal relations and structure. The national variations, although of considerable interest in their own right, can be subsumed by an analysis of the structures that articulate them. In the concluding chapter we will discuss policies which are oriented to a transformation of these structures.

In the consciousness of the vast majority of people who own

only property for consumption and not productive property, the major cognizance of stratification will be in terms of income differentials. This level of conceptualization tends not to consider the productive ownership of property but concentrates on aspects of occupations and earnings. It was through such an analysis that one particularly pervasive representation of the relational characteristics of class came to be widely accepted, debated and rejected. This has come to be known as the 'embourgeoisement thesis'. What was proposed was that the working class, particularly its skilled, wage-earning, manual members, was becoming increasingly affluent and thus taking on consumption patterns characteristic of the bourgeoisie; becoming, as it were, 'embourgeoisified'.

One of the earliest identifications of this process was by Zweig (1961), a theme to which he has since returned (Zweig, 1976). Zweig's original thesis noted the expansion of white-collar jobs, educational provision by the state, a narrowing of income differentials and a weakening of traditional working-class family and residential ties contingent upon the postwar restructuring of urban life and space. A number of consequences were seen to flow from these observations which were stressed in what came to be known as the 'myth' of the 'withering away of class' (Westergaard, 1972). It was assumed that the shape of the class structure of the advanced capitalist societies was taking on a 'diamond configuration'; that is, a swollen middle stratum with a small distribution towards the extremes, such that the 'ruling' and 'working' classes appeared to be now in decline. This thesis was tested as a hypothesis in a series of studies by Goldthorpe and his colleagues, notably in their volume *The Affluent Worker in the Class Structure* (1969).

To what extent did changing affluence change workers' collective representation or image of society? Had embourgeoisement been significant, Goldthorpe *et al.* expected that it should have led to a decline in the degree of collectivist, solidaristic and antagonistic images of social reality held by members of the working class. Three ideal typical variants among the working class had been posited by Lockwood (1966) in an earlier study. These were 'proletarian traditionalists', 'deferential traditionalists' and 'privatized workers'.

Proletarian traditionalists were characterized as those workers involved in occupational communities with a high degree of homogeneous identity. Typically this would be found among those engaged in jobs requiring courage, team-work and toughness, such as miners or steelworkers, where that occupation is the major work-identity available (because of the dominance of a particular industry in a specific community). Groups of workers like miners, who are the classic militant occupational community (Allen, 1981), overwhelmingly have a 'power' image of society divided into an 'us' and 'them' polarity, generated and reinforced by the double solidarism of work and community life.

It is not clear how realistic the 'traditional proletarian' characterization of the working class ever was. Moreover, the increasing economism of working-class unions of recent years is not a necessary and sufficient indication of the decline of the traditional proletarian. It has been precisely those workers who conform most nearly to the traditional proletarians who have until recently been most economistically militant. In addition, those alienated workers who have only an economic commitment to a firm have a work situation with a high propensity to militancy. As has often been remarked, a single-stranded cash nexus is easily snapped. Thus, in such a situation, the union takes on a decisive importance because it mediates between the individual-at-work and the wider political processes of 'free collective bargaining', 'arbitration', 'corporatism' or whatever. The centrality of the union in this way is a finding supported by studies in countries as diverse as Sweden (Korpi, 1978), France (Hamilton, 1967) and England (Coates and Silburn, 1973).

Deferential traditionalists typically work in small firms, in relatively isolated, low-density and economically autonomous communities which have a well-differentiated occupational structure as well as a fairly stable population. In such contexts, a diffuse paternalism can soften the class principle. Privatized workers were most relevant to the Luton study. Typically to be found in newer industries and housing estates, cut adrift from either local deference or solidarity, these protypical members of mass society are the authentic exemplars of 'embourgeoisification'. The anomie of affluent existence, contrasted with traditionalist types of workers, became a common leitmotif of studies of the working class. Hoggart (1958) and Young and Willmott (1957), for instance, reflected upon the decline of working-class community and its traditional forms of interaction, while the Luton studies focused on the rise of instrumentalism. In particular, following Bott's (1957) influential stress, they situated it in those immediate social experiences formed in networks of friends, neighbours and relatives. Affluent workers were far more likely to be privatized workers than they were likely to be proletarian traditionalists. They were recognizable as such by an instrumentalist orientation to work, unions and politics alike.

Instrumentalism is seen to be the cause for the break-up of

proletarian traditionalism; yet many of the affluent workers' responses suggest that they do hold a 'power' model of society. Comparison made between the empirically researched affluent workers and the ideal typical proletarian traditionalists is necessarily somewhat speculative. The ideal type is a construct and so any difference will be an effect of its construction.

Luton workers were sampled because they were not a physically concentrated, traditional, single-occupational community. Hence, it would not be legitimate to extrapolate a secular trend, in terms of the demise of the traditional proletarian, from a highly specific sample, as Benson has suggested:

> in essence, the central criticism being advanced is that the 'traditional' worker displays far too much of a tendency to appear in the guise of a *deus ex machina*, whose function it is to validate a prepared theoretical position. In moving from the ideal typical to the historical level of analysis, there occurs a corresponding tendency to treat as reality relationships which were previously only hypothesised, or presented in a somewhat tentative way (1978, p.156).

A further issue concerns the relationship between communal and class solidarity (Allcorn and Marsh, 1975, p.211). The former, with its particularistic emphasis, need not necessarily entail the more universalistic orientation of the latter. According to Allcorn and Marsh, an explicit distinction is required between notions of solidarity and sociability; the absence of the latter need not entail the absence of the former. Again, the sampling bias is evident. Luton workers were chosen in part because of their heterogeneous backgrounds, geographical mobility and lack of social roots. This, taken with the tendency of the researchers to explain orientations to work primarily in terms of factors external to work, tends to downplay work-related factors shaping the consciousness of workers. Additionally, consciousness is assumed to be fairly unitary and coherent.

It has been widely argued, however, that the consciousness of the working class is typically fragmentary and disorganized. If this is so, then we need not expect any necessary, direct, relationship between proletarian class position, its variable experience, and radical protest. Mann (1973a), for instance, has proposed that workers' images of society are only partially formed through immediate experience. More especially, they are selectively enacted from the whole media of signification in modern society. While some of these may place a general stress on meanings which are conducive to privatization, at a more personal level the lived experience of the worker will interpellate contradictory beliefs selected by and from other media. From this perspective the contradictions found in the responses by the workers questioned in the Luton study would simply indicate contradictions lodged in working-class experience. It is this interpretation, advocated by Parkin, which proposes the existence of not only a dominant ideology or meaning-system within worker' consciousness, but also a subordinate one:

> Studies of working class attitudes which rely on questions posed in general and non-situational terms are likely to produce findings which emphasise class consensus on values; this is because the dominant value system will tend to produce the moral frame of reference. Conversely, studies which specify particular social contexts of belief and action, or which rely on actual behavioural indices, are likely to find more evidence for a class differentiated value system; this is because in situational contexts of choice and action, the subordinate value system will tend to provide the moral frame of reference (Parkin, 1971, p.95).

Some empirical support has been given to these conclusions by Moorhouse and Chamberlain (1974), and they have been elaborated further by Allen (1975) and Moorhouse (1976).

In one basic sense the very notion of 'affluent' workers is problematic, not only in normative and relational terms, but also in economic ones. How affluent, relatively, are affluent workers? Members of the working class, even those relatively 'affluent' ones, remain lowly paid relative to members of the new middle classes throughout their life-cycle of employment. They will, on the average, earn slightly more in their thirties than in their twenties, but this income declines as they enter middle and old age, and 'slow down' in hours and pace of work, to a lower figure. These were the findings from British data of the early 1970s, interpreted by Westergaard and Resler (1976, p.78), and more recent data used by Reid (1981, pp.69-121) indicate that the general outline has not changed. Broadly speaking, the new middle classes earn around the median annual income of all income-earners, when all incomes are aggregated, while ruling-class incomes vary between a half to twice as much. The working classes, broadly speaking, earn up to 25 per cent less than the new-middle-class median (Reid, 1981, p.92), but work consistently longer hours and do more overtime to achieve this, under less favourable terms and conditions of employment (Wedderburn, 1972, p.177).

In respect of affluent workers typically displaying distinct orientations to work and an elective affinity for the range of

213

available jobs in the labour market, a number of points may be made about the labour market and its structure. It is assumed by the Luton studies that workers do have the ability to choose rationally between alternative jobs, according to their orientational priorities. Different types of workers may have different orientations and thus choose different types of jobs. However, as Blackburn and Mann (1979, pp.18-19) suggest, we may accept that while distinct orientations and actual choices exist, these none the less may characterize non-competing sections of the labour force. Differing orientations to work may in fact be stratified in non-competitive and, hence, non-alternative, niches in the labour market. Thus, differing groups may have differing orientations to work but exercise them in different segments of the labour market.

We have dwelt on the relationship between the working class and class consciousness at some length, because these issues have been at the centre of sociological enquiry, particularly in Britain (and Australia – e.g. Connell, 1977; Chamberlain, 1983). More recently, however, partly as a consequence of the Luton research and subsequent debate on the fragmentation of the working class (Roberts et al., 1977), interest has shifted towards a concern with the differentiation not just of working-class consciousness, but more especially working-class structure. Central to this concern is the structure of labour markets.

The labour market and the working class

The labour market is the central fact of life for the working class in capitalist society. Its formation in the Western European capitalist states followed roughly the same pattern in each case, albeit with local variations. In part, the industrial proletariat developed as a mass partly recruited from the peasantry by the process of rural exodus and expropriation which Marx described. This also fed the development of the white settler proletariat in the newer territories of the world economy, such as the white dominions of Australia, Canada and New Zealand, or America. Such a process of recruitment from, and slow decline of, the peasantry has been an underlying feature of the history of capitalism. However, closely allied with the decline of the rural peasantry was the process of demographic expansion in Europe, triggered by the growth of an international economy in foodstuffs (Wallerstein, 1974; Mols, 1976).

Initially, this labour market was quite total. It incorporated men, women and children, often from as early as three years old, at least until the first effective Factory Acts were won by working-class struggle. However, it was never an undifferentiated market, and considerable regional divisions occurred within and between states. Additionally, it was characterized by 'traditionally' lower wage rates for women than men, frequently justified on the grounds that if women were involved in wage-labour, then patriarchy in the disposition of a single wage could no longer prevail. It was thus considered appropriate that women's labour be less highly rewarded (Hamilton, 1978; Bergier, 1973).

Early employers were largely drawn from the same ranks as the industrial proletariat, as biographies of early industrialists demonstrate (Bergier, 1973, pp.409-11). It did not require much 'primitive accumulation' or initial saving of capital to become a capitalist (Tribe, 1975, p.36). Capital was easily acquired through Protestant asceticism and diligence, as Weber (1976) argued, or it could be obtained as a loan from a money-lender, the theological norms against usury being easily surmountable. As capitalism developed, however, and as the costs of entry became greater, capitalists came increasingly to be recruited from the upper strata of the bourgeoisie and landed aristocracy (Bergier, 1973, p.410). This was particularly the case in countries whose capitalist development occurred after its establishment in Britain. The latter, an early and rather special case, saw a distinctive institutional separation between mercantile-oriented aristocratic capital and industrially oriented bourgeois capital (Rubinstein, 1974). This was not to be as characteristic of developments elsewhere.

The industrial proletariat proper comes into being with the 'liquidation' of the means of production held by small independent commodity producers and their subordination to capitalist organization and control (Marglin, 1974). Concomitantly, there occurs the growth of an industrial workforce as a *mass*; that is, as an urban and industrial concentration of wage-labourers eking out its existence under common and frequently brutalizing conditions (Bergier, 1973). A further stage in the development of the proletariat is its maturation into a conscious social class with an articulate appreciation of common position, such as English Chartism offered. A third step is the organizational mobilization of the working class into political and trade bodies, 'the labour movement', with specific economic and political aims. This process, a part of the 'long revolution' of which Williams (1961) writes, is nowhere completed and indeed is still in its infancy at those margins only recently incorporated into the capitalist social economy. Even in the more fully developed capitalist social formations, organizational development involving and incorporating wage-earners continues to have such emphatic political and economic effect that one must hesitate to conclude that the process of working-class formation has anywhere reached finality. The most substantial effect of this ongoing process is that the future of the working class becomes ineradicably political; the structuring of the labour market, 'the whole complex of institutions and arrangements that make labour power a commodity, and keep it a commodity' (Connell and Irving, 1980, p.19), becomes itself structured through political class struggle. Marx recognized this clearly in his analysis of the struggle surrounding the Ten Hour Bill, as well as in his contribution to the First International, which insisted on the necessity of the working class forming itself into a political party (Marx, 1974, p.270).

All of the variegated forms of class conflict, fought for politically, culturally and economically, will actively make and shape the structure of the labour markets, for they are often complex, differentiated and segmented. Inasmuch as this conflict finds expression through political class struggle in the form of legislative concessions tending to transform the labour market in the working class's interests, it represents an element in the movement towards socialism, minimizing the conditions of a 'pure' competitive labour market, at the general level (Stephens, 1979, pp.10-11).

We have indicated the importance of the labour market as a central, structural element in capitalist society. In selling labour power to an employer, workers place themselves under the control of capital and it is through this exchange that workers come to experience the diverse mechanisms of surveillance and extraction of surplus labour that make them 'workers'. The actual selling of labour power and the terms and conditions of the labour market in which the worker offers up this 'capacity', have fundamental links to the structure of class power and domination in the wider society (Blackburn and Mann, 1979).

Some sociological discussion of labour markets has focused on them as structures of constraint and choice. Following from the formalist constructs of neoclassical economics, the choices have frequently seemed more pervasive than the constraints, as Coulson et al. (1967) have argued. The opacity of neoclassical formulations is an effect of an occluding set of assumptions concerning a system of free and equal exchange, based on rational choices, which occur in markets postulated in abstraction from any context of social relations which might structure them. Any such social relations of asymmetrical power which do occur are attributed to 'frictions', 'imperfections' or 'rigidities' in the market. Although such an exchange framework may provide us with a way of analysing some of the more explicit transactions of social life, it generally has little to say about the rules which govern these exchange processes, nor about how these have developed and operated. (See Heath (1976) and Clegg (1975, 1977) for a more detailed appraisal of exchange-based perspectives.)

Assumptions of free and equal exchange are not entirely absent from some sociological perspectives on economic life which stress the role of choice in labour markets (Coulson et al., 1967). It may be said to be implicit in the 'affluent worker' studies, for instance, in which there appears to be an indirect correlation between 'orientation' and preferences asserted in actual labour markets (Blackburn and Mann, 1979, pp.16-21). Our object in the section that follows, therefore, is to focus not only on important questions concerning workers' experience of the labour market, on which we have concentrated thus far, but also to examine the structures of the labour market and the forces from which these structures may be said to derive.

The predominant contemporary economic approaches to the structure of the labour market derive either from the neoclassical approach or from the 'institutionalist' perspective associated, in particular, with Kerr (1950, 1954). Contemporary variants of neoclassicism stress the importance of *human capital* (e.g. Becker, 1964). This concept is meant to represent wage-incomes as a return on investment as if analogous to entrepreneurial profit-incomes:

> The productivity, and hence the market value, of labour power increases with the amount of capital invested for the qualification of each worker. That is, inequality of life-earnings and occupational status are explained as being a consequence of unequal investments of 'human capital', i.e. of costs incurred for education, vocational training etc. (Kreckel, 1980, p.532).

There are, however, serious objections to such an individualistic approach to structural characteristics. It is not clear that aggregating an individual's 'human capital' in this way does entail a consistent and rational structure of income disparities, career paths and occupational statuses. Empirical research on mobility consistently demonstrates the low returns to education, for example (Heath, 1981). Additionally, it does not explain why people with the same 'human capital' investments but with different attributions of status as men/women, black/white, etc., in civil society, should have structurally dissimilar returns.

One variant of human capital recognizes the importance of these civil identities in qualifying suitability for the labour markets in which people are employed. Human capital inputs

217

become conceptualized as achieved 'signals' attached to people who, as specific types of person in civil society, can be characterized by 'indices' of identity. Identity in this context concerns such fixed ascriptive attributes as sex, age, ethnicity. Any employment exchange then becomes a matter of the participants' subjective evaluation and presentation of themselves as the appropriate mix of 'indices' and 'signals'. However, this approach (Spence, 1973) does not explain the differential estimates that produce structured inequalities of access and reward in labour markets, so much as redescribe them.

The *institutional* school works with a conception of institutionally, separate labour markets, constituted 'by rules, both formal and informal' (Kerr, 1954, p.93). The rules set the boundaries of access and closure for both employers and employees in labour markets. They may be both constitutive and preferential rules, at their strongest; or, at their weakest, simply preferential. Typically they may be 'established by employers' associations, by the informal understanding of employers among each other (the "gentlemen's agreement"), by companies when they set up their personnel policies, by trade unions, by collective agreements, and by actions of governments' (Kerr, 1954, p.93).

In many ways, because of its notion of separate and competing labour markets, this perspective is similar to the *dualist* or *dual labour market* perspective. The major difference is that the latter realizes that the topography of labour markets admits of differentiation on more than merely the horizontal plane. Additionally, it considers the vertical dimension of labour-market structures.

The dualist perspective developed from a number of studies which sought to explain the cultural and institutional structuring underlying the concentration of specific categories of low-status workers, particularly blacks, in disadvantaged employment situations (Piore, 1979; Bluestone, 1970; Doeringer and Piore, 1971). Increasingly, this perspective has been co-opted to explain other structural characteristics such as women's subordination in the labour market (Barron and Norris, 1976; Beechey, 1977, 1982) and the historical development of dualism (Friedman, 1977) as a phenomenon of monopoly capitalism. We will first briefly recall the standard Marxist account and then consider Friedman's qualifications preparatory to a more general discussion.

In general, the slow honing of capitalist relations of production from the sixteenth to the nineteenth century, produced a workforce which, despite its many varied identities, was shaped to an increasingly homogeneous pattern. Of course there were variations, and it would be unwise to discount them, but, none the less, it may be deduced that the slow erosion of guild-based craft production as the dominant mode necessarily reduced the heterogeneous basis of actually existing production. At the same time it created the conditions under which a more homogeneous and undifferentiated mass of labourers might collectively organize and resist the conditions that were producing (and reproducing) them. For Marx the process was both deterministic and dialectical: 'As the number of co-operating labourers increases, so too does their resistance to the dominance of capital, and with it, the necessity for capital to overcome this resistance by counter-pressure' (Marx, 1976, p.313).

In the century since Marx constructed this formula, the actual work experience of many people in the advanced capitalist economies has been not so much one of an apparent homogenization but an apparent differentiation. One observer has noted the extent to which 'differences in pay and conditions based on workers' skills, age, sex, race, country of origin or firm size have persisted from [the phase of] modern industry to the present day' (Friedman, 1977, p.47). These differentials reflected the development of internal job structures which were to establish the basis for labour-market segmentation. An initial definition of this process is offered by Loveridge and Mok (1979, p.27) as the outcome of historical processes through which political–economic forces facilitate those mechanisms and institutions whereby the purchase and sale of labour power is arranged into separate sub-markets, or segments, distinguished by different labour-market characteristics and behavioural rules.

According to Friedman, the conditions of employment of working-class labour becomes a product of two simultaneous and contradictory processes towards both homogenization and differentiation. The working class becomes less homogeneous through both a horizontal differentiation into separate economic sectors and a vertical differentiation between various levels of the occupational hierarchy. As Collins (1978) notes, these two differentiation processes combine and intersect with sex, race, ethnic and other attributes of civil society to produce characteristic fractions or 'segments' within the proletariat. There are a number of different models of these segments in the literature.

Dualist perspectives represent a model of the labour market bifurcated into primary and secondary segments:

> The primary and secondary segments . . . are differentiated mainly by stability characteristics. *Primary jobs* require and develop stable working habits; skills are often acquired on the job; wages are relatively high; and job ladders exist. *Secondary*

219

jobs do not encourage and often discourage stable working habits; wages are low; turnover is high; and job ladders are few. Secondary jobs are mainly (though not exclusively) filled by minority workers, women and youth.

Within the primary sector we see a segmentation between what we call 'subordinate' and 'independent' primary jobs. *Subordinate primary jobs* are routinized and encourage personality characteristics of dependability, discipline, responsiveness to rules and authority, and acceptance of a firm's goals. Both factory and office jobs are present in this segment. In contrast, *independent primary jobs* require creative, problem-solving, self initiating characteristics and often have professional standards for work. Voluntary turnover is high and individual motivation and achievement are highly rewarded (Reich *et al.*, 1973, p.359).

The authors of this definition have been in the forefront of radical dualist perspectives in the USA and have clearly influenced work elsewhere (Friedman (1977) and Barron and Norris (1976) in Britain, for example; Collins (1975, 1978) in Australia; also see Lever-Tracy's (1981) critique of the latter). The strengths of the perspective are evident in that structured inequalities are not only horizontal but vertical (*contra* the institutionalists). Additionally, they are regarded as structural effects of jobs rather than individual attributes (*contra* the 'human capitalists'). The weaknesses are less evident, but become clearer when placed in the context of their explanation of the existence of these structured inequalities and in the context of more empirical research. What is in question is an approach which admittedly overcomes the attribution of voluntarism to workers but only at the cost of simultaneously allowing it full rein for capitalists; the cunning of capital becomes the major explanatory variable for explaining the historical structure of labour markets. They are an effect of employers' purposive, intentional actions, a deliberate policy of 'divide and rule'. This strategy, it is argued, is intended both to prevent workers collectively mobilizing around common interests and to create a stable labour market for modern monopoly capitalism (Edwards *et al.*, 1975; Gordon, 1972).

We shall consider the 'divide and rule' argument first. The outcome of the division of the organizational workforce, it is argued, is to disunite workers. A number of authors argue that these consequences should be seen as a result of purposive employer strategies, and one major study of job structures in the US steel industry (Stone, 1974) concludes that this is the crucial impetus for segmentation. Stone's argument attempts to demonstrate that the creation in organizations of numerous formal status distinctions based on technical considerations has created hierarchical divisions within the working class. Moreover, it is claimed that company-specific employee benefits and 'welfare capitalism' (Brandes, 1976) also serve to fragment potential solidarity (Stone, 1974, pp.127-42). These differentiations thus serve to reduce class consciousness and united struggle, as Wachtel comments:

> The impact of the stratification process on consciousness is to
> divert workers' consciousness from a class orientation and
> replace it with an identification with one's strata in society,
> producing status consciousness. This, coupled with the inculca-
> tion of hierarchical forms of work organization is a twin-edged
> sword which had profound effects on the American working
> class (1974, p.12).

A broadly similar argument is advanced for Britain by Nichols and Armstrong (1976) and Nichols and Beynon (1977). These studies again argue that capital has deliberately pursued the development of elaborate but functionally meaningless organizational hierarchies. Historical analysis by Foster (1974) has focused on the evolution of strategies which led to the decline of revolutionary class consciousness in England. Much of this work has pointed to the incorporation of sections of the labour movement. This incorporation, it is proposed, occurs through specific conditions and remuneration which encourage the development of a more closely aligned and accommodative working-class sub-culture. The connections between class fragmentation and the emergence of non-threatening class-based experience has also been noted by Edwards, who concluded that:

> The development of twentieth-century . . . capitalism has
> fractured, rather than unified, the working class. Workers have
> been divided into separate groups, each with its distinct job
> experiences, distinct community cultures, and distinct con-
> sciousness. The inability of working-class-based political move-
> ments to overcome these divisions has doomed all efforts at
> serious structural reform (1979, p.184).

One major reservation about some dualist models concerns their obviously functionalist character. It is argued, for example, that capitalism 'requires' the segregation of its workforce and 'since these differences have been institutionalized in the economic structure of society, and more fundamentally since they serve the needs of capital accumulation, they persist' (Edwards,

1979, p.197). Moreover, the necessity of stratification is often viewed as a direct result of strategies consciously realized by capitalists: 'employers turned to strategies designed to divide and conquer the workforce' (Edwards *et al.*, 1975, p.xiii). It is not our intention to discount entirely these conclusions. Apart from the lack of evidence to indicate that there has ever been a united proletariat, it seems that analysis of labour-market segmentation would be better served if it focused on the structural outcomes of the development of production itself, rather than regard the divided working class as a product of manoeuvres by employers conscious of a need to preserve the structure of capitalism. Moreover, such an exclusive focus on the 'cunning of capital' neglects 'the possible impact of strategies of labour market segmentation sustained by various groups of workers and their representatives' (Kreckel, 1980, p.535).

Some aspects of the dualist argument do seem to be well supported. This is to concede that, as we have established, modern capitalist economies have a tendency to a dominant meso-sector of what has been termed 'monopoly capital', surrounded by much smaller, often symbiotic, petty bourgeois organizations. Within the former one will find primary-sector enterprises. These monopolistic, capital-intensive, highly profitable and technologically advanced firms and industries offer high wages, are highly unionized and have internal labour markets whereby promotion and training are sheltered within the enterprise, rather than being exposed to the rigours of the external market (Doeringer and Piore, 1971). As Blackburn and Mann (1979, p.22) observe, usually there will be an access point into the structure at both the unskilled and the skilled levels. It is at these ports of entry that the only real competition for jobs occurs. By contrast, secondary-sector markets are regarded as small, backward, usually labour-intensive firms operating in highly competitive conditions, with low rates of pay and unionization. These form a 'buffer-zone' of intermediate and small establishments, which provide the majority of low-qualification secondary jobs, whose incumbents are readily and easily hired, fired and rehired as the business cycle allows. In larger organizations, at the boundary of the primary labour market, there will be various groups of 'specialized' or 'semi-skilled' workers in subordinate primary jobs (Reich *et al.*, 1973).

In the primary sector two interconnected processes have been associated with the development of internal labour markets. According to Blackburn's and Mann's (1979, p.22) account, they are the increased degree of economic concentration and the increased capital intensity of this concentrated sector. One of the major benefits for primary-sector organizations of increased economic concentration is the potential it offers for oligopolistic control in the product market. This increase in certainty concerning its operating environment leads to a correlative desire for a reduction in the uncertainty of the internal organization, particularly where the technical core of capital intensity is concerned. To facilitate this, employers try to reduce uncertainty surrounding their labour force, particularly those parts of it in 'strategically contingent' (Hickson et al., 1971) positions. Thus, where economic factors have increased the inflexibility of production, it is hypothesized that employers will generally seek to establish internal labour markets.

High-cost, strategically contingent technical cores require constant operation for maximal profitability which is facilitated by isolation from labour disruption. One way of achieving this is through the promotion of stable, known, trusted and experienced workers into central and specialized positions which are also often more closely associated with the maintenance of managerial authority. Friedman (1977, p.110) notes that employers will try to co-opt the leaders of the unions or organizations representing such groups. The purpose of this is to establish procedures for inhibiting disputes and to protect employment when adjusting to short-run slumps in product demand by laying off more expendable workers first. Core sections of the labour market have associated with them what has been described as 'golden chains': fringe benefits such as sickness pay, holiday allowances and pensions – all linked to length of service. These jobs thus offer more stable employment with considerable job security and established patterns of career progression. What Mann (1973b) has described as a situation of 'mutual dependence' ensues in which neither employer nor employee wish to expose themselves to the uncertainties of the labour market.

This general structure of a partial reciprocity of interest between employers and unionists in the primary sector is one which, as Kreckel (1980, p.535) notes, is more appropriate to the analysis of big manufacturing industries. Consequently, it may not be so applicable to other important sectors of capitalist labour markets.

Further reservations regarding these studies concern the difficulties that have been encountered in empirically establishing the overall dichotomies posited. Even the most recent work of Gordon et al. (1982) suggests a greater deal of complexity and internal contradiction in labour markets than has heretofore been admitted. Studies in Europe reported in Loveridge and Mok (1979) demonstrate a less formal, more permeable structure of boundaries and career paths than the US studies have indicated:

> A move toward a multi-segmental model can only serve to
> reflect the complexity of social class and ethnic differences
> between marginal workers. This, in turn may enable the
> development of more precise analysis and prescription than has
> been possible hitherto with the cruder dual market concept
> (Loveridge and Mok, 1979, p.18).

A somewhat similar impression emerges from the body of research into segmentation and its interaction with economic crisis in Europe (Wilkinson, 1981; Berger and Piore, 1980).

In different economies the structural inequality of segmentation is likely to be multicausal. Kreckel (1980, p.541) suggests that there might be 'five major social mechanisms affecting bargaining strength in advanced capitalist labour markets'. The mechanisms delineated are termed *demarcation, exclusion, solidarism, inclusion* and *exposure*.

Demarcation consists of horizontal boundary maintenance against other categories of workers, in order to maintain the privileged space in which workers operate. Exclusion is vertically organized to ensure that the excluded competition is less privileged, while demarcation may be organized between equally privileged, but now singularly and non-competitively organized skills, all maximizing their privilege by rigorous boundary maintenance. Solidarism, the classic proletarian strategy, on the contrary, promotes an inclusive interpellation of solidarity as the overriding focus of identity. Inclusion is that strategy used by employers to contain skilled workers with a low liquidity preference within tight internal labour markets. It entails the 'deliberate creation of corporation-specific skills' (Sengenberger, 1978; Kreckel, 1980, p.541) through which internal labour markets may operate:

> Very frequently inclusion occurs as a by-product of capital
> concentration and monopolization; once there is only one
> bidder left in a labour 'market' who is prepared to employ a
> particular occupational qualification, this occupation has been
> successfully encircled and finds its bargaining power reduced
> (Kreckel, 1980, p.541).

Finally, the strongest strategy for employers of workers in jobs in the secondary labour market, is that of exposure. Simply, exposure entails that unskilled workers have no degree of uncoupling from the dictates of the business cycle, but are quite unshielded from its rhythms of supply and demand. Frequently, these workers will also be subject to exclusionary strategies from more skilled, and hence privileged, workers. A number of structural conditions characterize the most exposed workers in the secondary labour market. Work is easily performed by almost any workers – its skills are not at all contingently strategic; it is work which can easily be dropped from production schedules in conditions of failing demand; if demand resumes, then almost any replacement workers could do the jobs and would be available to do so; it is generally performed by workers who, when retrenched, will lack sufficient solidarity with other workers to cause significant disruption; and it is generally not associated with the maintenance of managerial authority. By structuring the organization of employment, management can create segments in which the wages and conditions of employment reflect the peripheral status of such work. Typically, foreign (Castles and Kosack, 1973; Piore, 1979) and women (Barron and Norris, 1976) workers largely dominate unskilled, manual production work. Young workers also constitute an important source of cheap labour crucial to some sections of capital, particularly retailing (Game and Pringle, 1983). Women, immigrants and racial minorities retain their peripheral status largely through a lack of solidarity with them by male, white, indigenous workers and the unions and organizations which represent them (Ward, 1975). In part this will reflect the general prejudices of the particular society (Curthoys and Markus, 1978).

Such status-group formation occurs initially through exclusionary control of the labour process (Berger and Piore, 1980). The locus of control is not wholly the province of an unencumbered management and capital, but will frequently be articulated through exclusivist strategies by other workers. For these workers solidarism appears to exclude, in particular, women, ethnic minorities and blacks, from more privileged primary-sector jobs maintained through the strategies of vertical exclusion and horizontal demarcation. Clearly, one of the easiest ways of doing this is to restrict access to the acquisition of skills to certain privileged groups and simultaneously to exclude certain stigmatized groups. The basis of stigmatization is variable with the range of identities in civil society: in Ulster it might be Catholics; in Israel, Arabs; in West Germany, Turkish *gastarbeiter*; in Britain, West Indians and Asians.

For the moment we will leave to one side the question of women's subordinate participation in the labour process. This is a universal feature of all existing civil society. We will argue that a specific explanation of the general facts of women's subordination may be sought in the social organization of male/female social relationships. The bases of ethnic and religious stigmatization, on

225

the other hand, are highly specific and highly variable.

The confinement of ethnic and other stigmatized groups has been assumed to arise because they have access to a second-best subsistence role as a functional alternative to wage-labour, for instance, in their native land, domestic household or wherever (Offe and Hinrichs, 1977). Blackburn and Mann (1979, p.32) suggest that:

> Collaboration between employers and established workers against newcomers is a normal feature of industrial relations throughout the development of capitalism. In the case of the treatment of foreign labour in Europe, native workers and their trade unions have generally supported the discriminatory legislation. Convinced that 'over-full' employment retards the growth of the economy, they consent to the importing of labour provided that it does not possess full labour rights, that it can be sent back home again if unemployment arises, that it cannot compete on the open labour market.

Secondary labour markets throughout the OECD display one important characteristic. The most exposed workers, women excluded, are ethnically/religiously stigmatized groups formed through negative ascription. As such, they are constituted by a process of exclusion from positions of greater power in the labour process by those who already share control of them. Often this is enshrined in custom and practice through a prolonged period of negotiation with and resistance to management. It will be particularly effective where a group of workers has made itself strategically contingent (Brown, 1973; Rimmer, 1972). Management will ordinarily share the attributes of the privileged group. What identities will be most exposed in which civil society is a question capable only of historical answer.

The question of women is somewhat different, if only because identity as a gendered person is a universal attribute of all members of all civil societies. Not all members may have a consciousness of their otherness as 'black' or 'white' in racially homogeneous civil societies; none may escape the biological basis of their own bodies even while seeking to transform the practices through which their identities as gendered persons are constructed. Chief amongst these practices are those pertaining to the structure of civil society as one of households in which 'limitations are placed on women's employment opportunities and their bargaining power in the labour market is weakened as a result of the division of labour in the household' (Garnsey, 1978, pp.235-6).

Employers mediate between households and the labour market

in the provision of jobs. To the extent that they particularly follow strategies of exposure in doing so, they connect the household division of labour, as it is ideologically defined, with divisions in the labour market. The requirements that workers must satisfy if they are to qualify for and remain in *unexposed* segments of the labour market are the following: long-term, uninterrupted employment; full-time work; and geographic mobility (Garnsey, 1978, p.237). However,

> these are precisely the conditions which the majority of women cannot meet because of the demands of their work in the household and the family. In particular, part-time work is treated as incompatible with enjoyment of the benefits of 'protected' employment; this is in the interests of employers and the majority of union membership (Garnsey, 1978, p.237).

It is in large part for these reasons that women are concentrated in the secondary sector of employment (Martin, 1980) – one principally of smaller, competitive firms with exposed jobs. Such employment structures ensure that wage levels and the level of unionization may be depressed in the economy as a whole (Blackburn and Mann, 1979, p.22). The propensity to join unions is more a function of one's occupational position in the division of labour than of the personal characteristics of job-holders, as Barron and Norris (1976) argue. Women's work roles tend to be concentrated in jobs with high rates of labour turnover and low rates of unionization, because of the reality of employment opportunities.

It is important to draw a distinction between the propensities of jobs and the characteristics of incumbents in those jobs. The unattractiveness of secondary-sector jobs is not the result of their incumbency by workers who are regarded as 'marginal'. Indeed, the contrary is the case. If certain groups are consistently found to occupy peripheral positions, the processes involved require adumbration. We have noted that one of the more frequently observed patterns of discrimination in labour markets concerns the differential nature of men's and women's access to, orientations towards and positions in the labour process (Power, 1975; Lloyd, 1975; Kuhn and Wolpe, 1978; Amsden, 1980).

Employment conditions for women are considerably worse than those for men. Women occupy positions which are typically less skilled as well as being largely excluded from promotion in internal labour markets, and hence tend to be less well paid on average (Barron and Norris, 1976). These circumstances may be the outcome of a complex of processes. Amongst these must be counted the ideological determinations which provide the support for the notion that men are the natural breadwinners and that women's natural place is as a (house)wife and mother. This is despite the reality that women's income is frequently vital to family living standards (Land, 1976) and that, in Britain for instance, around 20 per cent of women workers are the principal wage-earners in their household (Blackburn and Mann, 1979, p.284). The majority of women's employment conditions are scarcely such as to increase their work involvement at the expense of what is said to be their central life interests in the home and family (Brown, 1976, p.37).

Ideology is produced and reinforced by structural factors which militate against the development of institutional means for the provision of adequate childcare arrangements, for example. A further element in this subjugation is the neglect of women's issues by trade unions. In general, not only does the unpaid domestic labour of working-class women contribute to depressing the wages of male workers, it is also used to maintain women in work situations structurally unconducive to economistic or solidaristic struggles (Barron and Norris, 1976). The sexual division of labour is the major basis on which labour markets are segmented. Employers have consistently taken advantage of new technologies in order to 'feminize' deskilled work. The advantages accruing to employers in this process include the formation of a relatively compliant and inexpensive labour force: 'the internal labour market and other defences against insecurity exist on the backs of a secondary labour force . . . and that means largely on the backs of women' (Blackburn and Mann, 1979, p.284).

The reasons why solidaristic strategies are less often encountered amongst workers in the most exposed sectors of the labour market are in part an effect of the jobs themselves. Why have women members of the working class typically not become a repository of a highly solidaristic consciousness as either women or workers? Part of the answer may be found in the somewhat protracted 'domestic-labour debate' concerning whether or not women's household work is productive of the value of labour power (Seccombe, 1974, 1975; Coulson et al., 1975; Gardiner, 1975, 1977; Himmelweit and Mohun, 1977; Adamson et al., 1976; Molyneux, 1979). The outcome of that debate was always clear: domestic labour is socially necessary and functionally vital and hence of considerable significance in the class system (Garnsey, 1978). However, the specificity of women's oppression is not to be found by restrictive analyses which attempt to ascribe 'value' to activites ancillary to the capitalist production process itself. An immense range of both reproductive and non-reproductive activities takes place in households. The unpaid domestic labour performed by women clearly does provide considerable support for productive labour. Alternative means of relating domestic labour, consumption and women's wage-labour, which do not presuppose the household as the natural locale of female workers could be sought. It is to these options that the domestic-labour debate has drawn attention. The specific forms of women's dual participation in aspects of production and reproduction can be demonstrated without recourse to 'value' analysis whose purpose was never to categorize all forms of human labour.

The specificity of women's ambiguous relationship to the paid workforce is demonstrated by Williams's (1981) study of working-class families in an Australian mining town. The isolation of women and the associated primacy according to parenting and personal relations prevents the development of an oppositional milieu for them. This dissipation of protest into personal quarrels is most apparent in non-urban environments. None the less, it can be seen that under certain circumstances the working-class family can 'create the political space for working-class men's opposition to events' at the workplace (1981, p.191). Capitalism and patriarchal hierarchy are intertwined in a way that both deepens the oppression of women and facilitates the reproduction of a politicized, male, labour power.

Class and patriarchal ideologies support diverse forms of social relations in the family. Women are subject to a mass of competing and contradictory pressures, so that, for instance, domestic tasks can be commodified even in the guise of undermining the commodity form. Women are advised by advertisements on US day-time television to keep the family home for breakfast – rather than at a 'fast-food' stop' – by serving branded frozen croissants and pastries. The point is not so much that either way further commodification occurs, but that female resistance to household drudgery is orchestrated through a commodity form, rather than a questioning of 'normal' social relations of household production. On the other hand, there are contrary pressures to expand the commodity form of fast-food breakfasting, and with it female secondary-labour-market employment. This can occur at the same time as reduced state expenditures for secondary-sector employment and activities (health, childcare) are eroding women's work opportunities. The expansion of such opportunities as a result of technological changes to job structures should also be noted. What such changes frequently elicit by way of a response from already organized workers is an intensification of pressures for exclusion (Rubery, 1978). Moreover, 'these pressures alter over the course of major economic cycles, influencing consumption patterns and the structure of the labour market in ways which are to some extent irreversible' (Garnsey, 1978, p.238). Additionally, gender structuration is not simply a feature of 'capitalism' but characterizes other formations such as the state-socialist societies as well.

Discrimination on an ascriptive basis in a democratic society at least allows collective assertion that civil rights be protected. However, even where legislation has been achieved through 'equal pay' acts and so forth, the facts of labour-market segmentation and structurally unequal jobs usually remain (Wolff, 1977; Bruselid, 1980). Moreover, in the most exposed areas of the labour market there are workers for whom civil status cannot be assumed: the substantial number of illegal immigrants in all the advanced capitalist societies. The degree of illegal penetration will depend on the porosity of a state's boundaries – even in Australia there are not insignificant numbers of immigrants defined as 'illegal'. Kreckel (1980, p.543) observes that no open strategies of defence are available to officially criminal workers, whose major advantages will be their willingness to be exploited rather than exposed. The institutionalization of systems of *gastarbeiter* (Berger and Mohr, 1975) is a legal way of creating categories of workers who lack the attributes of citizenship; their main 'asset' is their legal compulsion to exit the state upon cessation of a fixed-term labour contract. In times of downturn, they are a means of initially externalizing unemployment and its associated costs, which would otherwise be borne by the domestic state for its own second-class citizens, as occurred in the early stages of the post-1974 recession in West Germany.

Strongest amongst working-class participants in the labour market are those who are resistant to both inclusion in internal labour markets as well as exposure to the economic climate. These are workers who possess 'general occupational qualifications' (Sengenberger, 1975), for whom several types of submarket may be identified (Kreckel, 1980). The strength of these workers is in their ability to substitute employers (at propitious moments of the economic cycle). They are not dependent on just one unit of capital despite their general dependence on capital as a whole. At its strongest this strategy is that of the new middle class – the academically, managerially and professionally qualified workers who were discussed in the previous chapter (see also Crompton and Jones, 1982). Beneath these positions are those workers whose skill capacity is expressed in general occupational qualifications which are both fully marketable and in demand. In such cases, 'the "exclusiveness" of a particular occupational skill may be turned into a bargaining asset' (Kreckel, 1980, p.544). However, where it has been, these workers may be subject to tendencies of occupational restructuring. Restructuring usually entails a dialectically linked process of deskilling, dequalification or devaluing of some aspects of existing jobs; with upgrading, hyper-qualification, or revaluing of others (Penn, 1982). Where this occurs, devalued general occupational qualifications become liable to strategies of inclusion by employers, as the market position of a particular skill is eroded. Where revaluation occurs, the basis for the formation of an 'independent' primary-market position occurs.

The revaluation and devaluation of general occupational qualifications thus have links with broader social processes. In particular, we must focus on the relationship between civil spheres of social reproduction and the labour process, whereby specific market situations and relations of domination are constructed as part of the normal reality of working-class life.

The organization of consciousness

In the past it may have been possible to engage in successful struggle at the point of production when middle-level line management had the authority to make concessions to workers with respect to conditions. However, senior management, in whom overall control is increasingly vested via centralized accounting and organizational control structures, is hence able to move the parameters of conflict to areas external to the competence of individual unions. As Hyman (1975, p.106) notes, transnational corporations can and do readily manipulate their internal accounting processes so as to disguise the profitability of any particular national operation, thus seriously inhibiting the formulation of union strategies. Decisions on the location of production, new investment and plant closures and redundancies are likely to be formulated on political and economic bases which lie wholly outside the territorial boundaries within which the relevant trade unions operate (Baldry et al., 1981).

It has been argued by Cressey and MacInnes (1982) that a growing awareness exists amongst trade unions of an expanding area of industrial activity outside of the ambit of collective bargaining. 'Issues such as investment, location, products development and pricing policy, which are the key determinants of the prospects in the longer term for workers' income levels and employment opportunities . . . are not included in the items for traditional collective bargaining' (1982, p.278). This situation is exacerbated by the tendency for 'strong, well developed union workplace organization' to be matched against multidivisional management structures within complex multi-company enterprises.

Capital has developed the organisational basis to emancipate aspects of its decision-making from market processes to a far greater extent than labour. The 'organizational base' is the modern heterogeneous multi-national enterprise which, although it is ultimately dependent on market pressures to accumulate capital and grow, can take strategic decisions about its 'internal' operations which do not depend on the market position of individual plants or divisions. . . . Enterprises can contain labour resistance as long as it is confined to the individual plant, because it is no longer likely to be dependent on any particular plant to be able to keep running profitably. In contrast, it is very difficult for trade union or unofficial organisations to spread beyond the individual plant (Cressey and MacInnes, 1982, p.289).

The difficulty for collective bargaining in raising decision areas outside of the ambit of the individual plant, on the one hand, or national labour markets on the other, must lead to a strengthening of the freedom of transnationally based enterprises to implement planning and control strategies which considerably weaken the basis of resistance at a particular point of production in particular states, as Baldry *et al.* (1981) have argued with respect to Massey-Ferguson and its Scottish operations.

It can be seen that market processes are such as to give only very limited control either to workers or to most individual capitalists. For the working class in general and for unqualified manual workers in particular, the market may best be characterized in terms of its uncertainty. The possibilities for any significant choice in the determination of economic status are so narrow for most workers as to be insignificant. Support for this argument is provided by data from Blackburn's and Mann's (1979) study which shows that the division of tasks associated with organizational hierarchies has little basis in the functional skill or technical requirements of production. Their examination of the intrinsic quality of jobs revealed that 'complex technical skills are rarely encountered among manual workers except at the top of the internal labour market and among qualified craftsmen' (1979, p.292) and, further, that even though job skills differed in accordance with various positions in the internal market, 'the *absolute* level of skill of all but the very highest jobs is . . . minimal' (1979, p.280). They estimated that 87 per cent of the manual workers in their study exercised less skill at work than they would in driving to work and that 95 per cent of jobs could be done by 85 per cent of workers. To accept these sobering conclusions is to realize that despite segmentation, nearly all manual workers make up a relatively homogeneous pool of interchangeable labour power in terms of skill requirements. What is crucial in differentiating them are structures of compliance arranged through internal labour markets. This would also provide significant support for the view which was advanced by Braverman (1974) of a 'degraded' or deskilled proletariat.

It is the structure of the labour market itself which provides the most formidable constraint to working-class action. First, the parameters of rational choice within the external labour market are so restricted that, objectively, there is little choice at all. Secondly, the major source of systematic structure in the availability of economic rewards results from the internal labour market and it is in this sphere that the least degree of control accrues to workers. Despite the existence of these structural impediments to the fulfilment of collective interests, a number of recent studies have been unanimous in their findings that the constraint of the market is not felt as such by workers. As Blackburn and Mann (1979) argue, workers 'have internalized the constraint and identify it as reality itself.' Other writers have made substantially similar points (e.g. Mann, 1973a; Willis, 1977; Nichols and Beynon, 1977; Pfeffer, 1979). There is thus a widespread acceptance of their disadvantaged market situation by unskilled manual workers which accords with the reality of their lives in the workplace and in the labour market.

Many of these occupational disadvantages and the acceptance of them are filtered by workers' perceptions of what is possible. Such perceptions, products of the social division of labour, become job-allocation mechanisms and are therefore crucial to the creation of interests and the formation of alliances (see Gagliani, 1981). Barriers to entry into particular occupations, including barriers derived from these informal processes of perception, exist and have become entrenched in all societies. In capitalist democracies where the use of coercive methods is generally deemed to be inappropriate, responsibility for most of the sifting process accrues to the education system. What emerges is that jobs with few formal educational requirements are disproportionately allocated to job-seekers from working-class families. Income differentials which lead to both qualitatively and quantitatively less education for low-income families are generally reinforced through artificially raised educational requirements for particular work. The actual skill and educational levels required for the performance of most occupational positions is scarcely reflected in the formal qualifications required of new applicants (Berg, 1973; Kumar, 1977). Further structural impediments noted by Bowles (1972) include tendencies for educational provision to be distributed unevenly on a regional basis with a clustering of better facilities in the areas favoured by already privileged groups. Finally, barriers to job allocation can be erected outside of the educational system, on quite intangible but explicit criteria of civil society (see Silverman and Jones, 1976). Salaman (1979, pp. 187-8) thus concludes from his study of selection processes in the British Army and Ford that

> despite the apparently rigorous and systematic nature of organisational selection procedures, the really salient qualities derive not from neutral process of job study, but from a desire to pick recruits with the 'proper', responsible attitudes and appropriate values. . . . These qualities are themselves culturally based and determined. And their interpretative use by the selecting officers shows how they can be employed to isolate and reward cultural qualities.

In most capitalist societies, all of the processes we have described are applied simultaneously and reinforce each other. These mechanisms illustrate the complementarity of political, economic and civil structuration. The principle of rewarding achievement ensures that responsibility for the unequal outcomes of education provision lies outside of the realm of values and reflects on the cultural or class predispositions of the proletariat (Bowles, 1972). The thrust of a number of studies of the perceptions and attitudes of working-class youth clearly points to the conclusion that such phenomena are a product of sexual, ethnic and class forces in educational provision and family structure, which are reproduced in working-class culture (Bowles and Gintis, 1976; Bourdieu, 1974; Karier, 1973). The significance of these conclusions lies not only in the insight they provide into the reproduction of the social division of labour, but also into the possibility of working-class struggle. There has been a marked tendency in the development of occupational structures in most capitalist labour markets for a simultaneous increase in both the upper and lower levels of non-manual working-class positions (Heath, 1981). In Gagliani's view (1981) this has permitted some upward mobility for certain categories of formerly manual workers as well as a significant increase in the labour-force participation of women. Both of these groups of workers are channelled through educational and other forms of discrimination into lower-level, non-manual positions in which there is a clear demarcation (in terms of pay and conditions) from manual workers. Thus, for non-manual workers who have experienced these processes as upward mobility there is a fundamental incentive to support the existing system and to ally themselves politically with it. 'The incentive is given by the opportunity to preserve the existing, biased, social division of labour which guarantees most non-manual workers a more-than-compensating wage' (Gagliani, 1981). The development of a working-class political alliance of manual and non-manual groups is thus inhibited by the material barriers which develop out of the social division of labour.

Power relationships dominate work settings; however, these rarely emerge at the level of conscious action, because, in these settings, power is to a large extent embedded rather than explicit. 'People experience a natural order of existence which they have grown up to accept and which therefore does not appear to involve power at all' (Sharp, 1969, p.1). Part of that natural order of existence is the appearance that workers who sell their labour power on a 'free market' are themselves expressing a freedom of choice which makes their bargain with employers seem a fair one: 'If you don't like it you can go somewhere else.' As all critics of the formal freedoms of liberalism emphasize, for unskilled manual workers such 'freedom of choice' is illusory. Yet many workers see themselves as failures, so that workers' own judgments begin to deny the importance of broader social relationships (Nichols and Beynon, 1977). The Nichols and Beynon study shows that workers try to make sense of their situation: they live from day to day; they construct reasonably co-herent pasts and futures; and they maintain respect for themselves. Where a collective political strategy is ill-developed they are thrown back upon readily accessible individualistic explanations of personal inadequacy, with which they cope by 'making out' in work constructed as a series of implicit 'games'. While treating some aspects of work like a game makes it more bearable for individual workers, at the same time taking part in something conceived as a game 'generates consent with respect to its rules'. Consent is manufactured in and through work with which individual workers make bearable the terms under which they are obliged to sell and exercise their labour power. By recasting what they can into a ritualized, game-like sense of episodes, of work and resistance, workers distance themselves from the objective conditions of work. This created 'space' then serves to reproduce such conditions, as Burawoy (1979, p.81) has argued.

The complex articulation of meanings uncovered by ethno-graphic studies suggests a cohesive link between a set of broadly held ideological assumptions and their referents in everyday aspects of work and its organization. The articulations are thus the result of social processes in the wider civil society where people talk together, comprehend vocabularies, make assertions and 'understand' each other. The degree of politicization of the 'nature' of civil society and its articulation through the state and economy will vary between different groups, different work settings and different points in time. Where it operates most effectively is in 'defining' for members of work organizations what is possible or impossible, inevitable or challengeable, in their economic and political situation. The normalcy of civil society is pervasive. This is nowhere more clearly indicated than in the comments of workers studied by Willis, who concludes:

> Although inequalities are often seen, exploitation recognised, and injustices and contradictions experienced every day, none of these things seems to point in the same direction. They do not have a common cause. If some exploit and some are exploited, if some are equal and others unequal this does not happen with the systematisation of classes. . . . A quite marked degree of disenchantment with the prevailing system and a degree of knowledge of exploitation, coupled with culturally mediated (though distorted) and partially lived out penetrations of the capitalist system, can co-exist with a calm acceptance of the system and belief that there is no systematic suppression of personal chances in life. Suppression is recognized, but as no more than a random part of the human condition. Human nature, not capitalism, is the trap. Ideology has helped to produce that – though not simply from its own resources; it is believed, because it is partly self-made. (1977, p.165).

What these studies show is that power will be revealed much less in positive acts of decision-making involving conflict and choice over alternative policies, than in everyday application of those assumptions which give priority to private capital accumulation and market exchange in the use and distribution of resources. Phenomenologically, this is mediated through categories of an abstracted individualism and routine experience; thus, as Westergaard and Resler (1976, p.424) note, 'power is to be found more in uneventful routine than in conscious and active exercise of will.' The social relations and routines which are generally taken for granted in this way are those of private property and the market. Thus it is perfectly 'normal' that profit should be the yardstick of investment in most areas of activity and that the economic well-being of the propertyless majority should be set primarily by the terms on which they may be able to sell their labour power.

The extent of the ideological nature of decisions and events within work organizations is frequently mystified, disguised and denied. Organizations and the technology they employ are frequently proposed as inevitable, neutral and rational phenomena, yet behind this façade exists an over-arching ideology expressed in terms of 'rationality'. In such usage, rationality may be used interchangeably with what is reasonable. However, this is to conceal the significance of Weber's distinction between formal rationality and substantive rationality. Substantive rationality applies certain criteria of ultimate ends to the calculation of economic action as distinct from the formal translation of such actions into numerically calculable terms (Weber, 1968, pp.85-6). Thus the assimilation of a *seemingly* apolitical instrumental logic with a formal rationality is a process which is profoundly political. Decisions which are inherently political – that is, concerned with interests and values – come to be seen as technical matters in which participation is limited to those whose interest or expertise is so designated. Social order and control within organizations can more easily be maintained if issues can be reduced to purely formal terms. It is formal rationality that is epitomized in the specialized roles and technical rules that constitute a bureaucratic structure of organization (Clegg and Dunkerley, 1980). Differences over what Weber terms the outcome and the spirit of the organization are minimized in the premises of decision-making: 'These premises are to be found in the "vocabulary" of the organisation, the structure of communication, rules and regulations and standard programs, selection criteria for personnel, and so on – in short, in the structural aspects' (Perrow, 1979, p.149).

The labour process and structures of control

One of the major strengths of Marxian and radical Weberian approaches to organizations which have been adumbrated elsewhere (Clegg and Dunkerley, 1980) is that they highlight the irremediable politics of organizational structure. In these 'radical' accounts, the design of work, the adjustment of the production process to accommodate new technologies and the structure of organization, are viewed as the end result of deliberate interventions. (Burrell and Morgan, 1979, summarize 'radical' approaches.) Marglin (1974), for instance, has attempted to demonstrate that the destruction and fragmentation of skilled craftwork dating from pre-industrial times had little to do with the technological superiority of large-scale machinery. 'The key to success of the factory, as well as its aspiration, was the substitution of capitalists' for workers' control of the production process' (1974, p.46). The most notable recent contribution to the sociological study of the labour process is that of Braverman whose *Labour and Monopoly Capital* (1974) initiated a major reformulation of theories of control in the study of organizations.

Braverman, following Marx, set forth a detailed exposition of the realization of capitalist control over the labour process. This account argued that scientific management provided the vehicle for effecting the progressive investment of decision-making powers in the hands of capitalists and the removal of control from workers. The management techniques elaborated in the systems of Taylor, Ford and others constitute the extension of capitalist relations to all levels of work organizations. These techniques were employed by the development of elaborate systems of stratification creating strictly demarcated hierarchies; the formulation of specific methods of wage payment, in particular piece-work rates and incentive payments; and the extended fragmentation and deskilling of the workforce through an elaborate division of labour and the creation of intermediate management functions. For Taylor the purpose of scientific-management intervention,

> both in order to ensure management control and to cheapen the worker, [required that] conception and execution must be rendered separate spheres of work, and for this purpose the study of work processes must be reserved to management and kept from workers, to whom its results are communicated only in the form of simplified job tasks governed by simplified instructions which it is thenceforth their duty to follow unthinkingly (Braverman, 1974, p.118).

Once skill or knowledge is thus removed from the control of workers and placed in the hands of 'management', whose task it is to plan and control the work process, there are significant advantages which accrue to capital. Labour is cheapened and made more easily transferable as aspects of planning and design of work are themselves now infused with managerial control and removed from labour. According to Braverman, skills formerly exercised by workers are absorbed not only by management but also by modern technological systems and the work arrangements upon which they are predicated. The significance of locating technology in this context is that it provides a clear mechanism for the extension of direct-control strategies under the guise of rationalization and technological progress (Cummings and Greenbaum, 1978). Braverman's thesis is that the logic of capitalist intervention into the labour process has focused on the differentiation of once unified functions of conception and execution. This now constitutes the major locus of differentiation in contemporary industry (Salaman, 1981). Finally, it is argued that the nature of these developments has been determined by conscious strategies of the contending classes:

> The bureaucratic reorganization of the labour process developed, then, not through some technological imperative but through a historically specific process of class struggle which was understood and articulated as such by the contending parties (Clawson, 1980, p.255).

A measure of the impact of *Labor and Monopoly Capital* is the critical debate which has surrounded its findings (e.g. Wood, 1982). Three major elements of this debate are important to the themes we have been developing and require elaboration. The comments which follow show that each of the critiques of Braverman has a similar focus.

The first point is that the labour process is but one of a number of avenues through which influence and control are brought to bear on workers. Such control often appears redundant. It has been proposed by Hyman and Brough that

> the manifest absence of socially available justifications for uncompromisingly oppositional behaviour by workers – which would be dismissed as 'sheer bloody-mindedness' and hence irrational – is clearly an inhibiting factor against uncompromising resistance to managerial priorities in the course of the negotiation of order at workplace level (1975, p.207).

As we have suggested earlier, educational institutions, the family and the media of communication and socialization are scarcely likely to utilize a vocabulary of motives which could provide unskilled workers with a legitimate and plausible rationale for that resistance to managerial prerogatives which, in its rituals and rules, provides much of the sense of locale which is work (Burawoy, 1979). What is political is not experienced as political, but as simply the games people play to make work bearable. Those ethnographic studies which we addressed earlier suggest that it is more than likely that labour enters the workplace prepared to co-operate and contribute to a degree conventionally regarded as appropriate. Clearly, such conventions do not impact passively on working-class groups but are negotiated and modified in the light of objective conditions and experiences. Nevertheless, it seems likely that the forms of control of the labour process connnect with non-work experiences which reflect the valuations imposed by the distribution of economic and political power in the wider society. Thus, to emphasize control in the labour process is to obfuscate other structural forces whose impact may be overriding.

The second concern surrounding Braverman's analysis derives from the relative lack of emphasis on the consequences of working-class consciousness and resistance. This has led to the recognition that the development of a clear-cut relationship between capitalist production methods and the skill structure of the workforce is significantly constrained by worker resistance. While there may have been a general trend towards deskilling, the difficulty which Braverman's unidirectional thesis encounters is that when the fact of worker resistance is admitted, the theorization of class relations is thrown into disarray. The design of work involves a critical interaction of structures of management control, employee resistance and subsequent adjustments and counter-pressures which management attempts to employ (Littler, 1980, 1982; Friedman, 1977). There are two issues which flow from this contention. One is that Braverman's analysis proposes a mechanistic notion of a capitalist class whose degree of intersubjectivity is such as to determine a unitary capital-logic (Zimbalist, 1979; Aronowitz, 1978). The second point is that the actual levels of skill or technical knowledge employed by the worker in any particular location may be less relevant to employers' needs to control the labour process and to enhance the conditions for accumulation than the extent to which the workers have or have not 'been accepted as skilled within the politics of the workplace' (Lee, 1981, p.58). Clearly, the specific conditions circumscribing the actions of both labour and capital within the workplace affect the degree of intervention possible (Elger, 1979). This highlights the essential variability of the outcomes of worker resistance. 'Some changes are resisted more than others, some groups resist more than others, some groups achieve a "negotiated order", whilst some groups become a privileged elite' (Littler and Salaman, 1982, p.256). In this process both jobs and workers acquire certain social statuses to which accrue expectations and regulations concerning rates of pay and conditions (Lee, 1981). These differentials are not only intraorganizational (Clegg, 1981), but also become interorganizational and regionally specific in the worldwide division of labour, and hence, not specific to the politics of a particular labour process.

The third issue which has been raised with respect to Braverman's work concerns the complexity and variety of influences on the structure of employment. The development of mechanisms at the level of the workplace constitutes only one of a complex and interacting set of factors shaping the workforce. Included among these factors are changes in levels of national and international economic activity reflected in levels of employ- ment, interregional changes in the distribution of economic growth or the availability of political subsidies, development of new markets, changes in tax structures and the growth of new industries and products (Lee, 1981, p.59). Equally important to employers are alternative income sources external to the production process. Factors such as commodity and currency speculation, money market transactions and credit manipulation have important consequences for the development of economic activity. Thus, accumulation may have more important origins in mechanisms in the sphere of circulation than in the labour process (Littler and Salaman, 1982). As we have noted in our discussion of the middle class, the 'realization' issues will in many instances exercise the attention of capital rather more than production itself. For many capitalists, control over the labour process may become only one of a number of sources of accumulation. Clearly, the calculations of the controllers of capitalist industrial enterprises are not solely governed by the requisites of production. Indeed, where workplace relations have assumed a 'negotiated order' and where the expression of industrial conflict has been routinized through structural and procedural mechanisms, employers will be placed in a situation allowing them to devote a considerable proportion of their energies to concerns other than production.

Reservation is clearly in order concerning Braverman's con- centration on the notion of an 'imperative of control'. Such an imperative is not sufficiently located in patterns of economic activity and the interrelated changes in economic and political factors at the level of national economies (Cutler, 1978). In order effectively to incorporate an account of these factors, analysis is required of the manner in which the organization of the labour process and the design of work relate to exigencies and contradictory features of accumulation strategies in particular historical conjunctures. It has been argued in this context that the contemporary forms of the capitalist mode of production are a complex mediation by diverse organizations of state and enter- prises to cyclical, social–historical forces that are themselves interdependent with the process of accumulation. There is, for example, an argument which suggests that cyclical factors surrounding crises in accumulation in the 1930s and again in the 1970s created the circumstances in which large numbers of workers were effectively deskilled (Boreham and Dow, 1980;

Lee, 1981). In this analysis it is the articulation of technological innovation and accumulation, and particularly the cycle of fixed-capital renewal, that must provide the focus of analysis of contemporary changes in the mode of production. These changes may, once in motion, generate dislocation and crises which activate the search for alternative strategies for valorization and accumulation. The orientation and 'success' of capitalist strategies to redress the outcomes of such crises must be viewed as contingent upon the response of working-class organizations and their political practice (Boreham, 1980). However, as Rutigliano (1977) has pointed out, almost all that labour has sought to do is defensively to oppose some of the grosser exploitative features of the reorganization of work. These may be adopted because the modes of political action which seem to be available or appropriate are structured not only by historical and immediate material conditions, and by the formal nature of trade union organization and action, but also by the historical and contemporary bonds between workers' organizations and labour parties. The structural limitations of a trade unionism which is confined to the role of permanent opposition permit the bargaining of conditions and rewards within work organizations but restrict the occasions for any direct promotion of macro-level social and economic change.

The processes characterized by Braverman and others as deskilling (Baxandall *et al.*, 1976; Zimbalist, 1979; Clawson, 1980; Burawoy, 1978, 1979) impact on the labour force in a manner which is not only uneven in its general application to production because automation is deployed unevenly across branches of industry, but also because it is specific in its location in particular sectors of industry. The postwar valorization and accumulation strategies of capital have influenced the formation not of a deskilled proletariat of unskilled manual labour, but semi-skilled workers 'embodying a limited heterogeneity of forms of training and experience' (Elger, 1979, p.87). In this context, workers' struggles over specific workplace practices (in areas such as staffing levels and deployment of work groups) have acquired certain advantages ranging from their command over the training and 'seniority' requirements associated with particular jobs to the vulnerability of highly integrated and automated 'flow' production to disruption by industrial action on the part of a small number of workers. Of course, the shopfloor level does not constitute the only terrain on which the battles between capital and labour are fought. Equally, by focusing narrowly on the process of capital accumulation we cannot account for the *structure* of the working class in contemporary capitalism. Such a structure is never more than emergent in the alliances and struggles between groups. Braverman has correctly shown that the reorganization of work promoted the conditions for a fundamental ideological division between mental and manual labour (Sohn-Rethel, 1978; Stark, 1980). But there is no direct correspondence between the social division of labour and class structuration. The creation of occupational groups broadly representative of mental labour within industrial production, and also the state bureaucracies, has made redundant former strategies of class struggle based on industrial confrontation and has gradually shifted the emphasis to struggles and alliances at the national political level.

One of the underlying problems which has inhibited analysis and debate surrounding labour strategies at the political level is the inadequate theorization of control in analyses of the labour process. Capitalists have been vested with qualities which imply a 'logic of control' as an end in itself. However, direct control of labour power is necessary only to the extent that the absence of such control inhibits accumulation. Clearly, an important first step is to provide a more complex typification of forms of control as well as to link these forms to tendencies and crises in accumulation. Recently, a number of writers have focused on the organization of the labour process as a totality which is a *structure-in-process*. Regarded thus, the way is clear for a delimitation of types of control, linked to stages in the development of accumulation, whose motive force can be explained as the articulation of contradiction generated by each stage of development.

The idea of types of control which do not necessarily correspond to a uni-directional evolution of deskilling is offered by Edwards (1978) in an argument which parallels Friedman (1977). He begins by criticizing Braverman's weaknesses, while acknowledging the strengths of the analysis. Edwards's (1978, p.110) major criticism is that 'Braverman has left class conflict out of his analysis of the labour process.' The analysis reinstates class conflict, by focusing on the development of discrete systems of control. Control of the labour process embodies three elements: the direction of work tasks; the evaluation of the work done; and the rewarding and disciplining of workers (Edwards, 1978, p.112).

Three 'historically important and essentially quite different ways of organising these three elements' are identified. First, there is 'simple control', which is direct, open and interpersonal. This simple control seems to correspond more or less to Simon's (1952) notion of direct, extensive formal control (Offe, 1976;

Clegg, 1979, p.118). Second is 'technical control', where 'the control mechanism is embedded in the physical technology of the firm.' Third is 'bureaucratic control' where 'control becomes embedded in the social organization of the enterprise, in the contrived social relations of production at the point of production.' The key feature of this social organization is the widespread acceptance and use of Weber's (1968) formally rational ideal type of legal rational bureaucracy. The latter two types of control are 'structural'.

The argument is that the transition from simple control to either technical or bureaucratic control developed from employers' efforts to control conflict in the production areas of firms in the former case, and in the area of administrative functions in the latter. One cannot make such a simple identification today, because of 'the incompleteness of technical control and the increasingly factory character of administrative work' (Edwards, 1978, p.112). Additionally, it is not only the employers, but also the unions who staff and manage the contemporary forms of bureaucratic control.

In Edwards's argument, technical control is embedded in the organization of production 'based on a technology that paces and directs the labour process' (1979, p.113). Production arrangements embodied in technical control contribute a further impetus to the homogenization process leading to a workforce dominated by unskilled and semi-skilled machine operatives. While this does not differ greatly from Braverman's account, alternative conclusions are suggested. Such homogenizing forms of control carry within them the seeds of organized, united resistance – a resistance fostered by reliance on highly integrated technological production which is susceptible to disruption. Such forms of control therefore find their most effective application in non-unionized, peripheral workforces in which workers know that they may easily be replaced.

The second form of control both evolved from and reflected the 'managerial revolution' which overtook the modern corporation by the 1940s. Edwards argues that management viewed 'bureaucratic control' as a basis for labour–management relations that by-passed the forms of collective negotiation with unions which were in many ways a product of technical control. Bureaucratic control led to the routinization of management itself, enabling the management process to operate without conscious intervention by capitalists. Power relations emanate from the structure of formal organizations and the need formally to exercise authority is therefore minimized. As Edwards puts it: 'control is embedded in the social and organisational structure of the firm and is built into job categories, work rules, promotion procedures, discipline, wage scales, definition of responsibilities and the like' (1979, p.131). An important corollary of bureaucratic forms of control is that certain structural requisites established in order to draw on and enhance workers' dependency and loyalty to the corporation significantly reduce employer flexibility in the labour market. Job security and advancement procedures, whilst destructive of collective solidarity nevertheless serve to some extent to protect workers from displacement. The result is that labour costs are shifted from a variable to a 'fixed' basis. Workers who would formerly have been dispensable during periods of economic downturn now have some guarantees of tenure, the costs of which assume an increasing importance to capitalists in their decisions to invest in new equipment requiring additional 'fixed' labour costs.

An intense form of bureaucratic control is exemplified in Japanese corporate arrangements which embrace workers in a system which equates career and organization (Littler, 1980). This system is paralleled by recruitment practices which ensure that opportunities for advancement other than through commitment to a single corporation are severely limited. More importantly, the lack of portability of employee benefits and welfare schemes in Japanese corporations relies on the inadequacy of public welfare arrangements in order to achieve the full effect of increasing dependency (Littler and Salaman, 1982, pp.261-3). It is scarcely surprising in these circumstances that the development of welfare state arrangements has met consistent opposition from Japanese employers (Crawkour, 1978).

The rigidity which bureaucratic control lends to the employment of labour has encouraged capitalist enterprises to develop alternative strategies to re-establish an element of flexibility within their production arrangements. First, as we described earlier in our account of labour markets, bureaucratic control strategies have largely been applied to the activities of core or strategically contingent members of the workforce. Discontinuities in internal labour markets ensure that for a majority of workers in peripheral, lower-level positions, technical control and homogenization of work is the preferred strategy. Firms will also generally hive off large segments of production entirely through sub-contracting, thus allowing considerable flexibility through their option to discontinue contracts in times of recession. A further element of flexibility derives from the practice of locating production in developing countries – especially within so-called 'free trade zones' – where workers are unlikely to be protected from dismissal or other forms of industrial exploitation through labour regulation or social legislation.

These examples indicate that it is not entirely correct to suggest that bureaucratic control is either replacing technical control or is not subject to reversal. It is none the less true that the elaboration of formal, legally sanctioned rights and responsibilities surrounding employment has impelled industrial conflict into a broader political arena. Structural mechanisms designed to socialize some of the costs of employment provisions – such as workers' compensation arrangements, superannuation legislation and nationalized health schemes – allow employers' reproduction costs to be met out of public expenditure. However, because these are now matters for the public agenda they provide for the intrusion into industrial conflict of a wider class politics.

It is clear that there is a developmental logic at work in Edwards's analysis when he observes that developments within the firm reflected and interacted with a broader reorganization. This was the development of monopoly capitalism responding to the 'driving force' of capital accumulation. Indeed, he argues that 'each form of control corresponds to a definite stage in the development of the "representative" or most important firms, and so the systems of control correspond to or characterize stages of capitalism' (1978, p.112). The development of these systems of control has been one of uneven articulation across different sectors of the economy.

Edwards's analysis, while insightful, retains some lacunae. Most significantly, it does not contain an adequate theorization of the organization as a complex unity of distinct types of control. It neglects the critical relations within the working class between forms of control and labour-market structuration (Penn, 1982, p.102). It simply identifies the three types in a developmental logic. Furthermore, although Edwards offers a distinction between the monopoly and competitive sectors of a modern economy, this is hardly adequate as a realistic sectorization, largely because of the absence of a consideration of the role of the state.

Aglietta's (1979) work, on the other hand, attempts to integrate the type of concrete history which Edwards mentions with a more rigorous analysis of the laws of motion of the capitalist accumulation process which underlie the changes in control. This leads to the idea of the labour process conceived as a complex unity which is a 'structure in motion'. Aglietta's key concepts are the changing regulation of structural forms, with changes in regulation conditioned by crises, which as Davis (1978, p.212) argues, are 'creative ruptures in the continuity of the reproduction of social relations which lead to their restructuring in new forms.' Structural forms, such as organizations, are complex social relations which are, amongst other things, historical products of the class struggle and changing cycles of capital accumulation. Recognition of this leads to a periodic succession of intraorganizational regimes constructed as if to correspond with the averaged succession of Kondratief 'long waves' (Davis, 1978, p.259; Mandel, 1975; Barr, 1979). Major changes in the organization of the labour process thus undergo an historically rational evolution. They emerge as a response by dominant agents within organizations to changed conditions of accumulation. In order to try to reconstruct more profitable conditions, reorganization takes place. New underlying principles of organization are tried, widely adopted and become the rule for particular aspects of particular labour processes. Such rules are not randomly distributed in their genesis and adoption but are conditioned by fundamental movements in phases of capitalist accumulation.

Organizations are complex structures-in-motion. Their essence is control. Differential controls apply to people involved at different levels of the social relations of production. The major variable conditioning the general historical determination of these controls is the effect of cyclical and general changes in accumulation as they are mediated by the calculations of organizationally dominant members, the intraorganizational elite representative of the corporate ruling class. Cressey and MacInnes (1982) argue, in similar terms, that a structure of control exists in which there occurs a hierarchy of planning decisions and production activities. Within this hierarchy, capital increasingly dominates certain strategically important decision-making areas, as well as providing the structural framework through which these decisions are translated into the technical forms of production. What is being suggested here is that there are important constraints placed on alternative strategies which focus exclusively on particular segments of control over production. As Cressey and MacInnes put it, 'unless the character of the forces of production are challenged within capitalism it is difficult to see how social relations of production can be meaningfully changed by a revolution in the superstructure of the relations of distribution, or indeed what such a revolution would consist of' (1982, p.290).

Industrial struggles over control of the labour process are not sufficient. The material realization of alternative forms of production is possible only within the ambit of a broader political and ideological struggle within civil society and the state. Ultimately, we would argue that this will involve the development of changed political and social relations of the state. The conclusion towards which our analysis of the labour process leads must be that to focus too rigidly on the labour process not only limits our attention to only part of the arena for struggle, but also neglects the synchronization of production and phases of accumulation and valorization with class relations beyond production. We must also consider the necessity for analysis to apprehend contingent questions about class structuration in specific national formations. Deskilling, for instance, has not necessarily led to a correlative change in the technical, strategic and social capacity of craft labour to resist the incursion of forces which might erode its economic status. So, not only is the relationship between the logic of accumulation and transformations of the labour process multidimensional and indirect, but so too are the linkages between changes in the labour process and the identification of class interests.

We have argued that a great deal of recent theoretical work on the labour process has adopted an explicitly mechanistic and one-dimensional conception of capitalist control in which little space is reserved for any active role on the part of labour in influencing either the technical or social conditions of production. Moreover, 'labour' remains an undifferentiated category. We have also suggested that these accounts lead to an under-emphasis of the political and ideological forces which also determine the structure and direction of production. What is needed is more than a reassertion in the labour process perspective of worker reaction and resistance. One of the salutary effects of the important work on dual and segmented labour markets which we described earlier is that it draws our attention to the qualitatively different employment practices which exist both within and between labour markets. Consequently, we are sceptical that there can be a theory which purports to explain 'the capitalist labour process'. Recurrent problems of control over production have their origins in the political and economic forces which lie behind historical cycles or crises in production and it is an understanding of these forces that must inform work on labour processes, together with national and sectoral accounts of the broader forces which set the context of production.

An adequate theorization of capitalist production will emerge only within an analysis of the full ambit of capitalist accumulation. This will entail locating the exploitation and appropriation of surplus in the labour process in relation to the differentiated structure of labour markets, as well as in relation to realization of profit. The key to understanding the organization of production lies in an analysis of phases of accumulation and their articulation within class relations beyond production, but framed at the point of production in the struggles over wages and profits. Furthermore, we have argued that labour-process theories have been weakened through their insistence on a uni-dimensional notion of control, identified solely with capitalist prerogatives.

Class, industrial conflict and party

Perhaps no single point has been reiterated more emphatically in the debates on the labour-process perspective than the importance of studying resistance to organizational controls. Resistance can take many forms – from rule-breaking, slowdowns and working to rule, to more explicit forms of sabotage and collective action. The most explicit collective action, of course, is the strike, defined as a temporary stoppage of work by a group of employees who withdraw their labour in order to express a grievance or enforce a demand (Griffin, 1939). From a labour-process perspective, strikes as a collective form of action and resistance are regarded as a sign of working-class power. We will argue a contrary case.

Our interpretation suggests that shopfloor power is real enough but less potent than other strategies that may be open to a labour movement, when viewed in a comparative perspective. Compared thus, we would suggest, that in the aggregate a high level of strikes is not a necessary or sufficient index of shopfloor power.

The general framework of analysis that we have proposed in this book presupposes that the social relations which embrace people in production are the fundamental starting-point for an analysis of the structure of society. The basic cleavage in this structure is between those who own the means of production and buy labour power, and those who do not possess means of production and can sell only their labour power on the market. With their labour power they necessarily sell their own time and their disposition over it. Once an employment contract is entered into, the buyer of labour power enjoys both the legal and the actual subordination of the seller.

We should not treat this exchange as if it were simply between individual buyers and sellers of labour power. Outside of certain simplistic conceptions of what markets ought ideally to be like, an optimal balance of power between a small number of individuals possessing the labour power of a vast number of other people, rarely pertains. If it did, the distribution of power resources would be overwhelmingly in the buyers', rather than the sellers', favour.

Collective action changes the picture. In the next chapter we will consider the opposing power of collectively organized labour and capital and will propose that the balance lies, in the abstract, with capital rather than labour, because of the much greater salience and heterogeneity of civil society and its attributes in the lived experience of labour, as opposed to capital. However, this is an abstract model; it does not refer to particular organizations of labour and capital, but simply to a general model. What it demonstrates is that the class principle is not a necessary basis for collective action – civil society, in particular formations, might occlude it, while certain state formations and governing parties might seek to repress it. As we note in the next chapter, the most propitious circumstances in which the class principle might flourish would be those of civil equality in both a formal and substantive sense and democratic equality in terms of suffrage. The former prepares the ground for industrial organization, while the latter prepares the ground for political organization. Additional aspects of social organization would include

> a high level of union organization, industrial rather than craft unionism, co-operation between blue-collar and white-collar unions, a strong union central authority which co-ordinates the actions of different unions, and close co-operation between this central confederation and a party that clearly dominates on the left (Korpi and Shalev, 1980, p.307).

These considerations add comparative dimensions to the general framework we are developing. While this framework leads us to conclude that almost all sellers of labour power are structurally unequal compared to all but the smallest buyers, we have noted some aspects of the structuration of these inequities through labour-market segmentation. Furthermore, when we consider this distribution of power resources comparatively and historically, we clearly find variable degrees of inequality.

An elucidation of these variable degrees of inequality lies in an appreciation of the linkages between the political and industrial spheres, political parties and collective action. These linkages are constituted through a 'power-difference' model of conflict, as Korpi (1974, 1978) terms it. The less unequal the parties are in a social relationship the more it will be marked by social conflict. The more unequal the parties are in a social relationship the less it will be marked by social conflict. The reasons for this are simple. Manifest conflict typified by the exercise of power (getting others to do something they would not otherwise have done, even against their resistance) occurs only where the weaker party is at least strong enough to formulate and act on an alternative course of action. In other words, 'a great disadvantage in power resources makes successful action by the weaker party unlikely' (Korpi and Shalev, 1980, p.307). Where there is a smaller or, over time, decreasing power-difference, one would anticipate that there would be an increase in conflict 'since the weaker party will attempt to change the unequal terms of exchange and the stronger party to maintain them' (1980, p.308). Moreover, where there is more than just one arena of conflict, it is advantageous to the weaker party to move the power process and its conflict manifestations to the arena in which they have least disadvantage.

In liberal democracy (the coexistence of formally equal bases of political representation and parliamentary/presidential governance with formally unequal relations of production, grounded in private property), there is ample evidence to suggest that the working class is at a greater disadvantage in the realm of private property and its relations of production than in the political sphere. Not least is the fact that, in the latter, equal and universal suffrage allows for the sacking of the political masters by the mass; no such power resides in the normal organization of relations of production. Hence, given the achievement of universal suffrage, then

to the extent that the working class through its organisations for collective action is able to achieve strong and stable control over the executive, the conflicts of interest between labour and capital will increasingly be fought out in the political arena and industrial conflict will decline (Korpi and Shalev, 1980, p.308).

A different theorization of industrial conflict to that implied in the labour-process perspective is therefore suggested. Shorter and Tilly (1974) have conceptualized strikes as 'politics by other means'. Having compared data on strike levels for thirteen countries in the postwar period to 1968, they demonstrated that the level of strike activity appeared to be inversely related to the extent to which the government during that period was weighted towards labour party representation. Where this representation was institutionalized over a period then strike rates fell, because, they proposed, workers had become accepted into the polity. Consequently, strikes, as a second-best strategy to the political, declined in importance. This finding has been further supported by data reported by Hibbs (1976, 1978).

The interpretation that Hibbs provides appears to confirm Castles's (1978) analysis of social democracy. Social democracy does deliver real benefits to the working class. Strike levels decline partly because political class struggle in the state, to the extent that it succeeds, removes pressure for the industrial strategy of free collective bargaining, mobilized through strikes. Economistic struggles lose their salience as the 'social wage' increases, because gains in the market wage will in all probability contribute not so much to personal but public welfare through the effects of taxation. Additionally, to the extent that a political strategy appears to succeed, unions are more likely to commit resources to it rather than to strike-fund payments.

We would propose that high levels of strikes do not necessarily signal a strong and highly resistant labour movement. This may appear to be the case as a result of an exclusive focus on the point of production and resistance to it within a specific national framework. We would, however, propose a different relationship between class, politics and strikes. High levels of strike action may in fact be interpreted as a sign of blockage of the working class at the more effective level of class action and mobilization: the political level. Moreover, it signals that the institutional arrangements arrived at in the political arena are themselves partly an effect of the balance of class forces at any particular conjuncture. Certain institutional aspects of past victories or defeats will be inscribed within this arena in a sedimented form, shaping further struggles of class forces.

Within this arena the central focus of struggle will be, as Lindblom (1977, p.14) suggests, 'the degree to which market replaces government or government replaces market.' Perhaps the most significant issue over which this struggle will occur will be that of economic policy, because of its impact upon property rights, relations of production, the control of the labour process and the labour market. These are the central structural features of the industrial sphere. To the extent that labour movements attempt to affect these, they may do so through a number of strategies. Two polar ideal types were identified by Sidney and Beatrice Webb (1924); these are 'the method of legal enactment' and 'the method of collective bargaining'. The former method is one whose primary locus is the political sphere of the state, while the latter focuses on specific industries and firms as its more appropriate site. Hence, the former may be termed a political strategy, oriented towards the subsumption of market to government, while the latter is a market strategy oriented towards 'free' (i.e. without state interference and regulation) collective bargaining. As ideal types, such strategies will never be found in reality in their pure form, but always as somewhat mixed and contradictory. The balance of class forces and the development of a labour movement strategy are, of course, never voluntaristically 'chosen'. Nor are they subject to endogenous determination alone. No state is a political island. All states are part of an international network of alliances and oppositions which necessarily have effects on the balance of domestic forces. Perhaps nowhere is this more noticeable than in the contortions of European mass Communist Parties in France, Spain and Italy in the last decade as they have tried to formulate an independent Euro-strategy, outside of the 'Moscow line' (Carrillo, 1977; Della Torre *et al.*, 1979).

Strikes have been a central issue of concern in society at large, ever since their efficacy began to be registered in legislative attempts to neutralize or outlaw them, at the end of the eighteenth century in Britain. A leitmotif of much of the writing done by industrial relations specialists in the 1950s and early 1960s on the social structure of the advanced societies, was the 'withering away of class', as Westergaard (1965, 1972) has extensively documented. Linking class and struggle was the finding that strikes, as the dramatic focus of their expressive unity, were at the centre of this 'withering' (Ross and Hartman, 1960). It became conventional wisdom to point to the decline in strikes, internationally, as a postwar trend. Trends, however, have often been constructed out of what, with hindsight, proves to have been an extrapolation from a cycle rather than a linear tendency. This appears to have been the case in the interpretation of comparative data on industrial conflict which are usually constructed by international agencies such as the International Labour Organization (ILO) or the Organization for Economic Co-operation and Development (OECD).

With all due caution (ILO, 1934, p.37; Shalev, 1979), it may be observed that the level of strike activity in the world's advanced capitalist economies increased quite notably in the period from 1969, such that some commentators have spoken of the outbreak of a world strike wave (Sweet and Jackson, 1977, 1978; Jackson and Sweet, 1979a, 1979b). After 1968/9 through to 1976, in the OECD states, the total number of working days lost in disputes, on the average, more than doubled compared with the 1951–67 period. The incidence of this strike wave has been put in an historical context by the work of Korpi and Shalev (1980) for eighteen industrial capitalist societies from 1900 to 1976. The focus of this analysis is the extent of non-agricultural workforce involvement in strike activity.

The post-1968/9 strike wave is not the first this century. The period from the turn of the century until 1920 saw an upward trend in strike activity (except in the USA and Canada), with the years around 1920 providing the benchmarks for an international strike wave, which was followed by a decrease in the 1920s.

During the latter part of the 1930s in about half of the major OECD countries, there was an increase in strike activity (the exceptions were countries in which Fascism was dominant or in which a labour party had gained office). Immediately after the Second World War there was another international strike wave of short duration, giving way to quite divergent postwar patterns.

After the Second World War, in Sweden, Norway, Austria, Germany, Netherlands and Switzerland, strike activity fell to what were historically low levels. The reference-points for each country differ, but the trend is the same. A further six countries showed a marked increase from the interwar years. These were Italy, Australia, France, Finland, New Zealand and Japan. In the remaining six countries of the UK, Belgium, Denmark, the USA, Canada and Ireland, the level of relative involvement was somewhat more stable and at average levels, in comparative terms, since the interwar period. After 1968/9, with slight lags, there has been a resurgence of conflict. This has not receded to the more quiescent levels of the 1950s and early 1960s, even in the period of economic depression which has developed after the 1974 peak of the strike wave. Korpi and Shalev grouped the eighteen countries under examination according to criteria of left labour strength in political (share of votes over a period) and industrial (union membership) spheres. Both working-class mobilization and degree of political control were used to categorize measures of strike activity. They produced the following national groupings of relative strike involvement (1980, p.320):

(i)   high labour mobilization with stable left political control (Sweden, Austria, Norway);
(ii) high labour mobilization with occasional leftist control of politics (Denmark, New Zealand, UK, Belgium);
(iii) medium–high labour mobilization with little left political control (Australia, Finland, France, Italy, Japan);
(iv) low labour mobilization with exclusion of leftist influence in politics (Canada, US, Ireland);
(v)   low–medium labour mobilization but partial left political participation in politics (Germany, The Netherlands, Switzerland).

The correlations between the different patterns of industrial mobilization and political involvement are striking. In the three 'social democrat' examples of a political strategy of high mobilization and stable control, the level of involvement and volume of strikes are very low. What makes these findings more striking is that in the period before the social democrats became the normal party of government in both Sweden and Norway (which, unlike Austria, did not have a Fascist prewar government), the strike volume and involvement was very high. This declined sharply with the accession to government of the social democrats (1932 in Sweden, 1945 in Norway).

The countries which are characterized by a high level of working-class mobilization and occasional or unstable labour party control have had a fairly stable level of strike involvement since the war, with the exception of New Zealand. However, these strikes have not lasted as long as the great prewar confrontations, such as the General Strike. Consequently, the extent, or volume, of strikes has declined. The left parties have not become the natural parties of government, despite some pretensions to the contrary in the UK. Hence, there has been no widespread displacement of conflict from the industrial to the political sphere, while a degree of intermittent 'bargained' corporatism has held down the average of strike involvement, despite the post-1968/9 strike wave.

The group of countries with a relatively highly mobilized labour movement in the industrial sphere, but which had signally failed to win commensurate strength in the political sphere, include Australia, France, Italy, Japan and Finland. Each of these countries experienced a split labour movement at the level of political representation. It is in these countries that the level of strike involvement has escalated relatively dramatically since the war. Indeed, in France, Italy and Australia one could say the escalation was not only relatively but absolutely substantial. The reasons for this are clear: it reflects 'a situation where a relatively highly mobilised working class is limited to carrying out its conflicts of interest with capital entirely in the industrial arena, with the government generally sympathetic to the viewpoint of capital' (Korpi and Shalev, 1980, pp.320-3). It is here, and in the less well-organized Irish, US and Canadian cases that industrial strife reflects political blockage most sharply. In the latter cases strikes occur between large capital and large labour unions, primarily organized as set-piece battles in the wages round, displaying an orderly, routinely long-lived character. There are fewer strikes but they last longer, hence the volume of strikes is high. In the remaining case, both Switzerland and Germany have been characterized by a high level of migrant *gastarbeiter* labour-force participation. Moreover, both Switzerland and the Netherlands are religiously divided, while Switzerland also has major regional, linguistic and gender cleavages as bases of political representation (and in the case of the latter, non-representation). Perhaps these aspects of civil society (and in the German case, the Eastern example of another kind of state) have contributed to the weaknesses of class mobilization on both fronts?

Sweden is the strongest illustrative case of the general argument for a political strategy, for it is only after the beginning of social democratic rule from 1932 onwards that its high and prolonged levels of strike action receded. Their decrease was due to the emergence of a set of economic and social policies which partially transformed the reproduction of capitalist relations of production towards the goal of a public interest. To argue this account of the changing pattern of strike action in Sweden is to distance ourselves from some alternative accounts. Conventionally, the reasons that are often produced for the lessening of strike action under democratic socialist governments stress the ability of 'parliamentary socialism' (Miliband, 1962) to incorporate the working-class leadership, which is then prevailed upon to extend this incorporation to the rank and file, in order more efficiently to manage capitalism. The question of specific policies as more or less reproductive/transformative of particular class-structured inequalities will be the concern of our final chapter.

Concluding remarks

The comparative perspective on strike activity adumbrated in the previous section leads, paradoxically, not towards a de-emphasis on the labour process but to a reassertion of the renewed importance for labour strategies of the internal organization of work. Freed from the fetters of a conception of work organization which represents only the implementation of capitalist control and worker resistance at the point of production, the agenda of the labour movement might incorporate alternative formulations of work design and its organization. These would not simply be struggles of resistance through 'alternative corporate plans' to capital-logic, but would be part of broader political and economic strategies. The articulation of forms of job redesign with a coherent political strategy, such as those that have characterized Swedish trade union and labour movement debates (Meidner, 1978; Korpi, 1978; Higgins, 1980, 1983; Apple and Higgins, 1982; Higgins and Apple, 1983) and to a lesser extent the French and Italian union federations (Kelly, 1982), offer one of the major avenues for a renewed impetus to the political programmes of the working class. In making these assertions we are cognizant of the arguments that such strategies are merely reformist and inexorably lead to an accommodation or incorporation of working-class interests within the broad thrust of capitalist development (Strinati, 1982; Burns et al., 1979; Scase, 1980; Crouch and Pizzorno, 1978; and Lehmbruch and Schmitter, 1982).

It is important to realize that our analysis leads away from a concern with struggle in the labour process *per se*. Collective bargaining and labour-process resistance is based necessarily on market tactics. Markets enter into the segmentary and occupationally differentiated bases of union formation, while workers and their unions can ordinarily react only tactically to initiatives taken by management and the state. At another extreme to market tactics as a basis for struggle would be a political strategy, with a more strategic but labour-market response lying midway. A political strategy entails a commitment to using the state to transform the balance of modes of production in a given formation, not only through social contacts and price and income policies, but also through a widespread extension of civil rights from the sphere of a liberal polity to an illiberal and anti-democratic economy. While individual citizens may have recourse to procedures which redress injustices which occur under the jurisdiction of the former, they are relatively powerless in the latter:

In most societies the law broadly prohibits one person from inflicting injury on another; prohibits, for example, physical assault, theft, libel, and conspiracy to injure. But it leaves one great exception; injury through termination of an exchange relation. It is easy to see why it must allow that exception if a market system is to persist. But it is an exception, one to which classical liberal theory on liberty seems blind (Lindblom, 1977, p.48).

Somewhat surprisingly, and detrimentally, as Hirst (1982) has argued in the British context, trade unions have often displayed an ambivalent attitude towards this lacuna in liberal theory or have been unable to do more than seize the opportunities implicit in liberalism's espousal of unfettered rights of bargaining over market exchange. The ambivalence of many unions to alternative strategies reflects a well-founded degree of suspicion and cynicism about the possibility of a genuine economic democracy and an aversion to policies which may lead to further incorporation into structures moulded by the interests of capital.

Tensions generated by the restructuring of political rights and expectations since the onset of recession in the 1970s necessitate that the linkages which labour movement strategies seem to cement between the political and industrial spheres require careful reappraisal. Analysis of class structure therefore has to include consideration of political class struggle. It is not sufficient to examine the structure of social classes without relating this structure to political parties and the ways in which differing 'class interests' are formulated as such through representation both in and to the state. While the state is the major structure through which a political strategy can be pursued by the organizations of the working class, macro-economic policy is the major vehicle of such a strategy. A necessary prerequisite of the policy proposals with which we shall conclude this investigation must be an empirically and theoretically adequate account of the state. Our interest in economic policy is precisely to demarcate a stratagem of 'class politics' which are less than reproductive of the existing structure of classes. Indeed, our aim is to further the cause of a working-class-based politics capable of popular articulation and aggregation not only of the core constituency, but also of the ranks of a disaffected middle class.

8 Class organization and the state

Class struggle, in as much as it is formally organized into interest-mediating associations in the industrial sphere, occurs between trade unions and employers' groups. In the final chapter we will analyse the *processes* of this struggle. We may define these processes in terms of actions which result in more or less transformation or reproduction of a given relationship between capital and labour. For each class, the success of class struggle will be determined by the extent to which either class gains greater control over the capitalist system as a whole (in the long term, the stakes are somewhat higher of course). We will consider this struggle subsequently in terms of changing patterns of reinvestment of surplus for accumulation and its effects on changing patterns of class shares of total income, in the variable framework of stages of economic development. In this chapter we investigate the relationship between the state, civil society and the *organization* of the two contending parties to this struggle. Through this investigation we establish that 'capital' and 'labour' cannot be adequately conceptualized as plural, countervailing powers. On the contrary, we argue – against much popular wisdom – that trade unions are not 'too strong' or 'capable of holding the country to ransom', but tend to be routinely more disorganized than the capital they confront, because of the characteristic structures of civil society and the state and the respective salience of these for the opposing powers. Class organization is never likely to be an unambiguous matter.

Class structure and organization

Organizations structure the terrain on which are inscribed the basic class features of capitalist societies. Without organization there can be no 'class interests'. The notion of a class having a collective interest can only ever gain credence inasmuch as organizations are formed whose mandate entails the representation of 'class interests'. Interests, in other words, cannot ordinarily be said to exist prior to their articulation as such. To speak of 'real interests' outside of or concealed behind actual interest representation through organization is to refer not to empirical phenomena, but to theoretical constructs. Such theoretical constructs should not be dismissed out of hand. They may well fulfil an important heuristic function. Empirically, in so far as the major classes do find their interests represented through organization, then this organization takes place primarily through trade unions, employers' associations and political parties.

To the extent that there exist relations of solidarity and co-operation in either unions or employers' associations, these describe classes engaged in practices of struggle. What might appear on the surface to be equivalent – one class organization countervailing another class organization – is not, on further reflection, an equal positing of one interest group against another.

A major difference results from the history of class formation. Without the benefits of association in trade unions, workers would have had no bargaining power over the amount of time their labour power was available. Individual workers who tried to limit their own availability or to improve their exchange value would have been replaced by other workers or, if skilled, by machines (Marglin, 1974). The association of workers is thus a response by the individually powerless to the power of the fusion of innumerable units of 'dead labour' under the unitary control of a relatively seamless capital.

Trade unions are organizations constituted on the terrain of class structure inasmuch as they organize labour, but they necessarily do so in terms of statuses inscribed in the development of civil society. The most evident of these is already signified, for many countries, in the term 'trade' unions: unions are frequently organized on occupational bases, which function under many circumstances as potential sources of division within the working class. These are most probable when capitalism develops upon an already established tradition of guild, occupational and craft structures (Clegg and Dunkerley, 1980, pp.41-57). Such divisions may form the basis for significant strata within the working class, particularly where they intersect with labour-market advantages and domestic or ideological cleavages.

Only workers can be organized by unions. Workers must already be in employment in other organizations. Thus, unions are 'secondary' organizations able to organize only those who have already been organized by capital or the state into 'primary' organizations (Hyman and Fryer, 1975, p.158; Offe and Wiesenthal, 1980, p.72).

Capital organizes workers by combining labour, machines and raw materials in a labour process oriented to the production of surplus value. The combination is achieved through the form of a contract. A contract to purchase the fruits of congealed labour, raw materials and machines, is an unproblematic transfer of money capital for particular raw materials and machinery.

Contracts with living labour are more problematic for employers. First, it is not labour itself which is purchased, but labour power, a capacity for labour. This capacity has to be translated into actual practice and action, into 'labour efficiency', the central substance of which is the control of human effort in the labour process (Baldamus, 1961; Clegg and Dunkerley, 1980). The fundamental problem is that this effort is not physically separable from the labourer. In order to control it, incentives, force, ideology and all the practices of the management of complex organizations have to be applied to the bearers of this labour power, this potential effort, in order to obtain maximum efficiency. Yet the effort always remains under the physical control of the worker, whose work it is, even though it legally 'belongs' to the employing organization. Formal contractual relations notwithstanding, the equivalence of a certain amount of labour and a certain wage is an effort bargain – constantly renegotiated in the daily rhythms of everyday work life.

The effort bargained over concerns the potential valorization inherent in any specific organization of the working day and the amount of value exchanged for the labour power acquired. Individual workers have little opportunity to affect the terms of this bargain, except in rare cases of high demand for specific and unsubstitutable skills which are in short supply, or where, organizationally, they are collectively able to simulate these conditions. In the absence of such limiting conditions, the individual worker remains a discrete objectification of a general capacity-for-labour, confronted by capital which is usually more unified compared to the competitive atomization and division of living labour power. Capital is liquid by definition, while labour is always non-liquid. '*Workers cannot "merge": at best, they can associate* in order to partly compensate for the power advantage that capital derives from the liquidity of "dead" labour' (Offe and Wiesenthal, 1980, p.74).

Capitalists are physically separate from the capital they individually control, in contrast to the relationship between

261

labourers and labour power. One consequence of this difference is that capitalists are 'free' to dissociate themselves from the actual functioning of their capital (in various forms of property) in ways in which labour cannot. Capital possesses the peculiar property of appearing to be self-expanding. It grows, seemingly, of its own accord. It can be used up by capitalists in the 'cultivation' of a wide range of interests in civil society and yet still be replenished while these interests are being satisfied elsewhere.

Labourers are less fortunate. They are both 'the subject and the object of the exchange of labour power' (Offe and Wiesenthal, 1980, p.75). Their interests in their involvement in the labour process cannot be conveniently and quantitatively reduced to a single 'bottom line' of economic calculation. Their involvement is always qualitative as well as quantitative. It includes

> not only material rewards but also such things as job satisfaction, health, leisure time, and continuity of employment. Therefore, unions are confronted with the task of organizing the entire spectrum of needs that people have when they are employed as wage workers. This multitude of needs of 'living' labour is not only comparatively more difficult to organize for quantitative reasons, but also for the reason that there is no common denominator to which all these heterogeneous and often conflicting needs can be reduced so as to 'optimize' demands and tactics. How much in wages, for instance, can 'rationally' be given up in exchange for which amount of increase in job satisfaction? The answer to this question cannot be found by any calculus that could be objectively applied; it can only be found as the result of the collective deliberation of the members of the organization (Offe and Wiesenthal, 1980, p.75).

Further dissimilarities emerge from these different organizational possibilities. While capitalists can, and under competitive pressures, must be engaged in rational economic calculation about the efficiency of their reproduction of capital, labour has no opportunity to increase the efficiency of its reproduction because it takes place outside the sphere of capitalist production. Changes in the efficiency of the domestic sphere have no effects in capitalist employment of the labour reproduced. The implications of this have been elaborated by Harvey (1982, p.447):

> though labour power is a commodity the labourer is not. And though capitalists may view them as 'hands' possessed of

stomachs, 'like some lowly creatures on the sea shore', as Dickens once put it, the labourers themselves are human beings possessed of all manner of sentiments, hopes and fears, struggling to fashion a life for themselves that contains at least minimal satisfactions. The conditions of production and reproduction of labour powers of different quantity and quality exist at the very centre of that life. And though susceptible of all manner of influence through bourgeois institutions and culture, nothing in the end can subvert the control workers exercise over certain very basic processes of their own reproduction. Their lives, their culture and, above all, their children are for them to reproduce.

Once reproduced, however, labour is dependent, in most circumstances, upon being employed by capital. It is only in exceptional circumstances of natural bounty, unencumbered land and non-residence in large urban conglomerations that property-less labour is able to subsist other than through entering into production relations. Hence, workers are dependent upon the well-being of capitalists rather more than capitalists are dependent on the well-being of workers. Ordinarily, capital hires labour rather than the other way around. Given these contractual and legally defined relations, then the contractor is at liberty to substitute greater amounts of capital for labour in the form of productivity-enhancing techniques. The labourer legally contracts the sale of labour power while physically retaining possession of the 'alienated' commodity. This produces a concurrent separation of legal control over labour power (in terms of its disposition within the overall system of law) together with a unity of the labour as subject of the object thus disposed. Labour is thus 'at the same time the object of what is sold in the labour market transaction and the partner in the labour contract, object and subject of the exchange relation' (Offe and Wiesenthal, 1980, p.92). A *unit* of labour is just that but is always also a *unique* unit: a particular subject with unique consciousness, identity and self-conception. From this paradoxical position flow most of the classic ambiguities of organizing labour,

namely the ambiguity between individualistic versus collective improvement of one's condition, between economic versus political concepts of one's interests, between the identities as consumer and producer, between the priorities of higher wages versus better working conditions and more secure employment, and between the behavioural alternatives of individual com-petitiveness and class solidarity (Offe and Wiesenthal, 1980, p.93).

Organized struggle by the working class depends upon the mobilization of the membership resources, their motivation and co-ordination, to achieve concerted action disruptive of the valorization process. This may be working-to-rule or striking or whatever. For unions this involves overcoming *all* the divisions of civil society – of gender, age, race, region, occupation, etc. – by defining all of these as of less value than solidarity.

The achievement of such solidarity, rather than becoming simpler and more condensed with the development of capitalism as a mode of production, would, on the contrary, seem to have become more difficult with the emergence of conglomerate enterprise structures. Cressey and MacInnes (1982, pp.276-78) established that although large concentrations of capital have become organized on an enterprise basis, so that one nominal centre of calculation can centralize many different plants, it is unusual for one to find a comparable centralization (in Britain) of co-ordinative activity between the different unions in the many plants. A Commission on Industrial Relations study of sixty multiplant undertakings also noted that

> as multi-plant companies grow and change in structure with, in many cases, a centralization of industrial relations policies or issues relating to them, trade union power has, relative to this development, tended to become decreasingly decentralized in its operation (1974, p.6).

The structure of enterprise calculation in countries such as Britain or Australia, confronted with a fragmented and somewhat inchoate organization of trade unions (compared to unions in Sweden or West Germany, for example) appears to offer substantial political leverage in decision-making. Labour union struggle, particularly in these less favourable comparative circumstances, requires a massive organizational effort to overcome not only the civil but also the capital-logic heterogeneity of workers' interests. The salience of this argument is nowhere more apparent than in circumstances where labour, engaged in a struggle at one point of production, can be resisted and eroded by simply altering the balance of multiple sourcing to take up any slack in production schedules that collective action in one plant can disrupt. To be effective in these circumstances labour has to be organized on a multiplant basis (see Cressey and MacInnes's (1982) analysis of shop-steward combine committees in Britain).

In general, the heterogeneity of union members' interests is the result of the twofold intersection of the specific class position of being propertyless labour whilst being formed in civil society. Whatever interests are acquired in the latter can be satisfied only through work in the former. Labour, unlike capital, has no equivalent 'liquidity preference' or 'relative autonomy'. Any of life's central interests can be followed only through participation in labour; almost any of these interests, such as the policy aspects of health, safety, welfare, environmental or defence legislation, may be constituted as a relevant interest for labour. Moreover, producers in class positions are also consumers of other producers' commodities. This can lead to the frequently noted anti-union attitudes of workers who are themselves unionists: as consumers they resent effects that as producers they must strive to achieve if they are to increase control over their wages, the labour market and the labour process (Moorhouse and Chamberlain, 1974).

It is clearly the case that, in contrast to labour, capital has only one easily quantifiable and calculable interest to organise: the profitability of individual firms. However, to the extent that employers' associations such as the Confederation of British Industry (CBI) represents the views of all member firms, then we may note the following qualifications. First, the association may, and in this instance does, include nationalized as well as private capital. The significance of this is clearly contextually variable. It is often observed that such nationalized industries are run as if they were profit-oriented: indeed, this is certainly the experience with entities such as British Steel. A second consequence of the representational, interest-mediating function of associations such as the CBI is that they supposedly do represent all members, both large and small companies. Empirically, however, there is evidence to suggest that 'large companies, and indeed a small clique of representatives from such companies, dominated CBI policy' (Fidler, 1981, p.235). Not only may there be contradictions between large and small companies, there may also be quite real divisions between different sectors and branches of capital. Third, there may not be the same degree of representation in a singular body for capital as there is for labour: the singular representation of capital seems to be more an effect of moves in a 'corporatist' direction than is the case with labour. Thus, for instance, at the start of the renewed development of corporatism in Australia, which the National Economic Summit Conference of April 1983 presaged, employers were universally regarded as less well organized than was labour, because they were less singularly organized than was labour, due to the unitary intermediation which was orchestrated through the auspices of the Australian Council of Trade Unions (ACTU).

It has been further suggested by Offe and Wiesenthal that civil society generally provides capital with a more explicit and

265

legitimate ideology, in the form of media coverage. Certainly, researchers such as the Glasgow Media Group (1976, 1979) argue that media representation of labour spokespersons and their views is more 'negative' than that of employers and capitalists generally. There is some evidence to suggest that for business people themselves, particular elements of the media, such as television, relay an anti-capitalist bias (Fidler, 1981, pp.241-2). In part the belief that this is the case derives from a perception of business people as poor representers of capitalist interests when they do appear on television. Additionally, it is seen to derive from the short-term focus of the media on particular, not necessarily long-lived or representative aspects of business, such as a super-profit earned in inflationary circumstances. Consequently, many large corporations advertise not just their products or their services but a corporate image designed to foster consensus on their inherent value. Given this advertising, it may not be reasonable to argue, as Offe and Wiesenthal (1980, p.85) do, that there is already existing 'a presupposed consensus as to social, cultural, and political values to which one can always refer'.

Offe and Wiesenthal also argue that the degree of structural compatibility between the state and capital leads to a situation in which the relationship between the ideology and the practice of the state is different for each class. For members of the working class, the lived experience of the state's ideology as neutral arbiter in its practice in civil society poses more contradictions than it does for capital. Consequently, the probability that members of the working class will come to recognize their own prior perceptions and constitutions of interest (as they have already been produced in civil society), as erroneous and distorted, is greater than for members of the capitalist class. The capitalist class is structured so as to be more complementary with the state. Labour is not. This reflects its very different constitution in civil society and, of course, differential class positions.

The differential class positions of agents of capital and labour results in very different forms of interest intermediation (Schmitter, 1979). Working-class organization in trade unions is the locus of workers' interest intermediation. It is, in other words, these organizations in which and through which the central life interests of labour come to be learnt, articulated, repressed or controlled. It is not that there are interests waiting to be organized but organizations which attempt to organize their memberships into differently intermediated interests. Thus, such organizations do not simply 'represent' an already pre-given definition of interests.

Instead, these organizations are simply one of many such bodies in civil society which attempt to define what exists, what is possible and what is right for working people. This is a consequence of the organizations themselves. In large measure, they create the relevant interests.

The normal condition of existence for most people is one of uncertainty, equivocality, opacity, and a cacophony of competing interpellations. For the organization of capital, this is less problematic, inasmuch as the processes of interpellation and interest intermediation can all be funnelled into one issue: the quantitative expression of profitability. Even then, it never emerges in an uncontradictory manner. It is always a fractured, partial and contradictory result (Hawley, 1980, p.52).

The greater ambiguity, opacity and equivocality in the relation of practice to ideology in the lived experience of members of the working class means that their political organization will always display a tension between the organizational processes of discursive will-formation in dialogue, debate and exchange, and processes of political action in terms of the existing political and economic structures. While the mechanisms of the former are those of practical reason, where free subjects argue and debate the nature of their interests without fear or hindrance, in order to arrive at collectively agreed principles and policies, the mechanisms of the latter are those of technical reason: the ability to 'know the rules', to work within them to advantage and to specialize expertise on this ability. The former mechanism of collective will-formation stresses democratic processes while the latter stresses bureaucratic processes. The tension between these two modes of operating is more deeply inscribed in labour organization than in capital (Offe and Wiesenthal, 1980; Therborn, 1978).

This tension between democracy and bureaucracy is more deeply inscribed in labour organization because the different practices of civil society have differential effects on different class positions, constituted in a different relation to the state. Capital is not only more unified in terms of its interpellation in civil society, particularly as far as gender is concerned. Its interest intermediation is capable of a far simpler organization than that of labour. Further, it has a more immediately registerable effect upon state policy, through the mechanism of business confidence, than is open to labour.

At the structural level, the representation of capital and labour interests, because of differences in class formation in civil society, does yield some interesting contrasts. If we were to contrast the markets for capital and labour respectively, as spheres of social action, then crucial differences between the two become apparent. The stock exchange is characterized by extensive spatial configurations articulated through a dense and tightly coupled network of exchanges in which major switching and investment decisions are capable of almost instantaneous response to any datum constituted as relevant.

The labour market is also characterized by extensive spatial configurations. These, however, are organized through exchanges which are both far more numerous and far less centralized than stock exchanges. Labour exchanges are also far more loosely coupled with each other and the global economy. They are essentially local. On the stock exchange transactions are immediately capable of creating effects whose 'intentional causes' can be interpreted in the subsequent, almost immediate, social action surrounding price movements. Contrast this with labour's position. Transactions on the labour market occur in two kinds of exchange with two kinds of effects. On the one hand, there is the labour exchange (or job or employment centre). Here, exchanges always have to be initiated by one side to the exchange – either employing units or labour, mediated through the local exchange. Exchange is not necessarily completed from one end of the chain labour → labour exchange → employing unit. The registration of labour does not necessarily entail an exchange with an employer, while for an employing unit the registration of a vacancy usually does entail the exchange with a unit of labour power. Labour's role in the exchange can only ever be reactive to vacancies notified (and the exchange is legally empowered to insist that particular units of labour accept the offers). No legal compulsion makes it necessary for capital to provide labour with work, although workers can and have been required to supply capital with labour.

Exchange also takes place, of course, between workers and employing units as well as between unemployed workers and agencies for their registration. Although these have immediate effects in terms of the capital market's articulation of a response to strikes and settlements of grievances, there is no similar, seemingly impersonal mechanism whereby a response to pre-emptive action on capital markets can be immediately registered in and through labour markets.

Labour exchanges are far more dependent on capital exchanges; they are far less tightly coupled, much more mediated, and have much less immediate effect on the markets of labour. Under capitalist relations of production the latter are far more dependent and coupled to the former. Collectively, this power differential is inscribed in class conflicts, institutionalized in the markets for capital and labour, and mediated by the state. Indeed, according to some recent formulations the state is the factor of cohesion which serves to ensure the reproduction of capitalist economic domination in all these spheres.

The state and political parties

We have proposed that civil society is the terrain upon which definitions of the possible are given presence, condensed, materialized and fought over, by classes and by other bases of social mobilization. A crucial resource to be fought for, over and within, is the state. We conceive of the state as a complex of organizational resources oriented to the construction of the economy and of civility in various determinate modes. These modes centre on diverse forms of representation, intervention and regulation. Various state and civil modes can articulate with the same mode of production. Hence, as we will observe, capitalism as a mode of production has been capable of articulation through state forms as diverse as Fascism, national government, liberal democracy and democratic socialism. No necessary relationship or evolutionary path exists in the relation between state form and mode of production.

The links between capitalism and democracy appear to be deflected and mediated in the state through struggle in civil society – usually through either a destruction of a pre-existing non-democratic state form in warfare or a wartime national mobilization whose popular impetus is sustained into a struggle for representation across a broad front (Therborn, 1977). Capitalist development has aided such struggles indirectly, through stimulating concentration of urban space and work, literacy, and improved communications, but it cannot be said to 'cause' democracy or to have a special functional relationship to it.

The state, as a centre of representation, intervention and regulation, exhibits a degree of centredness and inclusivity which is unique amongst the organizational apparatus of modern society. It touches upon, shapes and moulds everyone to some extent. No one can escape its presence, surveillance and materialization. The state is the fundamental social relation of modernity. Although the state's social relations are frequently bathed in an ether of legitimacy acquired through either active consent or passive acquiescence by the mass of the people, it would be mistaken to assume that the state requires consent to achieve hegemony over civil society. Such a condition may sometimes hold, but it need not. Historically, there appears to be no compelling evidence to suggest that states without a certain legitimacy or hegemonic presence in civil society will necessarily falter. Ordinarily they require additional pressure for this to happen. We may note, for instance, that in recent memory it took an external state and its army to cause both Amin's Ugandan state and Pol Pot's Kampuchea to fall. Innumerable other examples could be cited of states founded less on moral or passive accord and more on officially sanctioned terror.

This discussion serves to underscore the fact that force is the underlying basis of any state. At the minimum, state power rests on an effective monopoly of the means of violence within a given territory. Where it falters it tends to do so not so much on the basis of a lack of legitimacy as on the basis of a countervailing might or through defeat and defection at the hands of either another state or another organized claimant to its power.

The state is not necessarily an external, coercive phenomena *vis-à-vis* its citizens. Initially, state power developed not to oppress its citizens but to constitute them as such, as *citizens*, under its protection; protection against other competitive powers aspiring to similar strategies of 'organization' of a populace. (Organization can take diverse forms. Historically, it has ranged from plunder, through to slavery, subjugation, exploitation, etc.) We should not regard 'the people' and 'the state' as implying that the former are under the yoke of the latter. There are simply different state forms for organizing a populace into a people. Conceptions of the state which invoke it as an external interference in the 'normal' functioning of civil society are necessarily mistaken. State intervention and regulation, of one sort or another, is necessarily pervasive. It has been ever since the construction of the state as an organizational complex for safeguarding the interests of its constituent associations during princely absolutism. Monopoly over the means of violence always has a potential for use against citizens of the state in question, but has its origins more especially defined against the citizens of other states or the people of other territories, in pursuit of issues constructed as being in a particular 'national interest'.

This is not to argue that the authoritarian, repressive state is absent from the modern world, any more than is state terror. It is too easy to find counterfactual cases to maintain such a view. However, the dominance of the 'repressive apparatus' (as Althusser (1971) termed it) is not typical of the state form of the leading postwar advanced societies in the capitalist world. The state form which could be regarded as being more characteristic of the major OECD nations is that of 'liberal democracy'. Liberal democracy emerged in states where liberal freedoms of private property and wage labour appeared long before they were democratic. Democracy came only after prolonged struggle by those excluded from the liberal state, a state which was narrowly founded on the enfranchisement of propertied males. Progressively, under pressure from below, usually accompanied, as Therborn (1977) suggests, by external pressure on the state during warfare, the franchise was extended to the male working class, women, blacks and other groups disenfranchised on the basis of some salient status attribute.

In the struggle for the franchise it was collective action by groups such as workers, women and blacks, which settled the issue after a bloody process. However, what was won was entry into an electoral contest in which the status of citizen was uniquely privileged in the ritual of most people's participation in politics. Through the act of voting one's individual status as a citizen rather than one's collective identity as a worker, for instance, becomes compelling. Whatever the qualities that are inscribed in one's statuses in civil society are abstracted away in the solitary act of representation by voting, in favour of the socially and economically naked individual. To be a citizen with full civil rights comes to be defined as being an abstract individual recognizable as such through a number of legally constituted activities, notably voting.

The vote is cast for parties which, historically, organized their interest mediation on the basis of class divisions within the economy, or, in some instances, status in civil society, such as the religious or ethnic/linguistic community parties of Western Europe. However, the nature of party organization involves both articulation and aggregation in order to gain political office. Within the advanced capitalist democracies the *raison d'être* of party organization has been rather more the aggregation of votes sufficient to gain office than the articulation of an interest constituency *per se*. Moreover, articulation always proceeds through a process where the interest-constituency is itself given shape by representation, under the imperatives of efficient aggregation: in other words, getting the numbers. Consequently, the requirements of the electoral system, the electoral boundaries and technical rules for registering the values of votes cast, tend to become the dominant influence on the party organization and, through it, frequently the party platform. Thus, although parties tend to a class core (or a religious or ethnic/linguistic core) in the articulation of a constituency, there are good organizational reasons why they might tend to weaken this through an appeal to potential aggregates of voters. However, throughout the OECD there are explicit 'free enterprise', and 'socialist' or labour parties (except in the USA, where the latter is absent).

Mass parties (as opposed to populist 'cadre parties', a term which Harrison (1980, p.99) uses to characterize parties such as the Gaullist Party in France) are bureaucratic organizations dependent for financial and other resources on a mass membership. While the ideology of the party is precisely what attracts a party membership, either this often has to be compromised by the exigencies of gaining an aggregate electoral support or, less frequently, the ideology has to become the basis for widespread education of the electorate to acceptance of the party views. The latter case would conform with Lindblom's (1977) model of 'persuasion'. In the former case, Harrison (1980, p.100) suggests that a division is likely to occur between parliamentary representatives, who have to practise compromise in implementation, and constituency members attracted to the ideology but unsullied by the exigencies of office-holding. The educational alternative would be one where the party was committed to educating both parliamentarians and the potential constituency in political choices. Usually, both of these strategies will occur simultaneously, with differing weight, as different parties come to embody different emphases in quite different states, economies and civil societies. To mention a key variable in each sphere, it is clearly important whether or not parties' election costs are publicly subsidized; whether or not the private concentration of media power is high; and whether or not the civil society is characterized by a dense network of workers' education (such as is found throughout Scandinavia). Where costs are met, media access to left views seriously endorsed and widespread workers' education in social and political issues a norm, then the party will face less of an aggregative tension and be better able to move towards an articulatory stance. Where the political scene presents a more diverse set of bases of representation than a simple class cleavage and a relatively homogeneous civil society, then the more variegated the demands of civil society the less able is a party in a two-party system to contain such demands manageably within an articulatory mode. Pragmatism rather than principle, numbers rather than ideology, tend to predominate in the latter situation, unless popular education can overcome civil differences in articulating a genuinely popular programme. The notion of education proposed here would clearly be two-way and would constitute policy just as much as it would teach it.

From the point of view of the electoral mobilization of a labour party, an articulatory strategy, rather than one which is piecemeal and aggregative, represents a stronger organizational base. This is because the latter is always prone to special interest group defections if the contending conservative parties can succeed in framing and marketing policies designed to appeal to them. However, an articulatory strategy cannot simply rely on any *a priori* asumption of a given class interest or community, as Hindess (1980) has made particularly clear. An electoral majority has to be mobilized around a programme. We would argue that the strength of the programme as a project of structural rather than piecemeal reform is the crucial variable in facilitating an articulatory mode of representation (Himmelstrand *et al.*, 1981, pp.191-209). We will return to this issue in the concluding chapter.

Current theories of democratic pluralism tend to a view of politics which regards parties primarily as aggregative, rather than articulatory agencies. Articulation and education tend to be subordinated in this view to the mobilization of aggregate demand and party supply in the political market place. On the one hand, there are parties competing on the political market; on the other hand, there are various bases for representation within civil society. Through organization these can be orchestrated as elective affinities by individual voters responding to the platform that the party organization and leaders sell in the 'market'.

This metaphor of the market, as Macpherson (1977, pp.88-90) argues, is hardly credible. If a market it be, it is one which is highly oligopolistic and characteristically low on consumer sovereignty, with few sellers, offering broadly undifferentiated products, on terms that they manipulate. Credibility, maintains Wells (1981, pp.156-7), is indeed stretched past breaking-point:

> Whereas individuals in a market choose between specific alternatives in the light of a general framework, namely the prevailing structure of prices, voters choose between competing general frameworks in the light of their specific interest and position. Liberal democratic elections, in fact, reverse market processes. In the market, choice, by and large, has a specific feedback because it is the choice of a specific action: purchase of commodity A leads to consumption of commodity A, a certain selling-price implies a certain rate of profit etc. Conversely, the voter's choice of a general framework can only have a general diffuse feedback, and the link between his specific interest and position on the one hand and the general result of the vote on the other is therefore constantly in danger of being obscured. . . . It follows that any analogy with the market can only be maintained if this tenuous link between the specific and the general is preserved and reinforced within the electoral process itself. Instead we find the opposite.

Moreover, voting has become increasingly plebiscitary in character as electoral contests have become a competition between two or more active elites, organized in parties, and the mass of passive citizenry 'choosing' between brands of personal identity constructed as specific individuals who will lead the passive mass. The process of identity-construction, of course, has become a highly complex matter of psephology and public relations firms working through the mass media of modern society. The infrequent, secret, ritualistic casting of the vote thus becomes the high-note of politics, obscuring the political context of this 'public performance politics'.

The political context of these public performances operates through the field of political 'issues' which, in a modern state, are overwhelmingly those of 'the economy'. But this 'economy', the site of class relations, appears in the guise of, as both Wells (1981) and Emmison (1983) have argued, a 'fetish'. The economy appears as a problem of citizens, as voters, thus as a 'national issue', while in reality these problems of 'the nation' are those of the capitals operative within it. 'By defining the contradictions of capital as national problems, and voters as abstract citizens in relation to these national problems, liberal democratic elections enable capital to appear as identical with the national interest' (Wells, 1981, p.159). The basis for this is inherent in the class relations of capitalist production. It is seemingly through capital and capital alone, that labour power can be used to generate growth, accumulation and employment. Getting the economy working again becomes identical with getting capital back to work. The national interest, standing mystically outside of and over those people whose actions comprise it, requires a formal homology between, on the one hand, alienated workers and voters and, on the other hand, a reified economy and politics, fused in the representation of all abstract individuals: the nation, condensed in the centralized administration of the state as its technical rational–legal apparatus.

The unity of physical protection and legal regulation defines the state as a specific complex of organizations which, in Urry's (1981, p.104) words, implement policy 'through the application of predetermined rules by hierarchically organized bureaucrats' with 'little possibility of innovative action'. Such people are generally regarded as the more or less ideal embodiment of the bureaucratic type identifed by Weber in *Economy and Society*. This type was organized around what Wilson (1983, p.154) has referred to as three basic clusters of characteristics. The scalar cluster comprises principles of hierarchy, discipline, formal authority and rule orientation; the functional cluster demarcates spheres of competence, principles of selection and advancement and the technical bases for identifying these; finally, the career cluster provides the formally meritocratic rationale for submission to bureaucratic work, with its principles of free selection and contract, the separation from the means of administration of the official, with a career defined in terms of a full-time, salaried and revokable appointment. Collectively, these principles have, quite rightly in our opinion, been seen as an appropriate means for achieving efficient and formally equitable administration. They are the bedrock for any view of the state as an apparatus of neutral, technical and apolitical efficiency in its means of achieving goals which are politically defined elsewhere, by a party.

It has been argued by Poggi (1978, p.129) that the traditional neutral view of the state depended upon a conception of civil society which was, in fact, subsumed to the competitive market. There were two reasons for this. First, the competitive market (at least as it appeared in its representation in economic theory) was self-equilibrating: it did not require, in theory, any regulation and intervention by the state. Second, for so long as the market remained competitive it produced no power relations among economic factors other than a generalized dependency of all upon 'the market'. Thus, the state could appear as the only leviathan in the nation (the church/state battle having been fought and won by the state). However, the fiction of self-equilibrating markets could hardly survive the growth of centralized and concentrated business power in firms which maximized not only profits, but also control over markets, one another and the wider society. Consequently, with the increasing dependence of civil society as a whole upon the success or failure of these giant enterprises, the state, of necessity, has to attempt to achieve some degree of equilibration of what can no longer be assumed to be self-equilibrating. Consequently, as conservatives such as Durkheim feared, the liberal distinction between state and civil society becomes blurred by widespread state interventions, but these are an effect of the grossness of the economic factors rather than the 'external' coercion of the state itself.

The view of the state as a benignly neutral instrument is now generally regarded as archaic, more ideological than real, and even as somewhat whimsical. In its place, however, stands no clear alternative view. Indeed, the concept and theory of the state has been one of the most contested areas of debate within social science in the recent past. Despite numerous surveys of and contributions to these debates (Therborn, 1978; Jessop, 1977, 1978a, 1982; Urry, 1981; Frankel, 1978, 1979; Holloway and Piccioto, 1977), the notion of the state remains essentially contested in what are quite explicitly, and not surprisingly, terms of political debate.

Theories of the state

Most conservative characterizations of the state tend to over-emphasize the autonomy of politics (narrowly defined) and to under-emphasize the politics of administration. On the other hand, many recent Marxist theories have under-stated both by collapsing the distinction between the state as a social relation and the state as a complex of organizations into a theory of the state *per se*, without reference to the components of the state in anything other than functional terms.

The genesis of this 'collapsing' may be located, despite the differences of emphasis, in the classical Marxist texts (Jessop, 1977, 1978b). The earliest of these derive from 1842–3 when Marx sharpened his ideas in the context of a *Critique of Hegel's Philosophy of the State* (1970b) and 'A Contribution to the Critique of Hegel's *Philosophy of Right*' (1975). Hegel (1967) had developed a theory of the state as the universal synthetic institution created through a series of mediations between civil and political society. Marx envisaged this function as redundant in a genuine democracy: thus, he regarded the present state, in which the bureaucracy functioned sectionally rather than neutrally, as a parasite on the people. In his later writings this view was elaborated into a conception of the state as an instrument of class rule: it 'is nothing more than the form of organisation which the bourgeois necessarily adopts both for internal and external purposes, for the mutual guarantee of their property and interests' (Marx and Engels, 1969, p.59). It is this theme which Lenin developed when he defined the state as the oppression of one class by another in *The State and Revolution* (1921).

The state is an instrument of power which develops with the emergence of class exploitation and which finds expression in a body of officials functionally specialized in administration and repression. Later analyses by Althusser (1971) and Poulantzas (1973) take this theme but give it a distinctively structuralist impetus. This is derived from the centrality in their work of a particular conception of Marx's *Capital* (Althusser and Balibar, 1970). In this interpretation, *Capital* is an analysis of the concept of a 'pure' mode of production as an abstraction. In actual instances, the capitalist mode of production develops in an uneven articulation between the several distinct fractions of capital. This necessitates the existence of an institution concerned with the maintenance of the mode of production's overall cohesion and equilibrium. This cannot simply be a state which functions in the interests of capital-in-general, except in the very broadest of senses; for example, the preservation of private property relations. There is no such thing as capital-in-general because of the conflicting interests of the different fractions and because of the different historical and institutional circumstances under which capital formation and accumulation takes place. It is for these reasons that it is argued that the state requires a degree of 'relative autonomy' so that it can establish the general framework in which the particular fractions of capital function. This general framework almost always entails the sacrifice of some particular interests and fractions. Thus, the state is conceptualized as oppressive, not only *of* the working class, but *for* ruling-class interests. This may entail state actions which are not reproductive of the whole of capital, although they are cohesive of a formation in which dominant classes continue to dominate through the unhindered *process*, yet changing structure, of capital accumulation (Poulantzas, 1973, pp.44-50, 1975, pp.78-81). From this perspective the key feature of the state is its reproductive character, its ability to be able to reproduce the conditions of production. In Althusser's (1977) work this leads to a stress on the role of ideology, conflated into a concept of the ideological state apparatus, which fulfils the functions of the state together with the more familiar repressive state apparatuses.

In these views, the state is pre-defined, because of its reproduction/ideology function, as a capitalist state, because that is the character of the society being reproduced (Crouch, 1979). It could cease to be capitalist only if capitalism itself ceased to exist. If the state functions always as the institutional source of capitalist cohesion in a capitalist society, there is little point in attempting to gain concessions or reforms from it – they will always (in the long run) be in the interests of capital. This induces either a fatalistic acceptance of the state or a utopian belief in the possibility of somehow radically 'smashing' it.

A further consequence of this view is that it suggests that the nature of the capitalist state is such that it has no capacity to be able to respond positively to working-class demands, through the forcing of radical reforms or the granting of concessions. Empirically, given the degree of mobilization, contestation and struggle which has occurred around the state in liberal capitalist democracies by combatants in the class struggle, this view must be regarded with little credence. Some state policies do work to the advantage of workers; some work against the interests of capital. The normal course of economic development regularly

277

and predictably presents fissures in the extent to which the state operates unambiguously in the interests of capitalists:

> The state imposes on each capital various laws, rules, conditions, procedures and taxations which govern the operation of these separate units. And these result significantly from the force and organisation of working-class and popular politics, from the determined resistance of the working-class and others to reproduce the conditions of their own reproduction. Such working-class resistance is never straightforward since it will entail alliances and coalitions with other classes, fractions and social forces. And it will always meet the constraints of action imposed by the existing degree and forms of capital accumulation, the relationship of national to international capital, the movements of money capital and the constraints of the balance of payments, etc. (Urry, 1981, p.115).

The state apparatuses are thus the site of a constant battle between different organizations of labour and capital for control of the resources they have available to them. This is a struggle which is historically patterned. The power of state organizations as they enforce legal obligations or fulfil welfare functions for 'social problems' unresolved through the market is the object of contestation. These state organizations develop not only their own internal structures of bureaucratic control but must do so in the absence of the external discipline of the rationality of the market and subject to the, perhaps, irrational pressures of a plurality of organizations, classes and fractions in civil society. Their ability to do so will be contingent upon the opportunities provided by the 'boom–recession cycle' in capital accumulation.

If the inputs into state organizations are mediated by class struggle, this entails that the outputs – specific state interventions – will always be problematic for the capitalist class. The crucial intervening variable is the nature of the transformation processes – organization/public administration – which intervenes between class struggle, popular demands, executive dictate, organizational imperatives, pressure group activity and specific state decisions.

The transformation processes are structured in a number of class-specific ways. These include, first, the role of interrelated elites from common social backgrounds in the formulation of policy inputs to the executive; second, the structure of hegemony incorporated into the state organizations' taken-for-granted practices of administration; third, the structures affecting the range of relevant issues and interests with which the state has to deal.

Miliband (1969, 1977) has focused specifically on the role of elite personnel in the state apparatus. This view of the state tends to leave its 'functions' and 'organizational form' untheorized. It is regarded rather more as a tool or instrument (hence it is frequently referred to as an *instrumental* approach) which different elites can use for different purposes. Elites are the key focus, defined as those 'people who are located in the commanding heights of the state, in the executive, judicial, repressive and legislative branches' (Miliband, 1977, p.68). Miliband (1969) bases his argument on a wealth of empirical evidence which demonstrates that the state elite has tended to have a relatively homogeneous class background in common with elites in other economic and cultural heights of society. On the basis of Miliband's ample comparative data, it seems warrantable to argue that the major but certainly not the only determinant of access to these most privileged jobs would be a privileged background. In this case it would seem not unreasonable to argue that the individual ruling-elite members are very largely drawn, intergenerationally, from a ruling class which is largely self-reproductive (Stanworth and Giddens, 1974; Higley et al., 1976).

The significance attaching to these studies hinges on one or other (or both) of two assumptions. One has been termed the 'representative bureaucracy' thesis. Initially, this was advanced by Kingsley (1944), albeit in a milder form than is usually advanced today (see Sheriff, 1974, p.448). What is suggested is that unless the upper levels of the state's apparatus of organizations, in particular the public administration, are filled by people who are broadly representative of the population as a whole, in terms of variables such as ethnicity, sex, region and class, then the administration may be less than wholly public in its orientation: it may neglect the needs and interests of those status groups or sectors of the public that are excluded in the recruitment process. Such ideas are behind 'equal opportunity' legislation which establishes quota allocations for various categories of (qualified) people in public administration. This may give rise to a tension between 'meritocracy' and 'representativeness', as Sheriff observed. This tension is frequently observed empirically (Boreham et al., 1979; Royal Commission on Australian Government Administration, 1976, p.23).

The second assumption governing concern about elite recruitment is that this unrepresentative commonality of background results in a common world-view of cultural, political and broadly ideological perspectives. There may be no overall unanimity of views on specific issues but there is a framework of consensus; parameters whose self-evidence is never questioned. These constitute a definite 'hegemony' of conservative, ruling, dominant interests.

In its stronger versions the 'hegemonic' argument is unsupportable. If there were such ruling-class hegemony then no social change would be possible. (Marcuse's (1964) 'one-dimensional' thesis is a case in point.) Clearly, this has not been the case: liberal, democratic capitalist societies have a degree of openness to social change, from which, in part, their legitimacy derives. It is doubtful that there is any knowable content for such an emphatic hegemony; nor is it likely that its mechanisms could unproblematically adjust to changing requirements which do from time to time, inevitably, arise.

There are other objections. Although a correlation between a state elite and an economically dominant class can be and has been established, this relationship has not always held historically. The nature of the exceptions are significant. In nineteenth-century Britain, for instance, the aristocracy ruled politically while the emergent bourgeoisie did not rule. Nor did their representatives, as Ricardo's campaign against the Corn Laws demonstrated. But there can be little doubt concerning the class character of the later-nineteenth-century British state as capitalist (Corrigan, 1980). One is obliged to concur with Miliband, after the salutary experience of his celebrated debate with Poulantzas, that 'the class bias of the state is not determined, or at least not decisively and conclusively determined, by the social origins of its leading personnel' (1977, p.71).

As we have noted, the view of the state adopted by Miliband's (1969) earlier work is instrumentalist: the state is regarded as an instrument for the promotion of ruling-class interests. However, if it is an instrument our discussion suggests that it is poorly tuned for the purpose suggested. Despite a relative degree of homogeneity in the background of elite personnel, there still remain substantial differences and a low correlation between social background and ideological position. Identical private schools can produce 'radical' labourites or 'wet' conservatives, while the products of similar state schools may also be quite dissimilar. Moreover, no such thing as the interest of capital in general appears to exist over and above the particular interests of particular capitals. Additionally, these are always open to reformulation in quite ambiguous ways by the organization and interest mediation of the state itself, as Block (1977, p.13) observes. Once inserted into the state apparatus, 'ruling class members who devote substantial energy to policy formulation become atypical of their class, since they are forced to look at the world from the perspective of state managers. They are quite likely to diverge ideologically from politically unengaged ruling class opinion.' As we shall observe presently, a more structural and less personalistic account is more adequate.

It seems, therefore, that elite recruitment into the state apparatus is facilitative of class rule, but it is not determinant of it. This is one of the reasons why the nature of state outputs in terms of specific policies and interventions remain problematic for the ruling class. All things being equal, however, ruling-elite recruitment may be considered a significant but not determinant aspect of the politics of public administration and the state.

Some elements of the instrumentalist position are useful in detailing the ways in which members of the state apparatus are able to develop a concern with 'reproduction'. The ruling class is able directly to influence the state through the normal processes of lobbying, bribing and informally pressing for actions which it regards as conducive to the interests of the particular contributors to valorization under its control, such as tax relief, tariff policies, budgets, devaluation/revaluation decisions. All groups of capitalists are 'obliged to become politically active, not just to articulate their own views on collective class interests, but also to defend their particular interests' (Mandel, 1974, p.480). In periods of expansion, these interests tend towards securing increasingly favourable state interventions, in the socialization of costs, risks and losses. Additionally, capital may attempt to secure guarantees and subsidies from the state for profitable accumulation opportunities. Despite the often competitive particularity of interests being promoted 'the overall effect of this proliferation of influence channels is to make those who run the state more likely to reject modes of thought and behaviour that conflict with the logic of capitalism' (Block, 1977, p.13).

All states are composed of complex and often internally contradictory and inconsistent organizational apparatuses. However, these organizations are dissimilar to capitalist organizations in a number of ways which conservative governments who seek to recommodify state activities have not been slow to acknowledge. This entails an *organizational* perspective on the state. Within capitalist organizations the fact of competition between many organizations (at least in the competitive sector) leads to precise calculation within them and to an adoption of rationality. But it can be argued that there is no analogous objective social mechanism in the state sector by which state organizations can reduce costs and orient themselves towards an ideal of rationality. On the contrary, where state organization is governed by the principle of an allocative economy, there may be a 'permanent wastage of resources to the extent that all individuals active in it have a material interest in increasing these allocations' (Mandel, 1975, p.579). The reason for this material interest is simple: in an allocative economy any saving on expenditure leads to a reduction in allocations. In terms of the dynamics of power and status within organizations, increased or large allocations are potent resources of both a material and symbolic nature. Hence the need for private capital to control the costs of the managerial labour process and, by contrast, the ambiguous and contradictory location of those state personnel charged with similar control, but at the same time seeking to increase their allocation. Mandel argues that the allocation principle, whereby expenditures are under a constant and automatic inflationary pressure, 'governs all public administration in a commodity-producing society'. This has also been argued at length by Wildavsky (1964). Such arguments suppose that no internal auditing according to politically derived standards of accountability and efficiency is possible. Arguments such as those proposed by Mandel (1975) are generally relevant in circumstances where an executive faces a bureaucracy with strongly organized solutions to possible problems, including an executive wishing to develop the means to implement a sophisticated audit of expenditures and achievement of goals.

State organizations may thus be governed by an allocative economy and so become formally irrational, or at least only partially rational, in terms of purely legal or administrative fiat. An example of the latter would be the existence of staff ceilings which, quantitatively, may be rational (in terms of a cost-reduction exercise) but qualitatively may be irrational inasmuch as they diminish the quality of a service whose rationale justifies their existence. Additionally, these organizations may be characterized by a tendency to a reactive avoidance of responsible planning in the face of competing and contradictory pressure and conflicts, not only from fractions of capital but also from labour, as well as other popular forces in civil society. However, to the extent that these possibilities are realized, the charges of 'administrative overload' and endemic inefficiency that have surfaced since the 1970s, achieve legitimacy.

State organization is constructed in the absence of market mechanisms. Without the discipline they ideally imply, or some alternative such as a public audit, terms such as effectiveness and efficiency lose their focus. The outcome of this rationality–deficit is that public administration comes to be characterized less by its rational goal-orientation and more by its subjective goal-orientation, where subjectivities are, instrumentalists suggest, already preconstituted in a bourgeois, elite mode. This subjective irrationality also has objective organizational determinants. These have been well captured in a definition of organization which has been proposed by Cohen *et al.* (1972). This definition refers only to an organization which characteristically displays problematic preferences, unclear technology (because it lacks any rational rules for monitoring, reflecting and reformulating what it is doing) and fluid participants (who vary in the amount of time and effort they devote to the decision process). These three properties of organized anarchies are particularly conspicuous in public organizations.

The model of 'organized anarchy' stands many current assumptions on their head. Organization has to occur without consistent, shared goals due to changing political interpretation of electoral mandates; so decision-making often proceeds under ambiguity. When a decision is made it is often without recourse to either explicit bargaining or markets; rather, it seems to relate more to the phenomenological attention of members to topics. Here, phenomenology is constituted through the active 'bringing to attention of the administration' by agents, agencies, lobbies, ministers, issues and classes 'outside' the formally constituted bureaucracy whose socially constructed subjectivities – of habit, thinking, feeling, being – may be more or less in, or of, the bureaucracy. Organization, as well as being a process, in such a setting becomes a set of procedures

> through which organisational participants arrive at an interpre-
> tation of what they are doing and what they have done while in
> the process of doing it. From this point of view, an
> organization is a collection of choices looking for problems,
> issues and feelings looking for decision situations in which they
> might be aired, solutions looking for issues to which they might
> be the answer, and decision makers looking for work (Cohen *et
> al.*, 1972, p.4).

There are four elements of organization in this process. First, organization problems, as they are registered by the organization; second, organization solutions – answers looking for questions to attach themselves to; third, participants, who, as has already been pointed out, constitute an 'unrepresentative' and elite-centred bureaucracy; and, finally, choice situations where various kinds of organization personnel, problems and solutions come together. Some of the 'selection rules' guiding these choice situations have been specified by Weick (1969, pp.72-3). For instance, organization members will typically select those choices which require least effort on their part; choices that have occurred most frequently in the past; that have been most successful and predictable in the past; that will produce the least disruption to the organization; that will produce the most stable changes; that can be completed most rapidly; that are available and are not involved in commitments elsewhere; that will utilize the most- rather than the least-experienced personnel; that appear the most relevant given the form in which the problem is registered; and that appear most rewarding.

These criteria serve to reinforce the conservative ethos of elite recruitment through providing an objective context of organizational conservatism: an organizational climate geared to organizationally easy action. (This is why Weber (1978) favoured charismatic leadership – it could disrupt routine in ways in which leadership produced according to such rational criteria would not.) This is not peculiar to public administration, of course, but would be common to most large-scale organizations. What is peculiar to public administration as opposed to private organization is that this conservatism is not subject to any external requirements other than those registered as political demands – usually mediated through the minister. However, as ministerial experience has shown, the politics of bureaucracy can frequently serve to counter ambiguity by subverting political ends with administrative means, or 'ploys', as Meacher (1980) and Blackstone (1983) have suggested.

One author who has been concerned to incorporate similar qualifications is Crouch (1979). The state may well have its primary function oriented to preserving the prosperity of capital accumulation, but, in addition, in order to preserve electoral legitimacy, governments are not readily able to ignore popular pressure even where it conflicts with what they define as the interest of capital. This pressure finds expression in demands for material prosperity – employment and stable prices, for example. Before Thatcherism, stability seemed to be the key: the politics of public administration is inherently conservative. Crouch unwittingly uncovers what may be a clue to the apparent failure of recent attempts to dismantle and deregulate the panoply of the modern state:

> The state's personnel ordinarily have a strong interest in maintaining the stability of institutions which stand between the society and the collapse into civil war; the ease of their own jobs, the prestige of the institutions with which they are identified, ultimately perhaps their own physical safety and (in the case of elected politicians and those about them) their

survival in office all depend on continuing social stability. It is that pursuit of stability which provides the clue to the ultimate motivation of state action (1979, p.40).

Once prosperity passes and is unable to provide the basis for stability, vested interest and institutional inertia take over. But archaic forms of state action remain, until overlaid by a new generation of rules, procedures, practices and collective behaviours.

A considerable advantage of this perspective is that it unhinges the actions of the state apparatuses from the conscious direction of some sector of the ruling classes and regards them rather more as the outcome of a conflict between distinct sets of agents – the capitalist class, the working class, other movements within civil society, and the administrators and managers of the state apparatus. The stress on the routine organizational practices of these state employees, the higher civil service, also focuses our attention not simply on the class-specific inputs to and outputs of the state, but the actual processes of transformation which occur within the state apparatus, quite independently of the consciousness of any particular group (Block, 1977, pp.7-8).

The preceding characterization of the state moves away from the antimonies of *either* a structuralist *or* an instrumentalist perspective, and incorporates some aspects of the organizational perspective. It begins to focus attention on the limits of the state's *structural selectivity* (Offe, 1975) in attending to some issues, enacting some laws, formulating some policies, regulating some areas, *but not others*. In this view, the relative autonomy of the state is recognized, as well as the limits placed on this by its operating environment, and its form as a complex organization; indeed, it is precisely the latter that ensures that the state can never enact in any unmediated way any interest representation made to it.

Various aspects of the state have been analysed as conducive to the reproduction of capitalist interests, inasmuch as they are inscribed in the constitutional form of liberal democracy. A key variable is often elucidated in terms of the need of the state for the maintenance of a reasonable level of economic activity. More abstractly, it can be said that the state in capitalist society attempts to fulfil two basic but sometimes contradictory functions. These are 'accumulation' and 'legitimization'. On the one hand, the state in complex and frequently organizationally contradictory ways, seeks to maintain or create the conditions in which profitable accumulation is possible; but, on the other, it aspires to maintain hegemony. The state, in this argument, cannot afford to neglect the profitable accumulation of the key capitalist enterprises: to do so is to risk drying up the source of its own power – the surplus production capacity of the economic system, the taxes drawn from this surplus and the labour that produces it. Public support, in terms of the legitimacy ceded to the government and the state, may ordinarily be expected to decline sharply if the regime can be perceived as being responsible for social disasters, such as unemployment, inflation or resource shortages. (As we will note, the most common deception is to naturalize such disasters.) Further to this argument, the state has to maintain 'legitimacy' through retaining the loyalty, apathy or acquiescence of economically exploited and socially oppressed groups and classes, while, at the same time, it aids their further exploitation. However, 'those who accumulate capital are conscious of their interests as capitalists, but, in general they are not conscious of what is necessary to reproduce the social order in changing circumstances' (Block, 1977, p.10). The latter concern is a preoccupation which the managers of the state are structurally obliged to develop, because, as Crouch (1979) argues, their power rests on the basis of continued prosperity and political and economic order. The extent to which the state, through these managers, is able to respond to changing circumstances is a function not of individual but of collective consciousness (Clegg et al., 1983). Moreover, the capacity of state institutions to secure stability is subject to dramatic transformation itself, according to phases of capitalist expansion and recession. In addition, structural change in the economy generates quite altered 'functional' requirements from time to time, as well as time-lags in their implementation.

Of equal importance, if less immediately apparent, is the legitimacy ceded not by the electorate as a whole, but capitalists in particular. The withdrawal of legitimacy, or the weakening of tacit support by capital does not have to wait upon the procedural conventions of parliamentary elections. It can be registered much more immediately and subtly. This will be through the mechanism of individual capital's private investment decisions. Through these, capital may institute a collective veto over state policies. A failure, or even hesitancy, to invest in any specific nation state, will be interpreted as a crisis of 'business confidence': the amalgam of factors which coalesce in the capitalist community's evaluation of the risks and potentials – financial, social and political – attaching to any particular investments. Considerations of class control and conflict, of political stability and disorder, of a friendly or hostile government, will be all important in the evaluation of any nation state as a site for investment within the world economy. Consequently, as Edelman (1977), p.151) proposes, governments will grow increasingly responsive to the concentrations of wealth created, where they are not obliged to be responsive to the middle class, the working class, or the poor. These considerations can have very de-stabilizing consequences for left-of-centre social democratic governments. For instance, it has been documented that during the brief period of interruption to conservative rule in Australia (1972–5) which the Whitlam government represented, there was a substantial outflow of, mainly foreign, capital. After the constitutional crisis and dismissal of the Labor government on 11 November 1975, and the return to 'normal' conservative rule, this rapidly reverted to a situation of substantial capital inflow (AMWSU, 1977). However, as the Hawke government's 10 per cent devaluation after gaining office in Australia in 1983 demonstrates, such capital flows can be reversed. Olof Palme's 16 per cent devaluation in Sweden soon after re-election in September 1982 similarly shows that the conditions for currency instability can be self-fulfilling once a 'run' on foreign reserves is initiated.

A possible scenario drawn largely from the experience of the Allende government in Chile has been sketched by Block (1977, pp.17-19). Whenever the left wins an election business confidence declines; this is expressed in speculative activity against the national currency, in anticipation of reformist or extravagant or inflationary policies being adopted. Such anticipation, even given the Keynesian/Kaleckian origins of reformist policies by social democrats, is unwarranted. It is commonly feared that such policies aim to redistribute national income away from profits and towards wages and benefits. A 'rational' response to these policies by capitalists would therefore be to prepare to compensate for any loss of profit by raising prices, a strategy which is especially available to capital operating in the oligopoly and monopoly sectors. In times of boom, inflationary pressures are set up by the bargaining power of a fully employed labour force; in times of recession, however, expansion of public sector spending cannot possibly be inflationary. The opposition to expansionary policies will derive from a fear of an expanded role for the state and from the enhanced participation in economic decision-making that is implied by high levels of investment (Kalecki, 1943). The problems peculiar to social democratic regimes in the context of recovery from the recession of the 1970s and 1980s are discussed in the last chapter. But at any time, these governments will face certain challenges.

In a situation of speculation against its currency, a social democratic government has basically two options. It can renounce its reformism in the face of external pressure from economic orthodoxy, domestic crisis, the International Monetary Fund, the Treasury and escalating inflation. This is the strategy adopted by the Callaghan Labour government in 1976 in Britain. Alternatively, it can carry on regardless, probably provoking a reduced rate of investment and a possible monetary crisis. This in turn would provoke such a response from autonomous capital that quite unprecedented, and probably electorally unpopular, defensive measures would be required by the state to preserve national integrity. In such a situation, a continuing commitment to reformism would mean that the economy would need to be isolated from the world economy, by some combination of price controls, import controls and exchange controls: the various versions of an Alternative Economic Strategy (AES) which we will consider in the last chapter postulate such a package.

Business confidence, the psychological representation of the investment cycle, is the crucial variable. This, of course, is not something which is disorganized or left to individual calculation. There exist organized indices of business confidence to assist internationally mobile capital. For instance, capital can consult the world index of political risks for investors calculated by the American Business Environment Risk Index Institute, or the World Political Risk Forecast Institute, which has noted of Singapore, for example, that excellent economic prospectives rise in inverse proportion to political opposition.

It is through such means that capital, in its investment decisions, is able to set a range of powerful limits on the possibilities of state action. However, in so far as the state is an effect of class struggle, the effectiveness of working-class struggle as well as the actions of capital must be considered. This is demonstrated clearly in Marx's analysis of the length of the working day. As we have already indicated, there was, at the time of the Ten Hour Bill, little business confidence in the wisdom of the Act. Apologists for capital, such as Nassau Senior, rallied against a policy which they argued would eliminate the most profitable part of the day – the last few hours of work! However, working-class agitation and aristocratic parliamentarians were able to win in debate, and the Ten Hour Bill became law.

In addition to identifying struggle *within* the state, such as the Ten Hour Bill, one can identify those mechanisms *about* which class conflict will have to be constructed to undermine overall reproduction. This is to differentiate class conflict *within* the political form of the state from class conflict *about* this form. Class conflict within the state is that conflict which is able to manifest itself within the given organizational and procedural *rules of the game*, in the actually existing state structures. This conflict concerns

> which political forms are most conducive to the articulation of the undistorted interest of various classes; supposedly each class tries to generalise and institutionalise those political forms which are most conducive to the self-enlightenment of the members of that class as to its 'true' interest and which, at the same time, minimize the adversary class's chance of articulating its interests (Offe and Wiesenthal, 1980, p.95).

The national interest and capitalist interest can, it has been demonstrated, frequently be orchestrated in harmony. However, we have been at pains to demonstrate that one cannot maintain that the state's output of legal enactments, the key resource available to the state in defining the 'rules of the game' in civil society and the economy generally, will necessarily be reproductive. Law is *the* intermediary between civil society, the economy and the state. Political and class struggles are manifested materially in the changing regulation and legal forms enacted by the state. The subjects engaged in these struggles are, of course, always already constituted as legal subjects by the state. Thus, neither the state, nor its constitution of subjects, is neutral or independent of these struggles. Forms both of the state and of subjects are an object of class struggle.

The state, as a social relation which embodies the class struggle (and other struggles generated by major social cleavages produced by interpellations of ethnicity, race, gender, region, nation, and so on), is never wholly determined within the 'rules of the game'. In consequence, the central question concerning state interventions will be the extent to which their actual content is a result of ruling-class domination or contrary popular pressure. This, along with differing accumulation strategies favoured by different segments of capital (Jessop, 1983), may produce interventions which are not optimally reproductive: they may, for instance, be compatible whilst at the same time having contradictory effects (Clegg and Dunkerley, 1980, pp.550-5). Under sufficient popular pressure they may even be non-reproductive: that is, they may be transformative of the underlying principles of organization of the state and society. Struggle may materialize about the state. The state, in other words, may become an instrument for translating the interests of labour into redistributive and egalitarian practice. With this conception, the theory of the state achieves a position in which elements of both the instrumental, structural, organizational and structural selectivity approaches can be incorporated.

A conception of the state as a social relation informed Marx's *Capital*, albeit in implicit terms. The success of working-class struggle in shortening the working day was the decisive factor in the transition from what Marx termed the formal to the real subordination of labour and the move from the absolute to the relative exploitation of surplus value. This is indicative of the general point: class struggle is a decisive factor in the transformation of both the state and capitalism. The state is changed by taking on new functions and apparatuses as a result of the changed legal statutes, while capital has to reconsider its competitive possibilities in terms of the changed limits to its activity, prescribed by the state. It is for this reason that working-class struggles against the depredations of the market society have been instrumental in facilitating both the further development of capitalism and the expansion of the state. With this process, as we have argued, the state's expansion began to develop its own logic, under the pressure of state managers operating in an allocative economy.

The translation of working-class pressure into state reforms and capitalist rationality is not an unproblematic and smoothly functioning process for a number of reasons. Working-class demands are rarely granted in their original form. Anticipation of this can often lead to an inflation of demands in expectation of a negotiated settlement. Elements of repression can co-exist with concessions. Considerable time-lags invariably occur between concessions being granted after working-class pressure and the development of state powers which are proposed to enable enhanced accumulation. Radical demands are ceded which cannot be translated into potential benefits for capital. Occupational health and safety legislation often falls into this category. Where there is pressure for reform, state managers in both the government and civil service have to balance a delicate equation. If reforms of a critical issue are blocked or refused, there may well be an escalation of class antagonisms. This can exacerbate any problems of business confidence, such that a mildly reformist government may appear more stable to large capital interests than a more conservative one (Block, 1977).

Once again, it is important not to over-state the case. The perceived threat to business confidence has in many cases not been sufficient to prevent potentially radical reforms, particularly during periods of national mobilization such as depression, war and postwar reconstruction. It is in such periods that the role of the state has quantitatively expanded for different reasons. During war the importance of international business confidence declines in the face of the generally patriotic climate and the high levels of economic activity engendered by military production. In serious depressions or postwar reconstruction the dynamics are different. Should state policy attempt to revive the economy it is probable that business confidence will emerge as a key variable as the political balance shifts. Other possibilities are discussed later. One important theoretical consideration is the gap between reform in law and in actual practice. Not all legal changes are enacted in the spirit which might have guided their drafting. Further, not all forms of reform achieved in these 'exceptional' periods succeed in outlasting them (Lowe, 1975). Reform, in itself, is simply a substantive means oriented to a particular end, the end being the continuing implementation of the reforms in practice. It is the mechanisms whereby the state manages this implementation which are crucial.

State management has to be accomplished through state managers. Many state managers hold beliefs which affirm their personally neutral roles, beliefs which co-exist with a belief in institutions they have supported. To accept the contradiction of a neutral ideology and a partial practice is to live out the mythologies of the roles attached to the positions these managers occupy 'while at the same time maintaining a measure of personal integrity by recognizing facts inconsistent with the role' (Edelman, 1977, p.151). Hence, the naturalization of the state as a social relation is an effect of practices whose partiality, as self-interested exceptions, can be seen to affirm the eidolon of neutrality. Liberal, neutral ethics, however flawed in practice, can be used as an operational device, in the pursuit of specific substantive ends. A realistic party programme that seeks to articulate a constituency, despite alliances it may build in the economy and civil society, will still need some mechanisms for the generation and implementation of its programme. Ethics of neutrality, even as ideology, may be seen to have purpose. To overcome fetishistic tendencies in a state whose managers equate their 'normal' practices with neutrality, parties must make *difference* their key-note. This is precisely because it is the denial of difference which has become the hallmark not only of certain 'tough-minded' conservative parties, but also of the state more generally. Abstract impossibilities of existence have been promoted which serve to narrow the range of possibilities for state action through practices such as

> the constant 'rewriting of history' to materialize what has been, in fact, an extremely changeable set of State relations, to claim that there is, and always has been, one 'optimal institutional structure' which is what 'any' civilization needs; and . . . to

marginalize (disrupt, deny, destroy, dilute . . .) all alternative forms of State, particularly any which announce any form of organization that establishes *difference* at the level of the national social formation (Corrigan *et al.*, 1980, p.17).

Since 1979 the resolute reiteration by the British Prime Minister Margaret Thatcher that 'there is no alternative' to her economic policies of monetarism (TINA, as her opponents have dubbed this refrain) has served to illustrate the validity of this analysis in its sharpest form.

Paradoxically, to the extent that difference can be ruled out, an aggregative party can succeed in also being an articulatory party, by persuading the variegated populace that it articulates what is seemingly the only rational option. Under such circumstances, as has been remarked elsewhere,

> Little effort is expended in critique or counter-strategy, because the weapons of critique are not available. Unemployment, inflation or wage cuts can come to be accepted as normal, as natural, as something which could not have been otherwise, as their sense is constituted in and through hegemonic forms of theorizing (Clegg, 1979, p.88).

To the extent that the exclusion of alternatives is couched in terms of a programme justified through categories derived from the dominance of liberal democracy, notably individual freedom and social order, secured through the market, then any counter-hegemonic strategy will have to seize these categories to demonstrate how its programme extends and deepens them.

State and strategy

It has been suggested that in the post-1974 world recession the fate of liberal democracy and its coupling to capitalist economy is once more in question (Offe, 1983). We will argue that this conjuncture offers a real opportunity not so much for uncoupling liberal democracy from the capitalist economy, but for restructuring the latter in order to deepen the former.

To the extent that changes in postwar institutions and practices generated economic growth and capital accumulation, they did so through decisively transforming the structure and organization of class relationships. It is this changed structure of class relationships, we will argue, which is responsible for the present recessionary impasse. Hitherto, the dominant strategies for its resolution have been market-oriented: that is, they have adopted a market strategy of reaffirming the capitalist nature of the economy, which, while it has been cognisant of the decline of competitive markets, has either proposed remedies oriented to 'rigidities' in the labour market or has exhorted the verities of competition to a capital market increasingly dominated by large corporations. We have argued that it is primarily the changes in class organization which have produced large, merged private corporations whose unsocialized investment behaviours and strategies are the effective causes of recessionary downturns in economic activity.

The recession is a resultant of 'capital-logic' and its restructuring of class relations in different states and civil societies, particularly at the level of changes in the corporate organization of the ruling class and response to this by the working class. The restructuring of capital which was punctuated by the last merger wave of the late 1960s and early 1970s took place after a prolonged period of accumulation which strengthened labour considerably. However, the subsequent changes to corporate organization have produced impediments to further accumulation which have weakened labour.

Politics is inscribed on this changing terrain of class relations. In terms of class politics, concentrating on Marx and Engels's two great classes, two rational strategies, appropriate respectively to capitalists and labourers, can be identified. The axis of differentiation is the extent to which each strategy is oriented towards reproduction: a socialist strategy would be oriented towards transformation.

The reproduction of the capital–labour relation poses a 'strategic dilemma' for capital: wages are a cost to production as well as the source of market demand for production. For these reasons, 'the capital relation constitutes an indeterminate terrain on which different interests compete to establish a definite course of accumulation' (Jessop, 1983, p.148). Accumulation itself becomes a strategy in which both the institutions of the state and the associations of particular capitals are involved under conditions of ambiguity given by disarticulation in the circuit of capital. Economic crises will affect the ability of the state to implement and regulate accumulation strategies. To the extent that finance capital, for example, facilitates the realization of value created in the industrial sector, an accumulation strategy can be perceived which has very different implications from one where financial interests can be pursued alongside a steady 'deindustrialization' (Jessop, 1983, p.150). The strategic choices available to the state in such instances will clearly be divergent enough to ensure prolonged contestation over models of economic growth, degrees of non-market infrastructural provisions, concessions to intra-

and interclass rivals, and so on. The extent to which either reproduction or transformation will be achieved will be an uncertain effect of those strategies. None the less, inasmuch as periods of disarticulation in the circuit of capital through the various manifestations of the 'value form' produce recessionary conjunctures, then existing accumulation strategies can be seen not to be wholly reproductive. Such conjunctures throw the whole issue of accumulation strategies into question. At such times alternative strategies, fashioned with transformative rather than merely reproductive goals in mind, can more readily contest the terrain of ideas in a labour movement for whom 'business as usual' no longer provides a natural hegemony.

The growth of modern complex organization in both the state and the economy structures classes in such a way that accumulation strategies intended, however uncertainly or imperfectly, to transform the capitalist value form in its circuit, need not necessarily be restricted in their attraction to a shrinking traditional proletariat. Salaried 'new-middle-class' employees, particularly in the blocked career paths of the lower orders of the state and economy, have a greater interest in accumulation *per se*, than in the strategy designed to accomplish it. Hence, where market-oriented accumulation strategies can be said to have failed and their own careers are in question, such a class may welcome a more explicitly political economy if it appears to offer functionally more efficient accumulation. Whether or not these possibilities will materialize is in large part conditional upon the strength of class organization which we discussed earlier in this chapter.

It is through an analysis of changes in the structure of capitalist accumulation, particularly as it is punctuated by recession, that the more explicitly political and party concerns enter into the determination of the forms these changing relationships will take. In recession, both aggregate profits and employment decline, irrespective of improvements that occur in a localized way in particular branches of the economy. Consequently, both capital and labour organization will be weakened. However, as this chapter has made clear, the decline will not be from a position of formally equivalent power. Moreover, recession can tilt this balance further towards capital because of the far greater liquidity of the latter. Labour is weakened by recession disproportionately, not only because of the lack of liquidity of labour, but also because recession further disorganizes workers through exacerbating and deepening the employed/unemployed division. Further, as Therborn (1979, p.9) hypothesizes, recession tends to generate class struggles whose outcome depends on the pre-crisis strength of capital and labour – not in any deterministic way, but in consequence of the fact that recessions do not automatically strengthen labour, unless there are additional, exogeneous factors at work serving to weaken state reproduction. Divergent political analyses of crisis or recession can be identified. We will consider these in the final chapter, particularly with a view to the strategies that ensue from them. In the past, capitalist development was supported by the propagation and expansion of the forms of liberal democracy. The current recession appears to some commentators to portend a restructured market-logic as its solution, while others propose a greater subsumption of market criteria to an extended notion of citizenship, one embracing economic as well as civil rights. It is the structural determinants of these choices and the possible outcomes they imply that we will analyse next.

Summary

The representation of the economy as comprised of two countervailing organized powers is one which is false. This misrepresentation becomes apparent in a number of important ways through a consideration of the state and civil society. The state and civil society are mediated through political parties and state regulation. Political parties hardly compete in a political marketplace, hence notions of political participation that focus primarily on voting are unduly restrictive. Politics embraces not only mass parties but also the state as a social relation of complex organization. The state is no more a neutral instrument than is the party. Each, in diverse ways, has generally good organizational reasons for organizationally easy action. However, the ideology of the state as a liberal, neutral instrument, has its uses. It may be articulated as a strategy by governing parties against those practices which run counter to the parties' manifesto. Rhetoric can be used to ensure particular practice. Such a strategy is particularly needed where aggregative parties operate in a variegated class structure and civil society. The combination of an aggregative party and a state whose organizationally conservative views concur, in an articulation of a lack of difference, presents the strongest challenge to any other party seeking to establish a different set of policies. It either has to attempt to aggregate the same ground and thus lose any major claims to difference or it must be engaged in a popular struggle to construct a different, alternative hegemony founded on workable alliances across the class and status differentia subsumed under the present hegemony. To do this requires some account of what a different politics and economics might be, its relation to the structure of class society and a programme for its implementation.

9 Class politics and the economy

The fundamental facts of class structuration always exist simultaneously with a wide variety of other social practices located in the state and civil society. It is the existence of distinct modalities characteristic of the process of capital accumulation which serve to structure the rhythm of class formation within the overall pattern of social processes. The distinctive form of capitalist accumulation is that of the boom–recession cycle. It is the cyclical, crisis-prone character of capitalist development which produces corporate restructuring and therefore provides heightened opportunities for state intervention, class organization and alternate accumulation and investment strategies.

Class struggle emerges when any collective effort to influence the fundamental processes of surplus appropriation and redeployment (valorization) involves conflict with the established organization of this class process. As such, although specific manifestations of class struggle are always possible during periods of capital accumulation, they are never inevitable. To the extent that non-class conflicts may affect the conditions which make surplus labour extraction possible, significant strategic opportunities for political and social change that *do* have effectivity for fundamental class conflicts may be in the process of constantly being produced. In this chapter we will outline how political struggles over the role of the state in particular national contexts can take the form of unambiguous class struggle, but we also note that even non-class conflicts may have effects on the potential for ongoing capital accumulation. We have already discussed the political impact, at crucial conjunctural moments, of the petty bourgeoisie and new middle class.

The state, in its normal functioning, regulates the conditions of social and economic life. It is none the less apparent that state regulation changes over time, partly as an effect of the technical skills and knowledge available at any given time, and partly as a response to those characteristics of the state's environment to which it selectively attends at any given time. Technique and selectivity are necessarily linked. For many commentators this union achieved a heightened form during the postwar growth of Keynesian-managed economies in many of the advanced states (although, of course, the postwar epoch saw a retreat from the greater regulation of the wartime command economy). Hence, 'Keynesian policy' has become almost an iconographic representation of 'state intervention' and its alleged failures.

Keynes and intervention

Both the neo-conservative and the radical assaults on the counter-cyclical and welfare-state consensus politics of the post-1945 decades have focused on the alleged inappropriateness of Keynesian interventions in the context of the current recession. Conservatives see the crisis as a result of the erosion of capitalist and managerial prerogatives by incipient statism, regulatory intrusions, expanding spheres of unproductive spending and overloaded government. On the other hand, some Marxist critiques of postwar Keynesianism point out that the development of a social security system, a social wage component of national income, infrastructure provision for private enterprise, industrial relations legislation and state economic management have simply built so many contradictory elements into the framework of the capitalist state that its failure to foresee or to avert inflationary consequences and monetarist responses is scarcely surprising.

We wish to clarify these disparate positions by re-examining the potential for democratic involvement in economic policy and by pointing to some of the structural determinants upon policies concerning public sector cutbacks and expansion, wage maintenance and moderation, joint employee–corporate–state consultative bodies and strategies, investment decisions, growth, distribution and inflation. Economic policy formation is the area of state activity most readily affected by changed political acumen of any of the major class groupings discussed previously.

The ambiguity and disparity of the available accounts of contemporary political conflicts derive in part from the unusual conditions that have characterized the depression that began in 1974. Compared with the 1930s, the current experience in most countries seems more intractable and less amenable to any single set of policy remedies – even though unemployment rates are far lower in the 1980s than they were at the peak of the 1930s depression. It seems that the institutional and political conditions for concerted commitments to full employment policies for the 1980s and beyond will be more difficult to secure this time than they were in the 1940s. Even then, the commitments were delayed for over a decade and abandoned soon after (Apple, 1983).

The difference between the two depressions is superficially signalled by the simultaneous presence of both unemployment and inflation in the 1980s. This conjunction of elements thought to be mutually incompatible because of the presumed existence of a 'trade-off' between them, led to the often proclaimed but inaccurately formulated conclusion that demand-stimulation remedies that were appropriate for the 1930s depression were self-defeating in the 1980s.

Consequently, anti-recessionary policy has been eschewed in almost every country in favour of anti-inflationary policy. Inflation is seen as the cause of the recession and expansionary policies are seen as inevitably inflationary. Policies designed to reduce public spending and to reduce the rate of wage increases have therefore been proposed as essential preconditions of permanent economic recovery. It is this presumed relationship between unemployment and inflation that appears to be misunderstood in most contemporary debate.

When Keynes in 1936 produced his intellectual justification (and rhetorical pleas) for an interventionist role for government, it was clear that the cause of economic downturn was the absence of mechanisms by which producers were able to match their output with consumer demand. Although Keynes arrived at his conclusions by considering the differential motivations of investors and savers, the problem with which he was dealing was precisely that which was revealed by the 'disproportionality' thesis in Marx's examination of the conditions for 'simple reproduction'. Chronic demand deficiency either generally or in certain sectors was a permanent possibility. A corollary of the absence of equilibrating mechanisms in a normally functioning private enterprise economy is obviously unemployment, sectoral imbalance, and a need for massive structural adjustment. This occurs for a variety of contingent reasons, such as disasters, unforeseeable changes in technology, preferences, etc., as well as for reasons of social organization, including the existence of speculative activities, and 'anarchy' of the market as an allocator of resources.

Keynes recognized that market mechanisms did not work to align the decisions of different groups in the community. In times of economic downturn, governments *could* deliberately expand the level of economic activity by initiating public expenditures, paying wages, increasing aggregate demand, and allowing multiplier effects to increase economic activity, incomes, production, employment and living standards. Thus, he maintained, they *should* do so. Keynes argued that any public expenditure would achieve these effects but implied that socially desirable and long-term capital-intensive projects should be preferred. But he seemed to sense as well the inevitable political objections:

> If the Treasury were to fill old bottles with banknotes, bury them at suitable depths in disused coalmines which are then filled up to the surface with town rubbish and leave it to private enterprise on well-tried principles of laissez-faire to dig the notes up again . . . there need be no more unemployment and, with the help of the repercussions, the real income of the community, and its capital wealth also, would probably become a good deal greater than it actually is. It would, indeed, be more sensible to build houses and the like; but if there are political and practical difficulties in the way of this, the above would be better than nothing (Keynes, 1936, p.129).

As we know now, of course, the political objections to expansionary policies were substantial, even in the 1930s. It was only the onset of the war that allowed the objections to be overcome and for full employment to be achieved. Some theorists, despite this wartime experience and despite the *political* nature of the objections to Keynes, still maintain that 'commonly orthodox Keynesianism . . . implies an exaggeration of the capacity of governments in capitalist countries to achieve their objectives' (Tomlinson, 1982, p.121). Such claims would require substantial evaluation of the extent of the state's autonomy. It is unduly rationalistic to assume that the failure to achieve a construct, an objective, is *a priori* a 'failure'. A great deal depends on the construct itself. Such matters cannot be settled out of context by formalist argument. Second, we can ironically note that amongst Keynesians themselves, there has been a recognition that the theory was blocked in practice not by an exaggeration of government capacity, but by its limitation. Joan Robinson, for instance, was well aware of the institutional hostility in the British Treasury to the remedies explicit in Keynesian policy:

> It was a joke in Germany that Hitler was planning to give employment in straightening the Crooked Lake, painting the Black Forest white and putting down linoleum in the Polish

Corridor. The Treasury view was that his unsound policies would soon bring him down. But the little group of Keynesians was despondent and frustrated. We were getting the theory clear at last, but it was going to be too late (Robinson, 1973, p.3).

So demand-stimulation aspects of Keynesianism were never implemented in peacetime in an authentic or comprehensive way. More important, however, is that policy makers seem never to have recognized that Keynesianism could not succeed whilst it was seen as merely a strategy for demand stimulation. Although Keynes did not pursue the issue, the real problem was one of structural change in the economy. Industry organized purely on the profit principle is incapable of perpetually meeting social needs, although it may achieve some short-run fit, because economic and social change periodically make some sectors and activities redundant and hence call forth new forms of economic expansion. Robinson (1972) has argued that if these issues had been recognized much earlier than they were, the possibilities of the Keynesian revolution would not have been so quickly dissipated. Economists involved in policy-making institutions at the time agree that Keynes's proposals were implemented too cautiously or too unspecifically (Myrdal, 1972, pp. 8, 19; Galbraith, 1975, p.138; Robinson, 1972).

Economic recessions are always the occasion for transition from one pattern of economic activity to another. Without planning mechanisms and mechanisms of structural adjustment, social disruption at such times is inevitable. Keynes accepted that a useful short-term solution would be for governments to hire unemployed people for short- and long-term projects which would stimulate demand, but the underlying problem would remain one of attending to the overall structure of the economy. It was on this basis that Keynes proposed much more substantial forms of government intervention than would be required by mere increases in public spending: 'There is no clear evidence from experience that the investment policy which is socially advantageous coincides with that which is most profitable' (1936, p.157). This is because there would be occasions when capitalists' long-term expectations would lead to a curtailment of investment. He advocated a much more democratic and collectivist input into the economic decision-making processes of mature capitalist economies on a permanent basis: 'I conceive, therefore, that a somewhat comprehensive socialization of investment will prove the only means of securing an approximation to full employment' (1936, p.378).

These key aspects of the *General Theory* were decisively ignored by the postwar policies of 'fine-tuning' (fiscal and monetary policy) which came to be regarded as authentic Keynesianism. For some analysts of the business cycle, the 'bastardization' of Keynes's prescriptions was not surprising. It is easier to see now than it was at the time that neither the institutional hostility to the anti-recessionary policies advocated by Keynes nor the short-lived periods of official commitment to policies of full employment can be adequately explained by the attitudes of policy-makers themselves. Nevertheless, the era of the long boom, a period during which government intervention was nominally accepted (and exemplified in the 'new economics' of the 'Kennedy Keynesians' (Cowling, 1982, p.121)), was not an era of public involvement in investment decisions. Public expenditure plans, other than military expenditures which neither compete with private investment nor subsidize public consumption, were emasculated. The condition that Keynes determined as necessary for the avoidance of slumps, namely 'the somewhat comprehensive socialization of investment', was conscientiously shunned. The lessons of both the 1930s depression and Keynes's theoretical interventions were not learned.

The political trade cycle

Although Keynesianism may have produced the technical basis for a systematic state intervention and regulation of a qualitatively different kind, Keynes's understanding of the state rarely exceeded that of a liberal world-view. In the absence of a more sophisticated understanding of the ability of government to effect policy solutions, Keynes was unreasonably sanguine. However, this confidence was not as evident among other economists who at roughly the same time advocated similar solutions to the problems that vexed Keynes. It has been pointed out by Robinson that a more realistic and prescient account of the likely behaviour of the state was provided by the Polish economist and wartime planner, Michal Kalecki (Robinson, 1976b). There is a political background in the opposition to the full-employment doctrine even though the arguments advanced are economic (Kalecki, 1943, p.324). Kalecki pointed out that business people would not favour prolonged full employment if it involved public investment in public enterprise, nor if it helped to erode the 'moral principle' of reward for effort, nor if 'factory discipline' was lost through growing self-assurance and class consciousness of the working class. To the extent that full employment would involve a shift in the locus of decision-making from private to collective auspices, it would be opposed. Faced with the choice between political control and profitability, capitalists will tend to sacrific the latter:

> It is true that profits would be higher under a regime of full employment than they are on average under laissez-faire; and even the rise in wages resulting from the stronger bargaining power of the workers is less likely to reduce profits than to increase prices, and thus affects adversely only the rentier interests. But 'discipline in the factories' and 'political stability' are more appreciated by the business leaders than profits (Kalecki, 1943, p.326).

This opposition, according to Kalecki, would come in both ideological and institutional forms. The social function of the doctrine of sound finance becomes apparent as it is invoked to keep the level of economic activity dependent on 'business confidence' rather than public intervention. None the less, since the 1930s it has not been theoretically consistent to deny the efficacy of government intervention *per se*, even if in practice such claims have acquired credence; so objections can be expected to centre on political *maintenance* of full employment. Once governments learned that it was possible to alleviate a slump, permanent full employment became a political possibility, and as it became apparent that the stimulation of private investment does not secure this, a permanent role for public investments was legitimated. To prevent the possibility (and to counteract the enhanced power to the working classes that full employment would provide), conservatives 'would probably find more than one economist to declare that the situation was manifestly unsound' (Kalecki, 1943, p.330). What Kalecki was anticipating was the era of the 'political trade cycle' where full employment was approached for electoral purposes from time to time, but where each period of expansion was followed by reductions in budget deficits in non-election years. He foresaw the era of 'stop–go' economic policy which accompanied the aborted Keynesian revolution all through the 1950s and 1960s.

The business cycle is a phenomenon which reflects objective consequences of the interrelated changes of investment decisions, overall capital accumulation and the volume of existing capital equipment. As Figure 9.1 indicates, these magnitudes do not rise and fall together. Kalecki's 1933 essay showed that investment (the formation of physical capacity rather than a set of financial flows) was the key to the operation of the business cycle (Beresford and McFarlane, 1980). When capitalists initiate investment orders, they call forth increases in production and after a

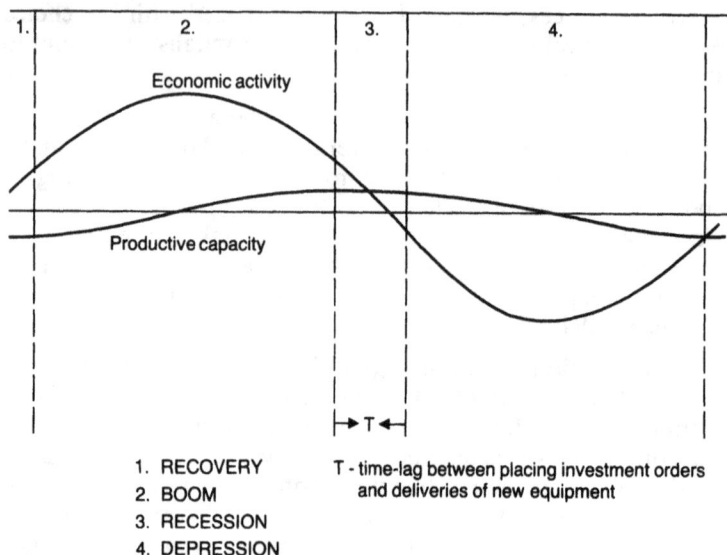

1. RECOVERY
2. BOOM
3. RECESSION
4. DEPRESSION

T - time-lag between placing investment orders
and deliveries of new equipment

FIGURE 9.1 *The business cycle produced by interrelated changes in investment orders, gross accumulation and levels of capital equipment*

Source: Kalecki (1933)

time the volume of capital equipment (productive capacity) in existence will have increased, leading, therefore, to a cessation of investment orders. In a recovery phase of the cycle, investment orders will *exceed* the replacement requirements and production will commence even though the volume of capital equipment is still low or shrinking (this was the condition which initiated the increase in investment decisions in the first place). Under these conditions, a boom may ensue – this will involve setting up new equipment, a consequent expansion of capital's capacity and an inevitable decline, first in further investment orders, and then in the production of investment goods. Consequently, during the recessionary phase, investment orders will be below the requirements for their replacement even though the volume of capital equipment is high or expanding. In the inevitable depression the continuing increase in capital equipment slows down and an increase in production of investment goods could be expected in the second half of the depression.

Conceptualization of an ideal type of economic cycle in this way, allowed Kalecki to illustrate not only the underlying determinants of fluctuations in economic activity (in less psychologistic terms than those used by Keynes), but also the possibility of quite technical definitions of the stages of the cycle. Recession, depression, recovery, and boom each manifest a different relationship between the level of economic activity and the level of productive capacity.

As we have argued, however, it is impossible to stabilize investment activity at a level appropriate to non-cyclical growth unless all investment is conducted according to planned production and in the context of prior decisions concerning the allocation of resources between investment and consumption and the distribution of income. This schematic model of the capitalist business cycle (Kalecki, 1933, pp.9-14) shows that capitalists as a whole do control their own (collective) destinies because of their control over investment. When capitalists spend money, on either investment or consumption goods, their money flows to other capitalists as profits. 'Workers spend what they get, capitalists get what they spend.'

The behaviour of economic aggregates at different stages of the business cycle has other elements. Kalecki was able to demonstrate that the distribution of income was not fixed in a capitalist economy but varied according to stages of the business cycle. He was able to argue, on the basis of both empirical and theoretical analysis (1954a) that in the early stages of a general downturn, the share of total income accruing to labour increases while the profit share declines. This is so even though real incomes will probably still be falling. It is not a consequence of increased bargaining strength of labour but rather due to the external factors giving rise to the depression itslf. The first indicators of recession are declines in turnover and hence in profitability. The downward phase is inevitable because increases in investment cannot go on indefinitely. When the rate of investment is allowed to fall, so too will the rate of profits. If the amount of productive capacity continues to be high or increasing when sales are not, the boom will break (Robinson, 1966, p.339). As excess capacity begins to appear, the wages share of total income rises.

When capital begins to respond to these conditions by reconstituting the labour market or by suppressing real wages or by increasing the degree of monopoly (retaliatory measures which all aim to arrest the decline in profitability), then the wages share will decline relative to the profits share. In the initial stage of the upswing it is usual for the wages share to decline and for capital's share to increase. It is in the upswing, furthermore, that raw material costs increase proportionately more rapidly than wage costs, and so too does the profit share. Profits are determined by capitalists' propensity to invest and consume. Investment is the key, because capitalists can decide to increase their share of national income simply by deciding to invest more.

It is clear, therefore, that the class distribution of income, and consequently the relative strength of the collective participants in industry, is linked not only to cyclical movements in capitalist economies but also to the more long-term secular and structural tendencies which emerge from them. Cowling (1982) has argued that the business cycle upswing is normally the occasion not only for an expansion of the share of profits in total income, but also for 'the degree of monopoly'. These increases, as we argued earlier, are the result not so much of any rationalistic economies of scale, but of the financial basis of the organization of a capitalist economy based on general credit availability. Economies of scale in finance are more important than those presumed to exist in technique. Indeed, to the extent that the real subordination of merged multiplant enterprises into the more rational multidivisional structure has been hotly resisted subsequent to mergers, then these economies scarcely exist. Financial economies of scale are the main lever of merger. Lower costs per unit of finance for larger firms, the use of size as a risk indicator for loan capital, and the source of much of this capital from institutional investors all contribute to the increased degree of monopoly.

For these reasons, the organizational form of capitalist industry is transformed at key stages of capitalist development, with crucial and determinant consequences for labour movement capacity to intervene in wage, health and safety, macro-policy or industrial democracy conflicts with employers. The influences on income distribution are not voluntarist but structural: but even the structural conditions may produce multiple determinations. In so far as there is a tendency to industrial concentration, workers in the more monopolized sectors may have enhanced bargaining power; yet in so far as these conditions exist in an expansionary phase, it is the profits share rather than the wages share which is increasing: 'the factors which determine the degree of monopoly will determine the share of wages irrespective of worker pressure; the higher the degree of monopoly the *lower* the wage share' (Cowling, 1982, p.104). The most important corollary of this argument is the lack of effectiveness of market-oriented policy for either investment determination or income determination.

Because income distribution changes at different stages of the cycle, no simple wages/profits trade–off can be presumed in a capitalist economy. If wages and profits shares respond simultaneously to investment cycles then it is clear that profits cannot be enhanced by depressing wages directly. It makes no sense to claim that wage reductions are essential for economic recovery. The determinants of cyclical movements in capitalist economies are of an external, secular or structural kind and are not given initially by changes in political power or the bargaining successes of organized labour. They are far more determined by investment decisions and by judgments concerning future capital requirements. It is not costs which determine production but investment behaviour.

In the modern epoch this behaviour is increasingly the result of, as well as contributor to, monopolistic tendencies. The erosion of competitive pressures is understandably accompanied by the existence of excess capacity in industry (because the otherwise effective drive towards efficiency and cost-cutting is eroded). Under these circumstances, extra-market power is used as a means of repressing activity and, therefore, of restraining the threat of labour. To some extent tendencies towards concentration which occur in expansionary phases, when profits are also expanding relative to wages, impose constraints upon any increase in labour's real income. But these two processes – an increasing profits share and increasing real wages – are not incompatible. However, as we shall argue later, an explicitly anti-recessionary programme will require the institution of a permanent incomes policy to control politically not only the pricing powers of corporations, but also distribution of income between labour and capital which is the outcome of the processes of expansion. Any growth phase enhances not only labour's bargaining power but also wage levels. Therefore, 'it is possible to envisage a higher wage share as a permanent gain from operating the economy closer to its potential output than capitalists would choose to do' (Cowling, 1982, p.97).

Consequently, nothing sensible is to be achieved through concessions by labour concerning 'wage restraint'. In fact, to the extent that organized labour is able to restrain price 'mark-ups' in industries with a high degree of monopoly,

a wage rise showing an increase in the trade union power leads – contrary to the precepts of classical economics – to an increase in employment. And conversely, a fall in wages showing a weakening in their bargaining power leads to a decline in employment. The weakness of trade unions in a depression manifested in permitting wage cuts contributes to a deepening of unemployment rather than to relieving it (Kalecki, 1971, p.163).

Wages are a component of consumption as well as of costs, so high wages will have a positive effect on overall profits in so far as they permit higher levels of aggregate demand, aggregate spending, economic activity and production. The 'wages as costs' tendency is always subordinate to the 'wages as contributor to expanding output' tendency because of these independent determinants of the class distribution of income. Thus the form and effectivity of class struggle changes at different stages of the cycle (Robinson, 1977, p.13).

A corollary of this reasoning is that the level of income is never independent of its distribution. This observation has important implications for macro-policy during recession. If the distribution of income between wages and profits is mirrored by the division of national output between workers' consumption (wages) and capitalists' consumption (investment), then the higher the proportion of investment in total output, the higher the share of profits relative to wages in national income (Kregel, 1979, p.55). When extended to the distribution of income within the class of consumers, it can also be seen that the more unevenly skewed is the distribution of income, the lower will be the overall levels of income. Consequently, a shift in income distribution alone (towards those with high propensity to consume) will have an expansionary effect on levels of economic activity (Worswick, 1977, p.26). Higher levels of incomes, employment and activity, themselves indicate a decline in inequalities. The converse is also true: unevenly distributed incomes are more likely during periods of low or declining total income. To the extent that macro-economic policy promotes either inequality or deflation, it automatically encourages both. The politics of restraint have a class bias far beyond that admitted in anti-inflationary rhetoric (Boddy and Crotty, 1975).

Political implications of this analysis abound. Incomes in capitalist society can be explained independently of any reference to the productivity of the recipients. Classes are not merely 'factors of production' which are rewarded in accordance with their contribution to production, but political actors able to influence the level, content, distribution and effects of that production:

It is no longer possible to justify unequal incomes on the basis of differential productivity nor the difference between wages and profits on the same grounds. Income differentials are thus neither natural nor economic facts, but the result of social and political custom and decisions, as well as market power' (Kregel, 1979, p.58).

In the 1980s especially, it is apparent that wages policies are intended to affect distribution (not only prices), and hence cannot be justified independently of an investment policy designed to achieve or avert full employment. In any capitalist economy, therefore, the key to overall economic performance is investment. For Kalecki (1954b) there would always be a lag between investment decisions and actual investment, so capacity could be growing when production was falling. As long as investment levels determined capitalists' profits, employment levels, and the overall trajectory of capitalist development, control over the content of investment will assume political and economic importance. As we have argued, in an unregulated private enterprise economy, private control of investment is unlikely to produce stable or long-term growth. Furthermore, high levels of reinvestment from profits increase not only growth rates for the economy generally but also the profit share of total output, to the detriment of wages. This means that labour movement programmes for economic expansion need to insist on high rates of growth to avoid slumps and unemployment, but need simultaneously to check the concentration of wealth and power that accrue to capital during such phases.

Public or planned control of investment can check its destabilising influences. If investments and associated distributions of income are known in advance, if productive capacity is designed to produce socially necessary products in the desired proportions, and if society could routinely expect that its needs were being systematically met, then cyclical patterns of employment, income and capacity utilization would not be necessary.

Expectations of economic stability are never authoritatively ordained or naturally given. They always need to be constructed in particular institutions and enterprises and around specific objectives. Centralized imposition of such objectives cannot be a sufficient alternative to market-determined decision-making because 'the effective subordination of all production decisions to a central agency implies capacities on the part of that central agency which are simply impossible to conceive of in any substantial economy' (Tomlinson, 1982, p.51). This is not what the Keynesian-derived criticisms of private control over investment would proffer. Central planning of the type conventionally scorned by anti-socialist thinkers could resolve problems of co-

309

ordination and disproportionality, but by itself could not ensure that different investment decisions with different priorities were embraced. The socialization of investment necessitates not only planning but responsiveness to democratically expressed social needs. Central planning is not omniscient in this respect. Economic democracy, possibly achieved through regionally and locally constituted processes, will, on the other hand, be able to control the content of economic activity in a way compatible with macro-economic stability. Without such control, economic conditions will remain capricious.

For these reasons, contemporary anti-recessionary programmes are unlikely to be successful unless they include a significant measure of economic democracy to bring new investment decisions into line with the requirements of full employment and industrial regeneration. Unforeseeable consequences are inevitably attendant upon capitalists' control of investment, whether in times of growth or in times when investment is being withheld.

These considerations on the cyclical nature of capitalist development led Kalecki firmly to conclude that full employment could not be permanently secured by capitalism unless 'new social and political institutions', to reflect the erosion of managerial prerogatives, were developed.

Collective control of investment, however, presumes not only new political and economic institutions and organizational forms, but also the construction of a different hegemony in civil society. Neither can be expected to emerge autonomously or unambiguously. Currently fashionable tripartite or corporatist arenas for 'discussion' of economic problems are most usually a parody of the new institutions Kalecki had in mind. Non-cyclical economic development would produce a major shift in the balance of class forces towards labour. Crucial economic decisions would be made according to different criteria (need rather than profit), resources would be allocated differently (according to political determination rather than market mechanisms), and much production would become decommodified (because public sector activities offer the most immediate outlets for dramatic increases in investment). State intervention has not yet had to meet those challenges that a commitment to permanent full employment implies. Permanently high levels of employment and non-cyclical accumulation strategies would be possible only in so far as planned and democratic bases for economic activity were established. New institutions would need to be seen not as mere anti-crisis improvisations but as permanent and fundamental reforms to the criteria by which capital accumulation occurs. The economic rationale for industrial democracy is thus inescapably established. This is why Kalecki concluded his discussion of the political business cycle thus:

> If capitalism can adjust itself to full employment a fundamental reform will have been incorporated in it. If not, it will show itself an outmoded system which must be scrapped. . . . The fight of the progressive forces for full employment is at the same time a way of preventing the recurrence of fascism (1943, p.331).

Inflation and class conflict

Keynes's policy prescriptions for the 1930s depression were at least notionally accepted during the postwar boom. Throughout this period, however, the radical implications of Keynesianism were forgotten. Keynesianism was seen as the economics of depression and therefore as dispensable once full employment was approximated.

The decline of Keynesianism was even more stridently celebrated in the 1970s when it became possible to claim that its policies were appropriate *only* to the phenomenon of unemployment. Once the concurrence of unemployment and inflation appeared, previously accepted remedies were declared either anachronistic or counter-productive.

Yet Keynes and Kalecki both recognized that in times of full employment, when the bargaining strength of unions was enhanced, there would be irresistible pressures towards inflation. This understanding of inflation is not as irrelevant to conditions of widespread unemployment as it may initially appear.

The equation of Keynesianism with inflationary tendencies is a product of the economics of the 'new right'. Such prognoses are based on monetarist theory concerning the causes of inflation. But monetarism is not merely an analysis which exists in opposition to that of the 'post-Keynesian' theorists. It is in fact a theory which addresses a different kind of inflation.

Monetarism is a doctrine, originating with the classical economists, which holds that increases in the 'money supply' (definable in various ways to include or exclude deposits in as wide a range of financial institutions as is deemed appropriate) are a crucial variable in any economy. Specifically, the 'Quantity Theory of Money', as it was formally called, maintains that the overall level of prices in an economy is determined by the amount of money in circulation. It is a notion which dates back to Hume and J.S. Mill and is meant to connote that we cannot have more than we produce: if we try to take more from the system in the form of money than has been or can be produced, then the only result will be a rise in prices (the market equivalent of queuing). The policy corollary is obviously that we should not put money into the system except at a rate that can be matched by the real availability of goods and services. This theory is the origin of monetary policy and it is the source of the doctrine of monetarism.

If monetarism holds that only price levels are determined by the money supply (and not their exchange ratios or any other 'real' relations in the economy), then for monetarists, money is seen as a 'veil' over real economic conditions or as a lubricant which facilitates exchange but which does not determine anything. The Keynesian view is quite contrary. In this framework, money matters. Money does not remain a neutral link between transactions in real things, but, rather, produces a dichotomy between 'real' and 'monetary' aspects of economic phenomena. Money provides a link between the present and the future; it affects motives and decisions; it can be in short or excess supply; its availability can have consequences. For Keynesians, therefore, inflation is not merely a monetary phenomenon: it is a reflection of real forces (Davidson, 1972). For monetarists, money does not affect real relations: the basic principles of a barter economy remain. The only effect of money is to determine the overall level of prices.

All arguments which attribute inflation to excessive public spending rely on this 'Quantity Theory of Money'. Monetarists have produced elaborate statistical correlations between changes in the money supply and changes in income levels and these have been interpreted as indicating that changes in public-sector-initiated expenditure levels ultimately cause changes in price levels (inflation). The theoretical underpinnings depend upon the presumed *post hoc* equilibrium of the supply of and demand for money. The equation which demonstrates this relationship has four components: the price level (P), the volume of transactions (T), the quantity of money in existence at a moment of time (M) and the velocity of circulation of the money (V). Hence, the identity formula, $MV \equiv PT$, is meant (by monetarists) to imply that any instability of PT is a result of the instability of MV. This 'quantity equation' could be interpreted in a number of different ways. It could imply that if any increase over a definable period in PT as a result of either an increase in employment/output or in costs/prices has not been matched by an increase in the velocity of circulation of money, then the money supply must have increased. However, this interpretation has not usually been proffered; instead, 'the basis of the argument [was] that a change in the quantity of money will produce a more or less proportionate change in the price level' (Robinson, 1971, p.78). Monetarists' arguments along these lines are intended to imply that when the supply of production is fixed (as it is at any single moment) no increase in the availability of money can miraculously usher forth more real wealth. Keynesians argue that there is no question of a sudden increase in liquidity to which the productive process will be unable to immediately respond, but rather that government demand-stimulation measures, if directed to the appropriate industries at the right time, in accordance with economic planning and a regard for the existing and desired structure of industry, *will* be able to engineer an increase in the volume of total output. Hopefully, demand stimulation will be an instrument of planning for the restructuring of industry and not the result of an unexpected increase in the availability of gold sovereigns (Hume) or 'helicopter' money (Friedman) (Gamble and Walton, 1976, p.63).

The Keynesian argument is that money supply increases are the result of increases in activity or in prices. The equation should be read from right to left instead of from left to right (Robinson, 1971, p.88). Increases in MV are a consequence, not a cause, of inflation.

Further criticisms of this key monetarist position concern the behaviour of the other variables, T and V. If only M is supposed crucially to influence PT, then clearly, for advocates of the 'Quantity Theory', both the velocity of circulation of money and the demand for money are assumed to be stable. In recession, however, it is possible to conceive of dramatic decreases in V which would therefore allow substantial increases in M without any effect upon PT. This proposition is taken up by Kaldor's recent reappraisal of the British Radcliffe Committee Report on the working of the monetary system (Kaldor, 1982). That 1959 report repudiated not only monetarist principles but the efficacy of monetary policy measures. This is primarily because nothing of an *a priori* kind can be said about the velocity of circulation of money. It certainly cannot be regarded as stable. Spending is not constrained by the amount of money in existence – the velocity of money, statistically and historically, can accommodate quite wide fluctuations in spending such that the money supply need not respond at all. 'The quantity theory of money stands or falls with the proposition that the velocity of circulation of money is stable and invariant . . . to changes in the quantity of money' (Kaldor, 1982, p.9). This means that there can be no direct or causal influence exerted by changes in the money supply on the level of prices.

Monetarists, furthermore, equate the money supply with public expenditure. They are disinclined to suggest that money supply increases should be curtailed by restraints on private sector activity. This is clearly a political preference to which alternatives could well exist. In any case, government spending and government-induced economic activity need not be inflationary and (depending upon how it is financed) need not increase the money supply.

Investigation of the causes of actual inflation can best proceed by recognizing that there are two types – 'demand-pull' and 'cost-push'. The first typically occurs during booms (or other extraordinary circumstances) when the problem is one of shortages (blockages) of particular commodities or of labour. The latter occurs when there exist specific influences on the costs of production – for example, wage increases, increased costs of materials, finance, etc. The inflation of the 1970s and 1980s is inflation specific to recessionary conditions. At times of under-employment of resources, industrial capacity and labour, inflation can not be caused by excess demand or by 'too much money chasing too few goods'.

The distinction made by Keynes between 'real' and 'monetary' phenomena has implications for the relation between income distribution and inflation. Trade unions have an ability to bargain for money wage increases, but they do not have any direct influence over the real purchasing power of those wages. Labour cannot directly influence the level of real incomes, nor the share of wages in relation to profits. Workers can and do struggle to influence the share of wages in total income, but as long as control of pricing and investment remains with those against whom they struggle, labour can never catch up – except with the specific acquiescence or default of employers.

Yet during prolonged periods of full employment, pressure for higher wages does build up and to the extent that enterprises and firms do not acquiesce in relation to their pricing and spending behaviour, the result will be inflation. Capitalists attempt to influence the profits share by their spending; workers try to influence the wages share by bargaining over the money wage rate. The extent to which these classes in conflict actually do influence the outcomes of their struggle is determined structurally – by the phase of economic development in the long term and by the state of the trade (business) cycle in the medium term. Consequently, production and distribution are closely related: 'ultimately the distribution of income will be determined by those who control capital'; hence, 'the success of class struggle is going to be determined by the extent to which workers are able to gain greater control over the capitalist system as a whole' (Cowling, 1982, pp.115, 121).

Cyclical changes in economic fortunes and bargaining strength also influence the 'degree of monopoly' and therefore the ability or otherwise of large corporations to increase prices *more than proportionately* following a rise in costs. The extent to which employing organizations are not subject to competitive pressures is the extent to which price mark-ups can be used to compensate for declining turnovers as well as cost increases. Power over pricing means that the wages–profits share is also a function of the degree of monopoly. In so far as prices will not fully restore cash-flows in a downturn, the wages share of total income will not decline as much as it will when, further into the cycle, corporations feel more able to use mark-ups to increase profitability. Therefore, to the extent that inflation is a consequence of the pricing policies of oligopolistic, non-competitive corporations, it will be the occasion for a shift in income distribution away from wage-earners. The share of production accruing to labour tends to decline as the extent of monopolization increases (Feiwel, 1975, p.202). Kalecki's emphasis on corporate power thus is understandable because of the direct and indirect effects it has on inflation – directly, through corporate determination of prices; and indirectly, through the influence pricing policy has (along with investment decisions) on the distribution of income and hence on the wage claims of unions.

A crucial difference between the depression of the 1930s and current conditions is the extent to which this monopoly power has enabled corporations to remain in business despite falling turnovers. The merger wave of the 1960s led to a far greater concentration of capital. In the 1930s, faced with sustained downturns in profitability, many enterprises simply ceased to exist. By the 1970s, this tendency for euthanasia had disappeared except in the economically significant competitive sector; corporations which have market power are able to increase unit costs to whatever level is necessary to ensure longevity. But the increase in organizational strength which has enabled capital in the current recession to fuel inflationary fires has had analogous implications for organized labour (Heilbroner, 1980; Cowling, 1982).

To a large extent, the strength of trade unions in the 1970s and 1980s has been such that the existence of very high unemployment has not prevented wage demands being put and, frequently, granted. That wage increases have become one of the two components of the inflationary spiral in the 1970s reflects a crucial difference between the institutional forms that prevail in the current epoch and those of the 1930s. This would not have surprised Keynes. In that depression money wages were reduced and unions did not have the ability to resist. In the 1970s money wage increases sought and received by well-organized unions, when abetted by price increases imposed by increasingly monopolistic corporations, became responsible for inflation. This is true even though real incomes of either or both of these groups might be falling. In times of recession, inflation is a symptom of the struggle between capital and labour to retain their respective shares of total income (Clegg et al., 1983). Yet once overall economic growth declines, this struggle (which is present in times of boom as well) intensifies and takes an inflationary form. Recessionary inflation reflects conflict over the distribution of income; it is an outcome of class struggle. Inflation is a consequence, not a cause, of recession.

Interestingly, monetarists do not see unions as the cause of inflation; it is the Keynesians who argue that wage rises (and price rises) cause inflation. Monetarism, however, is usually accompanied by a social philosphy which opposes the existence of unions *per se*, because they distort free-market mechanisms. Although Keynesians see union bargaining strength as a cause of inflation, this analysis is not accompanied by either the ascription of blame or any suggestion that wage demands should be restrained.

If inflation during recession is caused by conflict over the distribution of income, and if the distribution of income changes at different stages of the business cycle, then clearly there can be no effective anti-inflationary policy that is not at the same time an anti-cyclical or anti-recessionary policy. To the extent that inflation of this kind could be alleviated by prices and incomes policies designed to influence the distribution of income, then such 'contracts' between capital and labour seem justified. However, it is well known that social contracts, prices and incomes policies, and other attempted agreements between organized labour and the political parties of labour have often been the occasion for real wage reductions. The solution to inflation does require a consensus concerning income distribution, but many actual agreements which have initially attempted to achieve such a consensus have ended up facilitating wage cuts in the mistaken belief that it is high costs (including wage costs) that are the cause of economic downturn. For these reasons, contemporary unions are often, understandably, hostile to such policies (Tarling and Wilkinson, 1977; Panitch, 1976).

On the other hand, if the link between unemployment and inflation (i.e. between recession and class struggle) is conceptualized by economic policy institutions in Keynesian rather than monetarist terms, some useful political strategies can begin to be developed.

Most importantly, we need to heed the obvious lesson from both recessionary periods, that measures which aim to reduce inflation by undermining unions' organizational strength or by reducing real wages will, because of their effects on overall demand, increase unemployment and deepen a depression. Anti-inflationary policy is almost always iatrogenic, as the experience of Thatcherism reveals. But these circumstances cannot justify the claim that inflation causes unemployment, nor that inflation causes the recession, nor that wage costs are responsible for factory lay-offs, nor that inflation is the primary political problem, nor that there is a 'trade-off' between unemployment and inflation. The empirical reality of the Phillips curve (Phillips, 1958), which showed an apparent trade-off between the two for the first half of this century (in the UK), has little analytical relevance to the subsequent era when, due to altered institutional circumstances, both unemployment and inflation have been rising together. Unemployment and inflation have different causes, but closely connected solutions for which political will rather than economic orthodoxy is required.

The structural dimensions of each phenomenon were clear to writers in the post-Keynesian tradition long before the current recession developed and the prescriptions implied by the Phillips curve were revived. In 1958 Robinson made a strikingly prescient observation:

> Some people who do not remember the old days, or who remember and do not care, hanker for some unemployment again. . . . It may be that the new problem, of how to run a full employment economy without inflation, will soon be over-shadowed by the old one, of how to prevent a slump. But this will not solve the problem. It is more like curing a disease by killing the patient (Robinson, 1958, p.273).

The paradox of full employment, like the paradox of investment, is that it constantly calls forth the need for new, socially acceptable forms of economic activity (Kalecki, 1939, p.149). Even though the affluent capitalist countries have been spectacularly successful in finding such outlets for private enterprise, growth rates have been lower than they might have been had the 'age of growth' not also been an age of 'stop–go' policies (Pollard, 1982). Despite this context, the demands for wage reductions persist, diverting attention from the need for refla-tionary policies and activity (Dow, 1983).

The increasing acceptance by individual unionists that any pay increases cost the jobs of other unionists signals not only the contemporary weakness of organized labour, but also the hypocrisy of the advocates of wage restraint. Although the gains made by workers in any inflationary situation will be transient (Cowling, 1982, p.109), this cannot be a signal for workers to acquiesce in the struggle altogether, for then the losses would be magnified. If workers were to acquiesce, real wages would fall, as would demand, employment and the opportunities for renewed growth. If wages do not keep up with prices, the result is stagnation; if they do, inflation. This is the dilemma Keynes recognized (Robinson, 1976a). It is why strategies for economic recovery need to be linked to policies which make the distribution publicly explicit.

An incomes policy could operate unproblematically during recession because it would probably safeguard workers' incomes more reliably than would collective bargaining. But its real value would emerge during a recovery phase when the expansionary processes would make employers less willing to resist wage demands.

The profits side of the struggle over shares of national income would also be transformed during a recovery phase. As investment policy picks up and production, incomes, employment, etc., begin to increase, profits always gain proportionately more rapidly than wages. Yet, as the absolute value of all incomes is increasing as well, the bitterness of the struggle to maintain shares of total income would begin to dissipate. Clearly, then, the best long-term solution to the type of inflation we currently have is a reflationary economic strategy. Only in times of growth do the downward pressures on real incomes and the upward pressures on money wages disappear. Only in times of growth do unemployment levels fall; so that profit rates, investment, production, real incomes and living standards increase. These conditions indicate unequivocally that we should not promote an anti-inflationary policy that is not, at the same time, primarily an anti-recessionary policy.

Monetarism and the state

The arguments presented so far suggest that in the postwar era, the processes and institutions of economic policy formation have emerged as the major locus of political parties' struggles for a broadly based class support. From this it is clear that an adequate understanding of the economic role of the modern state cannot be achieved without a sustained analysis of the political and ideological struggles which have raged around and exerted influence upon state intervention into economic activity. The hostility of the 'new right' to the growth of government is usually quite explicit. Milton Friedman's classic (1962) enunciation of the virtues of economic freedom derived from an uncompromising libertarianism and has buttressed his subsequent monetarism. Friedman invokes the support of Adam Smith. However, he does so by abstracting away the context of Smith's advocacy of bourgeois institutions (*vis-à-vis* the aristocracy, the monarchy and the church), thus inserting the rhetoric which Smith used progressively to provide a basis for the first concerted sequences of capital accumulation, into the context of a mature capitalism whose two centuries of growth and accumulation have begun to instance unsurprising internal problems (Friedman, 1977). In his more recent writing, Friedman's argument is less abstract, more emphatically a polemic for the 1980s, with its attacks on regulatory controls, welfare systems, social security, compulsory and free education, consumer protection, minimum-wage legislation and taxation. *Free to Choose* details a series of 'simple truths' concerning inflation: inflation is a monetary phenomenon; governments do determine the quantity of money; there is only one cure for inflation – a slower rate of increase in the quantity of money; it takes years – not months – to 'cure' inflation; and the unpleasant side-effects of the cure are unavoidable. 'We have been misled by a false dichotomy: inflation or unemployment. That option is an illusion. The real option is only whether we have higher unemployment as a result of higher inflation or as a temporary side effect of curing inflation' (Friedman and Friedman, 1980, p.282).

If it is not clear from Friedman, it is quite so from ancillary commentators that monetarism is a guise for something more than a cure for inflation. In recent times, the traditional liberal preference for minimalist government has taken some innovative forms. An entire discourse, if not a spirited debate, has developed around the theme of 'overloaded government'. Assuming the end of Keynesianism as settled, contemporary minimalists have switched their rhetoric from a defensive advocacy of small government in philosophical, doctrinal or idealist terms (Hayek, 1948), to a more aggressive denunciation of what they have hailed as the accumulated costs, inefficiencies and absurdities of welfarist and interventionist measures in the postwar era. Government itself is the cause of this crisis (Rose, 1980).

Forgetting that laissez faire was itself an interventionist achievement, Bell (1976), for example, criticizes the 'revolution of rising expectations'. Thanks to the welfare state and the susceptibility of modern liberal democracy to unchecked constituency pressure for favours, subsidies, programmes, income supports, public services and state-provided infrastructures, the inhabitants of modern democracies have become accustomed to demanding too much. The political system has become too accustomed to acceding to lobbyists and pressure groups. People's expectations have blown out of all reasonable proportion. Liberal democracy has become undisciplined and flaccid. Government is incapable of meeting all democratic demands; budgets are in deficit; taxation is excessive; administration and regulation burgeon; regulations run rampant. The result is 'inflationary finance', one of the economic consequences of democracy (Brittan, 1975, 1978). There is, therefore, a need for restraint, for fiscal rectitude, for a deflation of unreasonable expectations. For these writers, the plethora of extra-parliamentary bodies – committees of enquiry, special task forces, semi autonomous boards – are testimony to administrative overload; modern societies have become ungovernable. Behind the claims is the suggestion that the modern epoch has produced an irremediable contradiction between growth and inflation. There is an excess of democracy (Bowles, 1978).

Bell also argues that the expansion of the state (in his words, it is the 'fiscal household') has occurred without explicit public debate or approval. Intervention by accretion, always illegitimate, has become indefensible as governments move from the provision of basic needs towards attempts to satisfy (unauthorized) wants. As the acknowledged realm of public intervention moves from income maintenance, public transport and health, etc., to embrace free education, childcare, community development and anti-discrimination legislation, fiscal crises develop. Then, as basic allocative mechanisms (the market) are usurped by overtly political criteria and the decommodification of some services, including labour, legitimation crises begin to develop. Private profitability as a criterion for investment gives way to a public 'submission to a heavy-handed bureaucratic Moloch' (Bell, 1976, p.257).

The resurgence of provocatively laissez-faire rhetoric in the 1970s has been accompanied by an impromptu theory of demographic–technological–political–economic change which suggests that the clamour for lower taxes and smaller government in some countries is underwritten by sound social analysis. With respect to the 'tax revolt' in Denmark, California and Australia, it has been noted that the claims to 'welfare overload' and 'welfare backlash' have been based upon a concern that a decreasing proportion of affluent nations' populations had become engaged in productive activity (because of longer schooling and training involvements, earlier retirements and ageing). In addition, technological change was seen to cause longer periods of structural unemployment and transitional employment; welfare expectations had similarly reduced productive participation in the economy; while incentives to work and invest seemed to have been eroded, reducing aggregate incomes. Consequently, fiscal demands on the taxation system had expanded disproportionately for those people still engaged in productive economic activity. Eventually, there was a tax revolt and a political lurch to the right (Stretton, 1980, p.44).

> That is the right-wing myth of the backlash. If it were true the backlash would be worst in countries where welfare is most generous and taxes are highest and the public sector is biggest. Those should also be the countries with the poorest economic growth. But in the real world, most of the facts are notoriously opposite to those expectations. With minor exceptions, the developed countries with the best welfare and the most taxes and the biggest public sectors tend to have the *least* backlash, and often also the *best* record of recent economic growth. . . . Get right to the bottom, to the meanest affluent white capitalist country in the world, which is Australia devoting 12.8 per cent of output to welfare, and you find, as you might expect, that the meanest country effectively invented the welfare backlash and pioneered the reactionary shift in the pattern of taxation. . . . Australia does not have a backlash because it has been generous with welfare, it has a backlash because it has been mean with welfare. It is the meanest of the mean countries in which conservative pressures against generous welfare have tended to prevail for a generation. 'Backlash' and 'tax revolt' are merely the current forms of the perpetual conservative pressures (Stretton, 1980, pp.44-5).

As we will argue later, this phenomenon of prolonged objection to intervention into competitive, free-market mechanisms has distorted not only debates about the size of the public sector and hence the quality of its offerings, but has also become an important component of the very political structures which subvert and discredit what have been successful and indispensable aspects of macro-economic policy. In some cases, evidenced especially by the British Labour Party's spectacular defeats in 1979 and 1983, 'we get the backlash before we get the reform' (Wilenski, 1980, p.312). Although *alternative*, nationally specific, policies for economic growth do exist, they have not been granted a hearing sufficient for them to outweigh the entrenched caution, the institutionalized orthodoxy, the middle-ground pragmatism and the monetarist-inspired anti-interventionism that makes the modern aggregative or 'catch-all' political party the major force in economic policy-making that it is today. It is not the inapplicability of the labour-derived alternatives but the intranational political and organizational forms of implementing them that pose the most severe constraints on full-employment policies.

The tenor of this political and sociological attack on the postwar welfare state consensus is quite all-embracing. There is a tendency to treat the epoch since the 1930s as if the Keynesian revolution had never been aborted. Hence, Skidelsky writes: 'Keynes alone provided an intellectually coherent justification for a certain type of government intervention, one which would save, not destroy, both capitalism and liberal democracy. . . . We have put this theory into operation and lived by it for the last thirty years' (1977, p.viii). On this basis, free-market advocates can subsequently claim that the 'established doctrine' is now 'theoretically sterile and politically inoperable' (Lilley, 1977, p.26). The tendency to identify the mixed economy with the implementation rather than the abrogation of Keynesian prescriptions has also allowed some commentators to argue that all state-induced stimulus to economic activity is unwarranted. This claim has produced a bizarre interpretation of the 'political trade cycle'. Instead of accounting for the persistence of unemployment, it is used to explain the pernicious consequences of full (or almost full) employment:

> It is possible to boost output and employment, at least for a while, by a monetary or fiscal stimulus, but at the cost of a higher eventual rate of inflation. . . . There is a lag between the effects of a monetary or fiscal boost on real activity and its inflationary consequences. Thus, in the run up to an election, it is possible to have all the benefits without all the costs of inflationary finance. . . . The electorate's memory is subject to fairly rapid decay, so that the incumbents lose less from high unemployment early on in their period of office than they gain from low unemployment nearer polling date (Brittan, 1978, p.168).

Brittan's analysis concludes with an equally startling reversal of the post-Keynesian ascription of inflation in recession to the institutional form of class conflict. The new right is afraid that inflation is a symptom of unreasonable pressure by coercive groups on a nation's *limited* capacity to produce. Even when inflation is reduced (not through growth, but by deflationary policies and a return to 'reasonable' expectations and balanced budgets), the 'dangers to democracy' would no longer be disguisable in the wage–price spiral: tensions will remain. The 'temporary solvent' of tension (inflation) has been a 'benign form of self-deception – governments will need to be openly insistent that democratic impulses are stifled. Whereas Keynesian policy prescriptions imply that inflation is always easier to control during periods of growth when the actual flow of production and incomes is increasing (i.e. that class conflict causes inflation), the contemporary appropriations of the 'Quantity Theory' maintain that no growth is possible unless it occurs autonomously and that the end of inflation would produce even more overt class tensions.

These confusions are under-scored by two biases that have a pre-Keynesian pedigree in monetarist thought. Hayek in 1931 complained that it was 'naive inflationism' to imagine that government spending could increase output. For Hayek, and all anti-classical subjectivist doctrines, the economic problem was not how to encourage growth but how to cope with scarcity. Keynes was derided for neglecting 'real scarcities'. Excess capacity, the social and technical ability to expand production in the short term, did not define an economic problem for theorists for whom economics was to be 'the science of allocation'.

Such a situation, in which abundant reserves of all kinds of resources, including all intermediate products, exist, may occasionally prevail in the depths of a depression. But it is certainly not a normal position on which a theory claiming general applicability could be based (Hayek, 1941, p.26).

Hayek's main concern is to insist that monetary stimulation cannot increase production, even though the Keynesian point was to show that any spending necessarily would have multiplier effects on employment, income and output; Keynesianism was never an advocacy of indiscriminate increases in the money supply. Subsequent analyses of the causes of the long boom after 1945 indicate unequivocally that it was the ability of labour movements to secure high wages with a sustained expansion of government spending and state intervention which was respon- sible (Steindl, 1966; Apple, 1983), but Hayek (1944) had a different objection to that. The real target of Hayek's ire is an expanded role for government. This is apparent in the writings of the contemporary new right as well; but the depoliticization of resource allocation has always been a concern of liberalism (Polanyi, 1944, pp.141-50). The connections between modern monetarism and the philosophical and political libertarianism of a generation ago is clear even to Hayek:

> It is probably no exaggeration to say that, although open inflation that manifests itself in a rise of prices is a great evil, it is less harmful than a repressed inflation. . . . Such repressed inflation makes the price mechanism wholly inoperative and leads to its progressive replacement by central direction of all economic activity (1972, p.115).

The second recurrent theme in anti-Keynesian writing is revealed by the recognition that the fundamental breakdown in theoretical orthodoxy was never conceded by the adherents to marginalism. It is clear from orthodox accounts which attempt to explain the rise of Keynesianism and its subsequent demise that monetarists never considered themselves unable to explain the cause of the 1930s depression: 'There existed already a body of monetary analysis that was quite capable of explaining both Britain's and the industrial world's unemployment problems as a consequence of monetary mismanagement.' Emphasis on non-monetary (real) causes inevitably 'led to the recommendation of *ad hoc* remedies such as public works that lacked any firm grounding in theory as generally understood' (Johnson, 1971, p.4). The 'dark years of Keynesian despotism' (1971, p.12) were the result of sociological and political, not intellectual, factors. Only when inflation replaces unemployment as the primary political problem will the 'monetarist counter-revolution' be able to displace Keynesianism's 'policies of proven or presumptive incompetence', that is, incomes policies, with the policy solutions of monetarism (1971, p.12).

This defence of orthodoxy has also been voiced by Friedman who claims that the major contraction of output, employment and prices in the 1930s could have been avoided by a *less* restrictive use of monetary policies (1972, p.12), conceding that monetary policy can be misapplied but not considered dispensable. On the one hand, monetary policies can have unanticipated and perverse outcomes; yet on the other, the Friedmans urge nations to be patient while the expected effects of the monetarist cure for inflation come to fruition (1980, p.282). There seems little occasion for confidence in monetarism's prescriptions when the protagonists are so diffident.

> We have been driven into a widespread system of arbitrary and tyrannical control over our economic life, not because 'economic laws are not working the way they used to', not because the classical medicine cannot, if properly applied, halt

inflation, but because the public at large has been led to expect standards of performance that as economists we do not know how to achieve. . . . Perhaps, the random perturbations inherent in the economic system make it impossible to achieve such standards (Friedman, 1972, p.17).

These comments mark a crucial difference between the attitude to government held respectively by monetarists and Keynesians. Friedman's brief seems to be to convince the world that governments are structurally unable to perform most of the functions their advocates extravagantly promise. The caution is swathed, as often as not, in an appeal for a more realistic modesty. The Keynesians, embracing the realization which began with the Enlightenment, that social existence is and always has been amenable to volitional intervention, advocate policies that attempt to apply past experience to future possibilities. There is no doubt that demands which are unable to be met may be made, unreasonable expectations developed, and politically over-ambitious programmes drawn up. However, the primary concern of the opponents of laissez faire and its characteristic contemporary restraints is alleviation of the damage that non-involvement in public policy has caused in the past. 'The orthodox economists, still repeating incantations about equilibrium, encourage authorities to pursue these deflationary policies – the very same that Keynes in the thirties used to describe as sadistic' (Robinson and Wilkinson, 1977, p.13).

Considerable debate has developed around the question of whether or not monetarist policies work. The most commonly expressed objective of these policies is the control of inflation. They are unambiguously successful in this, both in terms of outcome (inflation rates in the UK and USA have fallen dramatically) and in terms of the means that have been used to break the inflationary spiral. Labour has been weakened both economically and politically. Monetarism has not, however, re-established the conditions for capital accumulation. In view of the role it plays in facilitating long-term tendencies towards deindustrialization, it is doubtful it was ever intended to do so. In fact, because inflation benefits debtors compared with creditors, finance capital has much to gain from anti-inflationary policy of the monetarist kind and nothing immediate to lose from the decline in domestic manufacturing. Yet claims persist that monetarism might still succeed in restoring competitiveness to industry (Glyn and Harrison, 1980, p.138; Harrison, 1982). 'Recent policies may not have regenerated industry but they have had enormous effects, many of which create severe difficulties for the implementation of socialist policies' . . . Tory policies have also created difficulties for the implementation of an alternative economic strategy' (Harrison, 1982, p.25).

Some branches of contemporary monetarism argue that this desired shift in political emphasis is made more difficult by the transformation of the monetary disease of inflation into a social-psychological one. Concern is commensurately expressed about the 'upward revision of inflationary expectations'. If people behave according to a modified extrapolation of past experience, then the 'expected' inflation rate will depend on past inflation rates; and if current expectations attempt to correct past 'errors', then there may be revisions to future expectations which, when translated into bargaining or 'ambit' claims, tend to become self-fulfilling (Laidler, 1973). When prices are increased, they are increased by more than is needed to cover costs. However, as Blackaby argues,

> Saying that they do this because . . . expectations have changed may to some extent be true, but it doesn't really add much. It comes down to the proposition that the movement of past prices is important in Trade Union push. To say that it is important because it changes expectations is rather by the way (1973, p.59).

Inflation cannot be abstracted from all the real, structural, phenomena of industrial change, market failures, institutional power and class tensions that Keynes and Kalecki anticipated.

We are left, however, with a need to account for the resurgence and contemporary popularity of monetarism. Kaldor (1982) has pointed out that the current experience represents the second time this century that monetarism has become official creed. Keynes, in 1925, noted that 'deflation does not reduce wages "automatically". It reduces them by causing unemployment.' The 'deliberate intensification of unemployment', in turn, was 'simply a campaign against the standard of life of the working classes' (1925, pp.259, 267). The suggestion Keynes made in the 1920 and which Kaldor endorses for the 1980s is that monetary policies are *intended* to attack specific industries and specific groups of people. In those earlier times, such policies were eventually abandoned and their opposite, 'a protective tariff on all manufactured goods', instituted in their stead. The result of this domestic protection of industry was 'the fastest rate of economic growth in British history' (Kaldor, 1982, p.ix). This experience suggests that deflationary policies and the economic downturns which accompany them are intended to restrain economic growth generally and to facilitate changes in industrial structure by less interventionist means than would otherwise acquire public endorsement.

The Keynesian view, of course, is that the postwar experience of high levels of employment, incomes, capacity utilization, output and productivity (compared with those which pertained in the 1920s and 1930s) vindicates the high-wage, pro-growth policies of structural change which the classical analyses and Keynes favoured. These are the policies which contemporary advocates of 'Alternative Economic Strategies' are attempting to assert against the policies of deindustrialization and against the theories espoused by Hayek, Thatcher and others. It is clear that conservative governments and conservative economic doctrines have recurrently kept levels of employment, income, production and living standards at lower levels than technically feasible – even during the long boom of the 1950s and 1960s (Simpson, 1983, p.81).

The connections between monetarist analysis and deflationary policies have more serious consequences than is sometimes acknowledged. It is these effects that give some indication of the dimensions of their contemporary adoption. In separate analyses, Pollard and Kaldor have highlighted the historical and institutional concomitants of prolonged refusal by governments to stimulate economic activity to the limits of resource availability. Even if the basic premises of the 'Quantity Theory of Money' were accepted, there would be alternative policy possibilities. Pollard has noted that it would make just as much sense to hold the rate of increase in the money supply steady (rather than reduce it) and to augment the flow of production. This would prevent the dismantling of industrial capacity that resolute application of monetarist policies entails. By continuing to place 'symbols before reality', contemporary policies of restraint, cutback and austerity have contributed to a 'law' seemingly covering the deterioration of British economic policies:

every government seems to have done more damage and to have succeeded in fewer things than the preceding one. . . . There is no important area of economic life in which the state of affairs is not such that it would have been regarded with horror or as impossible only a few years back. . . . The government seems to have ransacked the archives to come up with precisely those policies . . . which did the most damage and provided the least benefit in the depressed inter-war years. . . . Those who make our policy are prepared to tolerate the full horror and misery of mass unemployment . . .; they are willing to see whole industrial landscapes devastated, skills

CLASS POLITICS AND THE ECONOMY

lost, enterprise and originality thwarted and stifled (Pollard, 1982, pp.165-9).

There is, furthermore, a 'contempt for production' emanating from the institutions of economic policy advice. An unreasonable concern with 'responsible economic management' has entirely displaced the classical perspectives which would have encouraged a more sustained concern for the institutions and structure of the economy. There has been a 'single-minded obsession' on the part of Treasuries in the postwar era to subordinate real productive potential, manufacturing output and living standards to the icons of financial orthodoxy (price levels, budget deficits, balances of payments, etc.) (Pollard, 1982, pp.71-3). The 'sheer disregard' for policies of economic growth has produced the ambivalence and apparent omnipotence of contemporary government and created an environment where misinterpretation both of the past and of possibilities for the future has become rife. It has created too, the suggestion that, except in the UK, monetarism and the new right are at last on the defensive.

The long-term consequences of failure to invest and the interaction between long-term trends in capital accumulation and short-term policies of economic restraint are demonstrable and have permanent effects. Kalecki's expectations of governmental opposition to full employment seems to be echoed in Kaldor's evaluation of the reasons for and consequences of monetarist policies.

The true reason, one can surmise, lies in their success in transforming the labour market from a twentieth century sellers' market to a nineteenth century buyers' market, with wholesome effects on factory discipline, wage claims and proneness to strike. But the cost has been horrendous in terms of lost output, loss of social cohesion, and sheer misery of the unemployed, particularly the young. . . . When the present policies are finally abandoned (whether by the Conservatives or their opponents) the 'supply side' of the British economy will be found to have shrunk a great deal. The numerous factory closures which have *not* been balanced by the building of new factories, the roads and houses which have *not* been built, the social infrastructure (including higher education) which has been allowed to deteriorate are losses which can never be recouped – however much present policies are put into reverse, the real income of Britain at any particular future date will always be lower than it would have been if the Thatcher experiment had never taken place (Kaldor, 1982, pp.xii-xiv).

Postwar Keynesianism

In view of the failure of political conditions to secure an interventionist hegemony throughout the postwar period, it is not surprising that a British Prime Minister was able to make the following remarks to a party conference in 1976:

> We used to think that you could just spend your way out of a recession and increase employment by cutting taxes and boosting government spending. I tell you, in all candour that that option no longer exists, and that insofar as it ever did exist, it only worked by injecting bigger doses of inflation into the economy followed by higher levels of unemployment as the next step. That is the history of the past twenty years (Callaghan, 1980).

Monetarist theory (taken at face value), the official pronouncements of its institutional adherents, the ancillary literature on overloaded politics, ungovernability and administrative excess (Rose, 1980) and the occasional utterances of labour's elected representatives, however much they all misrepresent the nature of the crisis, do demonstrate the pervasiveness of the sense of failure of Keynesianism.

The real limits of Keynesianism, however, derive from its bastardization after 1951 and not from its inability to cope with the end of growth and the onslaught of 'fiscal crisis', as is implied by both Bowles (1982) and Bell and Kristol (1981, p.viii) who argue that stagnation and inflation is 'a Keynesian impossibility'.

The attack on the 'Keynesianism–collectivist consensus' (Harris, 1980, p.1) is understandable when it comes from an advocate of lower taxes, smaller governments, deregulation, fewer public services and less bureaucracy; but it assumes more significance when it appears in more concertedly analytical, Marxist-inspired social science.

Mandel, for example, admits to 'a certain similarity' between his own account of contemporary inflation and the 'Quantity Theory of Money' (1975, p.435). Like the orthodox monetarists, Mandel fails to distinguish between boom-inflation and inflation in a slump. He cites the long-term expansion of credit by 'leading firms' and deficit financing by the state throughout this century: 'The role of public expenditure as the main source of inflation became even more pronounced in the Second World War. . . . Henceforward the main source of inflation became the expansion of overdrafts on current accounts granted by banks to the private sector' (1975, p.417). Other Marxists have also sought to distance themselves from the 'left-Keynesian' view of inflation. Rowthorn, for example (1977, 1980) argues that 'inflation is the outcome, sometimes deliberate and sometimes not, of attempts by the state to promote capital accumulation, through expansionary monetary and fiscal policies' (1980, p.10), while O'Connor writes of the state's propensity 'to finance budgetary expansion through inflation' (1973, p.229), and Mattick claims 'deficit financing is also an inflationary process, although it can be held in check by the limitations imposed on the state debt' (1978, p.33). All these views fail to appreciate either the non-inevitability of inflation during sustained growth (to which the long postwar boom surely attests) or the non-inevitability of simple wages/profits trade-offs at different stages of the economic cycle. In these arguments there is occasionally a suggestion that wage rises are not inflationary in any direct sense but that, to the extent that profitability is impaired by wage increases, contradictions are manifested in the process of capital accumulation to which the state may in turn respond by infrastructural or other supports which are themselves inevitably inflationary. Hence, for some Marxists, the postwar era of state expansion has produced intractable inflationary results; consequently, it is argued that state policy is unable permanently to alleviate the built-in structural contradictions.

There is an analogous tendency in some political sociology to characterize 'the bundle of state institutions and practices [which] . . . has been developed in western capitalism' as 'the Keynesian welfare state' (Offe, 1983). The Keynesian welfare state, synonymous with 'the mixed economy', has been responsible both for the 'unprecedented and extended economic boom' and encouraged a 'distribution-centred' institutionalization of class conflict. It is important to note that postwar state interventionism has created the age of growth; it is misleading to argue that it was capable of delivering high standards of living only while growth persisted (Jessop, 1980, p.39). For Offe, Keynesianism has not been inherently inflationary, but it was established in the context of such specific political and representational expectations that its demise is likely whenever the terms of this 'postwar settlement' come under challenge. To the extent that 'external economic effects' and 'paradoxes of its internal mode of operation' have begun to exhaust the potential of the Keynesian welfare state satisfactorily to reconcile the 'welfarist' decommodification of certain services and certain aspects of wage-labour with demand stimulatory economic policies, it may be increasingly unable to fulfil the multiple tasks thrust upon it. Offe's argument has the advantage of seeing the differential origins of the 'Keynesian' and 'welfare' aspects of what he still terms the Keynesian welfare state; therefore it is possible to appreciate that redistributive policy accoutrements were attached by labour and social democratic polities to anti-cyclical and therefore anti-laissez-faire growth policies.

In only very few European states did revisionist debates at the turn of the century become the basis for a theoretical understanding of the transformative potential of forcing a capitalist economy into a high-growth, non-cyclical path of continuous capital accumulation (Higgins, 1983). Ernst Wigforss's contributions to Swedish social democratic strategy (which, like those of his British contemporary, G.D.H. Cole, were premised on economic democracy as a basis for representation), provide an exception. Yet as Offe points out, in most liberal democracies, the increasing non-class expression of political opposition and the tendency towards non-party, non-representative and non-public forms of public policy formation may stifle the 'class-effectivity' of such developments elsewhere.

Offe draws on a suggestion by Bowles (1982) that Keynesian–welfare interventions since 1945 may have been a successful response to a specific type of need which, since the 1970s, has been dramatically transformed. Bowles's reference is to 'the postwar internationalist–Keynesian–welfare state accumulation process', which needed to ensure adequate levels of surplus value realization and found the demand-stimulation strategies of the Keynesian era highly appropriate policy solutions to a unique situation. He speculates, however, that since the 1970s the crucial impediment to capital accumulation has been inadequate physical production and its consequently diminished levels of exploitation and accumulation. The problems of most Western economies have switched emphatically from Keynesian to classical preoccupations, implying that a simple reaffirmation of the welfare state and Keynesian full-employment policies is unlikely to provide a viable long-term platform for labour.

While this presumed inadvisability of a return to demand-stimulatory Keynesianism as a policy strategy for the 1980s is one we share, Bowles's argument concerning the transition from problems of realization to exploitation seems to us unconvincing. As Bowles himself suggests, both requirements are perennial in capitalist development. At any stage of this development process, Keynesian policies could be regarded as apposite only to the extent that they embraced structural, as well as demand, issues. The dissipation of these aspects of the Keynesian revolution in both theory and practice has certainly made orderly structural change more difficult in the economies of the 1980s than it might have been had 'the socialization of investment' been achieved in the 1930s or 1940s; but the two elements are necessarily intertwined at all times. In the current context, economic growth is being constrained not by an under-exploitation but by fear of the consequences of expanded accumulation. Hence, while an appropriate response for labour would be to insist upon growth and renewed accumulation, this would both require and secure enhanced purchasing power, enhanced real wages and enhanced participation in decisions affecting the dynamics of the economy. In general, capital accumulation strengthens labour; economic downturns do the opposite. Under-utilization of existing resources and capacities (including those of labour) means that an expansion of production and an expansion of labour movement politics is both possible and desirable.

The apparent unwillingness of contemporary political parties to embrace a commitment to the structural changes that would be demanded by an alternative strategy of economic expansion has been interpreted as implying not only that the economic crisis of the 1980s is wreaking its most significant manifestations in the sphere of politics, but also that the attendant political issues (new divisions, new movements, party decomposition, institutional unresponsiveness) have displaced class as a relevant indicator of the contemporary malaise. Bauman (1982), for example, has argued that the experience of post-1945 economic growth produced an unwarranted and oppressive 'economization' of politics. Non-economic interests (control over people's lives) have been subsumed by interests reflected in distributional struggles. In this view, class conflict is redundant in the context of overall economic decline; politics should be emancipated from industrial conflict and economic policy and become less concerned with these nineteenth-century conceptions.

Contemporary analysts such as Offe, Bauman and Bowles argue that class conflict has been dissipated by the development of heterogeneous political demands and distinct non-class-specific behaviours. The politics of civil society is said to have overtaken that of class.

Consequently, Bowles proposes that it is no longer the case that 'the capitalist accumulation process simultaneously expands the relative size of the working class and unifies its constituent parts' (1982, p.47). There may be aspects of the accumulation process itself which ideologically or politically weaken the working class.

The post-1945 'accord' between capital and labour was accepted, argues Bowles, without any formal or contractual agreements. It relied on diverse institutional innovations, legislative enactments and organizational developments whose common elements for labour were to secure the logic of profitability and market allocation in return for full-employment pledges, high wages, trade union rights and state intervention (Bowles, 1982, p.51; Offe, 1983, pp.62-3).

It has been argued by Apple (1983), however, that these immediate postwar 'settlements', although they involved distinctive patterns of working-class mobilization, were only partial victories for the labour movement. 'In virtually all countries the full employment commitment was watered down or defeated. . . . The various roads to full employment capitalism were paved with a series of ideological and political defeats suffered . . . in the 1945–51 period' (1983, p.73). Even during the Bretton Woods discussion, US negotiators opposed the development of international institutions which could have prevented the imposition of deflationary policies on other countries. Internally, fierce resistance was also mounted to the planning institutions and investment boards that were considered necessary for any permanent full-employment capitalism.

> Between 1951 and 1964 no working class political party ever held central office in Canada, France, US, Italy, Germany, Japan, Australia or Britain. . . . This meant that the crucial relationship between the trade union movement and working class parties evolved during a long period in opposition (Apple, 1983, p.106).

The welfare state was constructed under conditions of bourgeois political rule. Although there are national peculiarities the cumulative effect of the defeat of full employment was spectacular. Any evaluation of the subsequent Keynesian–welfare state era needs to recognize that the form was born out of working-class defeat and not out of overwhelming strength. This was the setting, as well, for the emergence of bastard Keynesianism and the era of unplanned growth combined with periodic unemployment and inflation, the era of 'stop–go' (Robinson, 1976a). The full employment that was experienced was accompanied by a deterioration in union solidarity and the widespread electoral decline of the parties of labour (Apple, 1983, p.108). Most important of all, however, was the non-development of planning agencies which became the most consequential legacy of the era of postwar reconstruction for the 1970s and 1980s. For only ten of the past forty years has there been full employment on any generalized basis (1983, p.108). Clearly, the politically sponsored dilution of full-employment proposals after 1944 is responsible for the traumas currently being experienced. Sweden, notably, seems to have been able to maintain a class-based commitment to full employment, based on a well-articulated and conscious mobilization of labour, a wages and profits stance that was geared to influencing the overall structure of the economy, an active labour-market policy and the creation of large public investment funds through which the labour movement could influence the direction of economy-wide investment processes.

Although the resurgence of bourgeois assault on working-class conditions, wages, participation and mobilization in the 1980s signals a change in relationship between workers as workers and workers as citizens, it is clear from Apple's survey that a high level of class identification and class-effective struggle has not been the norm in most countries during the period Bowles sees as marked by a unification of interests. None the less, it is necessary to be reminded that the contemporary weakness of labour will make the attainment of an effective counter-hegemony more difficult than has been the case in periods of boom. It is probably not correct to argue, as Bowles does, however, that an 'elimination by capital of imaginable and practical alternatives to capitalism' has been ensured (1982, p.71).

The explanation we prefer is almost entirely contrary to this. The implementation of full employment policies over time, even in the invidious form which such implementation actually assumed, especially when combined with the expansion of expectations and interest-group representation whose influence Bell *et al.* deplore and which Offe *et al.* ratify, produces broader consequences for capitalist social relations than has been commonly appreciated.

> If Keynesian policies convert a system with periodic bouts of heavy unemployment into one in which workers can always expect to find work then the working class will gain in power and confidence to the detriment of capitalist interests. . . . As a result we would expect that at certain points in time full employment policies would be jettisoned in the longer term interests of capital. . . . We can also expect a secular tendency away from Keynesian policies as the fruits of a prolonged period of prosperity and the elimination of severe cyclical fluctuations in employment are evident in terms of rising worker confidence and militancy (Cowling, 1982, p.121).

This formulation of historical and sociological limits to Keynesianism in practice suggests that something more than policy ultimately determines policy outcomes, and that something more than political rhetoric needs to be mobilized if the opportunities set up by permanent full employment are to be exploited as the basis for significant social transformation rather than used yet again for its postponement, displacement and denigration.

Parties and policies

We have already noted the metaphysical pathos with which a British Labour Prime Minister conceived the inability of left-wing governments in the 1970s to deploy expansionary economic policy. The foregoing analysis of Keynesian theory and postwar experience has argued that Callaghan was quite wrong so emphatically to concede the terrain of policy debate and struggle to the proponents of political impotence. The specular abnegation of the politically necessary fight for full employment, economic growth and industrial expansion that characterized parties of labour in the 1970s has of course made it impossible for those parties to offer an expansionary alternative in the 1980s. The recent revindication of Thatcherism and the associated declarations against all other priorities reflect something that was endorsed ideologically by the left throughout the previous decade. And now that the regime of the political trade cycle has passed (in the sense that employment and popularity deficits no longer necessitate pre-election expansion), the scenario is being replayed in other countries.

France is experiencing a return to the policies of austerity in a way that further discredits the public claims to legitimacy and relevance of the post-Keynesian reflationary option. Well before the radical restructuring that was portended in Mitterrand's pre-election commitments could begin to take hold, their necessary macro-economic underpinnings have been withdrawn. The autonomy of party as an instigator of policy seems less decisive in the French case than in the British (Ross and Jenson, 1983).

Elsewhere, the experience of countries with long periods of single-party hegemony disrupted by sudden shifts in party control (e.g. Australia, 1972-5; Sweden 1976-82) might be seen as further refutation of the ability of parties consciously to effect macro-economic outcomes (Castles, 1982, p.16). The re-election of a labour party to office in Australia in 1983, followed as it was by a spectacular corporatist initiative (in the form of a 'summit' conference conducted explicitly within the parameters of a renegotiated government–union 'accord' with respect to incomes, prices and industrial restructuring), and an almost immediate capitulation to Treasury orthodoxy (in the form of a retraction of election promises for expansion and a use of the projected budget deficit figures to justify postponement of reflation), further instantiates the pressures to which parties of labour can be subjected when they attempt any radical 'post-Keynesian' strategy of economic expansion.

Determinants of macro-economic outcomes within national contexts are not identified, however, solely by reference to particular political decisions, to bureaucratic complexions or to public gestures towards 'consensus'. Such knowledge requires sustained and precise investigation. In view of the apparent ease with which deflationary policies can be endorsed (compared with the obstacles to authenticating politically a reflationary alternative), there is a *prima facie* case for the supremacy of class politics as an independent variable in socioeconomic enquiry. The frequency with which parties of the left disappoint expectations by abandoning anti-recessionary policies suggests that more than volitional factors are involved.

An interesting and complicating aspect of this demise of postwar consensus, the decline of Keynesian politics and the renewal of political uncertainty attendant upon the apparent inability of existing political forms to eliminate unemployment and inflation, is the tendency for formerly stable party-political electoral constituencies to break up. Esping-Andersen has sought the specific causes of this 'party decomposition' in an analysis of the differential effects of the current economic crisis in Denmark and Sweden. He argues that traditionally strong social democratic electoral performances are being challenged from both ends of the political spectrum. 'The right struggles against too much social democratic state power, particularly too much welfare; the left struggles against too much social democratic powerlessness, in particular with respect to control over capital' (1980, p.550). In Scandinavia as well as in Britain, there is a suggestion that social democratic and labour parties have reached a structural impasse – an historical conjuncture where the ability to meet legitimate constituency demands has evaporated.

Of course, this political dilemma for parties does not exist with equal immediacy in all national instances; but in times when monetarist-inspired governments have created massive public pessimism while neutralizing and demoralizing their labour oppositions in portentous and historically unprecedented ways, something clearly has happened. It is as if the arguments of Bell and the new conservatives have been embraced as definitive by labour's former supporters, and as if public faith in traditionally structured political abilities is as sound as its faith in economists. Given that we have suggested that policy alternatives to continued depression do exist, this warrants further investigation.

Esping-Andersen's comparison of the plight of Danish and Swedish Social Democratic Parties indicates that historical and structural conditions in each country must be invoked to explain party decomposition, electoral disillusionment and policy failures. In Sweden, it is not likely that social democracy is decomposing.

> The social democratic party would be more likely to decompose, and working class politics would be more likely to fragment and polarize, when social democratic governments were less capable of expanding control over private capital, which in turn should be seen as an important pre-condition for the emergence of a welfare state revolt (1980, p.620).

The conclusions are that strong, nationally independent concentrated capitalist economies with homogeneous industrial unionism are likely to produce 'class politics'. Fragmented labour movements, problematic union–party links, relatively active petty bourgeoisies and party coalitions are likely to impede the development of state policy with a class component. Clearly, then, there is a need for ongoing investigation of 'the ways in which different political ideas, expressed through parties, factions and groups, interact with social and economic structures to produce the diversity of public outcomes that characterise modern states' (Castles, 1982, p.1). Castles argues that comparative investigation of public policy, rejecting 'futile debate about the primacy of political, social or economic explanation', shows that there is ample evidence of an interplay between political and socioeconomic factors in the determination of public policy (1982, p.7), with some policy outcomes more likely to be responsive to political prerogatives than others. Not surprisingly, the control of unemployment and inflation, because of the integral relation these have to socioeconomic structures, will be subject to a broader range of influences than political demands which rest solely within the ambit of state policy. It is therefore the case that the partisan composition of government alone will not be a sufficient indicator of ability to implement macroeconomic policy; thus, it will probably also be the case that the socioeconomic history which produces particular national instances of unemployment and inflation will also have produced a distinctive pattern of class organization and therefore of party-political assertiveness.

From these observations, there emerge three testable hypotheses concerning the political control of the economy. These have recently been subject to exhaustive scrutiny for twenty-one OECD countries at different stages of the postwar period by Schmidt (1982). First is the proposition that party control does matter for the ensuing pattern of economic development; second is the argument that it is not political choice but socioeconomic imperatives laid down by past developments in the capitalist mode of production which are determinant; and third there is a hypothesis assigning determinate influence to 'the political constellation of social forces in extra-parliamentary arenas' – the class politics hypothesis (Schmidt, 1982, pp.99-104). The conditions necessary to establish the first two of these are so diverse and interactive that only the class politics hypothesis can be supported.

Although the success of social democratic parties in controlling economic imbalances and maintaining a priority for full employment supports the hypothesis that 'party control does matter', this view does inevitably rest on 'a particular model of the relationship between civil society and the political system' (Schmidt, 1982, p.102). The assumptions here are that governments are not overly constrained by the economic structure in implementing policy goals; that social democratic parties are always willing to utilize state institutions maximally; and that capitalism itself is amenable to effective political intervention. It is not necessarily the case that these can be justified. In view of our knowledge of the variables which respond to conditions which produce either an abstract or political trade cycle, it seems unlikely that they ever could be.

In seeking an explanation for the taxation-financed public sector expansions of the postwar era, Schmidt finds that different conditions seemed to have been operative in the years of postwar reconstruction compared with the years of the long boom. In the 1950s, increasing state intervention occurred most usually when bourgeois political tendencies were split and economic growth rates were high; but as there were exceptions (Australia, Italy), it is clear that in this period 'social democratic political ascendency is a sufficient rather than a necessary condition for the expansion of the tax state' (Schmidt, 1982, p.119).

Throughout the 1960s and until approximately 1974, welfare state expansion occurred in correlation with increasingly strong labour movements: 'Under these conditions, even conservative parties are, more often than not, under strong indirect pressure to adopt some of the demands aggregated by the opposition parties' (Schmidt, 1982, p.121). The suggestion is that the resurgence of class conflict throughout the 1960s and early 1970s, imposed an impetus for government intervention and innovative forms of conflict resolution.

Once the crisis of the 1970s appeared, however, various indicators of the extra-parliamentary distribution of power (strength of the left-wing vote, trade union organization, corporatist arrangements, high wage-labour proportions in the labour force) tended to have most influence over government policies regardless of which parties are in office (Schmidt, 1982, p.127).

Schmidt's survey of political determinants of macro-economic policy, having tentatively concluded that 'class politics' can be considered a major causal determinant of large public sectors, proceeds then to examine the effects of the ensuing degrees of intervention upon more specific economic indicators – unemployment and inflation. Such an analysis is necessitated by the presumption among conservative commentators from Hayek to Keith Joseph that governments are unable to have other than perverse effects on economic outcomes, that market mechanisms ultimately prevail and that conscious intervention cannot permanently secure, except at unreasonable cost, non-market equilibria.

Keynesian and post-Keynesian projections are more than amply vindicated by empirical testing. Furthermore, some support for quite radical programmes of active labour-market policies is unambiguously provided. Not only does unemployment tend to be low in situations of relative isolation from the vicissitudes of the world market (an extension of Keynes's expectations about the undesirability of market-determined optimality at the domestic level), but unemployment is consistently lower in economies with little or no labour-market segmentation (Schmidt, 1982, p.130). It is correct to argue not only that ghettoized segments of the labour force bear the brunt of unemployment and become the industrial reserve army, but also that the existence of these identifiable groups allows the creation of unemployment which otherwise can be resisted. The implications of this finding are far-reaching: any Alternative Economic Strategy cannot succeed except to the extent that it eliminates completely the existence of poorly remunerated and ethnically, socially or sexually exclusive categories of jobs. The feminist critique of strategies involving simple expansion of employment opportunities, on the basis that in the future they would be much the same as they have been in the past, dissipates once one realizes that certain categories of employment and certain categories of discriminately treated labour, linked through the formation of particular status groups, cannot be countenanced by any political strategy for permanent full employment. The argument is as much functional as moral.

The extent to which the differential impact of unemployment has devolved on particular ethnic, regional, age or gender groupings has been the subject of sociological scrutiny throughout the postwar period. Studies of unemployment were typically undertaken within the context of enquiries into contemporary poverty and revealed, along with the persistence of long-term ineradicable unemployment even during the boom, that generalized growth and non-specific stimulatory measures had never been able to eliminate all involuntary unemployment (Sinfield, 1976).

To this extent, a return to growth will not solve all problems with respect to the differential experience of economic crisis; and the feminist critique of policies and strategies which do not take account of a broader range of issues than was considered appropriate prior to 1974 thus becomes entirely appropriate. Policies will be required which could generate and utilize an expanded knowledge of the specific circumstances in different industrial sectors, the implementation of technological change, redundancy, training, retraining, the relationship between guaranteed incomes and work incentives, the difficulties faced by minority groups and women, new forms of public sector employment and unemployment-induced poverty. There is ample evidence to suggest that they could be implemented only within the context of an accumulation strategy which did not reproduce existing market relations (Esping-Andersen et al., 1976).

A corollary of this argument is that unemployment is reduced to the extent that labour markets do not actually operate as markets at all. To the extent that a politicization of the conditions under which labour is hired and fired occurs, to the extent that welfare supports, trade union bargaining over wage levels, guaranteed minimum incomes and security of employment erode market mechanisms and employer 'rights', unemployment tends to be lower. This is a surprising finding given the long-nurtured hostility to the alleged destructive defensiveness of trade unions in contemporary Britain; but it is not at all surprising in the context of the theoretical arguments we have canvassed above. The strength of the anti-market milieu is inversely related to the level of unemployment (Schmidt, 1982, p.141). This is why the ideological and organizational cohesion of bourgeois tendencies becomes an independent variable in most circumstances.

In so far as these non-market developments feature in contemporary capitalism, however, they may be seen as indicators of the political and industrial weakness of labour rather than as an affirmation that 'class politics' is evolving in the interests of labour. Hence, there are two contradictory hypotheses concerning the link between corporatist structures and unemployment. If labour is weakened by 'incorporation', then unemployment will be higher under such conditions; if labour's influence is more equal than would be implied under laissez faire, unemployment should be lower. In fact, examination of determinants of unemployment during the 1970s confirms the proposition that corporatist structures (and extra-parliamentary class politics) tend to be associated with low levels of unemployment (Schmidt, 1982, pp.137, 141). Furthermore, unemployment is lowest in those countries with the highest proportion of working-age people in the total population – thus indicating that socioeconomic structure is a more important determinant of unemployment than normally defined economic factors (e.g. supply of and demand for labour):

All the countries with low rates of unemployment during the crisis of the 1970s were characterized by either strong or medium degrees of corporatist conflict resolution. A strong corporatism is a sufficient, but not a necessary condition for low rates of unemployment. . . . The opposite holds true for countries in which class conflict is regulated in either an authoritarian or competitive manner: a weak corporatism is a sufficient, but not a necessary, condition for high rates of unemployment (Schmidt, 1982, pp.141-2).

The mechanisms which institutionalize this fit are those we have already anticipated, namely political pressure on the part of labour to retain unemployment as a salient political issue, incomes policies which are associated with policies to redirect the pace, direction and warrant of capital accumulation, labour 'hoarding' (over-staffing) by industry which is denied the right to fire workers indiscriminately during recession, counter-cyclical demand policies in association with active labour-market interventions, and protective policies (Schmidt, 1982, p.144). Enterprise productivity should not be achieved by shedding labour and responsibility, but by forcing enterprises to find efficient uses for a workforce which is continuously involved in any rationalization of operations.

Theoretical and empirical support for non-market control over the economy is overwhelming. However, political objections exist suggesting a divergence between the effects of intervention to control labour markets and the effects on inflation. The orthodox and Friedmanite view is, of course, that inflation, because of its distorting effect on resource allocation, leads to high unemployment. The presumption has been that an inverse relationship between unemployment and inflation persists (Phillips, 1958), and that the social democratic preference is for a low-unemployment/high-inflation mix. The evidence reported by Schmidt, however, reveals neither a tolerance for nor the presence of high rates of inflation where there is a 'strong left milieu' and low unemployment. Table 9.7 (page 355) confirms the lack of any systematic or necessary relation between the size of the public sector and the rate of inflation. We have already argued that the best anti-inflationary strategy is an anti-recessionary strategy. This is instanced as well by Schmidt's empirical observations:

> The probability of a low inflation rate is high where the dominant mode of conflict resolution is corporatist in character, where industrial conflict is largely absent, and where the economy is wealthy and has a dominant role in the world market. If any one or more of these conditions is unfulfilled, there will be a strong probability of highish inflation (1982, p.153).

In so far as inflation does take hold and leads to either heavy-handed attempts to regulate wages or deflationary policies, it tends to cause a reaction which in turn exacerbates the recovery process and the inflationary process itself. The institutional preconditions for high levels of employment themselves provide the most effective check on inflationary pressures.

Schmidt's survey shows that complete control over the economy has not been achieved under any political constellation. The implication is surely that comprehensive and successful control is not possible, even by social democratic governments. It is none the less clear that although 'the dynamics of the economic and its structurally given instabilities' (1982, p.151) do tend to undermine efforts to achieve specific macro goals, the degree of party and policy impotence varies both with the extent of government (size of public sector) and the degree of interventionism. Economic instability is most likely to be controlled under conditions of 'active welfare capitalism' and least likely to be controlled in 'passive market economies'. Unemployment tends to be lower when social democratic hegemony and corporatism prevail; it tends to be highest under bourgeois regimes with competitive modes of regulation.

In general, although most hypotheses resting on the primacy of economic factors are not confirmed, it is still the case that the autonomy of the capitalist economy remains considerable, irrespective of political strategies adopted. The general levels of economic growth, including the patterns of development experienced in the past retain importance as determinants of the extent of possible political control of the economy. None the less, neither these processes of accumulation, nor the industrial structure that results from them, are resistant to conscious policy manipulation. In turn, the structure and trajectory of the economy determines the nature and extent of successful party interventions. If the links between the economy and institutional intervention are mediated by societal and political factors in the ways suggested, then substantial support for the importance of 'class politics' is won.

> The structures and outcomes of extra-parliamentary political arenas, the development of corporatist structures and the power distribution between left-wing and bourgeois milieux seem to be vital factors in determining the success or failure of macroeconomic policy, more or less irrespective of the party in office (Schmidt, 1982, p.164).

Furthermore, because each of these conditions is interactive rather than merely additive (Stephens, 1979, p.94), the formation of an effective social and economic policy through tripartite bargaining will be commensurately ineffective to the extent that any one of them is absent.

These general results from a range of OECD member states reiterate a very significant conclusion from the theoretical analyses of full employment that derive from Kaleckian insights. It is well established that full employment occurs most probably when market mechanisms are undermined and decommodified production relations are extended. For Kalecki, the implication was that full employment and capitalism are ultimately incompatible, so, to the extent that working-class mobilization occurred under that policy rubric, the transition to a matured, industrially sophisticated pattern of capitalist development was simultaneously a transition beyond capitalism to less market-centred, less commodified, less profit-oriented patterns of production. The struggle for full employment was seen as co-terminous with the struggle for democratic socialism; and these manoeuvres could not be confined to the realm of parliamentary politics and policy-centred reformism, but would necessitate the wholesale endorsement of a conscious and motivated labour movement. In so far as this reformism aims to develop institutions for the control of investment and elimination of inflation, the transitional potential of 'full employment' is immense.

Yet the analytical strength of the Kaleckian perspective is missing from many of the specific comparative studies of political effectivity and crisis management which, like Schmidt's, would otherwise vindicate the 'class politics' paradigm.

Kesselman's (1982) evaluation of the 'prospects for democratic socialism' in Sweden and France, for example, compares the 'parliamentary reformist' and 'confrontational' strategies of class conflict and compromise that typify the respective countries' patterns of political life. He acknowledges that both the French working class and the French economy are weaker than their Swedish counterparts as a result of this strategy. Like many other writers (e.g. Esping-Andersen *et al.*, 1976), Kesselman is concerned that some results of 'class politics' may 'merely' strengthen (or reproduce) capitalist social relations while others will tend to hasten 'democratic socialist transition' (1982, p.401). In both countries, 'class politics' is cited as a determinant of existing configurations; but he proposes that whereas Sweden's reformism will not lead to socialism, France's confrontationism might. He argues that 'social democracy can be characterized as a variant of advanced capitalism. . . . [It] institutes a kind of Janus-faced arrangement between capitalism and socialism. . . . [It] reduces the possibility of socialist transition' (1982, pp.401-3). On the other hand, capital–labour relations in France 'are among the most politicized and conflicted of any advanced capitalist nation' (1982, p.420). These are said to favour a socialist transition; while increasing control over investment merely imposes 'bureaucratic control' in the name of workers (1982, p.435).

An entirely different conclusion is reached in Webber's (1982) comparison of crisis management in Sweden and West Germany. The greater political strength of the social democratic movement in Sweden is held to account for that country's lower unemployment throughout the late 1970s and early 1980s compared with Germany's – although Germany's inflation rate has been lower and its growth rate higher. Figure 9.5 (page 349) highlights the urgency of the need for a restructuring of Swedish industry; but that country's political momentum at least recognizes the danger of (and determination to avoid) a 'plunge into a Swedish Thatcherism' (Webber, 1982, p.40).

The determinant role of 'class politics' has become increasingly important as the advanced capitalist economies encounter structural crisis and as political forces within them struggle to influence the form of response to it. The primacy of 'class politics' coincident with the development of a post-laissez-faire state has produced what Ferraresi calls 'institutional transformations' (1983, p.129) which have tended to escape systematic analysis. In some national instances there may be the 'particularistic allegiances', handouts, inefficiencies, and irrational corruptions associated with a bourgeois clamour for bureaucratic favours and clientelism. In other instances, we have noted the differential consequences of 'aggregative parties' representing a diversity of sectional interests and 'articulatory parties' which more consistently attempt to advance a programmatic thrust for a specific constituency. As we have argued, the form of political representation most conducive to predictable economic outcomes and economic restructuring is the latter. To the extent that 'competitive party democracy' (Offe, 1983) produces the 'catch-all' party as a dominant form of political expression, then not only do problems of legitimation and overloaded government expand, but the prospects of both economic management and economic transition diminish.

To the extent that 'every private problem becomes politicized', the state's capacity to exert responsibility is eroded and its 'authority to counter excessive participation' is enhanced (Esping-Andersen and Friedland, 1982, p.3). This is a paradox which is taking quite a decisive turn in Thatcherist Britain.

Profiles of crisis

The foregoing discussion has suggested that there can be no general experience or theory of crisis. The 'ideal type' of cyclical development presented earlier (Figure 9.1, p.304) cannot be observed in any pure form in any specific capitalist economy. Kalecki's argument is that in particular contexts a host of normally operative conditions will give to actual growth trajectories their characteristic and eccentric contours. Among these are population growth, size of the economy, pattern of technological change, degree of monopoly, income distribution, unproductive consumption, organic composition of capital, history and degree of state intervention, industrial structure, organizational and institutional conditions, relation to other domestic economies and the degree of public economic planning (Kalecki, 1954b, pp.145-61).

The accompanying figures show quite unambiguously that the current economic recession began in 1974 (Figure 9.2) and that the crisis has steadily deepened into the 1980s. For the twenty-four OECD countries which had been experiencing a total unemployment rate of 3–4 per cent, unemployment jumped very quickly to 5 per cent and has continued to grow ever since, accelerating again since 1980. For North America, the figures are much higher; for Japan, considerably lower.

At the same time, other measures of economic well-being might allow the claim that there have been two recessions, both short-lived, since 1974. Indices of industrial production show emphatic declines for most countries and the OECD total in 1974–5, with another drop in 1980 (Figure 9.3). It seems important to us that the pertinent interpretation of the conditions these figures represent is that the current crisis is now a decade old and that the structural aspects of it clearly militate against any

per cent of total labour force
seasonally adjusted

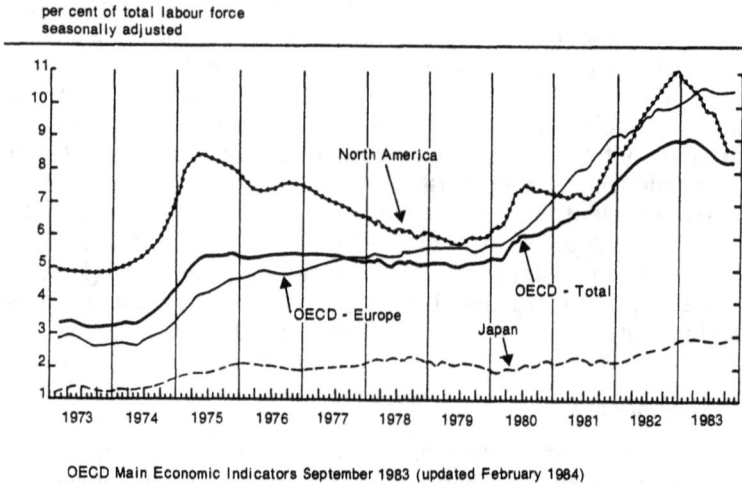

OECD Main Economic Indicators September 1983 (updated February 1984)

FIGURE 9.2   *Unemployment*

seasonally adjusted, 1975=100

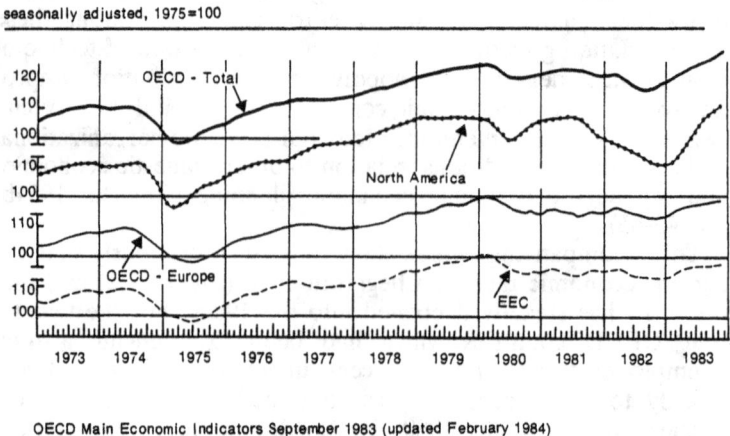

OECD Main Economic Indicators September 1983 (updated February 1984)

FIGURE 9.3   *Industrial production*

simple strategy for its resolution. The structural nature of the
recession is shown by consideration of Figures 9.2, 9.3 and 9.4
together. Overall production levels have continued to increase
since 1975 despite a massive increase in the percentage of the
available workforce excluded from production. In addition, the
rate of growth of employment is well below the rate of growth of

production, suggesting that even substantial reflation of some parts of some economies would not in itself eliminate symptoms of recession. For the OECD as a whole, manufacturing production has increased 21 per cent since 1975, while the size of the employed workforce has risen 5 per cent and that of the industrial reserve army by 52 per cent (since 1975; 130 per cent since 1974) (Figure 9.4).

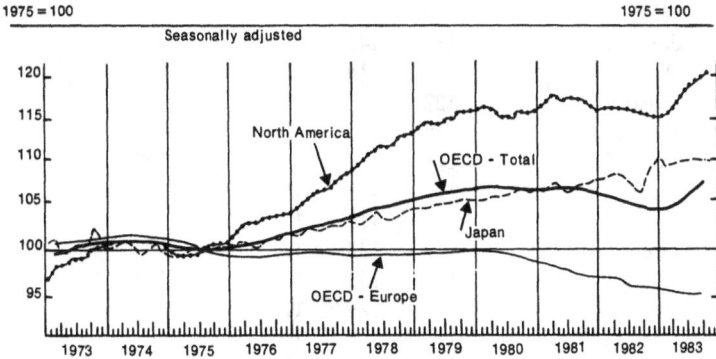

OECD Main Economic Indicators September 1983 (updated February 1984)

FIGURE 9.4 *Total employment*

With such irrefutable evidence of change occurring in the structure of economic activity (a characteristic of any recession), it is clear that general palliatives such as those implied by orthodox Keynesian demand-stimulation interventions could not be adequate to the task of regenerating the Western capitalist economies. As we have insisted, it was never a plausible claim. Decisive industry policies formulated on national, bilateral or multilaterial terrains are necessary.

A significant aspect of any crisis is its differential form and impact in different nation states. The general impact of the crisis is demonstrated by the production and unemployment figures already cited; but the diversity in national impacts is also significant as an indicator of the overall argument we have advanced concerning the impossibility of a general cause or theory of capitalist crisis.

In North America and Japan, for example, the size of the employed workforce has continued to grow during the crisis (by 15 per cent and 10 per cent, respectively), while that of Europe has declined by almost 5 per cent since 1975 (Figure 9.4).

TABLE 9.1 *Indices of industrial production (1975 = 100)*

	1979	1980	1981	1982 (1st quarter)
Canada	118	116	117	109
US	129	125	128	120
Japan	133	142	146	149
Australia	114	114	117	115
Austria	122	125	124	126
Belgium	116	115	112	113
Finland	118	128	129	128
France	118	118	117	113
Germany	117	117	116	117
Greece	129	130	129	129
Ireland	135	133	136	137
Italy	121	128	125	132
Luxembourg	111	108	100	103
Netherlands	112	111	109	109
Norway	125	132	132	135
Portugal	134	141	142	145
Spain	115	117	115	114
Sweden	98	98	94	93
Switzerland	109	114	115	113
UK	115	108	103	104
OECD Total	123	123	124	121

Source: *OECD Indicators of Industrial Activity*, 1982 II, p.20.

In the OECD as a whole, industrial production has increased 21 per cent since 1975. The countries with higher-than-average increases include Japan (49 per cent), Portugal (45 per cent), Ireland (37 per cent), Norway (35 per cent), and Greece (29 per cent); those below average include the UK (4 per cent), Canada (9 per cent), the Netherlands (9 per cent), France (13 per cent), and Australia (15 per cent). Most notable of all, however, is Sweden's performance: alone in the OECD, its industrial production in the period 1976–82 declined (by 2 per cent). (Table 9.1; Figure 9.5).

1975=100   seasonally adjusted

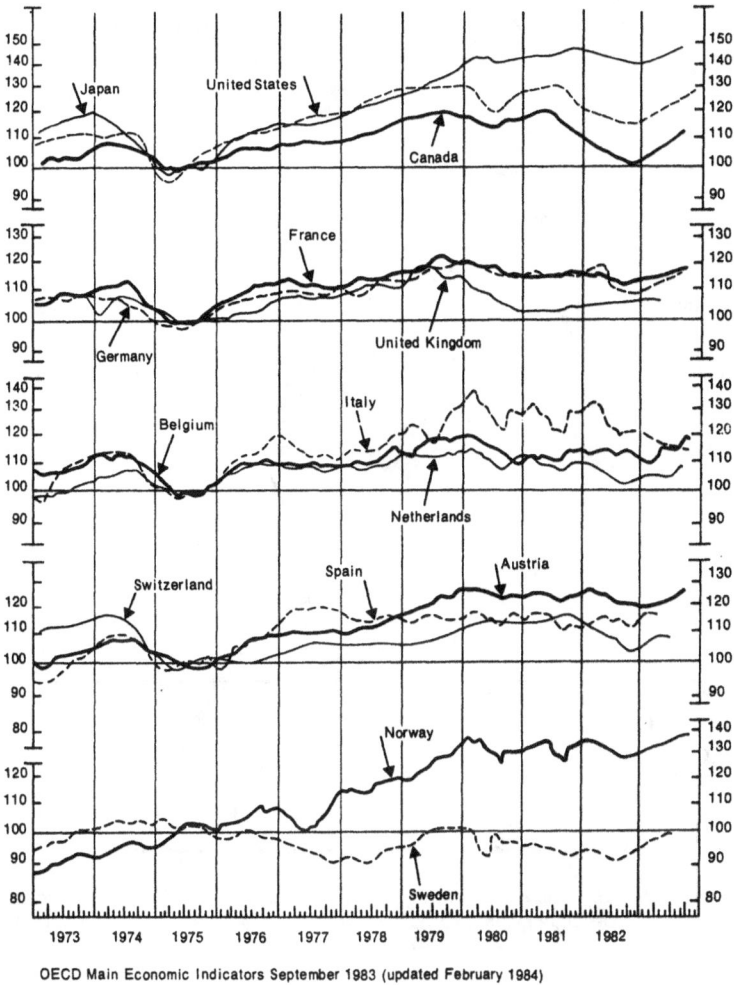

OECD Main Economic Indicators September 1983 (updated February 1984)

FIGURE 9.5   *Industrial production*

These industrial conditions are reflected quite unevenly in unemployment figures. Countries above the OECD average (8 per cent, 1982) include Spain, the UK, Belgium, the Netherlands, the USA and Canada; those below include Japan, Sweden, Austria, Norway and Germany. Sweden has the lowest unemployment of all the European industrial nations, despite falling

349

production for six years (Table 9.2), implying the structural supports for the workforce, the erosion of entrepreneurial rights, and the active labour-market interventions that have existed there (Regini and Esping-Andersen, 1980, p.110).

TABLE 9.2 *Unemployment (percentage)*

	1965	*1970*	*1974*	*1979*	*1980*	*1981*	*1982*
Canada	3.6	5.6	5.3	7.4	7.5	7.5	10.9
US	4.4	4.8	5.4	5.7	7.0	7.5	9.5
Japan	1.2	1.1	1.4	2.1	2.0	2.2	2.4
Australia	1.5	1.6	2.6	6.2	6.0	5.7	7.0
Austria	1.9	1.4	1.4	2.1	1.9	2.5	3.4
Belgium	1.8	2.1	3.1	8.4	9.0	10.9	13.0
Finland	1.4	1.9	1.7	6.0	4.7	5.2	6.1
France	1.5	2.4	2.8	5.9	6.3	7.6	8.0
Germany	0.3	0.8	1.6	3.2	3.1	4.3	6.1
Italy	5.3	5.3	5.3	7.5	7.4	8.3	8.9
Netherlands	0.5	0.9	2.8	4.2	4.9	7.5	10.2
Norway	1.8	1.6	1.5	2.0	1.7	2.0	2.6
Spain	2.5	2.4	2.6	8.5	11.2	14.0	15.9
Sweden	1.2	1.5	2.0	2.1	2.0	2.5	3.1
UK	2.3	3.1	2.9	5.7	7.3	11.3	12.7
Total OECD	2.6	2.7	3.0	5.1	5.8	6.8	7.9
OECD (Europe)				5.6	6.2	8.1	9.2
OECD (North America)				5.9	7.0	7.5	8.6

Source: *OECD Main Economic Indicators*, June 1982; *OECD Economic Outlook* 30, December 1981; *OECD Quarterly Labour Force Statistics*, no. 1, 1983.

Structural differences emerge also when consideration is given to inflation. For the period 1975–82, hourly earnings increased by 136 per cent in the OECD as a whole (a yearly average of 19 per cent); while the yearly average in Japan was 3.4 per cent; in the US, 10.4 per cent; in the UK, 18.7 per cent; in Germany, 6.4 per cent; in Sweden, 11.7 per cent; and in Australia, 13.9 per cent. But inflation is usually measured in terms of consumer prices. The OECD rate is currently 8.4 per cent, with a range from 2.3 per cent (Japan) to 15.3 per cent (Italy). Germany's rate is 5.3

per cent, Sweden's 8.5 per cent, France's 13.8 per cent, Australia's 10.5 per cent, and the USA's 6.7 per cent. Interestingly, there are two countries where producer prices have risen more rapidly than consumer prices: Denmark and Sweden, reflecting, presumably, the fact that the consumer goods and services available to the populace are subsidized or provided in decommodified form (Tables 9.3 and 9.4).

Neither Norway nor Sweden experienced the otherwise general downturn in 1974–5. Norway's industrial production has risen without significant interruption since the early 1970s. Sweden experienced its downturn three years after the rest of the world, reflecting the effects of export-dependency, a change of government and a very stable level of unemployment (implying a less spectacular impact on domestic demand (Figure 9.5). Only Sweden has demonstrated no dramatic increase in unemployment since 1974, although, as Table 9.8 (page 355) shows, the extent of 'deindustrialization' is more marked in Sweden than anywhere else. Apart from Japan, the countries with expanding industrial employment are those where the structural role of industry in the economy (measured in terms of employment) is lowest.

TABLE 9.3 *Index of hourly earnings (1975 = 100)*

	1979	1980	1981	1982	*Average yearly increase %*
US	139	151	165	173	10.4
Japan	139	150	159	164	9.1
Australia	148	164	181	197	13.9
Denmark	153	170	185	196	13.7
France	164	189	216	234	19.1
Germany	127	135	142	145	6.4
Italy	215	263			32.6
Norway	144	159	175	172	10.3
Sweden	147	160	177	182	11.7
UK	170	200	219	231	18.7
OECD Total	156	176	197	236	19

Source: *OECD Main Economic Indicators*, June 1982.

TABLE 9.4 *Index of consumer prices/producer prices (1975 = 100)*

	1979	1980	1981	1982	Current rate %
US	135/133	153/151	169/165	176/170	6.7/ 3.0
Japan	127/113	137/129	144/131	146/132	2.3/ 0.7
Australia	150/152	164/174	181/188	193/198	10.5/ 8.1
Denmark	146/133	164/156	183/181	195/193	9.4/ 9.5
France	145/134	165/146	187/165	197/174	13.8/ 7.4
Germany	116/113	122/121	130/128	134/132	5.3/ 4.7
Italy	178/174	216/205	258/242	284/266	15.3/14.4
Norway	135/130	150/150	170/166	183/174	11.1/ 4.8
Sweden	145/144	165/163	185/180	189/196	8.5/12.8
UK	166/172	196/200	219/221	231/230	9.5/ 8.7
OECD Total	140/134	158/154	175/169	184/177	8.4/ 7.1
OECD (Europe)	149/140	170/161	191/183	204/195	11.1/10.8

Source: *OECD Main Economic Indicators*, June 1982.

Further evidence that the structure of the economy is of decisive importance for the effects of economic crisis can be given by comparing inflation rates with the size of the public sector (government outlays as a percentage of Gross Domestic Product) and the rate of increase in the size of the public sector (Table 9.7). No clear relationship exists. The country with the largest and fastest-growing public sector (Sweden) has the fourth-lowest inflation rate; other countries with low inflation (Germany, Denmark) have large public sectors. There are outstanding examples of small public sectors coinciding with low inflation (the USA, Japan); but even here Japan has a rapidly expanding public sector. One country with a very small public sector (Australia) has relatively high inflation. Clearly, there is no necessary linkage.

Other aspects of these figures can be less conclusively interpreted. Table 9.5 shows that the wages share of GDP has been systematically increasing for the last two decades. The increase is as decisive before as after the onset of recession.

TABLE 9.5 *Wages–profits share of GDP (selected OECD countries)*

	1960	1970	1980
US	72/28	77/23	79/21
Australia	64/36	67/33	68/32
France	58/42	64/36	73/27
Germany	60/40	68/32	73/27
Italy	52/48	59/41	66/34
Sweden	66/34	76/24	80/20
UK	73/27	77/23	80/20
OECD Total	60/40	66/34	68/32

Source: *OECD National Accounts Main Aggregates Volume 1 1952-1981.*

However, the increases in wages share has not been a sign of increasing standards of living (real wages) as Table 9.4 indicates a greater inflationary burden has fallen upon consumers than upon producers (except in Denmark and Sweden). An important implication of this data is that wages/profits shares are not primarily influenced by parties in government or by labour movement bargaining strength. There is even the suggestion here that social democratic government may not necessarily enhance working-class material benefits relative to more conservative governments (Armingeon, 1982, p.270). An amalgam of influences is involved.

The class dimensions of national variations begin to emerge from consideration of the relative sizes of public sectors (Table 9.6). In Sweden the size of the public sector continued to expand dramatically even during the bourgeois interregnum, having doubled in two decades. Both Sweden's subsequent economic performance (where the outcomes with respect to levels of production are not reflected in unemployment and inflation) and the diversity of macroeconomic outcomes in the countries with small public sectors (USA, Japan, Australia) demonstrate very strongly the salience of the range of political and class influences on patterns of capital accumulation which we identified earlier. Table 9.8 shows the differential extent of declines in industrial

TABLE 9.6 *Total outlays of government as percentage of GDP*

	1960	1965	1974	1979	20-year growth %
US	27.8	28.0	32.9	33.1	19
Japan	18.3	18.6	24.5	31.5	72
Germany	32.0	36.3	43.4	46.4	45
France	34.6	38.4	39.7	45.3	31
UK	32.6	36.4	45.2	43.5	33
Italy	30.1	34.3	37.9	45.5	51
Canada	28.9	29.1	37.4	39.0	35
Denmark	24.6	29.6	42.0	44.1	79
Netherlands	33.7	38.7	50.8	59.5	77
Norway	32.0	34.2	44.6	51.4	61
Sweden	31.1	36.0	48.1	61.3	97
Australia	22.1	25.6	30.4	33.7	52
Total OECD	28.4	29.8	35.0	37.9	33
OECD (Europe)	30.9	34.5	40.3	45.1	46

Source: *OECD Economic Outlook* 30, December 1981.

activity relative to other components of economic activity. Surprisingly small proportions of the employed workforce are engaged in industrial production in most OECD countries.

The lack of fit between the involvement of the workforce in manufacturing industry and the economic and political power of the working class through unions and parties is not made apparent in these figures. Korpi and Shalev's (1980) categorization of countries with varying combinations of class mobilization and political control (as measured by strike involvements), which was presented in chapter 7, is partially reinforced by the typology represented in Table 9.9: countries with an 'active welfare capitalism' throughout the current recession have tended to be those with low rates of unemployment, large public sectors and left-wing governments; those with 'passive market economies' tended to be those with high unemployment, small public sectors and bourgeois parties dominant. Countries with low unemployment are those with highly mobilized and politically well-represented labour movements.

TABLE 9.7 *Ranking of selected OECD members*

Highest	Size of public sector	Rate of growth of public sector	Inflation
1	Sweden	Sweden	Italy
2	Norway	Denmark	France
3	Germany	Japan	Norway
4	Italy	Norway	Australia
5	France	Australia	UK
6	Denmark	Italy	Denmark
7	UK	Germany	Sweden
8	Australia	UK	US
9	US	France	Germany
10	Japan	US	Japan

Lowest

Source: Compiled from Tables 9.5 and 9.6, *OECD Economic Outlook* 30, December 1981.

TABLE 9.8 *Indexes of employment in industry 1982 (1975 = 100) and proportion of industrial employees in total civilian employment*

	Index	per cent (1982)
Canada	103	26
US	108	28
Japan	105	35
Australia	96	30
France	92	35
Germany	93	43
Italy	99	37
Sweden	86	31
UK	93	34

Source: *OECD Quarterly Labour Force Statistics* no. 1, 1983.

TABLE 9.9   *Modes of political and economic regulation*

Active welfare capitalism corporatist regulation	Passive welfare capitalism liberal regulation	Active market economies paternalist regulation	Passive market economies competitive regulation
Austria	Denmark	New Zealand	Australia
Luxembourg	Germany	Japan	Canada
Norway	UK	Iceland	Italy
Sweden	Finland	Switzerland	US
	Netherlands		

Source: Manfred Schmidt, *The Role of Parties in Shaping Macroeconomic Policy* (1982) (adapted).

Alternative accumulation strategies

Much of our analysis of the national specificity of the current crisis has presumed that nationally oriented strategic responses are possible. We have suggested that autonomous national recoveries from the current recession are likely to be more difficult in the 1980s than was the case in the 1930s, primarily because the types of reconstruction of the international division of production (Fröbel *et al.*, 1980) and the restructuring of particular labour processes (Clegg and Dunkerley, 1980) are occurring in ways which suggest that any anticipated 'next' phase of capital accumulation will occur not in the advanced industrialized capitalist countries, but in peripheral or semi-peripheral global locations where transnational rather than national capital will benefit (Holland, 1979; Wallerstein, 1979, 1980; MacEwan, 1981; Block and Hirschhorn, 1979; Weisskopf, 1981; Crough and Wheelwright, 1982). We have chosen not to elaborate these themes here. Our concern instead is to outline the institutional and political conditions which, in the light of the preceding chapters, we judge will be necessary for domestic economic recovery. The national dimension is therefore crucial to our consideration both of the particular forms of crisis and of the policy strategies which would need to be embraced by class-specific labour movement mobilizations for economic expansion and full employment.

356

It has been argued by Aglietta that within nations there are both 'characteristic difficulties' and 'persistent differentiations' which have influenced patterns of capital accumulation in the past and will therefore constrain political responses in the future. One of the contributors to the intractability of the current crisis has been the convergence of conditions of production in different capitalist nations and 'the accumulation of tensions that derive from the ultimate incompatibility of national modes of regulation' (1982, p.6).

For these reasons, politically inspired attempts to regenerate capital accumulation (within those countries upon which we have been basing our analysis of the relationship between class structure and economic developments) will need to intervene in processes which are resiting the locus of accumulation. Inevitably, to be successful, this would need to involve a quite complex political strategy involving various industrial and institutional transformations in particular nation states or groups of nation states. Just as processes of accumulation have shaped class structures and the practices of civil society in the past, so too will alternative accumulation strategies (Jessop, 1983), which could be developed to orient current tendencies in alternative directions, need to accommodate specific political realities and specific sedimented structures and constraints. We are now in a position to suggest what the class dimensions of such alternative accumulation strategies will be, the terrain on which they will need to be constructed, and the national or multilateral constraints with which they will need to contend.

At any given time the economic sovereignty of nations will be subject to both integrative and disintegrative tendencies. During the current recession these contradictory forces are evident in changing patterns of state regulation in different national contexts, as governing parties in diverse contexts attempt to cope with an accumulation of disintegrative tendencies. The disequilibrium is a result of significant structural transformations in the world economy. Many recent commentators, including Aglietta (1982) and Kaldor (1978), have pointed to the decline of the USA from a position of dominance in the international hierarchy of national growth systems. No longer is the USA the leading economy in the diffusion of manufacturing activities. 'Complementary' international linkages have been undermined by the erosion of national growth-rate differentials and the implied weakening of industrial specialization. The global pattern has become manifested in 'periodic overaccumulation' (that is, labour shortage) and generalized stagflation (Aglietta, 1982; Glyn and Harrison, 1980, p.11). A continuation of current reluctance to deploy industrial regeneration schemes would necessitate defensive protection and prolonged stagnation. A further fracturing of the world economy and subsequent declines in the economic performance and general standards of living in the advanced capitalist economies would result.

Some directions out of the impasse are clearly possible in theory. One scenario might see the USA and Japan use their evident potential for technologically based expansion in order to restore the pre-recessionary pattern of dominance in the world economy. A further possibility, much favoured by the British left groupings (Rowthorn, 1982; Holland, 1978), is for the economies of Europe to develop a series of regional renewal strategies which integrate the political strength of their labour movements with both anti-recessionary and anti-repressive social legislation to secure an industrially led regeneration based on an 'Alternative Economic Strategy'. Such an alternative has been conceived in distinction from the non-expansionary and deflationary preferences of monetarism. As such, although some of its elements derive from the post-Keynesian tradition, others, in Britain at least, derive from a reappraisal of ideas which were embraced during the 1930s and to some extent advocated, often uncritically, ever since.

Probably the initial formulation of the basic framework of an anti-recessionary Alternative Economic Strategy (AES) occurred with the publication in 1974 of a British government White Paper, *The Regeneration of British Industry*, by the then Secretary of State for Industry, Tony Benn. The principal features of that document were, first, a call for an expansion of public enterprise via an extension of the activities of the (British) National Enterprise Board and by the creation of further nationalized industry and, second, the decision to implement compulsory 'planning agreements' whereby all crucial decisions by remaining private sector enterprises concerning investment, expansion, contraction, technological change, product development, location, redeployment or closure would proceed only after consultation or in accordance with government and unions. The aim was clearly to counter pressures from the International Monetary Fund and various internal institutions on labour governments in order to stop the deindustrialization that had seemingly been a feature of the British economy since the turn of the century. It proposed policies, some aspects of which had been advocated by Keynes and generally opposed by Treasuries and Labour right-wingers, and therefore more or less abrogated, throughout the postwar years.

Although the AES began as an official set of policy alternatives designed in compliance with the British Labour Party's election manifesto as a means of ensuring that expansionary policies were not abandoned in office, it has since become neither distinctively British, nor located in or confined to any single political or intellectual grouping.

It has become an 'ideal type' of national reflationary strategy – implying both a set of policies to deal with unemployment and inflation by regenerating and restructuring the economy, and a set of political priorities to ensure widespread labour movement support for the combination of proposals that it necessitates.

As an economic package, the AES is sound enough. It recognizes that reflation of the economy requires a significant extension of economic planning, the public sector and public enterprises. It affirms the need for incomes policies not to depress living standards, but to secure political (non-cyclical) control over income distribution, to redress the dismantling of the postwar 'Keynes–Beveridge consensus' (CSE London Working Group, 1980, p.3), to impose whatever import controls are necessary for the restructuring of domestic industry and to establish conditions whereby the deliberate imposition of recessionary solutions to problems of capital accumulation cannot be contemplated again.

The three major elaborations of an AES for Britain all recognize that opposition to policies of expansion will be mounted (Aaronovitch, 1981, pp.83-8, 109-18; CSE London Working Group, 1980, pp.40-5; Holland, 1975, pp.204-6, 234-8). Such opposition is to be expected to policies which are explicitly addressed to the transformation of much of what conventional policy and parties have sought to conserve. For instance, the alternatives include proposals for both union and enterprise democracy, for greater access to information flows coupled with more general notions of public accountability on the part of enterprises, for tripartite negotiations over investment and incomes, and a restriction of the capacities inherent in corporate dominance of highly concentrated sectors of the economy (Holland, 1980, p.67). As our discussion of the state and parties in chapter 8 suggested, the opposition, just as much as the proposition, is founded on the notion of 'difference'. On the one hand, its impossibility; on the other hand, its possbility.

The Conference of Socialist Economists' (CSE) version of the AES notes the difficulty of opting for rapid economic growth:

> Both monetarists and non-monetarists have made the case that it is simply not possible to expand the economy by reflating, but that it is necessary to cut public spending and reduce public

sector borrowing. It is a tragedy that such ideas should have gained credence in sections of the Labour movement; it is important that they be openly contested. . . . Monetarism is not just a theory of inflation. It is a series of propositions stating that fiscal policy is useless, that all economic management is counterproductive, that all unemployment is voluntary, and that economic welfare is maximised by giving the greatest possible freedom to the operation of market forces. These propositions are embedded in a political and economic philosophy which is profoundly hostile to the public sector and deeply reactionary in its implications. It is the ideology of market capitalism par excellence (CSE, 1980, pp.40-1).

For all its endorsement, criticism, supplementation, amendment and reformulation by a range of political, institutional, factional and academic protagonists, the AES has still not been taken seriously by the groupings whose support it demands most – the more conservative, pragmatic personnel on the right-wing of the labour movement. As long as support for radical restructuring and reflation of the Western economies is not forthcoming from these sources, the parties of labour will seem disunited, their alternative policies uncommunicated and their strategies discredited. From this viewpoint, the 1979 and 1983 defeats of the British Labour Party were probably secured from the moment James Callaghan 'candidly' delivered his now famous 1976 pronouncement.

It is now clear that the British version of the AES, despite its claims to be a political strategy for transition as well as an economic programme for industrial regeneration, is unlikely ever to be effected. None of the conditions cited by Schmidt as sufficient for an alternative strategy seem possible within the time-frame necessary to prevent irreversible deindustrialization in Britain. The package of proposals offered by the AES all seem to be prefaced on the presumed impetus of 'the next Labour government'. No significant part of an alternative accumulation strategy – planning, 'planned trade', workplace democracy, challenges to multinational corporations, controlling inflation without repression – can be even commenced in isolation from the others.

This is because current 'pre-Keynesian' policies are accentuating trends which have been operating for some time in Britain. 'No other country comes close to matching this degree of deindustrialisation' (Coutts et al., 1981, p.86). The magnitude of the problem is given not only by the extent of industrial closure already experienced, but by the kind of conscious class mobilization that an alternative would require. For all the difficulties which may be anticipated, though, we are not advocating that the project be abandoned.

For a variety of reasons, therefore, the AES seeks to increase labour movement and state intervention into the developed economies in the hope of reversing not only the monetarist policies of restraint and public sector cutback, but also the long-term tendencies towards 'deindustrialization'. The cogency of the argument against market determination has been established by Singh's analysis of the long-term decline in the importance of manufacturing in the British economy. This long-term perspective shows that structural imbalance cannot be regarded as a temporary disequilibrium nor as a characteristic of a domestic economy alone. Real structural maladjustment may be a potential consequence of free trade for any mature or maturing industrial economy. 'Liberalization of trade has been detrimental to British industry, since it has inevitably led to a much faster increase in imports of manufactures without a concomitant rise in exports' (Singh, 1977, p.114). The adverse consequences of free trade and an open economy are evidenced by the development of non-complementary (competitive) productive capacities elsewhere in the world for more than a century. However, the dynamic balance between complementarity and competitiveness in the world economic expansion is always experienced unevenly, the complementary aspects of different national economies seemingly predominating from 1945 until the late 1960s.

The potential for participation in the international economy to lead to deindustrialization is exacerbated to the extent that a country has either a tradition of investing abroad (switching investment 'off-shore') or more domestically located multinational companies than its competitors (Singh, 1977, p.119). Orthodox policy measures to correct these tendencies will normally make matters worse, setting up a pattern of 'cumulative and circular causation'. For instance, attempts to enhance competitiveness by reducing wage costs will in fact depress demand, lower the rate of investment, impair technical progress, productivity and growth and hence produce an even weaker competitive position than before. Other policies of restraint, austerity and deflation will have similar effects. A long-term contraction in manufacturing industry causes concern not only because of the historically predominant role these activities have played in the advanced economies' growth, but because it is in manufacturing (rather than, say, the service sector, which seems to account for an increasing share of employment) that productivity growth, technical progress, economies of scale and internal multiplier effects more often originate (Singh, 1977, p.122).

The tendency towards deindustrialization of some former 'workshops of the world' has also been a tendency towards 'delabourization' (McQueen, 1982, pp.217-21). As suggested by Figures 9.3 and 9.4, a smaller proportion of the available workforce is able to produce higher levels of aggregate industrial production. Since the onset of recession, the share of the proportion of the labour force employed in British manufacturing has declined even more dramatically than it had in the previous decade (Singh, 1977, p.124), while the share of manufacturing output in total GDP has fallen only since 1973. These features are common to most OECD economies as a long-term structural characteristic; they imply not only that a further downward spiral could result from the declines experienced thus far in industrial production, but also that the contemporary 'shake-outs' are not leading to improved productivity (in contrast to previous recessions) (Singh, 1977, p.127). In Australia, the proportion of the workforce employed in manufacturing is now only 20 per cent and still falling (Crough and Wheelwright, 1982, p.102). The process is a conscious one in which 'deregulation' and 'denation-alization' of industry play a facilitative role. At the 'meso-economic' level (Holland, 1975), deindustrialization occurs in synchrony with the 'complementation' schemes of internationally rationalized and restructured producers (e.g. those which are now a contributor to the 'world car': a project which insulates corporate producers from temporary supply or production problems in any particular nation state by siting plants at various geographically strategic locations in an international network of production and distribution).

Deindustrialization is not merely a secular experience for specific economies attendant upon particular stages of maturity and manifested in import penetration, low productivity growth, entrepreneurial ineptitude, industrial relations problems, low design quality or balance of payments difficulties. Rather, it is an attempt by corporations to restructure their sphere of operations – a programme which creates internal economic dislocation while at the same time undermining the range of alternative political responses.

The worldwide mobility of capital (and, to a lesser extent, of labour) has internationalized economic activity and greatly reduced the ability of each national government to manage its own economic activity. The most striking example is the ineffectiveness of domestic countercyclic policy in the presence of significant capital mobility. . . . But the internationalization of capital itself is responsible in no small degree for the re-emergence of a polycentric world capitalist system in which no single state can exercise decisive leadership (Bowles, 1978, p.264).

In this view, an increase in competition from manufacturing located 'off-shore' will be met by reduced investment in the corresponding manufacturing centres which remain and seriously exacerbate already damaging tendencies (Singh, 1977, p.138). Deindustrialization is clearly not a symptom of 'the British disease' or of national failure to achieve an export surplus, which is the major focus of the 'Cambridge' view (Cairncross, 1979, p.10). It reflects more importantly a phase of global relocation of industrial activity which organizations such as the Trilateral Commission are anxious to sponsor (Sklar, 1980) and to which other international agencies such as the IMF have thus far responded with quite myopic and restrictive censures. Regardless, however, of whether alternative accumulation strategies opt for domestic or multilateral retaliations, the structural disequilibria have become deep-seated, and the economic and political possibilities so stifled by deflation and recession that it will not be possible to institute the required modifications in production without fundamental institutional changes and the permanent abandonment of the regime of free trade that the various formulations of the AES suggest (Singh, 1977, p.134). Import controls are central to policies to thwart deindustrialization, not because they will operate on a balance of payments impasse, but because they will help engender a regeneration of manufacturing industry (Kaldor, 1979, p.23).

Cripps and Godley are quite unequivocal: 'Fiscal expansion by direct control of imports (whether through tariffs or quotas) is the only practical means by which the UK, and probably several other industrial countries, can sustain expansion of national output sufficient to restore full employment in the next decade' (1978, p.327). Such policies need not reduce the volume of world trade and need not constitute a 'beggar-my-neighbour' approach (Robinson, 1935). They will perpetuate inefficiency only if they subsidize obsolete processes; in the context of fiscal and industrial expansion, this need not be the case.

Consequently, import controls would need to be supplemented by a series of industrial policies 'drastically' to increase investment; but as this is unlikely before the 'trough' of the depression, it is unlikely to come from the private sector. Appropriate public sector alternatives could be developed only as a consequence of labour movement pressure. Equally, however, industry policy requires a permanent incomes policy, accelerated growth, labour movement co-operation 'over a large field' and the abandonment of anti-inflationary policies (Balogh, 1979, p.200). At the same time, however, as the interlocking experiences of industrial decline suggest an expansive political programme for its reversal, substantial dispute exists concerning some of the elements in an alternative strategy.

Despite the strong case that exists for limiting the extent to which national economies are subject to international economic forces, a substantial criticism of the AES derives from doubts concerning the desirability or practicality of import controls. Both right- and left-wing critics of the AES point to 'the connection between the decline of liberal trade and the rise of militarism and fascism during the 1930s' (Willoughby, 1982, p.196). Protection has always been a major factor in the high rates of economic growth enjoyed by the core capitalist economies as Kaldor's criticism of the Gold Standard indicated. Whereas, in the past, protectionist policies were associated with imperialist politics and national rivalries, the domestic class structures of the major capitalist nations have now changed to such an extent that a radical AES-sponsored protectionism would not recreate imperial spheres of influence, but would help to undermine existing tendencies towards 'internationalization' of production. A radical AES implies a

breaking away from dependence on exports and imports from other metropolitan countries. . . . A radical programme of trade control would represent an attempt by workers within an economically depressed nation-state to escape the burden of maintaining themselves within the imperialist centre (Willoughby, 1982, p.209).

Although *ad hoc* protectionism is sometimes thought adversely to affect developmental aspirations within some industrializing nations, Cripps's and Godley's analysis indicates that a more powerful stimulus to industrialization of the South would be a radical acceleration of growth in the North. However, such progressive intervention in contemporary processes of global integration requires a restructuring of internal social relations and, thereby, a further restriction of external capital mobility (Willoughby, 1982, p.210).

New political institutions

Regardless of which political, social and economic futures the

364

advanced capitalist economies adopt throughout the 1980s and beyond, new organizational forms are inevitable. If the deflationary and non-expansionary policies that have, over the past decade, become familiar in formerly core countries are continued, it seems inevitable that more authoritarian structures will be necessary in civil society to adjudicate the unmet demands and needs thrown up by an expansion of deregulated market criteria in the economy. If, on the other hand, the 'left milieu' that has been suggested as a necessary condition for full-employment-led transitional strategies of renewed accumulation is in fact developed in those countries, then a variety of explicitly political decisions will demand to be the cynosure of organizational and class analysis.

Internal organizational consequences of labour-movement-initiated transitions were an unheralded aspect of capital accumulation even before labour began to exert an influence on the state and its economic policies. Effective worker organization is a precondition for the erosion of the premises of pure capitalism for historical reasons. 'Organisation appears as a source of power in capitalism for the first time in Marx's theory because capitalism is the first mode of production which puts the subordinate class in a situation in which it can organize' (Stephens, 1979, p.7). In the contemporary context, differences in class organization have been shown to explain quite substantial disparities in the degree of support for collective capital formation as a strategy for combining economic growth, worker solidarity and economic democracy in Denmark and Sweden (Esping-Andersen, 1981). Stephens iterates the organizational attributes that need to be secured when he points out that 'the state is not an independent force but, in fact, is highly dependent on the distribution of power in civil society' (1979, p.71). This implies that its policies and structures need not be constrained by a pre-given public opinion, but rather seen as the outcome of political and social forces. It is possible, therefore, to recognize a range of corporate decision-making which is normally outside the ambit of legislative regulation. Familiar labour reformism founders on such corporate obduracy; collective ownership becomes a preferred form of intervention. Stephens shows (1979, pp.145-9), as do Apple et al. (1981), that the failure of successive British governments to implement Keynesian reflationary policies, coupled with subsequent reversions to austerity, has been an indicator of the weakness of organized labour (Apple and Higgins, 1982; Higgins and Apple, 1983). In Sweden, wage restraint and deflation has been replaced by policies to effect structural changes in the economy. Lack of organizational acumen elsewhere has had profound political consequences whose genesis seems still unappreciated. 'It is ironic that a party which prides itself on ideological openness as compared to its supposedly more dogmatic Marxist sister parties has actually been one of the least innovative social democratic parties in Europe' (Stephens, 1979, p.148). Wage equalization and structural rationalization can be achieved only when a well-organized labour movement exists. Resistance to capitalist rationalization is always a defensive response and is not a viable alternative to recessionary policies.

In Kalecki's terms new political institutions will need to be developed to reflect this increased involvement of the working class. There will be two broad functions: control over investment and control over distribution of income. We have already argued that politically explicit, democratically inured, publicly debated criteria for investment decisions are absolutely essential for any anti-recessionary strategy. This will involve the creation not only of forums for discussion, but of centres for research, evaluation and planning of possible increments to economic activity. Accumulation will need to take place under socially desirable rather than privately profitable auspices.

Given the crucial relationships established by Kalecki and the post-Keynesian analyses between the class distribution of income and the level and rate of growth of economic activity, there will be a need for institutions to decide explicitly the distribution of surplus between consumption and accumulation requirements. If income distribution is allowed to become too unevenly skewed, recovery may be impeded; if unconsidered pressures are brought to bear on either wages' or profits' shares of total income at times when the balance between them is being shaped by phases of accumulation independently of policy decisions, then depression can be exacerbated. Outcomes which have appeared immutable in the past (relativities within the class of wage-earners; rewards to rentiers versus wage-earners) need to be seen for what they are: susceptible to conscious, responsive intervention and social reorganization.

Already there have been forms of organizational development which have usurped these roles. There is also a wide range of criticism of them (Newman, 1981; Schmitter and Lehmbruch, 1979; Lehmbruch and Schmitter, 1982; Berger, 1981b; Panitch, 1979, 1980; Westergaard, 1977; Birnbaum, 1982). It seems to us that provided the labour movement is able to develop its own hegemony over economic policy formation, a corporatist form is a necessary political development for political control of the economy. Tripartite decision-making structures (where capital and labour within state forums decide investment and accumulation strategies) and social contracts (where labour formally determines the level and conditions of its remuneration in exchange for guarantees with respect to state economic policy and corporate industrial priorities) should therefore be embraced as a necessary part of any anti-recessionary strategy in a post-market-determined economy. Not unexpectedly, there will be a variety of potentialities and dangers to be anticipated and accommodated.

The tripartite organizations which seem to be required by any non-authoritarian alternative accumulation strategy will obviously demand the participation, on a routinized basis, of capital, labour and the state. For capital, the advantage of participation in such arrangements derives from the reduced uncertainty concerning capital–labour conflicts over wages and the less capricious environment for industrial investment provided by the guarantees of contractually or legislatively binding tripartism. On the other hand, managerial prerogatives with respect to employment conditions and investment would be undeniably diminished. Class conflict would not be eliminated. The development of new forums for its expression and resolution would have the effect of transforming the terms through which this conflict has traditionally been expressed: by elimination of profitability as the criterion for investment; by replacing the market as the prime mechanism for resource allocation with overtly political mechanisms; and by decommodifying an increasing proportion of social production.

For labour, the advantages of involvement in institutions which are structured to allow a more broadly democratic determination of the scale, content and trajectory of capital accumulation, derive from the political implications of the Kaleckian analysis of full-employment capitalism. Implicit in this is the recognition that insistence on permanent full employment and production for use is ultimately incompatible with capitalism's underlying social relations. The caveats that have been sounded to labour involvement derive from either the experience of past incorporation into wages policy determination on unequal or unsustainable terms (Panitch, 1979), or else from a civil and pluralist constitution of labour as just one of a number of interest groups which are entitled to representation. This latter point is one which Offe (1981, 1983) cites in his claims that fragmented political conflict is increasingly unaccommodatable in the mechanisms of competitive party democracy. As the resulting tensions and limitations on the ability of the state to respond have become more apparent, a consequential 'wave of postpluralist realism' has created a perception of malfunctioning in the institutions of

CLASS POLITICS AND THE ECONOMY

democratic representative government 'which are serious enough to explain the resort to corporatist political structures' (Offe, 1981, pp.129, 146). Pluralist corporatism, by adjudicating multifarious civil demands, systematically presupposes consensus and therefore discriminates against labour organizations seeking to change the 'rules of the game' (Offe, 1981, p.153). Under such conditions familiar bargaining over wages and unfamiliar demands for economic democracy at a macro-economic level can be met only by the displacement of pluralist assumptions or by sustained repression. What is required of new institutions is not a problem-solving conflict resolution, but a regeneration of forums for a conflictual politics.

The most likely outcome is given, however, not by abstractly formulated political possibilities but by the history and forms of working-class mobilization that have existed in particular national circumstances. Regini and Esping-Andersen (1980) have pointed out that where unions have adopted macro-economic goals (full employment and economic growth) in addition to goals which benefit only their own members, they tend to acquire greater public legitimacy and therefore to be more politically effective.

As class unions acting in the political market, they should on the one hand be able to ensure that [social expenditure] is used to sustain growth and employment; on the other they should be particularly sensitive to the possibility of creating jobs in this way, as full employment means not only greater market power for the employed workers but also, by enlarging the size of the working class, more power for the unions in the political market (1980, p.1908).

Where unions seek to participate in social and economic policy decisions on a non-subordinate bias, they are clearly able to reconcile the demands of both the macro-economy and their own memberships.

It is important to examine the extent of internal organizational impediments to labour movement initiatives in the realm of economic policy and Alternative Economic Strategies. The development of new institutional norms may well have effects on the ability of political strategies to influence capital accumulation.

Explicitly political and non-repressive strategies which respond to 'post-pluralist' conditions are premised on what Regini (1983) has called a 'class-oriented' rather than an associational basis of representation. Under these circumstances, unions seek to represent a much wider constituency than simply their own members, through having political status attributed to them. What this entails is a delegation of public functions to the union

368

and their possible incorporation within the state. Certain organizational effects of this process have been noted, particularly the resultant tendency for the union's organization to become more bureaucratized and for interunion organization to become more centralized than would be the case where a market, rather than political, strategy has predominated. It has been suggested that there are three main reasons why a political strategy entails a greater degree of centralization: to ensure representation, to accumulate sufficient resources for comprehensive political education and to remove the leadership's representation from rank-and-file pressure (Draper and Palmer, 1982). More generally, it has been suggested that all interest organizations will tend to 'centralisation, bureaucratisation, co-optation of leaders, professionalisation of representatives and the use of experts, enhanced aggregation of demands, official recognition of their status, interdependence with public power, and long-term calculation of interests' (Regini, 1983, p.240). These tendencies will be greater for a labour movement which has followed an archetypal corporatist political strategy. Conventionally, these tendencies have been hypothesized as necessarily leading to a 'crisis of representation', one which is signalled by an increasing gulf between the interest-formulation of leaders and members. For instance, Esping-Andersen et al. (1976, p.197) have argued that corporatism 'is an internally contradictory mode of incorporating the working class'. It depends upon the union appointees retaining legitimacy in both their organizational role as union leaders and in their assigned role as state policy-makers.

Analyses that suggest that functional inevitability of a crisis of representation for unions following a corporatist strategy tend to be mechanistic in their assumption that there already exists a working-class interest, defined at the base, waiting to be sold out by interests distorted by their superstructural role. What this perspective omits is, first, a realization that any process of representation inevitably selects, mediates and therefore modifies the interests putatively being represented; and second, the national variability in the extent to which unions are able to combine the two goals of immediate income security for members and more politically defined full employment and economic growth for the working class as a whole (Regini and Esping-Andersen, 1980). It is, however, only partially correct to argue that interests are formed solely in the course of their representation. The 'fundamental' division between categories of economic actors is subject to periodic transformations of which these actors may be unaware, although issues which fire specific political demands will often not be of this type. Furthermore, the representation of wage negotiations may not comprehend the actual patterns of relationships between accumulation and distribution that we have specified. It is these considerations which account for the centrality of comprehensive political education in any political strategy (Carnoy, 1981). Any interest organization, especially a labour movement which seeks to follow a political strategy, carries out what Regini (1983, p.242) terms 'a profound modification of the specific and explicit demands' of its membership. The strategic concern is therefore to minimise the probability of representational crisis by maximizing participation in class-specific political decisions.

A primary safeguard is extensive internal democracy. This will entail that the determination, interpretation and articulation of members' demands is at base collectively decided, hence minimizing the risk of low levels of involvement and commitment to the policies which are transmitted. However, a political strategy entails a far wider constituency than simply the union's membership: it involves attempts to connect the demands formulated 'with those of social groups not forming part of the working class but potential allies of it' (Regini, 1983, p.244). One way of achieving this is to redefine shorter-term membership goals as compatible with a broader, longer-term strategy. This can be most strategically achieved to the extent that an anti-recessionary strategy is seen to be to the advantage of all groups seeking representation.

The crucial problem becomes one of sustaining long-term commitment. As Regini (1983, p.251) observes, this problem is always delicate because there is always a time-lag between the sacrifice of gains that might be acquired from free collective bargaining and uncertain future rewards from a general political strategy of renewed accumulation.

In the Swedish example, as well as others, such as Austria and Norway, the postwar era seemed to provide conditions that minimized the uncertainty surrounding political strategy. Most notable of these was the long period of governing control by working-class-based parties which did formulate policies of a general interest. The propitious patterns of economic growth experienced in these countries were, we have argued, a result of such strategies and policies. That links between state policy and transformative political and economic strategies exist, therefore, needs to be much more concisely incorporated into labour movement education programmes and negotiating practices. This is particularly urgent in the context of wage policy formation.

It has been argued that incomes policies in the past have been insufficiently cognizant of 'social obstacles' to their implementation (Hirst, 1982). Existing forms of collective bargaining (in the UK – the argument does not hold in countries with centralized or solidaristic wage-fixing systems) perpetuate non-functional relativities and entrench defensive modes of representation. The defensiveness and unwieldiness (Kilpatrick and Lawson, 1980) of collective bargaining is therefore criticized, and dogged adherence to it is cited as an impediment to a more practical and realistic incomes policy. However valid it is to insist that 'many potential issues of struggle in the enterprise cannot be expressed in terms of personal benefits' (Hirst, 1982, p.251), it is not correct to infer from this that collective efforts to defend real wage levels in times of recession are counter-productive to economic recovery, economic democracy and transitional political strategies. As we have argued, anti-recessionary policies demand real wage maintenance (admitting that an increasing proportion of this may be taken in the form of a decommodified, social wage); and deflationary policies always have the effect of depressing real living standards. The compliance (or otherwise) of trade unions with specific policies can never be a crucial determinant of strategic outcomes. Political power is decisive but this is given not by the working class alone, but by its capacities to mobilize the support of sufficient sections of the new middle class and the petty bourgeoisie to affect the direction of the whole economy. 'Where bargaining power is strong, but its political power weak, the likely outcome is a "British Disease", where sustained full employment compels labour to accept income policies and "lame-duck enterprise" subsidisation' (Esping-Andersen and Friedland, 1982, p.46).

Consequently, insistence upon incomes policies should not be expected to antedate the adoption of policies for industrial restructuring and reflation. It is unreasonable to argue that continuing commitment to free collective bargaining over levels of incomes undermines policies for full employment because, as we have already sought to establish, the control of inflation is much less problematic in an expansionary phase when real incomes are increasing and pressures on profits declining. To argue, as Hirst does, that income disparities produced in recession do not affect the bargaining strengths of those in continuing employment is to absolve from significance both the impact of unemployment on households where some members do still retain jobs and the increasing inability of unions to resist massive assaults on their organizational effectiveness. Hirst seems to suggest that monetarism is merely an ideological myopia: 'Far from being a fiendish capitalist plot, the depth of the British recession is a blunder consequent upon the stubborn persistence

371

in an unworkable policy derived from an irrelevant economic dogma' (1982, p.252). Our analysis has attempted to demonstrate that deflationary policies, policies which exacerbate cyclical tendencies that are structurally present anyway, are understandable in terms of the effects they achieve and the alternatives they deny. This holds for both the current recession and the objections to full-employment policies that were voiced in the 1930s.

Hirst's determination to see the differentials between wage-earners themselves is not only too Anglo-centric to provide a generalized case for incomes policies, but it also ignores the cyclical influences upon income distribution within the class of wage-earners that Kalecki's analysis highlighted. These disparities are always reduced as the level of total incomes increases. They are exacerbated to the extent that recession produces a capital flow to the secondary labour market as a consequence of union strength in the primary one (Regini and Esping-Andersen, 1980, p.121). The prime objective of social democratic policy must therefore always be towards full employment and balanced growth rather than to redistribution (Harcourt, 1977a). Policies oriented towards the latter can be effected only to the extent that the former is achieved.

Panitch's objections to any form of corporatism derive from his (1976) investigation of the experience of the British labour movement's acceptance, from time to time, of incomes policies. For Panitch, corporatism always means that eventually unions impose on their memberships bargaining restraints which are unreasonable and will ultimately reproduce the conditions favourable to continued capital accumulation and undermine the transformative potential and political power of organized labour. This has been the case, he maintains, whenever corporatist structures have been established in liberal democracies and is therefore likely to be the case if 'reformist' corporatism systematically emerges from current conditions. Tendencies towards corporatism exist, suggests Panitch, because of the manifest instability of orthodox economic management, the associated need to legitimate state policies of wage restraint and economic planning, and because it is no longer appropriate to leave the outcome of economic decisions to the unintegrated clash of market participants (1979, pp.121-2).

These suggestions warrant serious consideraton. If most social contracts and incomes policies in the past (including those negotiated by parties of labour) have been the occasion for reductions in real incomes of wage-earners, then any attempt to secure democratic and political control over the distribution of income as part of an 'alternative accumulation strategy' will invoke the suspicion of those who have been soured by past experience (Tarling and Wilkinson, 1977; Ormerod, 1981; Purdy, 1981). The commitment to real wage maintenance and guarantees concerning the wage and profit shares in total income would need to be unequivocal. There is no *prima facie* reason to suppose, however, that adequate public control over the class distribution of income is technically or administratively unachievable. The wartime success of wage and price controls in the USA shows that despite the likelihood of corporate avoidance tactics, control over all incomes can, with political will, be secured (Galbraith, 1974, part 5). The real obstacles will reside not in devising the appropriate political institutions but in ensuring insistence on economic expansion, which any full-employment accumulation strategy demands.

Concern is legitimately expressed, of course, about the imposition of radically altered institutional forms by stealth. Co-option of central trade union organizations to *ad hoc* bodies concerned with national economic planning and incomes policy 'has rarely, or at least only in very specific contexts been announced or even acknowledged as corporatist by politicians' (Panitch, 1979, p.121). These cautions, however, should not detract attention from the functional necessity of new institutional forums for macro-economic decision-making. Just as parliament has not been the site of these decisions in the past, the boardroom should not continue to be so in the future. The task is to bring labour, capital and the state together in ways which preclude the use of recession as a strategy for economic restructuring or workforce discipline. Neither should corporatist forms be used merely as forums for interest-group representation or as a surrogate parliament. New institutions will need to embrace representation from regional and particular lobbying interests at the time when actual investments are made (Abrahamsson and Broström, 1980), but they should not be expected to incorporate the multifarious representations that are constantly being formed and reformed in civil society. Labour's involvement in full-employment planning cannot be regarded as analogous to other specific political demands. Some objections to corporatism therefore seem to err by insisting, as for example Hall as done, that 'corporatism excludes the great mass of the people . . . the range of democratic participation is not expanded' (1983, p.197). Broadening the basis for political control of the economy involves the establishment of permanent and stable institutions whereby labour's participation is not an unequal or *ad hoc* matter.

If new political institutions are to be developed as a programme for industrial restructuring and a regeneration of a class-conscious politics; if functional representation of collective agencies of mobilization in socioeconomic policy-making is to be permanently ensured; if the 'massive inequality' which Macpherson regarded as always accompanying liberal freedoms and market allocation (1973, p.180) is to be displaced by 'post-liberal' organizational developments, then the instability and unresponsiveness of tripartite structures that is noted and feared by Panitch, Schmitter and Hall will need to be countered. Without the wholehearted participation of labour *qua* labour, unstable corporatisms will continue to be systems of 'interest representation' whereby demands are constrained (Schmitter, 1974, p.13). They need to be the opposite of this: institutional mechanisms which allow a socially responsive and democratically formulated allocation of enterprise surpluses to collectively controlled investment in a manner which accords with the distributional concomitants of such investment decisions and maximum levels of capital formation (Meidner, 1978, pp.13-18).

According to most critical observers of politics in Thatcherist Britain, 'authoritarian populism' has already arrived in the form of a concious, sustained and ruthless programme to dismantle the gains from the '1945 settlements'. Hall sees this realignment of political forces as a nationally specific continuation of circumstances that have existed periodically since the depression of the 1930s.

> The Callaghan episode – a squalid and disorganizing interlude – restored the now-classical repertoire of the social-democratic management of capitalist crisis, but on a markedly weakening political base. As that social-democratic repertoire was progressively eroded and exhausted the fissures in British society became everywhere more manifest (1980, p.157).

By weakening unions, making social institutions and legislation more repressive and by eschewing any economic alternative, Thatcherism is seeking to reverse the entire trajectory of postwar politics and to impose a more austere hegemony (Leys, 1980). As such, this political alternative, for all its efforts at deregulation in accordance with 'supply-side' polemicists (Heilbroner, 1981), is extraordinarily interventionist in the extent to which it seeks to transform the political forms of class conflict that were developed during the long boom. Its use of force as a social regulator is becoming the routine experience of an increasingly embittered part of the population. 'Creeping authoritarianism masked by the rituals of formal representation is what gives a peculiar historical specificity to the present phase of the crisis of the state/crisis of hegemony' (Hall, 1980, p.161). As the economic crisis has developed, various political possibilities have been raised for traditional modes of democratic representation. The path chosen by Thatcherism is one which appears to seek to 'uncouple' capitalism from democracy (Jessop, 1978a) and hence to foreclose certain alternative forms of resolution.

The analyses of general crisis tendencies in capitalist development, of the factors which produce trade cycles, of the influences upon effective economic policies and of the configurations of political strategies that have existed in the major capitalist countries have decisive implications. No postulated strategies for economic recovery that fail to consider the fundamental class divisions which shape processes of economic change can hope to attain analytical comprehensibility or political effectiveness.

Economic development and industrial restructuring during times of crisis change the basis upon which accumulation will recur in the future; hence, class capacities are being constantly reconstituted. The ways in which class formation has historically occurred have obviously structured late-twentieth-century political possibilities. This is what our argument throughout this chapter has sought to demonstrate. From the discussion we have provided of the organizational, institutional, national (and therefore non-general) terrains where class-based activities actually occur, it follows that class formation is 'an open-ended process with no fixed destination' (Therborn, 1983, p.39).

The ability of classes to affect social, political and economic outcomes is always contingent. It is this very susceptibility to political influence which decrees that policies aimed at regenerating the accumulation of capital according to *alternative* investment criteria will need to be comprehensive political strategies. The potential of such strategies to achieve their goals will depend less upon the formulation of the associated documents and statements than upon the capacities of classes to act and the forms of organization and practice thereby developed (Clegg *et al.*, 1983). Implications of this recognition that class (rather than simply policies, parties or parliaments *per se*) is the most autonomous variable provide the basis for recent attempts to develop a theory of capitalist politics (Therborn, 1983). Alternative strategies will be successful only to the extent that they are not incompatible with 'crucial moments' in the production, extraction, realization and accumulation of value (Jessop, 1983). There are always tenable and untenable alternative accumulation strategies.

It is conceivable, therefore, that the post-1949 and post-1974 defeats experienced by the parties and organizations of labour will help shape the economic future in ways which are not clearly amenable to working classes and democratic majorities in the advanced capitalist nations. By the time opportunities recur for the implementation of an AES in Britain, the process of deindustrialization may well have transformed class relations to such an extent that its programmatic elements will be entirely redundant. Certainly, the conditions under which democratic control of investment is likely to be secured in Sweden have been qualitatively distinct (and more favourable) for several decades compared with those pertaining in the UK. Even if restructure and reflation were to be flawlessly effected in Australia, France, Germany or the UK, the return to full employment could take several decades. The working class in each instance has an entirely divergent range of transformative involvements behind it and potentialities ahead. Interestingly, the Swedish labour movement's political thrust has been less dissipated by the plethora of non-class conflicts and non-class-specific demands than have appeared in civil society elsewhere (Offe, 1983; Webber, 1982; Korpi, 1982).

Although it is possible that the market-expanding proclivities of the British government will provide little comfort for industrial capital in Britain, it will almost certainly prevent the development of the 'radical corporatist' interventions that would be required for any programme of collective capital formation there. Subsequent societal development could be such that any future capital accumulation 'will produce far less proletarian unity or self conscious organisation' (Therborn, 1983, p.43). There is a possibility suggested also by Wright's (1983) examination of the likelihood of a post-capitalist future wherein labour plays a minimal strategic or structural role. If 'passive competitive' or authoritarian strategies are pursued, the dominance of capitalism in conjunction with liberal democratic political forms could give way to a 'statist' mode of production whose objective would still be accumulation, but whose main collective agency would be sections of the 'new middle class' – in Wright's terms, the 'technical intelligentsia'. These groups could assume bureaucratic and authoritative domination which would determine relations to the means of production and define the central mechanism of surplus labour appropriation:

> One of the pervasive dilemmas the working-class movement
> has always faced in capitalism has . . . been the systemic
> pressures towards a de-politicization of class conflict. . . . In
> statism on the other hand, economic class struggle – struggle

over the size and distribution of the surplus product – is immediately a political conflict. The politics of production become a form of political struggle involving the state. There is thus no tendency for struggles by direct producers to be purely economistic; they are always politicized by virtue of the social relations they confront (Wright, 1983, p.99).

Class politics, an assertion of the demise of market sureties, may not necessarily prefigure a liberatory involvement in accumulation strategies.

At the time of the Industrial Revolution, the emergent class, the bourgeoisie, was able to combine a formal (but limited) commitment to democratic politics with an expansive role in accumulation. Possibilities for an extension of liberalism to embrace economic and industrial democracy on a broad, macro, basis obviously exist in the 1980s; but equally obviously there are less sanguine possibilities too. The rise of the class of industrial capitalists stamped national economies and politics in now familiar ways; but this impact meant that the capacity of the working class decisively to influence cycles of development and political priorities has been fluctuating and uncertain. Alternative strategies aim for an epoch where the influence of traditional bourgeoisies is likely to decline, to make the labour movement's contribution more ascendant. However, although class capacities are always formed in the relationships that exist with other classes, the weakness of one (formerly hegemonic) class does not necessarily signal the ascendancy of another (Therborn, 1983, p.44). The usurpation of the market does not necessarily mean a heightened 'working-class collectivity'.

Moreover, as Therborn's account of the growth of 'labour-process collectivity' in Sweden shows, the ability of a class to influence national political and economic trajectories in a way favourable to its own constituency on a permanent basis, is at least partly dependent upon the specific composition of industrial production, the particular sectoral pattern of output, the 'regime of accumulation' (Therborn, 1983, p.42; Aglietta, 1979). Constraints upon labour movement assertiveness are stronger when accumulation takes place in mercantilist, financial and rentier forms compared with those which exist when a capitalist economy is dominated by industrial production. Workforce homogeneity, as we have argued, depends upon 'the sources of labour force recruitment, the skill structure of the work process, the system of remuneration and, more generally, the degree of integration of local labour markets' (Therborn, 1983, p.43). These organizational parameters have obviously been such in Sweden that the working class and labour movement there have been decisive forces.

Collective capital formation

We have hinted repeatedly throughout this chapter that Sweden provides an exceptional instance of the connections between working-class organizational acumen, determinate national policy and transitional economic strategies. Strategic lessons from the Swedish experience can be drawn by examining the potential this national instance has to provide a democratic, non-market road to high levels of industrial production and capital accumulation under non-bourgeois, consciously collective auspices.

Sweden is of political interest not only because of its history of concerted labour movement achievements with respect to welfare state provisions, wages, industrial democracy and corporate efficiency, but because of the formulation of and commitment to the development of 'employee investment funds' – the so-called Meidner Plan for collective capital formation to secure democratic control of the economy on a permanent basis (Meidner, 1978). Before we can adequately evaluate the 'Rehn-Meidner' proposals following their inclusion as a central feature in an electoral programme with which the Social Democratic Party was returned to office (September 1982), we need to examine the history of the labour movement's political struggles which have made such an alternative model feasible in the 1980s.

Most striking is the ability since the 1930s of a politically well-organized labour movement to adopt strategies and policies to increase economic growth, and for this experience of growth and stable political control to permit the evolution of longer-term political objectives in conjunction with the maturation of Swedish capitalism. Economic growth has strengthened labour and reduced inequalities; labour's strength has deployed the widespread egalitarianism and lack of effective organizational resistance by capital to ensure continued growth and continued ability to support social policies, taxation policy and labour-market interventions.

The radicalism of Swedish social democracy has its origins in the peculiar history of Sweden as a capitalist nation, in debates since the turn of the century concerning 'capitalism, socialism and democracy', and in the relationship between the political movement and political parties of labour especially during the uniquely long period of non-bourgeois rule from 1932 to 1976. The radicalism of this reformist politics which claimed adequacy to the goal of socialist transformation has been well articulated in the writings of politician and intellectual Ernst Wigforss since 1908 (Higgins, 1983).

Very early in the century, conditions were established which were to be long-lasting in their effects on the economy and polity of Sweden. A distinctive pattern of class conflict was created from the 1870s when industrialization and industrial unionism developed rapidly. From the end of the 1930s, when industrial conflict had been both open and bitter, changes in class organization occurred whereby a basic antagonism between the trade union confederation (LO) and the employers' federation (SAF) was established by the social democrats' decision to push relentlessly for economic growth as a means of undermining capitalist control of the economy.

The conflict existed even at the policy level. Employers seem to have been more aware of the transformative potential of any insistence on policies designed to achieve full employment and high growth. An exchange of letters between prominent Swedish industrialist Marcus Wallenberg and Keynes in 1933 reveals the incipient bourgeois hostility to the latter's proposals for demand stimulation and public borrowing. Not only would state intervention allegedly prevent a revival of entrepreneurial spirits, but it would need to be implemented by politicians who possess only 'some childish idea of the possibilities of tapping the well-to-do classes' and 'who believe that they can both eat the goose and have her lay eggs'. Against Keynes's suggestions, Wallenberg protested that however relevant public spending was to Britain, in Sweden it would be unnecessary and undesirable because it represented 'public extravagance and violation of economic laws'.

> The peasants complain. They always do. The industry complains. . . . The government is socialist. . . . Improvements are not all needed. Everything here is done. Slums do not exist in Swedish towns. Housing is up to date, and at least in Stockholm is too extravagant. The country is flooded by students, newspapers and books. . . . Very likely the whole scheme will lead to an uncontrollable inflation (quoted in Gårdlund, 1977, pp.89, 93).

Despite these objections, the 'politics of compromise' was abandoned, and with it any suggestion that socialist policies should be deferred pending a further maturation of Swedish capitalism.

In the postwar period, LO 'took the initiative from both party and state in developing a quite different strategy for the maintenance of stable growth and full employment without a damaging level of inflation' (Higgins, 1980, p.145). In addition, LO was able to co-ordinate wages policy and press other policy initiatives on the governing party (SAP). The 'Rehn-Meidner model', a policy initiative developed within the labour movement in the interwar period, was adopted in 1951 and set union priorities which from then on advocated a solidarity wages strategy to reduce incomes differentials, selective interventions in investment projects to reduce the indiscriminate impact of fiscal policies and an active labour-market policy to allay the effects of industry's rationalizations by facilitating mobility of labour to the more productive sectors.

The principles that were established exploited the historical weakness of the Swedish bourgeoisie as a mobilized political force by allowing the labour movement progressively to seek a dominant voice in investment decisions and capital formation. The adopted wages policy was not only solidaristic but such as to squeeze profit margins in uncompetitive or inefficient enterprises. Those which survived were highly productive, innovative and dominant in an increasingly concentrated Swedish capitalism. High profit levels were seen to be neither a necessary nor a sufficient condition for high rates of investment. Low profitability is just as compatible with capitalization and rationalization in industry as are high profits with low investment. Industrial restructuring was ensured by the Rehn-Meidner model's 'active labour market policy' through its corporatist organ *Arbetsmark-nadsstyrelsen* (AMS). These principles and institutions dictated that economic management would not resort to familiar wage and price controls, but control macro-economic aggregates by 'holding down demand and profit levels' so that the level and content of economic activity were always subject to political intervention. Growth was seen as more easily achievable in the context of high wages, high levels of investment from profits and relocation/ retraining schemes to accommodate structural readjustments which were expected to be recurrent.

Consequently, investment funds were established first by tax concessions and then from employer-funded pension funds. Under public control, these would be judiciously released as part of anti-cyclical and capital accumulation strategies (Higgins, 1980, p.146). This all amounted to what Higgins calls a permanent retreat from laissez faire. New worker participation and job protection laws in the 1970s have threatened even managerial rights to hire and fire labour (Higgins, 1980, pp.149, 153), further weakening the *class* capacity of the bourgeoisie. In fact, as Kaleckian insights would have predicted, the erosion of market integrity as a criterion of resource allocation, income distribution, wealth accumulation and economic rationality has been precisely what has facilitated growth. For stable growth, the nexus between private appropriation for profit and the use of labour and productive capacity needs to be broken (Figure 9.1, page 304; Higgins, 1980, p.151). Only then can control over the *content* of economic activity, crucial to any democratically acceptable *level* of economic activity, be ensured. To a large extent this has been the pattern established by the Swedish labour movement's participation in economic policy-making. The effect has been to strengthen the hand of labour itself (high unionization, high wages, low unemployment) and systematically to undermine capitalist social relations (guaranteed incomes, publicly provided services, economic and industrial democracy).

Legislative enactments (especially the 1976 Co-determination Act) mean that the participation of labour in closure, restructuring, relocation or establishment of enterprises is guaranteed and that disclosures and negotiation by employers is compulsory. Capital strikes and threats of 'lay-offs' are not an easy option for Swedish employers. Public investment funds, increasingly used (since 1974) for direct investment in companies, are also available for explicitly political direction, for example in low-cost housing, regional development and sectoral redeployment (Regini and Esping-Andersen, 1980, p.113). This has led to recent demands for the establishment of fully fledged wage-earners' funds.

For twenty-five years until the proposals were accepted by LO in 1976, Rudolph Meidner, an economist employed by LO, had been arguing, on the basis of Ernst Wigforss's earlier proposals, for some form of collective capital formation to solve the problem of excess profits which accrued in efficient industries (as a result of solidaristic restraints on pay in those companies where capacity to pay was high) and as a way of extending employee involvement in investment (Meidner, 1978; Higgins, 1983). To ensure that solidarity wages policy did not lead to accumulation of excess profits and untapped potentials for wage increases in some industries, Meidner sought

> legislation requiring all medium and large firms to pay free of tax a fixed proportion of their profits into funds collectively owned and controlled by employees in those industries and invested in the share capital of the firms concerned. . . . If the proposals were implemented, and 20 per cent of pre-tax profits were paid into funds, the trade union movement or its derivatives would own and control 52 per cent of the share capital of the firms affected within twenty years (Higgins, 1980, p.154).

For Meidner, *löntagarfonder* (wage-earner funds) were the solution to a specific problem: how the increase in private capital caused by high profits could be converted into democratic control over the process of capital formation (1978, p.14). The link between growth and a shift in the distribution of wealth towards capital and away from labour was clear to Meidner: 'Some form of employee funds will probably provide the long term solution to the prevailing conflict between the growth of capital and the distribution of wealth' (1978, p.16). The entrenched demand for full employment could be satisfied only if a high level of capital formation was also ensured and this is increasingly unlikely under private, market auspices.

The importance of the programme is that it produces a socialization of future economic activity with no state financial expenditure while at the same time providing new sources of capital formation which can be used for industrial restructuring and renewed growth without threat to present capital. It is in these respects that lessons can be gleaned for other countries. Almost everywhere, high rates of investment are necessary (Stephens, 1979, p.205). The Swedish proposals have always sought radical avenues for economic expansion and social justice which do not threaten the strength of the economy itself, but which seek to restructure industry or to enhance its efficiency by dissipating private enterprise.

> Probably few trade union movements are as positive as the Swedish one in their attitude to a high level of investment, to the steady expansion and technological regeneration of the apparatus of production. This can be attributed not solely to a ready appreciation of economic relationships but primarily to a successful employment and labour market policy (Meidner, 1978, p.17).

It is quite important to recognize the crucial differences between the Swedish scheme and quite dissimilar profit-sharing and co-determination proposals advocated in other countries under more liberal assumptions (Esping-Andersen, 1981; Webber, 1982; Himmelstrand et al., 1981). The Swedish experiments are designed to transcend the bounds of 'welfare capitalism' by hastening capitalism's maturation to the point where full employment can be provided only under fundamentally transformed social relations. This is the impetus for social and economic transformation. It is an extension of class struggle which does not suppose that class represents the whole domain of societal conflict (Himmelstrand et al., 1981, p.150), but which does recognize that control of production, investment, work and

CLASS POLITICS AND THE ECONOMY

modes of remuneration are of such fundamental significance that
major shifts in the locus of such controls can have structural
significance:

Even reformist working class organizations may be pushed into
a struggle for profound socialist transformation of society; and
they could well turn out to be more efficient than revolutionary
groups lacking the necessary strength and unity. . . . By
'revolutionary force' we mean a force which is instrumental in
transforming our present system beyond the kind of welfare
capitalism which we have today into a system where labourers
have major control over production, the organisation of work
and the use of the surplus, regardless of whether 'revolutionary
means' were used or not in attaining this measure of control
(Himmelstrand et al., 1981, p.91).

Meaningful transformation is possible, of course, only provided
that capitalism's familiar relationships between productive capacity and economic well-being are fundamentally transformed.
This possibility is, we have argued, given by the conditions of
maturing capitalism itself. But these conditions generate not only
increasing concentration of capital, but an increasing inability of
capital to discern acceptable applications for its productive
capacities. Economic democracy on a large scale is therefore a
means of permanently averting the dislocations which ensue
when private investors 'lose confidence', as well as a way of
allowing 'the material conditions required for the creation of
new, higher social relations of production to mature in the womb
of the old capitalist society' (Himmelstrand et al., 1981, p.309).
Swedish experience demonstrates that the trade union movement has been able to develop and have its policies implemented
only by developing its own structure of expertise over policy
options, and over planning and strategic information. State
structures, like any other complex organizational forms, normally
embody rigidities and bureaucratic inertia. They cannot be
expected to transform themselves or to undermine their own
implicit objectives. Hence the importance of new organizational
forms, organized not within a capitalist policy state but as ones
responsible to labour, becomes evident. The success of the
Swedish experience thus far demonstrates the necessity of
economic and political democracy being adopted together in a
broad strategy. However, investment decisions, even in the shape
of a formal democracy, might still be subordinated to the real
power of expertise and its 'mobilisation of bias'. Thus, these
proposals do not propose unrealizable goals. They accept the
functional superiority, in terms of efficiency, of some elements of

383

task-discontinuity and divided labour in any organization. So, within these constraints, the proposals formulate a democratic framework for their operation. A commensurate model of 'immediate democracy' already exists in Weber's (1947) work. As Weber proposed it, a democratic organization would include fixed (and short) terms of office; liability to recall at any time; rotation or selection by lot in filling offices so that every eligible member takes a turn at some time; guarantees that positions of power would not be attained by technicians with a long command of 'official secrets'; strictly defined mandates for the conduct of representative office laid down by the members; strict obligations for officials to account for their official actions to the assembly of members; obligation to submit every unusual or unforeseen issue to an assembly of members or a committee representing them; distribution of powers among a large number of offices, each with a prescribed function; and the treatment of office as a vocation rather than as a full-time occupation. Such a model, which recognizes the existence of task-discontinuity, would need to underwrite the administration and deployment of the wage-earners' funds in the process of restructuring organizations to prevent the emergence of a separate locus of external power. Such a model would then be able gradually to eradicate the influence of existing legal entitlements to the means of production, and to prevent non-representative managements pursuing their own separate interests.

Where a division of labour proves functionally or technically inevitable, or if job rotation is impractical because of the degree of specialist skill vested in the accomplishment of the task, then a different type of planning principle would be required. Within the organization, wherever policy is dependent on a major input from particular and specific skills, the plan proposed by the initial experts should always be matched by an independent plan developed by the planning branch of the fund administration for that particular region or industry. In this way, unions and their members can be sure of receiving technically informed advice which is neither sectionally nor personally interested.

What is being proposed is not that the technical bases of social action be abrogated, but that the social bases of technical action be apparent. The development of collective capital substitutes the relatively narrow interests of shareholders and corporate managers with those of practically involved and broadly committed workers – including the employed managers – operating as equally franchised economic citizens; citizens of an enterprise, region or state. As such, their interests will extend beyond those 'bottom-line' interests of private investors. Keynes's concerns will thus be meliorated.

Abrahamsson and Broström (1980) have proposed that the wage-earners' funds also provide the basis for a democratic system of political representation, incorporating organizational democracy, which will abet the achievement of the full-employment goal. 'The primary means of attaining this goal is the combination of *the right to make decisions* concerning production and *the right to execute the decisions*' (1980, p.234). The mechanisms for achieving this synthesis hinge on a new basis for political representation, based not simply on the abstract category of citizen but on each person's status as either employed or not employed. Actively employed people, it is proposed, would nominate and elect representatives through their work organizations, while those not employed would be represented on the basis of a geographical division. Hence, the first tier of proposed representation would be at the regional level, based on the two types of constituency. The constituencies would also elect representatives to a national assembly, in each case, on a proportional basis.

The representative bodies would share decision-making on capital formation with organizationally democratized enterprises, formed under the control of workers whose collective ownership would be vested in the wage-earners' funds. Such enterprises would still function as 'profit centres' through market-oriented operations, although, given the gradual euthanasia of rentier involvements, it would be more appropriate to speak of 'revenue centres'. Revenue is conceptualized as consisting of three parts, with the distribution between them being a matter for political decision, ultimately vested at the central level; a level, none the less, which is not at all independent of the other constituencies nor one which entails orthodox central planning of production.

Revenue would accrue to either wages, the investment funds, or as a social surplus. Abrahamsson and Broström (1980, p.236) suggest that the surplus itself be subject to further division. One element might contribute to income improvements for workers; a further element might be allocated to ensure enterprise solvency; while the remainder could consist of externally distributed funds for the provision of collective goods, reducing discretionary incomes according to representative decision-making. Necessarily, all decision-making would become aspects of a *political* economy, albeit one which functioned through markets, but in which markets would not be the main register of interests.

Problems of regional or industry inequities will obviously arise. For this reason, the tiers of fund representation need to be based on regional and sectoral constituencies, as well as on employed/

not employed status. In a political economy these issues cannot be left to the market to resolve. Political struggle is quintessential.

Of overwhelming importance to Swedish labour movement strategies has been the insistence upon fundamental class conflict as an organizing principle and as a principle according to which economic interventions are planned. But industrial unions (LO) and 'white-collar' unions (TCO) accept the principle of solidarity wage bargaining – 'wage earners do not want to use the trade unions to defend their separate professional interests but rather their collective interests as wage earners' (Korpi, 1982, p.136). Sweden's high degree of unionization (86 per cent in the early 1980s) has meant that a class-based rather than professional collectivism has developed, especially since the 1970s. Political parties, on the other hand, continue to operate 'along the lines of social stratification among the citizens' (Korpi, 1982, p.136), in part explaining the apparent discrepancy between the bourgeois interregnum of 1976–82 and the breakdown of the 'historical compromise' in the 1970s. A palpable political effect of labour-market strength (despite the absence of a socialist bloc majority in the Riksdag from 1976) is that the social democrats have been able to force the bourgeois parties to accept full-employment policy even during the 1970s, thus moving Swedish politics emphatically to the left.

The break-up of the 1938 agreement that the state should not be used to intervene legislatively on behalf of labour to undermine managerial prerogatives meant that long-term strategies for industrial democracy (in the 1980s) could be developed. Hence, labour is in a position to negotiate with the party to legislate the implementation of the wage-earner funds proposal. The success of this proposal depends on the maintenance of the class-solidarity principle. If full employment and the extension of democracy remain the major concerns of all sections of the workforce, then this is likely; if some wage-earners decide to abandon the collective principle in favour of a fragmented struggle over income distribution or 'new political issues', then wage-earner funds are unlikely to achieve their full potential. If the cohesion and striking power of wage-earners is maintained, then the beginnings in the 1980s and beyond of collective capital formation will seek to preserve full employment and therefore undermine the most important tenets of capitalism. Wage-earners will remain a vital force for societal transformation (Korpi, 1982, p.140).

The long history of social democratic theory and policy formation has been one characterized by an insistence upon both the need to extend the principles of liberalism into the economic arena and the need to transcend the inefficiencies of capitalist production. Abrahamsson and Broström refer to these as the extension of democracy from civil rights to labour rights where individual or enterprise 'egoism' is replaced by 'functional socialism' (1980, pp.229-52). For Wigforss this dual thrust was always central to a coherent social democratic philosophy based on a Marxist interpretation of capitalist development (Higgins, 1983, p.5). The achievement was clearly to have been able to translate analytical perceptions into implementable social policies. Wigforss recognized that capitalist competition itself was wasteful, inefficient and sometimes backwards: 'overall social wealth is much less than it could be, given our technical development, because of economic disorganisation' (Wigforss, quoted in Higgins, 1983, p.10). Wigforss argued that worker involvement could enhance productive efficiency, a claim amply vindicated by contemporary studies (Hodgson, 1982, 1983).

The development of an open-ended concept of state regulation in Sweden was one which took a long time and involved the frustrating experience of ultimately unworkable alliances with liberals. Economic liberation was a less tolerable force than the progressive ideas of liberal democracy had led the social democrats to expect: laissez faire is necessarily deflationary. During the crisis of the 1930s, but following the social democrats' success in government, the employers (SAF) withdrew their parliamentary obstructionism in favour of direct negotiations with the government and trade unions and in support of policies of production and expansion. The political and economic developments thus engendered strengthened the interventionist proclivities of the social democrats even further in the period of postwar reconstruction.

The bourgeois challenge at the end of the reconstruction period was defeated: 'In Sweden it was the labour movement that would build the welfare state, consolidate the full employment economy on its own terms and preside over the long boom' (Higgins, 1980, p.33). This was a unique conjuncture for European social democracy during these decisive years (Apple, 1983). The struggle against market ideology was a prolonged and important one during the 1950s and 1960s. The success of the Rehn-Meidner proposals and their successors was secured by emphatic insistence that the mission of social democracy was not the consolidation of past gains but the perpetual struggle against the limitations of economic liberalism. The political battle for a rational economic organization was simultaneously a struggle to overcome forms of domination and subordination. The Swedish labour movement's development of a transitional reformism has

387

always been an attempt to move beyond the welfare state. Full-employment policies do create problems for both capital and labour, especially in the form of inflation, but this is not so much an unresolvable contradiction on which capitalism founders, as it is an indication of the need to embark upon active programmes to ensure that the potential implied by high rates of capital formation itself breaks the impasse. 'Too few goods' is a phenomenon of under-production; it should not be seen as an opportunity for wage reductions or deflationary policies. The alternative to inflation in both boom and recession is to dismantle bourgeois monopoly over the organization of production. In this context, Swedish politics has been the terrain on which the influence of policy on capital accumulation and vice versa has been most clearly exemplified.

The Swedish experience demonstrates not only that anti-recessionary policy is possible, but that in order to develop such a political strategy, a long-term, openly political confrontation with laissez faire is necessary. 'Firms should become more like foundations without owners', Wigforss has said.

But more important, despite the impossibility of replicating Sweden's economic history and political institutions on other national terrains, is the prime lesson of twentieth-century capitalist experience. Not only does recovery from a recession demand a class-based politics, but the fundamental class forces which always underscore processes of economic development in good times and bad need to be confronted openly and explicitly. There can be no full employment by stealth. Social practices of profound consequence are nurtured by the doctrines of laissez faire. The struggle against social and economic irrationality is a struggle of a deeply political nature. The instruments for the moment are those provided by economic policy choices; but the long-term reorientation from economic caution, deflation, unemployment and repression requires a long-term alternative accumulation strategy under democratic control. This is the potential of collective capital formation.

Conclusion

The central aim of our concluding chapter has been to show that class inequality is sustained by processes that are created in the normal operations of the economy. Cycles of economic activity, systematically, though not mechanically, affect the political strength and personal fortunes of the major class groupings. Evidence for this can be assembled from surveys of life chances and sentiments of communal status as well as through analysis of the relationships between the differential categories of earned and unearned income.

Economic recessions become the customary way of effecting rationalization in a capitalist economy only because liberal institutional mechanisms provide a predominant role in the determination of economic policy for what are conventionally termed 'bourgeois interests'. As our preceding chapters established, these interests are typically those of a quite small ruling class whose rule is premised less on intended actions than on the consequences of structural mechanisms characteristic of class structuration in advanced capitalist societies. The most important of these mechanisms are those producing the class hegemony of large-scale capital, and the divided nature of the middle class and working class. As we have argued, both these unities and divisions are indeterminate outcomes not only of economically structured interests themselves, but also of their intersection with the milieu of civil society.

Generally, where a broad labour movement is able to subsume and co-ordinate civil issues within its economic policy framework, and win popular support, then the opportunity to intervene in economic policy determination exists. To the extent that democratic control of investment can be imposed upon the traditional custodians of capitalist enterprise, and to the extent that bourgeois prerogatives are undermined by a systematic transition from market control to political control of the economy, then a fundamental transference in class power will have been effected.

It is capitalist relations of production and the class politics which accompanies them that give to capitalist economies their cyclical and frequently capricious patterns of development. Only a regeneration of labour movement organizational strength and interventionist strategies will permit a more efficient, less wasteful, transitional process of economic growth. Just as permanent full employment and capitalism are incompatible, a sustained mobilization by the labour movement to achieve full employment will be resisted for as long as possible by the class forces arraigned against labour.

For these reasons, labour movement and social democratic policies need to be long-term political strategies to gain control of the accumulation of capital. Political control of the economy can be accomplished only to the extent that an economic and industrial structure can be planned and patterns of output eventually altered. Although this is a slow and initially ambiguous task, it is in no sense a pragmatic retreat from the radical and transformative politics implied by an understanding of capitalist economic development. It involves intervention into the structure of industry, the development of alternative modes of capital formation and the use of a more collectivist rationale for capital accumulation.

At the same time as more socialized investment, new political institutions and alternative accumulation strategies are being developed, the potential for their deployment against the interests of the labour movement will remain. A conflictual politics is inevitable: labour must use each strategic advantage as the basis for even more fundamental assaults on the rights of capital.

The assertion of the rights of labour, the implementation of innovative forms of economic democracy, and the construction of a more democratic, less liberal economy will be the occasion not only for higher material and political standards for a majority, but for a transition from advanced affluent capitalist economies to advanced affluent post-capitalist economies.

Bibliography

Aaronovitch, S. (1981), *The Road from Thatcherism: The Alternative Economic Strategy*, London, Lawrence & Wishart.

Abell, P. (1975), *Organizations as Bargaining and Influence Systems*, London, Heinemann.

Abercrombie, N. (1980), *Class Structure and Knowledge*, Oxford, Blackwell.

Abercrombie, N., Hill, S. and Turner, B.S. (1980), *The Dominant Ideology Thesis*, London, Allen & Unwin.

Abrahamsson, B. (1977), *Bureaucracy or Participation: The Logic of Organization*, London, Sage.

Abrahamsson, B. and Broström, A. (1980), *The Rights of Labor*, London, Sage.

Adamson, O., Brown, C., Harrison, J. and Price, J. (1976), 'Women's Oppression under Capitalism', *Revolutionary Communist*, 5, pp.2-48.

Aglietta, M. (1979), *A Theory of Capitalist Regulation: The US Experience*, London, New Left Books.

Aglietta, M. (1982), 'World Capitalism in the Eighties', *New Left Review*, 136, pp.5-41.

Aldrich, H. (1979), *Organizations and Environments*, Englewood Cliffs, NJ, Prentice-Hall.

Aldrich, H. and Weiss, J. (1981), 'Differentiation within the US Capitalist Class: Workforce Size and Income Differences', *American Sociological Review*, 46, pp.279-90.

Allcorn, D.H. and Marsh, C.M. (1975), 'Occupational Communities – Communities of What?', in M. Bulmer (ed.), *Working Class Images of Society*, London, Routledge & Kegan Paul, pp.206-18.

Allen, G.C. (1965), *A Short Economic History of Modern Japan, 1867-1937*, London, Allen & Unwin.

Allen, M.P. (1974), 'The Structure of Interorganizational Elite Cooptation: Interlocking Corporate Directorates', *American Sociological Review*, 39, pp.393-406.

Allen, M.P. (1981), 'Power and Privilege in the Large Corporation: Corporate Control and Managerial Compensation', *American Journal of Sociology*, 86, 5, pp.1112-23.

Allen, V.L. (1975), *Social Analysis: A Marxist Critique and Alternative*, London, Longman.

Allen, V.L. (1977), 'The Differentiation of the Working Class', in A. Hunt (ed.), *Class and Class Structure*, London, Lawrence & Wishart, pp.61-79.

Allen, V.L. (1981), *The Militancy of British Miners*, Shipley, Moor Press.

Althusser, L. (1969), *For Marx*, London, Allen Lane.

Althusser, L. (1971), *Lenin and Philosophy and Other Essays*, London, New Left Books.

Althusser, L. and Balibar, E. (1970), *Reading Capital*, London, New Left Books.

Amin, S. (1979), 'The Class Structure of the Contemporary Imperialist System', *Monthly Review*, 31, pp.9-26.

Amsden, A.H. (ed.) (1980), *The Economics of Women and Work*, Harmondsworth, Penguin.

AMWSU (Amalgamated Metalworkers' and Shipwrights' Union) (1977), *Australia Ripped Off*, Sydney, AMWSU.

Anderson, D.S., Western, J.S. and Boreham, P.R. (1978), 'Law and the Making of Legal Practitioners', in R. Tomasic (ed.), *Understanding Lawyers: Perspectives on the Legal Profession in Australia*, Sydney, Allen & Unwin, pp.181-98.

Anderson, P. (1965), 'Origins of the Present Crisis', in P. Anderson and R. Blackburn (eds), *Towards Socialism*, London, Fontana, pp.11-52.

Anderson, P. (1980), *Arguments Within English Marxism*, London, Verso.

Apple, M.W. (1979), *Ideology and Curriculum*, London, Routledge & Kegan Paul.

Apple, N. (1983), 'The Historical Transformation of Class Struggle in Late Capitalist Liberal Democracies', in S. Clegg, G. Dow and P. Boreham (eds), *The State, Class and the Recession*, London, Croom Helm, pp.72-128.

Apple, N. and Higgins, W. (1982), 'Vad gör reformisterna när de reformerar?', *Häften för kritiska studier*, Stockholm, 15, 6, pp.5-29.

Apple, N., Higgins, W. and Wright, M. (1981), *Class Mobilization and Economic Policy: The Struggles over Full Employment in Britain and Sweden 1930-1980*, Stockholm, Arbetslivscentrum Working Papers.

Armingeon, K. (1982), 'Determining the Level of Wages: The Role of Parties and Trade Unions', in F.G. Castles (ed.), *The Impact of Parties: Politics and Policies in Democratic Capitalist States*, London, Sage, pp.225-82.

Aronowitz, S. (1978), 'Marx, Braverman and the Logic of Capital', *The Insurgent Sociologist*, 8, 2/3, pp.126-46.

Aronowitz, S. (1979), 'The Professional–Managerial Class or Middle Strata', in P. Walker (ed.), *Between Labor and Capital*, Boston, South End Press, pp.213-42.

Aronowitz, S. (1981), *The Crisis in Historical Materialism: Class Politics and Culture in Marxist Theory*, New York, Praeger.

Asimakopulos, A. (1977), 'Post Keynesian Growth Theory', in S. Weintraub (ed.), *Modern Economic Thought*, Oxford, Blackwell, pp.369-88.

Averitt, R.T. (1968), *The Dual Economy: The Dynamics of American Industry Structure*, New York, Norton.

Bacon, J. and Brown, J.K. (1977), *The Board of Directors: Perspectives and Practices in Nine Countries*, New York, Conference Board.

Bachrach, P. and Baratz, M.S. (1962), 'Two Faces of Power', *American Political Science Review*, 56, pp.947-52.

Baldamus, W. (1961), *Efficiency and Effort*, London, Tavistock.

Baldry, C., Haworth, N. and Ramsay, H. (1981), 'Multinational Capital in Scotland and the Closure of the Massey-Ferguson Plant, Kilmarnock', paper presented at the Organization, Economy and Society Conference, Griffith University, Brisbane.

Balogh, T. (1979), 'De-industrialization and Industrial Policy: Comment' in F. Blackaby (ed.), *De-industrialization*, London, Heinemann, pp.196-201.

Baltzell, E.D. (1958), *An American Business Aristocracy*, Chicago, Free Press.

Baltzell, E.D. (1967), ' "Who's Who in America" and "The Social Register": Elite and Upper Class Indexes in Metropolitan America', in R. Bendix and S.M. Lipset (eds), *Class, Status and Power: Social Stratification in Comparative Perspective*, London, Routledge & Kegan Paul, pp.266-75.

Barbalet, J.M. (1980), 'Principles of Stratification in Max Weber', *British Journal of Sociology*, xxxi, 3, pp.401-18.

Barber, R. (1970), *The American Corporation*, London, MacGibbon & Kee.

Barnett, R.J. and Muller, R.E. (1974), *Global Reach: The Power of the Multinational Corporations*, London, Jonathan Cape.

Barr, K. (1979), 'Long Waves: A Selective, Annotated Bibliography', *Review*, 11, 4, pp.675-718.

Barrett, M. (1980), *Women's Oppression Today: Problems in Marxist Feminist Analysis*, London, Verso.

Barron, J. and Bielby, B. (1983), 'The Organization of Work in a Segmented Economy', unpublished paper, Graduate School of Business, Stanford University.

Barron, R.D. and Norris, G.M. (1976), 'Sexual Divisions and the Dual Labour Market', in D.L. Barker and S. Allen (eds), *Dependence and Exploitation in Work and Marriage*, London, Longman, pp.47-69.

Bauman, Z. (1982), *Memories of Class: The Pre-history and After-life of Class*, London, Routledge & Kegan Paul.

Baxandall, R. *et al* (1976), *Technology, The Labor Process and the Working Class*, New York, Monthly Review Press.

Bearden, J., Attwood, W., Freitag, P., Hendricks, C., Mintz, B. and Schwartz, M. (1975), 'The Nature and Extent of Bank Centrality in Corporate Networks', paper presented to the American Sociological Association, Annual Meeting, San Francisco, August 1975.

Bechhofer, F. and Elliott, B. (1976), 'Persistence and Change: The

Petite Bourgeoisie in the Industrial Society', *European Journal of Sociology*, xvii, pp.74-99.

Bechhofer, F. Elliott, B. and Rushforth, M. (1971), 'The Market Situation of Small Shopkeepers', *Scottish Journal of Political Economy* 18, 2, pp.161-80.

Bechhofer, F., Elliott, B., Rushworth, M. and Bland, R. (1974), 'The Petite Bourgeois in the Class Structure: The Case of the Small Shopkeepers', in F. Parkin (ed.), *Social Analysis of Class Structure*, London, Tavistock, pp. 103-28.

Becker, G.S. (1964), *Human Capital: A Theoretical and Empirical Analysis with Special Reference to Education*, New York, Columbia University Press.

Becker, L.C. (1977), *Property Rights: Philosophic Foundations*, London, Routledge & Kegan Paul.

Beechey, V. (1977), 'Some Problems in the Analysis of Female Wage Labour in the Capitalist Mode of Production', *Capital and Class*, 3, pp.45-66.

Beechey, V. (1982), 'The Sexual Division of Labour and the Labour Process: A Critical Assessment of Braverman', in S. Wood (ed.), *The Degradation of Work? Skill, Deskilling and the Labour Process*, London, Hutchinson, pp.54-73.

Bell, D. (1974), *The Coming of Post-industrial Society: A Venture in Social Forecasting*, London, Heinemann.

Bell, D. (1976), *The Cultural Contradictions of Capitalism*, New York, Basic Books.

Bell, D. and Kristol, I. (eds) (1981), *The Crisis in Economic Theory*, New York, Basic Books.

Bendix, R. (1956), *Work and Authority in Industry*, New York, Wiley.

Benson, L. (1978), *Proletarians and Parties*, London, Methuen.

Beresford, M. and McFarlane, B. (1980), 'Economic Theory as Ideology: A Kaleckian Analysis of the Australian Economic Crisis', in P. Boreham and G. Dow (eds), *Work and Inequality: Vol. 1, Workers Economic Crisis and the State*, Melbourne, Macmillan, pp.215-35.

Berg, I. (1973), *Education and Jobs: The Great Training Robbery*, Harmondsworth, Penguin.

Berger, J. and Mohr, J. (1975), *A Seventh Man: The Story of a Migrant Worker in Europe*, Harmondsworth, Penguin.

Berger, S. (1981a), 'The Uses of the Traditional Sector in Italy: Why Declining Classes Survive', in F. Bechhofer and B. Elliott (eds), *The Petite Bourgeoisie: Comparative Studies of the Uneasy Stratum*, London, Macmillan, pp.71-89.

Berger, S. (ed.) (1981b), *Organizing Interests in Western Europe: Pluralism, Corporatism and the Transformation of Politics*, Cambridge University Press.

Berger, S. and Piore, M.J. (1980), *Dualism and Discontinuity in Industrial Societies*, London, Cambridge University Press.

Bergier, J.F. (1973), 'The Industrial Bourgeoisie and the Rise of the Working Class 1700-1914', in C.M. Cipolla (ed.), *The Fontana Economic History of Europe: The Industrial Revolution*, Glasgow,

Fontana, pp.397-451.
Berlant, J.L. (1975), *Profession and Monopoly: A Study of Medicine in the United States and Great Britain*, Berkeley, University of California Press.
Berle, A.A. and Means, G.C. (1932), *The Modern Corporation and Private Property*, New York, Macmillan.
Bernstein, B. (1975), *Class, Codes and Control*, London, Routledge & Kegan Paul.
Binks, M. (1979), 'Finance for Expansion in the Small Firm', *Lloyds Bank Review*, 134, pp.33-45.
Birnbaum, P. (1982), 'The State versus Corporatism', *Politics and Society*, vol. 11 (4).
Blackaby, F. (1973), 'Incomes and Inflation', in J. Robinson (ed.), *After Keynes*, Oxford, Blackwell, pp.55-70.
Blackaby, F. (ed.) (1979), *De-industrialization*, London, Heinemann.
Blackburn, R. (1972), 'The New Capitalism' in R. Blackburn (ed.), *Ideology in Social Science*, London, Fontana, pp.164-86.
Blackburn, R.M. and Mann, M. (1979), *The Working Class in the Labour Market*, London, Macmillan.
Blackstone, T. (1983), 'No Minister', *New Socialist*, 9, pp.42-5.
Blair, J.M. (1972), *Economic Concentration: Structure, Behaviour and Public Policy*, New York, Harcourt, Brace, Jovanovitch.
Bland, R., Elliott, B. and Bechhoffer, F. (1978), 'Social Mobility and the Petite Bourgeoisie', *Acta Sociologica*, 21, pp.229-48.
Blau, P.M. and Duncan, O.D. (1967), *The American Occupational Structure*, New York, Wiley.
Blauner, R. (1964), *Alienation and Freedom*, University of Chicago Press.
Bleaney, M. (1976), *Underconsumption Theories: A History and Critical Analysis*, London, Lawrence & Wishart.
Bléton, P. (1966), *Le Capitalisme français*, Paris, Éditions Ouvrières.
Block, F. (1977), 'The Ruling Class does not Rule: Notes on the Marxist Theory of the State', *Socialist Revolution*, May–June, pp.6-28.
Block, F. (1978), 'Class Consciousness and Capitalist Rationalization: A Reply to Critics', *Socialist Review*, 8, pp.212-20.
Block, F. and Hirschhorn, L. (1979), 'New Productive Forces and the Contradictions of Contemporary Capitalism', *Theory and Society*, 7, 3, May, pp.363-95.
Bluestone, B.F. (1970), 'The Tripartite Economy: Labor Markets and the Working Poor', *Poverty and Human Resources*, July/August.
Blumberg, P.I. (1975), *The Megacorporation in American Society*, Englewood Cliffs, NJ, Prentice-Hall.
Boddy, R. and Crotty, J. (1975), 'Class Conflict and Macro Policy: The Political Business Cycle', *Review of Radical Political Economics*, 7, 1. pp.1-19.
Boreham, P. (1980), 'The Dialectic of Theory and Control: Capitalist Crisis and the Organization of Labour', in D. Dunkerley and G. Salaman (eds), *The International Yearbook of Organization Studies 1980*, London, Routledge & Kegan Paul, pp.16-35.

Boreham, P. (1983), 'Indetermination: Professional Knowledge, Organization and Control', *Sociological Review*, 31, 4, pp.693-718.
Boreham, P., Cass, M. and McCallum, M. (1979), 'The Australian Bureaucratic Elite: The Importance of Social Backgrounds and Occupational Experience', *Australian and New Zealand Journal of Sociology*, 15, 2, pp.45-55.
Boreham, P. and Dow, G. (1980), 'The Labour Process and Capitalist Crisis', in P. Boreham and G. Dow (eds), *Work and Inequality: Vol. 1, Workers, Economic Crisis and the State*, Melbourne, Macmillan, pp.1-27.
Boreham, P., Pemberton, A. and Wilson, P. (eds) (1976), *The Professions in Australia: A Critical Appraisal*, St Lucia, University of Queensland Press.
Bott, E. (1957), *Family and Social Network*, London, Tavistock.
Bourdieu, P. (1973), 'Cultural Reproduction and Social Reproduction', in R. Brown (ed.), *Knowledge, Education and Cultural Change*, London, Tavistock, pp.71-112.
Bourdieu, P. (1974), 'The School as a Conservative Force: Scholastic and Cultural Inequalities', in J. Egglestone (ed.), *Contemporary Research in the Sociology of Education*, London, Methuen, pp.32-46.
Bourdieu, P., Boltanski, L. and de St Martin, M. (1973), 'Les Strategies de reconversion', *Social Science Information*, 12, pp.61-113.
Bourdieu, P. and Passeron, C.J. (1977), *Reproduction in Education, Society and Culture*, London, Sage.
Bowles, S. (1972), 'Unequal Education and the Reproduction of the Social Division of Labour', in M. Carnoy (ed.), *Schooling in a Corporate Society: The Political Economy of Education in America*, New York, David Mackay, pp.36-64.
Bowles, S. (1978), 'The Trilateral Commission: Have Capitalism and Democracy Come to a Parting of the Ways?', in The Union for Radical Political Economics, (ed.), *US Capitalism in Crisis*, New York, (URPE), pp.262-65.
Bowles, S. (1982), 'The Post-Keynesian Capital–Labor Stalemate', *Socialist Review*, 12, 5, pp.44-72.
Bowles, S. and Gintis, H. (1976), *Schooling in Capitalist America: Educational Reform and the Contradiction of Economic Life*, London, Routledge & Kegan Paul.
Bradley, I. and Howard, M. (eds) (1982), *Classical and Marxian Political Economy: Essays in Honour of Ronald L. Meek*, London, Macmillan.
Brandes, S. (1976), *American Welfare Capitalism, 1880-1940*, University of Chicago Press.
Braverman, H. (1974), *Labor and Monopoly Capital: The Degradation of Work in the Twentieth Century*, New York, Monthly Review Press.
Brittan, S. (1975), 'The Economic Contradictions of Democracy', *British Journal of Political Science*, 5, 2, pp.129-59.
Brittan, S. (1978), 'Inflation and Democracy', in F. Hirsch and J. Goldthorpe (eds), *The Political Economy of Inflation*, London, Martin Robertson, pp.161-85.
Brown, S. (1976), 'Women as Employees: Some Comments on Research

in Industrial Sociology', in D.L. Barker and S. Allen (eds), *Dependence and Exploitation in Work and Marriage*, London, Longman, pp.21-40.

Brown, R. (1982), 'Work Histories, Career Strategies and the Class Structure', in A. Giddens and G. Mackenzie (eds), *Social Class and the Division of Labour: Essays in Honour of Ilya Neustadt*, Cambridge University Press, pp.119-36.

Brown, W. (1973), *Piecework Bargaining*, London, Heinemann.

Bruselid, L. (1980), 'Women, Class and State: Evaluating Social Policy and Political Demands', in P. Boreham and G. Dow (eds), *Work and Inequality, Vol. 1, Workers, Economic Crisis and the State*, Melbourne, Macmillan, pp.107-26.

Burawoy, M. (1978), 'Toward a Marxist Theory of the Labour Process: Braverman and Beyond', *Politics and Society*, 8, pp.247-312.

Burawoy, M. (1979), *Manufacturing Consent*, University of Chicago Press.

Burch, P.H. (1972), *The Managerial Revolution Reassessed*, Massachusetts, Lexington Books.

Burnham, J. (1941), *The Managerial Revolution*, Harmondsworth, Penguin.

Burns, T.R., Karlsson, L.E. and Rus, V. (eds) (1979), *Work, and Power: The Liberation of Work and the Control of Political Power*, London, Sage.

Burrell, G. and Morgan, G. (1979), *Sociological Paradigms and Organizational Analysis: Elements of the Sociology of Corporate Life*, London, Heinemann.

Burris, V. (1980), 'Capital Accumulation and the Rise of the New Middle Class', *Review of Radical Political Economics*, 12, pp.17-24.

Burt, R. (1979), 'A Structural Theory of Interlocking Corporate Directorates', *Social Networks*, 1, pp.415-35.

Burt, R. (1980a), 'On the Functional Form of Corporate Cooptation: Empirical Findings Linking Market Constraint with the Frequency of Directorate Ties', *Social Science Research*, 9, pp.146-77.

Burt, R. (1980b), 'Cooptive Corporate Actor Networks: A Reconsideration of Interlocking Directorates Involving American Manufacturing', *Administrative Science Quarterly*, 35, pp.557-82.

Burt, R., Christman, C.P. and Kilburn, H.C. (1980), 'Testing a Structural Theory of Corporate Cooptation', *American Sociological Review*, 45, pp.821-41.

Cairncross, A. (1979), 'What is De-industrialization?', in F. Blackaby (ed.), *De-industrialization*, London, Heinemann, pp.5-17.

Callaghan, J. (1980), Speech to Labour Party Conference, 28 September 1976, extracted in A.G. Frank, *Crisis: in the World Economy*, London, Heinemann.

Carchedi, G. (1975a), 'On the Economic Identification of the New Middle Class', *Economy and Society*, 4, pp.1-86.

Carchedi, G. (1975b), 'Reproduction of Social Classes at the Level of Production Relations', *Economy and Society*, 4, pp.361-417.

Carchedi, G. (1977), *On the Economic Identification of Social Classes*,

London, Routledge & Kegan Paul.

Carlin, J.E. (1966), *Lawyers' Ethics: A Survey of the New York City Bar*, New York, Russell Sage Foundation.

Carnoy, M. (1981), 'Education, Industrial Democracy and the State', *Economic and Industrial Democracy*, 2, 2, pp.243-60.

Carrillo, S. (1977), *'Eurocommunism' and the State*, London, Lawrence & Wishart.

Carroll, W.K., Fox, J., and Ornstein, M.D. (1982), 'The Network of Directorate Links among the Largest Canadian Firms', *Canadian Review of Sociology and Anthropology*, 19, 1, pp.44-69.

Castles, F.G. (1978), *The Social Democratic Image of Society*, London, Routledge & Kegan Paul.

Castles, F.G. (ed.) (1982), *The Impact of Parties: Politics and Policies in Democratic Capitalist States*, London, Sage, European Consortium for Political Research.

Castles, S. and Kosack, G. (1973), *Immigrant Workers and Class Structures in Western Europe*, Oxford University Press.

Castoriadis, C. (1982), 'From Ecology to Autonomy', *Thesis Eleven*, 3, pp.7-22.

Cervi, M. (1971), 'L'ombra della recessione sulle imprese minori: Fiat: 160 milia auto in meno', *Corriere delle Sera*, 18 December 1971.

Chamberlain, C. (1983), *Class Consciousness in Australia*, Sydney, Allen & Unwin.

Chandler, A.D. (1962), *Strategy and Structure*, Cambridge, Mass., MIT Press.

Chandler, M. (1975), 'It's Time to Clean Up the Boardroom', *Harvard Business Review*, 53, 5, pp.73-82.

Chapman, R.A. (1970), *The Higher Civil Service in Britain*, London, Constable.

Child, J. (1969), *The Business Enterprise in Modern Industrial Society*, London, Collier-Macmillan.

Child, J. (1972), 'Organization Structure, Environment and Performance: The Role of Strategic Choice', *Sociology*, 6, pp.1-22.

Child, J. (1982), 'Professionals in the Corporate World: Values, Interests and Control', in D. Dunkerley and G. Salaman (eds), *The International Yearbook of Organization Studies 1982*, London, Routledge & Kegan Paul, pp.212-41.

Child, J. and Francis, A. (1977), 'Strategy Formulation as a Structured Process', *International Studies of Management and Organization*, vii, 2, pp.110-26.

Clawson, D. (1980), *Bureaucracy and the Labor Process: The Transformation of US Industry, 1860-1920*, New York, Monthly Review Press.

Clegg, S. (1975), *Power, Rule and Domination: A Critical and Empirical Understanding of Power in Sociological Theory and Organizational Life*, London, Routledge & Kegan Paul.

Clegg, S. (1977), 'Power, Organization Theory, Marx and Critique', in S. Clegg and D. Dunkerley (eds), *Critical Issues in Organizations*, London, Routledge & Kegan Paul, pp.21-40.

Clegg, S. (1979), *The Theory of Power and Organization*, London, Routledge & Kegan Paul.

Clegg, S. (1981), 'Organization and Control', *Administrative Science Quarterly*, 26, 4, pp.545-62.

Clegg, S., Dow, G. and Boreham, P. (1983), 'Politics and Crisis: The State of the Recession', in S. Clegg, G. Dow and P. Boreham (eds), *The State, Class and the Recession*, London, Croom Helm, pp.1-50.

Clegg, S. and Dunkerley, D. (1980), *Organization, Class and Control*, London, Routledge & Kegan Paul.

Clement, W. (1975), *The Canadian Corporate Elite*, Toronto, McClelland Stewart.

Coates, K. and Silburn, S. (1973), *Poverty: The Forgotten Englishmen*, Harmondsworth, Penguin.

Cohen, G.A. (1979), *Karl Marx's Theory of History – A Defence*, Princeton University Press.

Cohen, J., Hazelrigg, L.E. and Pope, W. (1975), 'De-Parsonizing Weber: A Critique of Parsons' Interpretation of Weber's Sociology', *American Sociological Review*, 40, pp.229-41.

Cohen, M.D., March, J.G. and Olsen, J.P. (1972), 'A Garbage Can Model of Organizational Choice', *Administrative Science Quarterly*, 17, 1, pp.1-25.

Collins, J. (1975), 'The Political Economy of Post-war Immigration', in E.L. Wheelwright and K. Buckley (eds), *Essays in the Political Economy of Australian Capitalism, vol. 1*, Sydney, ANZ Book Co., pp.105-29.

Collins, J. (1978), 'Fragmentation of the Working Class', in E.L. Wheelwright and K. Buckley (eds), *Essays in the Political Economy of Australian Capitalism, vol. 3*, Sydney, ANZ Book Co., pp.42-85.

Collins, R. (1979), *The Credential Society: An Historical Sociology of Education and Stratification*, New York, Academic Press.

Collins, R. (1980), 'Weber's Last Theory of Capitalism: a Systematisation', *American Sociological Review*, 45, pp.925-42.

Commission on Industrial Relations (1974), *Industrial Relations in Multiplant Undertakings*, London, HMSO.

Connell, R.W. (1977), *Ruling Class, Ruling Culture: Studies of Conflict, Power and Hegemony in Australian Life*, Cambridge University Press.

Connell, R.W. and Goot, M. (1979), 'The End of Class, Re-Run', *Meanjin*, 38, 1, pp.3-25.

Connell, R.W. and Irving, T.H. (1978), 'The Making of the Australian Industrial Bourgeoisie, 1930-1975', *Intervention*, 10/11, pp.34-8.

Connell, R.W. and Irving, T.H. (1980), *Class Structure in Australian History: Documents, Narrative and Argument*, Melbourne, Longman Cheshire.

Conway, J.F. (1981), 'Agrarian Petit-bourgeois Responses to Capitalist Industrialization: The Case of Canada', in F. Bechhofer and B. Elliott (eds), *The Petite Bourgeoisie: Comparative Studies of the Uneasy Stratum*, London, Macmillan, pp.1-38.

Corrigan, P. (ed) (1980), *Capitalism, State Formation and Marxist Theory: Historical Investigations*, London, Quartet.

Corrigan, P., Ramsay, H. and Sayer, D. (1980), 'The State as a Relation of Production', in P. Corrigan (ed.), *Capitalism, State Formation and Marxist Theory: Historical Investigations*, London, Quartet, pp.1-25.

Coulson, M.A., Keil, E.T., Riddell, D.S. and Struthers, J.S. (1967), 'Towards a Sociological Theory of Occupational Choice: A Critique', *Sociological Review*, 15, 3, pp.301-9.

Coulson, M., Magas, B. and Wainwright, H. (1975), 'The Housewife and her Labour under Capitalism – a Critique', New Left Review, 89, pp.59-72.

Coutts, K., Tarling, R., Ward, T. and Wilkinson, F. (1981), 'The Economic Consequences of Mrs Thatcher', *Cambridge Journal of Economics*, 5, 1, pp.81-93.

Cowling, K. (1982), *Monopoly Capitalism*, London, Macmillan.

Crawcour, S. (1978), 'The Japanese Employment System', *Journal of Japanese Studies*, 4, 2, pp.225-45.

Cressey, P. and MacInnes, J. (1982), 'The Modern Enterprise, Shopfloor Organization and the Structure of Control', in D. Dunkerley and G. Salaman (eds), *The International Yearbook of Organization Studies*, London, Routledge & Kegan Paul, pp.271-302.

Cripps, F. and Godley, W. (1978), 'Control of Imports as a Means to Full Employment and the Expansion of World Trade: The UK's Case', *Cambridge Journal of Economics*, 2, 3, pp.327-34.

Crompton, R. (1976), 'Approaches to the Study of White Collar Unionism', *Sociology*, 10, pp.407-27.

Crompton, R. (1979), 'Trade Unionism and the Insurance Clerk', *Sociology*, 13, 3, pp.403-26.

Crompton, R. (1980), 'Class and Mobility in Modern Britain', *Sociology*, 14, pp.117-20.

Crompton, R and Gubbay, J. (1977), *Economy and Class Structure*, London, Macmillan.

Crompton, R. and Jones, G. (1982), 'Clerical "Proletarianization": Myth or Reality?', in G. Day (ed.), *Diversity and Decomposition in the Labour Market*, Aldershot, Gower.

Crouch, C. (1979), 'The State, Capital and Liberal Democracy' in C. Crouch (ed.), *State and Economy in Contemporary Capitalism*, London, Croom Helm, pp.13-54.

Crouch, C. and Pizzorno, A. (eds) (1978), *The Resurgence of Class Conflict in Western Europe Since 1968: Vol. 2, Comparative Analyses*, London, Macmillan.

Crough, G.J. (1977), *Foreign Investment and Transnational Corporations in Australia: An Annotated Bibliography*, Sydney, Alternative Publishing Company.

Crough, G. (1980a), 'The Australian Financial System', in G. Crough, T. Wheelwright and T. Wilshire (eds), *Australia and World Capitalism*, Ringwood, Penguin, pp.169-81.

Crough, G. (1980b), 'The Political Economy of the Mineral Industry', in G. Crough, T. Wheelwright and T. Wilshire (eds), *Australia and World Capitalism*, Ringwood, Penguin, pp.182-9.

Crough, G., Wheelwright, T. and Wilshire, T. (eds) (1980), *Australia and World Capitalism*, Ringwood, Penguin.

Crough, G. and Wheelwright, T. (1982), *Australia: A Client State*, Ringwood, Penguin.

CSE London Working Group (1980), *The Alternative Economic Strategy: A Response by the Labour Movement to the Economic Crisis*, London, CSE Books and Labour Co-ordinating Committee.

Cummings, L. and Greenbaum, J. (1978), 'The Struggle over Productivity: Workers, Management and Technology', in The Union for Radical Political Economics (ed.), *US Capitalism in Crisis*, New York, URPE, pp. 55-62.

Curthoys, A and Markus, A. (eds) (1978), *Who Are Our Enemies?: Racism and the Australian Working Class*, Sydney, Hale & Iremonger.

Cutler, A. (1978), 'The Romance of Labour', *Economy and Society*, 7, pp.74-95.

Cyert, R.M. and March, J.G. (1963), *A Behavioural Theory of the Firm*, Englewood Cliffs, NJ, Prentice-Hall.

Dahlström, E. (1979), *Division of Labour, Class Stratification and Cognitive Development*, Förskningsrapport, Sociologiska Institutionen, Göteborgs Universitet, 61.

Davidson, P. (1972), 'Money and the Real World', *Economic Journal*, 82, 325, pp.101-15.

Davis, E.W. and Yeoman, K.A. (1974), *Company Finance and the Capital Market: A Study of the Effects of Firm Size*, Cambridge University Press.

Davis, M. (1978), ' "Fordism" in Crisis: A Review of Michel Aglietta's "Regulation et Crises: L'expérience des États-Unis" ', *Review*, 11, pp.207-69.

Deal, T. and Kennedy, A. (1982), *Corporate Cultures: The Rites and the Rituals of Corporate Life*, New York, Addison-Wesley.

Deane, P. (1978), *The Evolution of Economic Ideas*, Cambridge University Press.

Della Torre, P.F., Mortimer, E. and Story, J. (eds) (1979), *Eurocommunism: Myth or Reality*, Harmondsworth, Penguin.

De Vroey, M. (1973), *Propriété et pouvoir dans les grandes enterprises*, Brussels, CRISP.

De Vroey, M. (1975), 'The Separation of Ownership and Control in Large Corporations', *Review of Radical Political Economics*, 7, pp.1-10.

Ditton, J. (1977), 'Alibis and Aliases', *Sociology*, 11, 2, p.233-56.

Dobb, M. (1937), *Political Economy and Capitalism: Some Essays in Economic Tradition*, London, Routledge & Kegan Paul.

Dobb, M. (1973), *Theories of Value and Distribution Since Adam Smith*, Cambridge University Press.

Doeringer, P. and Piore, M. (1971), *Internal Labor Markets and Manpower Analysis*, Lexington, Lexington Books.

Domar, E.D. (1957), *Essays in the Theory of Growth*, New York, Oxford University Press.

Domhoff, G.W. (1967), *Who Rules America?*, Englewood Cliffs, NJ, Prentice-Hall.

Domhoff, G.W. (1971), *The Higher Circles: The Governing Class in America*, New York, Vintage Books.

Domhoff, G.W. (1974), *The Bohemian Grove*, New York, Harper & Row.

Dooley, P.C. (1969), 'The Interlocking Directorate', *American Economic Review*, 59, pp.314-23.

Dore, R.P. (1973), *British Factory – Japanese Factory*, London, Allen & Unwin.

Dow, G. (1983), 'The Freeze Fallacy', *Australian Society*, 2, 1, pp.3-5.

Draper, A. and Palmer, D. (1982), 'A Political Exchange Theory of Trade Union Behaviour', mimeo, Stanford University.

Dunkerley, D. (1975), *The Foreman*, London, Routledge & Kegan Paul.

Dunkerley, D. (1980), 'Technological Change and Work: Upgrading or De-skilling', in P. Boreham and G. Dow (eds), *Work and Inequality: Vol. 2, Ideology and Control in the Capitalist Labour Process*, Melbourne, Macmillan, pp.163-79.

Dye, T.R. (1976), *Who's Running America?*, Englewood Cliffs, NJ, Prentice-Hall.

Edelman, M. (1977), *Political Language: Words that Succeed and Policies that Fail*, London, Academic Press.

Edwards, R. (1978), 'Social Relations of Production at the Point of Production', *Insurgent Sociologist*, 8, 2-3, pp.109-25.

Edwards, R. (1979), *Contested Terrain: the Transformation of the Workplace in the Twentieth Century*, New York, Basic Books.

Edwards, R.C., Reich, M. and Gordon, D. (eds) (1975), *Labor Market Segmentation*, Lexington, Mass., D.C. Heath.

EEC (European Economic Community) Commission (1976), *Fifth Report on Competition Policy*, Brussels.

Ehrenreich, B. and Ehrenreich, J. (1979), 'The Professional–Managerial Class', in P. Walker (ed.), *Between Labor and Capital*, Boston, South End Press, pp.5-45.

Eichner, A.S. (1976), *The Megacorp and Oligopoly: Micro Foundations of Macro Dynamics*, Cambridge University Press.

Elger, A. (1979), 'Valorization and Deskilling – A Critique of Braverman', *Capital and Class*, 7, pp.58-100.

Elliott, P. (1972), *The Sociology of the Professions*, London, Macmillan.

Emmanuel, A. (1972), *Unequal Exchange*, London, New Left Books.

Emmison, J.M. (1983), 'Lay Conceptions of the Economy: A Theoretical and Empirical Analysis of Ideology and Economic Life', PhD thesis, University of Queensland.

Encel, S. (1970), *Equality and Authority: A Study of Class, Status and Power in Australia*, Melbourne, Longman.

Epstein, L.K. (ed.) (1975), *Women in the Professions*, Lexington, D.C. Heath.

Esping-Andersen, G. (1980), *Social Class, Social Democracy and State Policy: Party Policy and Party Decomposition in Denmark and Sweden*, Copenhagen, New Social Science Monographs.

Esping-Andersen, G. (1981), 'From Welfare State to Democratic Socialism: The Politics of Economic Democracy in Denmark and

Sweden', in M. Zeitlin (ed.), *Political Power and Social Theory: A Research Annual*, vol. 2, pp.111-40.

Esping-Andersen, G. and Friedland, R. (1982), 'Class Coalitions in the Making of West European Economies', in G. Esping-Andersen and R. Friedland (eds), *Political Power and Social Theory: A Research Annual*, vol. 3, Greenwich, Cambridge, JAI Press, pp.1-52.

Esping-Andersen, G., Friedland, R. and Wright, E.O. (1976), 'Modes of Class Struggle and the Capitalist State', *Kapitalistate*, 4-5, pp.186-200.

Evan, W.M. (1966), 'The Organization-set: Toward a Theory of Interorganizational Relations', in J.D. Thompson (ed.), *Approaches to Organizational Design*, University of Pittsburgh Press, pp.175-91.

Feiwel, G.R. (1975), *The Intellectual Capital of Michal Kalecki: A Study in Economic Theory and Policy*, Knoxville, University of Tennessee Press.

Ferraresi, F. (1983), 'The Institutional Transformations of the Post *Laissez-Faire* State: Reflections on the Italian Case', in S. Clegg, G. Dow and P. Boreham (eds), *The State, Class and the Recession*, London, Croom Helm, pp.129-51.

Fidler, J. (1981), *The British Business Elite: Its Attitudes to Class, Status and Power*, London, Routledge & Kegan Paul.

Finniston, M. (1980), *Engineering our Future*, Report of the Committee of Inquiry into the Engineering Profession, London, HMSO.

Fleet, K. (1976), 'Triumph Meriden', in K. Coates (ed.), *The New Worker Co-operatives*, Nottingham, Spokesman Books, pp.88-108.

Fletcher, C. (1973), 'The End of Management', in J. Child (ed.), *Man and Organization*, London, Allen & Unwin, pp.135-57.

Fogelberg, G. and Laurent, C.R. (1973), 'Interlocking directorates: A study of large companies in New Zealand', *Journal of Business Policy*, 3, 2, pp.16–21.

Foster, J. (1974), *Class Struggle and the Industrial Revolution: Early Industrial Capitalism in Three English Towns*, London, Methuen.

Fox, A. (1974), *Beyond Contract: Work, Power and Trust Relations*, London, Faber & Faber.

Frankel, B. (1978), *Marxian Theories of the State: A Critique of Orthodoxy*, monograph no. 3, Melbourne, Arena Publications Association.

Frankel, B. (1979), 'On the State of the State: Marxist Theorists of the State after Leninism', *Theory and Society*, 7, pp.199-242.

Freeman, C. (1974), *The Economics of Industrial Innovation*, Harmondsworth, Penguin.

Freitag, P.J. (1975), 'The Cabinet and Big Business, a Study of Interlocks', *Social Problems*, 23, 2, pp.137-52.

Friedman, A.L. (1977), *Industry and Labour: Class Struggle at Work and Monopoly Capitalism*, London, Macmillan.

Friedman, M. (1962), *Capitalism and Freedom*, University of Chicago Press.

Friedman, M. (1972), 'Have Monetary Policies Failed?', *American Economic Review (Papers and Proceedings)*, 62, 2, pp.11-18.

Friedman, M. (1977), 'Adam Smith's Relevance for Today', *Challenge: The Magazine of Economic Affairs*, 20, 1, pp.6-12.

Friedman, M. and Friedman, R. (1980), *Free to Choose: A Personal Statement*, London, Secker & Warburg.

Fröbel, F., Heinrichs, J. and Kreye, O. (1978), 'The World Market for Labor and the World Market for Industrial Sites', *Journal of Economic Issues*, xii, 4, pp.843-58.

Fröbel, F. Heinrichs, J. and Kreye, O. (1980), *The New International Division of Labour: Structural Unemployment in Industrialized Countries and Industrialization in Developing Countries*, Cambridge University Press.

Gagliani, G. (1981), 'How Many Working Classes?', *American Journal of Sociology*, 87, 2, pp.259-85.

Galbraith, J.K. (1967), *The New Industrial State*, Harmondsworth, Penguin.

Galbraith, J.K. (1974), *Economics and the Public Purpose*, London, Andre Deutsch.

Galbraith, J.K. (1975), 'How Keynes Came to America', in M. Keynes (ed.), *Essays on John Maynard Keynes*, Cambridge University Press, pp.132-41.

Gallie, D. (1978), *In Search of the New Working Class: Automation and Social Integration within the Capitalist Enterprise*, Cambridge University Press.

Gallie, D. (1983), *Social Inequality and Class Radicalism in France and Britain*, Cambridge University Press.

Gamble, A. and Walton, P. (1976), *Capitalism in Crisis: Inflation and the State*, London, Macmillan.

Game, A. and Pringle, R. (1979), 'Sexuality and the Suburban Dream', *Australian and New Zealand Journal of Sociology*, 15, 2, pp.4-15.

Game, A. and Pringle, R. (1983), *Gender at Work*, Sydney, Allen & Unwin.

Garaudy, R. (1970), *The Turning-point of Socialism*, London, Fontana.

Gardiner, J. (1975), 'Women's Domestic Labour', *New Left Review*, 89, pp.47-58.

Gardiner, J. (1977), 'Women in the Labour Process', in A. Hunt (ed.), *Class and Class Structure*, London, Lawrence and Wishart, pp.155-63.

Gårdlund, T. (1977), '1933 års svenska krispolitik – Marcus Wallenbergs brevväxling med Strakosch och Keynes', in J. Herin and L. Werin (eds), *Ekonomisk debatt och Ekonomisk Politik: Nationalekonomiska Föreningen 100 år*, Lund, Norstedts, pp.85-99.

Garfinkel, H. (1967), *Studies in Ethnomethodology*, Englewood Cliffs, NJ, Prentice-Hall.

Garnsey, E. (1978), 'Women's Work and Theories of Class Stratification', *Sociology*, 12, 2, pp.223-43.

Gerry, C. and Birkbeck, C. (1981), 'The Petty Commodity Producer in Third World Cities: Petit Bourgeois or "Disguised" Proletarian?' in F. Bechhofer and B. Elliott (eds), *The Petite Bourgeoisie: Comparative Studies of the Uneasy Stratum*, London, Macmillan, pp.121-54.

Giddens, A. (1973), *The Class Structure of the Advanced Societies*,

London, Hutchinson.

Giddens, A. (1979), *Central Problems in Social Theory: Action, Structure and Contradiction in Social Analysis*, London, Macmillan.

Giddens, A. (1980), *The Class Structure of the Advanced Societies*, 2nd edn, London, Hutchinson.

Giddens, A. (1981), *A Contemporary Critique of Historical Materialism*, London, Macmillan.

Giddens, A and Stanworth, P. (1978), 'Elites and Privilege', in P. Abrams (ed.), *Work, Urbanism and Inequality: UK Society Today*, London Weidenfeld & Nicolson, pp.206-48.

Glasgow Media Group (1976), *Bad News*, London, Routledge & Kegan Paul.

Glasgow Media Group (1979), *More Bad News*, London, Routledge & Kegan Paul.

Glover, I.A. (1973), *Professional Engineers and Engineering in Britain: A Review of the Sociological and Industrial Relations Literature*, Edinburgh, Heriot-Watt University.

Glyn, A. and Harrison, J. (1980), *The British Economic Disaster*, London, Pluto Press.

Glyn, A and Sutcliffe, B. (1972), *British Capitalism, Workers, and the Profits Squeeze*, Harmondsworth, Penguin.

Goldthorpe, J.H. (1982), 'On the Service Class, its Formation and Future', in A. Giddens and G. Mackenzie (eds), *Social Class and the Division of Labour: Essays in Honour of Ilya Neustadt*, Cambridge University Press, pp.162-85.

Goldthorpe, J.H., Llewellyn, C. and Payne, C. (1980), *Social Mobility and Class Structure in Modern Britain*, Oxford, Clarendon Press.

Goldthorpe, J.H., Lockwood, D., Bechhofer, F. and Platt, J. (1969), *The Affluent Worker in the Class Structure*, Cambridge University Press.

Goodrich, C. (1975), *The Frontier of Control*, London, Pluto Press.

Gordon, D.M. (1972), *Theories of Poverty and Underemployment: Orthodoxy, Radical and Dual Labor Market Perspectives*, Lexington, Mass., D.C. Heath.

Gordon, D., Edwards, R.C. and Reich, M. (1982), *Segmented Work, Divided Workers*, Cambridge University Press.

Gordon, R.A. (1945), *Business Leadership in Large Corporations*, Washington, Brookings Institute.

Gorz, A. (1970), 'What Are the Lessons of the May Events?', in C. Posner (ed.), *Reflections on the Revolution in France: 1968*, Harmondsworth, Penguin, pp.251-265.

Gorz, A. (ed.) (1976), *The Division of Labour: The Labour Process and Class Struggle in Modern Capitalism*, Brighton, Harvester.

Gouldner, A.W. (1957), 'Cosmopolitans and Locals: Toward an Analysis of Latent Social Roles – I', *Administrative Science Quarterly*, 2, pp.281-306.

Gouldner, A.W. (1958), 'Cosmopolitans and Locals: Toward an Analysis of Latent Social Roles – II', *Administrative Science Quarterly*, 2, pp.444-80.

Gramsci, A. (1971), *Selections from the Prison Notebooks of Antonio Gramsci*, Q. Hoare and G.N. Smith (eds), London, Lawrence & Wishart.

Griffin, J.I. (1939), *Strikes: A Study in Quantitative Economics*, New York, Columbia University Press.

Gustavsen, B. (1976), 'The Social Context of Investment Decisions', *Acta Sociologica*, 19, 3, pp.273-84.

Gutman, H.G. (1976), *Work, Culture and Society in Industrializing America, 1815-1919*, New York, Knopf.

Hall, C.B. (1982), 'Interlocking Directorates in Australia: The Significance for Competition Policy', paper presented at the Eleventh Conference of Economists, Flinders University, August 1982.

Hall, S. (1978), 'The "Political" and the "Economic" in Marx's Theory of Classes', in A. Hunt (ed.), *Class and Class Structure*, London, Lawrence & Wishart, pp.15-60.

Hall, S. (1980), 'Popular-democratic vs Authoritarian Populism: Two ways of "Taking Democracy Seriously" ', in A. Hunt (ed.), *Marxism and Democracy*, London, Lawrence & Wishart, pp.157-85.

Hall, S. (1983), 'Thatcherism, Racism and the Left: An Interview', *Meanjin*, 42, 2, pp.191-202.

Halliday, J. (1975), *The Political History of Japanese Capitalism*, New York, Monthly Review Press.

Halsey, A.H., Heath, A.F. and Ridge, J.M. (1980), *Origins and Destinations: Family, Class and Education in Modern Britain*, Oxford, Clarendon Press.

Hamilton, R.F. (1967), *Affluence and the French Worker in the Fifth Republic*, Princeton University Press.

Hamilton, R. (1978), *The Liberation of Women: A Study of Patriarchy and Capitalism*, London, Allen & Unwin.

Harcourt, G.C. (1975), 'Much Ado about Something', *Economic Papers*, 49, pp.36-49.

Harcourt, G.C. (1977a), 'On Theories and Policies', in J.P. Nieuwenhuysen and P.J. Drake (eds), *Australian Economic Policy*, Melbourne University Press, pp.40-52.

Harcourt, G.C. (1977b), 'The Theoretical and Social Significance of the Cambridge Controversies in the Theory of Capital: An Evaluation', in J. Schwartz (ed.), *The Subtle Anatomy of Capitalism*, Santa Monica, Goodyear Publishing, pp.285-303.

Harcourt, G.C. and Laing, N.F. (eds) (1971), *Capital and Growth: Selected Readings*, Harmondsworth, Penguin.

Harris, Lord Ralph (1980), 'Taxation and Public Spending in a Modern Democracy', in J. Wilkes (ed.), *The Politics of Taxation*, Sydney, Hodder & Stoughton, pp.1-17.

Harrison, J. (1982), 'Thatcherism: Is It Working?', *Marxism Today*, 26, 7, pp.19-25.

Harrison, R.J. (1980), *Pluralism and Corporatism: The Political Evolution of Modern Democracies*, London, Allen & Unwin.

Harvey, D. (1982), *The Limits to Capital*, Oxford, Blackwell.

Hawley, J.P. (1980), 'Foreign Economic Policy, State Theory and the

Problem of "Interest": The Significance of the US Capital Programs, 1961-1974', paper presented at the American Sociological Association, Anual Conference, New York, August 1980.

Hawley, J.P. and Noble, C.I. (1980), 'The Internationalization of Capital and the Crisis of the Nation State', revised version of a paper presented to the American Sociological Association, Annual Conference, New York, August 1980.

Hayek, F.A. (1941), 'Keynes's Neglect of Scarcity' (1941) reprinted in *A Tiger by the Tail: The Keynesian Legacy of Inflation*, London, Institute of Economic Affairs, pp.23-9.

Hayek, F.A. (1944), *The Road to Serfdom*, London, Routledge & Kegan Paul.

Hayek, F.A. (1948), *Individualism and Economic Order*, South Bend, Indiana, Gateway Editions.

Hayek, F.A. (1972), 'The Outlook for the 1970s: Open or Repressed Inflation?', in *A Tiger by the Tail: The Keynesian Legacy of Inflation*, London, Institute of Economic Affairs, pp.113-19.

Hearn, J. (1977), 'Towards a Concept of Non-career', *Sociological Review*, 25, 2, pp.273-88.

Heath, A. (1976), *Rational Choice and Social Exchange*, Cambridge University Press.

Heath, A. (1981), *Social Mobility*, Glasgow, Fontana.

Hedenius, I. (1975), 'Analysen av äganderättsbegreppet', in B. Belfrage and L. Stille (eds), *Filosofi och Rattsvetenskap*, Lund, Bokförlaget Doxa, pp.37-61.

Hegel, G.W.F. (1967), *Philosophy of Right*, New York, Oxford University Press.

Heilbroner, R.L. (1980), 'The Inflation in Your Future', *New York Review of Books*, 27, 7, pp.6-10.

Heilbroner, R.L. (1981), 'The Demand for the Supply Side', *New York Review of Books*, 28, 10, pp.37-41.

Heritage, J. (1980), 'Class Situation, White collar Unionisation and the "Double Proletarianisation" Thesis: A Comment', *Sociology*, 14, pp.283-94.

Hibbs, D.A. (1976), 'Industrial Conflict in Advanced Industrial Societies', *American Political Science Review*, 70, 4, pp.1033-58.

Hibbs, D.A. (1978), 'On the Political Economy of Long-run Trends in Strike Activity', *British Journal of Political Science*, 8, pp.153-75.

Hickson, D.J., Hinings, C.R., Lee, C.A., Schneck, R.E. and Pennings, J.M. (1971), 'A Strategic Contingencies Theory of Intra-organizational Power', *Administrative Science Quarterly*, 16, pp.216-29.

Higgins, W. (1980), 'Working Class Mobilization and Socialism in Sweden: Lessons from Afar', in P. Boreham and G. Dow (eds), *Work and Inequality, Vol. 1: Workers, Economic Crisis and the State*, Melbourne, Macmillan, pp.143-61.

Higgins, W. (1983), 'Ernst Wigforss and the Renewal of Social Democratic Theory and Practice', unpublished mimeo.

Higgins, W. and Apple, N. (1983), 'How Limited is Reformism? A Critique of Panitch and Przeworski', *Theory and Society*, 12, 5, pp.603-30.

Higley, J. Field, G.L. and Grøholt, K. (1976), *Elite Structure and Ideology*, Oslo, Universitetsforlaget.

Hilferding, R. (1981), *Finance Capital*, London, Routledge & Kegan Paul.

Hill, S. (1980), 'Economic and Industrial Transformation: The Waves of Social Consequence from Technological Change', in P. Boreham and G. Dow (eds), *Work and Inequality, Vol. 1: Workers, Economic Crisis and the State*, Melbourne, Macmillan, pp.69-85.

Hill, S. (1981), *Competition and Control at Work: The New Industrial Sociology*, London, Heinemann.

Himmelstrand, U., Ahrne, G., Lundberg, L. and Lundberg, L. (1981), *Beyond Welfare Capitalism: Issues, Actors and Forces in Societal Change*, London, Heinemann.

Himmelweit, S. and Mohun, E. (1977), 'Domestic Labour and Capital', *Cambridge Journal of Economics*, 1, pp.26-44.

Hindess, B. (1980), 'Democracy and the Limitations of Parliamentary Democracy in Britain', *Politics and Power*, 1, London, Routledge & Kegan Paul, pp.103-24.

Hinings, C.R., Hickson, D.J., Pennings, J.M. and Schneck, R.E. (1974), 'Structural Conditions of Intraorganizational Power', *Administrative Science Quarterly*, 9, 1, pp.22-44.

Hirsch, A. (1981), *The French New Left: An Intellectual History from Sartre to Gorz*, Boston, South End Press.

Hirst, P. (1977), 'Economic Classes and Politics', in A. Hunt (ed.), *Class and Class Structure*, London, Lawrence & Wishart, pp.125-54.

Hirst, P. (1982), 'The Division of Labour, Incomes Policy and Industrial Democracy', in A. Giddens and G. Mackenzie (eds), *Social Class and the Division of Labour: Essays in Honour of Ilya Neustadt*, Cambridge University Press, pp.208-64.

Hobbes, T. (1962), *Leviathan*, M. Oakeshott (ed.), London, Collier-Macmillan.

Hobsbawm, E.J. (1975), *The Age of Capital: 1848-1875*, London, Weidenfeld & Nicolson.

Hodgson, G. (1982), 'Theoretical and Policy Implications of Variable Productivity', *Cambridge Journal of Economics*, 6, 3, pp.213-26.

Hodgson, G.M. (1983), 'Worker Participation and Macroeconomic Efficiency', *Journal of Post Keynesian Economics*, 5, 2, pp.266-75.

Hoggart, R. (1958), *The Uses of Literacy: Aspects of Working-class Life with Special Reference to Publications and Entertainments*, Harmondsworth, Penguin.

Holland, S. (1975), *The Socialist Challenge*, London, Quartet.

Holland, S. (ed.) (1978), *Beyond Capitalist Planning*, London, Blackwell.

Holland, S. (1979), 'Work, Workers and the Age of Uncertainty', *Social Alternatives*, 1, 4, pp.53-58.

Holland, S. (1980), 'Dominant Enterprise and Employment a Strategic Response', in P. Boreham and G. Dow (eds), *Work and Inequality, Vol. 1: Workers, Economic Crisis and the State*, Melbourne, Macmillan, pp.54-68.

Holloway, J. and Piccioto, S. (eds) (1977), *State and Capital: A Marxist*

Debate, London, Arnold.

Honoré, A.M. (1961), 'Ownership', in A.G. Guest (ed.), *Oxford Essays in Jurisprudence: A Collaborative Work*, London, Oxford University Press, pp.107-47.

Hunt, A. (1977a), 'Theory and Politics in the Identification of the Working Class,, in A. Hunt (ed.), *Class and Class Structure*, London, Lawrence & Wishart, pp.81-111.

Hunt, A. (ed.) (1977b), *Class and Class Structure*, London, Lawrence & Wishart.

Hunt, E.K. (1979), *History of Economic Thought: A Critical Perspective*, Belmont, Calif., Wadsworth Publishing.

Hunt, E.K. and Schwartz, J.G. (eds) (1972), *A Critique of Economic Theory: Selected Readings*, Harmondsworth, Penguin.

Hunter, A. (1961), 'Restrictive Practices and Monopolies in Australia', *Economic Record*, 27, pp.25-52.

Hussain, A. (1977), 'Crises and Tendencies of Capitalism', *Economy and Society*, 6, 4, pp.436-60.

Hyman, R. (1975), *Industrial Relations: A Marxist Introduction*, London, Macmillan.

Hyman, R. and Brough, I. (1975), *Social Values and Industrial Relations*, Oxford, Blackwell.

Hyman, R. and Fryer, R. (1975), 'Trade Unions: Sociology and Political Economy', in J.B. McKinlay (ed.), *Processing People: Cases in Organizational Behaviour*, London, Holt, Rinehart & Winston, pp.150-213.

Hymer, S. (1976), *The International Operations of National Firms*, Cambridge, Mass., MIT Press.

IDS (1981), *Professional Engineers and Scientists*, London, Income Data Services, study no. 239.

Ingham, G. (1982), 'Divisions within the Dominant Class and British "Exceptionalism" ', in A. Giddens and G. Mackenzie (eds), *Social Class and the Division of Labour: Essays in Honour of Ilya Neustadt*, Cambridge University Press, pp.209-27.

Jacques, E. (1956), *The Measure of Responsibility*, London, Tavistock.

James, D.R and Soref, M. (1981), 'Profit Constraints on Managerial Autonomy: Managerial Theory and the Unmaking of the Corporation President', *American Sociological Review*, 46, pp.1-18.

Jamous, H. and Peloille, B. (1970), 'Professions or Self-perpetuating Systems: Changes in the French University-hospital System', in J.A. Jackson (ed.), *Professions and Professionalisation*, Cambridge University Press, pp.109-52.

Jessop, B. (1977), 'Recent Theories of the Capitalist State', *Cambridge Journal of Economics*, 1, pp.353-73.

Jessop, B. (1978a), 'Capitalism and Democracy: The Best Possible Political Shell?' in G. Littlejohn, B. Smart, J. Wakeford and N. Yuval-Davies (eds), *Power and the State*, London, Croom Helm, pp.10-51.

Jessop, B. (1978b), 'Marx and Engels on the State', in S. Hibbin (ed.), *Politics, Ideology and the State*, London, Lawrence & Wishart, pp.40-68.

Jessop, B. (1980), 'The Transformation of the State in Post-war Britain', in R. Scase (ed.), *The State in Western Europe*, London, Croom Helm, pp.23-93.

Jessop, B. (1982), *The Capitalist State: Marxist Theories and Methods*, Oxford, Martin Robertson.

Jessop, B. (1983), 'The Capitalist State and the Rule of Capital: Problems in the Analysis of Business Associations', *West European Politics*, 6, 2, pp.139-62.

Johns, B.L., Dunlop, W.D. and Sheeman, W.J. (1978), *Small Business in Australia: Problems and Prospects*, Sydney, Allen & Unwin.

Johnson, H.G. (1971), 'The Keynesian Revolution and the Monetarist Counter Revolution', *American Economic Review (Papers and Proceedings)*, 61, 2, pp.1-14.

Johnson, P. (1978), 'Policies Towards Small Firms: Time for Caution?', *Lloyds Bank Review*, 129, pp.269-80.

Johnson, P. and Apps, R. (1979), 'Interlocking Directorates among the UK's Largest Companies', *Antitrust Bulletin*, 24, pp.357-69.

Johnson, T. (1977), 'What Is to be Known? The Structural Determination of Social Class', *Economy and Society*, 6, pp.194-233.

Johnson, T. (1982), 'The State and the Professions: Peculiarities of the British', in Giddens, A. and McKenzie, G. (eds), *Social Class and the Division of Labour: Essays in Honour of Illya Neustadt*, Cambridge University Press, pp.186-208.

Johnson, T. and Rattansi, A. (1981), 'Social Mobility without Class', *Economy and Society*, 10, 2, pp.203-34.

Kaldor, M. (1978), *The Disintegrating West*, Harmondsworth, Allen Lane.

Kaldor, N. (1979), 'What Is De-industrialization: Comment', in F. Blackaby (ed.), *De-industrialization*, London, Heinemann, pp.18-25.

Kaldor, N. (1982), *The Scourge of Monetarism*, Oxford University Press.

Kalecki, M. (1933), 'Outline of a Theory of the Business Cycle', in *Selected Essays on the Dynamics of the Capitalist Economy 1933-1971*, Cambridge University Press, pp.1-14.

Kalecki, M. (1939), *Essays in the Theory of Economic Fluctuations*, New York, Russell & Russell.

Kalecki, M. (1943), 'Political Aspects of Full Employment', *Political Quarterly*, 14, 4, pp.322-31.

Kalecki, M. (1954a), 'Distribution of National Income', in *Selected Essays on the Dynamics of the Capitalist Economy 1933-1971*, Cambridge University Press, pp.62-77.

Kalecki, M. (1954b), *Theory of Economic Dynamics: An Essay on Cyclical and Long Run Changes in Capitalist Economy*, London, Allen & Unwin.

Kalecki, M. (1971), 'Class Struggle and Distribution of National Income', in *Selected Essays in the Dynamics of the Capitalist Economy 1933-1971*, Cambridge University Press, pp.156-64.

Kanter, R.M. (1977), *Men and Women of the Corporation*, New York, Basic Books.

Karier, C.J. (1973), 'Business Values and the Educational State', in C.J.

Karier, P. Violas and J. Springs (eds), *Roots of Crisis: American Education in the Twentieth Century*, Chicago, Rand McNally, pp.6-29.

Kay, N.M. (1979), *The Innovating Firm: A Behavioural Theory of Corporate Rise and Decline*, London, Macmillan.

Kelly, J.E. (1982), 'Useful Work and Useless Toil', *Marxism Today*, 26, 8, pp.12-18.

Kerr, C. (1950), 'Labour Markets: Their Character and Consequences', *American Economic Review (Papers and Proceedings)*, 40, pp.278-91.

Kerr, C. (1954), 'The Balkanisation of Labour Markets', in E. Wight Bakke *et al.* (eds), *Labor Mobility and Economic Opportunity*, Cambridge, Mass., MIT Press, pp.92-110.

Kesselman, M. (1982), 'Prospects for Democratic Socialism in Advanced Capitalism: Class Struggle and Compromise in Sweden and France', *Politics and Society*, 11, 4, pp.397-438.

Keynes, J.M. (1925), 'The Economic Consequences of Mr Churchill', in *Essays in Persuasion*, New York, Norton & Norton, pp.244-70.

Keynes, J.M. (1936), *The General Theory of Employment, Interest and Money*, London, Macmillan.

Kilpatrick, A. and Lawson, T. (1980), 'On the Nature of Industrial Decline in the UK', *Cambridge Journal of Economics*, 4, 1, pp.85-102.

Kingsley, J.D. (1944), *Representative Bureaucracy*, Yellow Springs, Antioch Press.

Koenig, T. and Gogel, R. (1980), 'Interlocking Corporate Directorships as a Social Network', *American Journal of Economics and Sociology*, 40, 1, pp.37-50.

Koenig, T., Gogel, R. and Sonquist, J. (1979), 'Models of the Significance of Interlocking Directorates', *American Journal of Economics and Sociology*, 38, pp.173-86.

Kolko, G. (1962), *Wealth and Power in America*, London, Thames & Hudson.

Kondratief, N.D. (1979), 'The Long Waves in Economic Life', *Review*, 11, 4, pp.519-62.

Korpi, W. (1974), 'Conflict, Power and Relative Deprivation', *American Political Science Review*, lxviii, 4, pp.1569-78.

Korpi, W. (1978), *The Working Class in Welfare Capitalism: Work, Unions and Politics in Sweden*, London, Routledge & Kegan Paul.

Korpi, W. (1982), 'The Historical Compromise and its Dissolution', in B. Rydén and V. Bergström (eds), *Sweden: Choices for Economic and Social Policy in the 1980s*, London, Allen & Unwin, pp.124-41.

Korpi, W. and Shalev, M. (1980), 'Strikes, Power and Politics in the Western Nations, 1900-1976', in M. Zeitlin, (ed.), *Political Power and Social Theory: A Research Annual, Vol. 1*, Greenwich, Conn., JAI Press, pp.301-39.

Kreckel, R. (1980), 'Unequal Opportunity, Structure and Labour Market Segmentation', *Sociology*, 14, 4, pp.525-50.

Kregel, J.A. (1979), 'Income Distribution', in S. Eichner (ed.), *A Guide to Post-Keynesian Economics*, London, Macmillan, pp.46-60.

Krejci, J. (1976), *Social Structure in Divided Germany*, London, Croom Helm.

Kuhn, A. and Wolpe, A. (eds) (1978), *Feminism and Materialism*, London, Routledge & Kegan Paul.

Kumar, K. (1977), 'Continuities and Discontinuities in the Development of Industrial Societies', in R. Scase (ed.), *Industrial Society: Class, Cleavage and Control*, London, Allen & Unwin, pp.29-42.

Laidler, D. (1973), 'The Current Inflation – The Problem of Explanation and the Problem of Policy', in J. Robinson (ed.), *After Keynes*, Oxford, Blackwell, pp.37-54.

Land, H. (1976), 'Women: Supporters or Supported?', in D.L. Barker and S. Allen (eds), *Sexual Division and Society: Process and Change*, London Tavistock, pp.108-32.

Larner, R.J. (1960), *Management Control and the Large Corporation*, New York, Dunellen.

Larner, R.J. (1966), 'Ownership and Control in the 200 Largest Non-financial Corporations: 1929 and 1963', *American Economic Review*, 56, pp.777-87.

Larson, M.S. (1977), *The Rise of Professionalism: A Sociological Analysis*, Berkeley, University of California Press.

Lee, D.J. (1981), 'Skill, Craft and Class: A Theoretical Critique and a Critical Case', *Sociology*, 15, pp.56-78.

Lehmbruch, G. and Schmitter, P.C. (eds) (1982), *Patterns of Corporatist Policy-making*, London, Sage.

Lenin, V.I. (1921), *The State and Revolution*, Sydney, Australian Socialist Party.

Lenin, V.I. (1963), *Collected Works*, London, Lawrence & Wishart.

Lenski, G. (1966), *Power and Privilege*, New York, McGraw-Hill.

Lever-Tracey, C. (1981), 'In Reserve or Centre Forward? Immigrants and Capitalism', paper presented at the Organization, Economy and Society Conference, Brisbane, Griffith University.

Levine, J. (1972), 'The Sphere of Influence', *American Sociological Review*, 37, pp.14-27.

Lewellyn, W.G. and Huntsman, B. (1970), 'Managerial Pay and Corporate Performance', *American Economic Review*, 60, pp.710-20.

Leys, C. (1980), 'Neo-conservatism and the Organic Crisis in Britain', *Studies in Political Economy: A Socialist Review*, 4, pp.41-63.

Lieberson, S. and O'Connor, J.F. (1972), 'Leadership and Organizational Performance: A Study of Large Corporations', *American Sociological Review*, 37, 2, pp.117-30.

Lilley, P. (1977), 'Two Critics of Keynes: Friedman and Hayek', in R. Skidelsky (ed.), *The End of the Keynesian Era*, London, Macmillan, pp.25-32.

Lindblom, C.E. (1977), *Politics and Markets*, New York, Basic Books.

Littler, C.R. (1980), 'Internal Contract and the Transition to Modern Work Systems: Britain and Japan', in D. Dunkerley and G. Salaman (eds), *The International Yearbook of Organization Studies 1979*, London, Routledge & Kegan Paul.

Littler, C.R. (1982), 'Deskilling and Changing Structures of Control', in S. Wood (ed.), *The Degradation of Work? Skill, Deskilling and the Labour Process*, London, Hutchinson, pp.122-45.

Littler, C.R. and Salaman, G. (1982), 'Bravermania and Beyond: Recent Theories of the Labour Process', *Sociology*, 16, pp.251-69.

Lloyd, C.E. (ed.) (1975), *Sex, Discrimination, and the Division of Labour*, New York, Columbia University Press.

Lockwood, D. (1966), 'Sources of Variation in Working Class Images of Society', *Sociological Review*, 15, pp.249-67.

Loveridge, R. (1982), 'Business Strategy and Community Culture: Policy as a Structured Accommodation of Conflict', in D. Dunkerley and G. Salaman (eds), *The International Yearbook of Organization Studies 1981*, London, Routledge & Kegan Paul, pp.26-58.

Loveridge, R. and Mok, A.L. (1979), *Theories of Labour Market Segmentation: A Critique*, The Hague, Martinus Nijhoff.

Lowe, R. (1975), 'The Erosion of State Intervention in Britain 1917–24', *Economic History Review*, 31, 2, pp.270-86.

Lukács, G. (1971), *History and Class Consciousness*, London, Merlin.

Lukes, S. (1974), *Power: A Radical View*, London, Macmillan.

Mace, M.L. (1971), *Directors: Myth and Reality*, Harvard University Press.

McEachern, W.A. (1977), *Managerial Control and Performance*, Lexington, Mass., D.C. Heath.

MacEwan, A. (1981), 'International Economic Crisis and the Limits of Macro Policy', *Socialist Review*, no. 59, 11, 5, pp.113-38.

McFarlane, B. (1982), *Radical Economics*, London, Croom Helm.

McGee, T.D. (1978), 'The Decline of Engineering in the United States', *Engineering Education*, January, pp.339-43.

McGuire, J.W., Chiu, J.S. and Elbing, A.O. (1962), 'Executive Incomes, Sales and Profits', *American Economic Review*, 52, pp.753-61.

Mackenzie, G. (1982), 'Class Boundaries and the Labour Process', in A. Giddens and G. Mackenzie (eds), *Social Class and the Division of Labour: Essays in Honour of Ilya Neustadt*, Cambridge University Press, pp.63-86.

Mackenzie, G. and Silver, A. (1968), *Angels in Marble: Working Class Conservatives in Urban England*, London, Heinemann.

Macpherson, C.B. (1973), *Democratic Theory: Essays in Retrieval*, Oxford, Clarendon Press.

Macpherson, C.B. (1977), *The Political Theory of Possessive Individualism: Hobbes to Locke*, Oxford, Clarendon Press.

McQueen, H. (1982), *Gone Tomorrow: Australia in the 80s*, Sydney, Angus & Robertson.

Magdoff, H. (1969), *The Age of Imperialism: The Economics of US Foreign Policy*, New York, Monthly Review Press.

Mallet, S. (1975a), *The New Working Class*, Nottingham, Spokesman Books.

Mallet, S. (1975b), *Essays on the New Working Class* ed. and trans. by D. Howard and D. Savage, St Louis, Telos Press.

Mandel, E. (1975), *Late Capitalism*, London, New Left Books.

Mann, M. (1973a), *Consciousness and Action Among the Western Working Class*, London, Macmillan.

413

Mann, M. (1973b), *Workers on the Move: The Sociology of Relocation*, Cambridge University Press.

Marceau, J. (1976), 'Marriage, Role Division and Social Cohesion: The Case of Some French Upper-middle-class Families', in D.L. Barker and S. Allen (eds), *Dependence and Exploitation in Work and Marriage*, London, Longmans.

Marceau, J., Thomas, A.B. and Whitley, R. (1978), 'Business and the State: Management Education and Business Elites in France and Great Britain', in G. Littlejohn, B. Smart, J. Wakeford and N. Yuval-Davis (eds), *Power and the State*, London, Croom Helm, pp.128-57.

Marcuse, H. (1964), *One Dimensional Man: Studies in the Ideology of Advanced Industrial Societies*, London, Routledge & Kegan Paul.

Marglin, S.A. (1974), 'What Do Bosses Do? – The Origins and Functions of Hierarchy in Capitalist Production', *Review of Radical Political Economics*, 6, pp.60-112.

Mariolis, P. (1975), 'Interlocking Directorates and Control of Corporations: The Theory of Bank Control', *Social Science Quarterly*, 56, pp.425-39.

Martin, P.Y. (1980), 'Women, Labour Markets and Employing Organizations: A Critical Analysis', in D. Dunkerley and G. Salaman (eds), *The International Yearbook of Organization Studies*, London, Routledge & Kegan Paul, 128-50.

Marx, K. (1956), *The Poverty of Philosophy*, London, Lawrence and Wishart.

Marx, K. (1959), *Capital, vol. 3*, Moscow, Progress Publishers.

Marx, K. (1969a), *Theories of Surplus Value, vol. 2*, Moscow, Progress Publishers.

Marx, K. (1969b), 'Excerpts from "The Class Struggles in France, 1848 to 1850" ', in L.S. Feuer (ed.), *Marx and Engels: Basic Writings on Politics and Philosophy*, London, Fontana, pp.322-57.

Marx, K. (1969c), 'Excerpts from "The Eighteenth Brumaire of Louis Bonaparte" ', in L.S. Feuer (ed.), *Marx and Engels: Basic Writings on Politics and Philosophy*, London, Fontana, pp.358-88.

Marx, K. (1970a), *A Contribution to the Critique of Political Economy*, Moscow, Progress Publishers.

Marx, K. (1970b), *A Critique of Hegel's Philosophy of the State*, J.O. Malley (ed.), Cambridge University Press.

Marx, K. (1973a), *The Economic and Philosophical Manuscripts of 1844*, D.J. Struik (ed.), London, Lawrence & Wishart.

Marx, K. (1973b), *Grundrisse: Introduction to the Critique of Political Economy*, Harmondsworth, Penguin.

Marx, K. (1974), *Capital: A Critical Analysis of Capitalist Production, vol. 1*, Moscow, Progress Publishers.

Marx, K. (1975), 'A Contribution to the Critique of Hegel's Philosophy of Right', in L. Colletti (ed.), *Karl Marx, Early Writings*, Harmondsworth, Penguin, pp.243-58.

Marx, K. (1976), *Capital, vol. 1*, Harmondsworth, Penguin.

Marx, K. and Engels, F. (1969), *The Manifesto of the Communist Party*, in L.S. Feuer (ed.), *Marx and Engels: Basic Writings on Politics and*

Philosophy, London, Fontana, pp.43-82.

Mattick, P. (1978), *Economics, Politics and the Age of Inflation*, White Plains, New York, M.E. Sharpe.

Meacher, M. (1980), 'How the Mandarins Rule', *New Statesman*, 5 December, pp.14-15.

Meidner, R. (1978), *Employee Investment Funds: An Approach to Collective Capital Formation*, London, Allen & Unwin.

Meyer, J.W. (1977), 'The Effects of Education as an Institution', *American Journal of Sociology*, 83, 1, pp.55-77.

Meyer, J.W. and Rowan, B. (1977), 'Institutionalized Organizations: Formal Structure as Myth and Ceremony', *American Journal of Sociology*, 83, pp.340-63.

Miliband, R. (1962), *Parliamentary Socialism: A Study in the Politics of Labour*, London, Merlin Press.

Miliband, R. (1965), 'Marx and the State', in R. Miliband and J. Saville (eds), *The Socialist Register 1965*, London, Merlin.

Miliband, R. (1969), *The State in Capitalist Society*, London Quartet.

Miliband, R. (1977), *Marxism and Politics*, Oxford University Press.

Mills, C.W. (1959), *The Power Elite*, New York, Oxford University Press.

Mizruchi, M.S. (1982), *The American Corporate Network (1904-1974)*, London, Sage.

Mols, S.J.R. (1976), 'Population in Europe 1500-1700', in C.M. Cipolla (ed.), *The Fontana Economic History of Europe: The Sixteenth and Seventeenth Centuries*, Glasgow, Fontana, pp.15-82.

Molyneux, M. (1979), 'Beyond the Domestic Labour Debate', *New Left Review*, 116, pp.3-27.

Monsen, R.J., Jnr, Chiu, J.S. and Cooley, D.E (1968), 'The Effects of Separation of Ownership and Control on the Performance of the Large Firm', *Quarterly Journal of Economics*, 82, pp.435-51.

Montagna, P.D. (1973), 'The Public Accounting Profession: Organization, Ideology and Social Power', in E. Freidson (ed.), *The Professions and Their Prospects*, Beverly Hills, Sage, pp.135-51.

Moorhouse, H.F. (1976), 'Attitudes to Class and Class Relationships in Britain', *Sociology*, 10, pp.469-96.

Moorhouse, H.F. and Chamberlain, C.W. (1974), 'Lower Class Attitudes to Property: Aspects of the Counter-ideology', *Sociology*, 8, pp.387-405.

Morin, F. (1974), *La Structure financière du capitalisme français*, Paris, Calmann-Lévy.

Murray, R. (1971), 'The Internationalizaiton of Capital and the Nation State', *New Left Review*, 67, pp.84-109.

Myrdal, G. (1972), *Against the Stream: Critical Essays on Economics*, New York, Vintage Books.

Nankivell, P. (1980), 'Australian Agribusiness: Structure, Ownership and Control', in G. Crough, T. Wheelwright and T. Wilshire (eds), *Australia and World Capitalism*, Ringwood, Penguin, pp.160-8.

National Times (1978), Sydney, 15 October, p.11.

Newbould, G.D. (1970), *Management and Merger Activity*, Liverpool, Guthstead.

415

Newby, H., Rose, D., Saunders, P. and Bell, C. (1981), 'Farming for Survival: The Small Farmer in the Contemporary Class Structure', in F. Bechhofer and B. Elliott (eds), *The Petite Bourgeoisie: Comparative Studies of the Uneasy Stratum*, London, Macmillan, pp.38-71.

Newman, O. (1981), *The Challenge of Corporatism*, London, Macmillan.

Nichols, T. (1969), *Ownership, Control and Ideology*, London, Allen & Unwin.

Nichols, T. and Armstrong, P. (1976), *Workers Divided: A Study of Shopfloor Politics*, Glasgow, Fontana/Collins.

Nichols, T. and Beynon, H. (1977), *Living with Capitalism: Class Relations and the Modern Factory*, London, Routledge & Kegan Paul.

Noble, D. (1979), 'The PMC: A Critique', in P. Walker (ed.), *Between Labor and Capital*, Boston, South End Press, pp.121-42.

O'Connor, J. (1973), *The Fiscal Crisis of the State*, New York, St Martin's Press.

O'Connor, J. (1974), *The Corporations and the State*, New York, Harper Colophon.

Offe, C. (1975), 'The Theory of the Capitalist State, and the Problem of Policy Formation', in L.N. Lindberg, R. Alford, C. Crouch and C. Offe (eds), *Stress and Contradiction in Modern Capitalism: Public Policy and the Theory of the State*, New York, D.C. Heath, pp.125-44.

Offe, C. (1976), *Industry and Inequality: The Achievement Principle in Work and Social Status*, trans. and introd. by J. Wickham, London, Edward Arnold.

Offe, C. (1981), 'The Attribution of Public Status to Interest Groups: Observations on the West German Case', in S. Berger (ed.), *Organizing Interests in Western Europe: Pluralism, Corporatism and the Transformation of Politics*, Cambridge University Press, pp.123-58.

Offe, C. (1983), 'Competitive Party Democracy and the Keynesian Welfare State: Some Reflections on their Historical Limits', in S. Clegg, G. Dow and P. Boreham (eds), *The State, Class and the Recession*, London, Croom Helm, pp.51-71.

Offe, C. and Hinrichs, K. (1977), 'Sozialokonomie des Arbeitmarkes und die lage "benachteiligter" Gruppen von Arbeitnehmern', in C. Offe (ed.), *Opfer des Arbeitsmarktes: Zur Theorie der Strukturierken Arbeitslosigkeit*, Hewwied-Darmstadt, Luchterhand, pp.3-61.

Offe, C. and Wiesenthal, H. (1980), 'Two Logics of Collective Action: Theoretical Notes on Social Class and Organizational Form', in M. Zeitlin (ed.), *Political Power and Social Theory: A Research Annual*, vol. 1, Greenwich, Conn., JAI, pp.67-116.

Omodei, R.A. (1982), 'Beyond the Neo-Weberian Concept of Status', *Australian and New Zealand Journal of Sociology*, 18, 2, pp.196-213.

Oppenheimer, M. (1973), 'The Proletarianization of the Professional', in P. Halmos (ed.), *Professionalisation and Social Change*, Sociological Review Monograph 20, University of Keele, pp.213-27.

Ormerod, P. (1981), 'Inflation and Incomes Policy', in D. Currie and R. Smith (eds), *Socialist Economic Review 1981*, London, Merlin Press, pp.177-90.

Ornstein, M.D. (1976), 'The Boards and Executives of the Largest

Canadian Corporations: Size, Composition and Interlocks', *Canadian Journal of Sociology*, 1, 4, pp.411-37.

Pahl, R.E. and Pahl, J. (1971), *Managers and their Wives*, Harmondsworth, Penguin.

Pahl, R.E. and Winkler, J.T. (1974), 'The Economic Elite: Theory and Practice', in P. Stanworth and A. Giddens (eds), *Elites and Power in British Society*, Cambridge University Press, pp.102-22.

Palloix, C. (1976), 'The Labour Process: From Fordism to Neo-Fordism', in CSE Pamphlet no. 1, *The Labour Process and Class Struggle, Stage 1*, London, pp.46-67.

Palmer, D. (1983), 'Broken Ties: Interlocking Directorates and Intercorporate Coordination', *Administrative Science Quarterly*, 28, 1, pp.46-55.

Palmer, J.P. (1972), 'The Separation of Ownership from Control in Large US Industrial Corporations', *Quarterly Review of Economics and Business*, 12, 3, pp.55-62.

Panitch, L. (1976), *Social Democracy and Industrial Militancy: The Labour Party, Trade Unions and Incomes Policy 1945-1974*, Cambridge University Press.

Panitch, L. (1979), 'The Development of Corporatism in Liberal Democracies', in P.C. Schmitter and G. Lehmbruch (eds), *Trends Towards Corporatist Intermediation*, London, Sage, pp.119-46.

Panitch, L. (1980), 'Recent Theorizations of Corporatism: Reflections on a Growth Industry', *British Journal of Sociology*, 31, 2, pp.159-87.

Parkin, F. (1971), *Class Inequality and Political Order*, London, MacGibbon & Kee.

Parkin, F. (1979), *Marxism and Class Theory: A Bourgeois Critique*, London, Tavistock.

Parsons, T. (1970), *Sociological Theory and Modern Society*, New York, Free Press.

Patman Report (1968), *Commercial Banks and Their Trust Activities*, Staff Report for the Subcommittee on Domestic Finance, Committee on Banking and Currency, House of Representatives, 90th Congress, 2nd Session, Washington, DC, Government Printing Office.

Penn, R. (1982), ' "The Contested Terrain": A Critique of R.C. Edwards' Theory of Working Class Fractions and Politics', in G. Day (ed.), *Diversity and Decomposition in the Labour Market*, Aldershot, Gower, pp.93-103.

Pennings, J.M. (1980), *Interlocking Directorates*, San Francisco, Jossey Bass.

Perez-Diaz, V.M. (1978), *State, Bureaucracy and Civil Society*, London, Macmillan.

Perlo, V. (1958), ' "People's Capitalism" and Stock Ownership', *American Economic Review*, 48, pp.333-47.

Perrow, C. (1979), *Complex Organizations: A Critical Essay*, Glensview, Ill., Scott, Foresman.

Perrucci, R. (1973), 'Engineering: Professional Servant of Power', in E. Freidson, (ed.), *The Professions and their Prospects*, Beverly Hills, Sage, pp.119-33.

Perrucci, R. and Gerstl, J.E. (1969), *Professions Without Community: Engineers in American Society*, New York, Random House.

Peters. T.J. and Waterman, R. (1982), *In Search of Excellence: Lessons from America's Best Run Companies*, New York, Harper & Row.

Pfeffer, J. (1972), 'Size and Composition of Corporate Boards of Directors: The Organization and its Environment', *Administrative Science Quarterly*, 7, pp.218-28.

Pfeffer, J. and Salancik, G.R. (1978), *The External Control of Organizations*, New York, Harper & Row.

Pfeffer, R.M. (1979), *Working for Capitalism*, New York, Columbia University Press.

Phillips, A.W. (1958), 'The Relationship between Unemployment and the Rate of Change of Money Wage Rates in the United Kingdom, 1861-1957', *Economica*, 25, 100, pp.283-99.

Piore, M.J. (1969), 'On-the-job Training in the Dual Labor Market', in A. Weber *et al.* (eds), *Public–Private Manpower Policies*, Madison, Wis., Industrial Relations Research Association, pp.101-32.

Piore, M.J. (1979), *Birds of Passage: Migrant Labor in Industrial Society*, Cambridge University Press.

Playford, J. (1972), 'Who Rules Australia?', in J. Playford and D. Kirsner (eds), *Australian Capitalism: Towards a Socialist Critique*, Melbourne, Penguin, pp.108-55.

Poggi, G. (1978), *The Development of the Modern State: A Sociological Introduction*, London, Hutchinson.

Polanyi, K. (1944), *The Great Transformation: the Political and Economic Origins of our Time*, Boston, Beacon Press.

Pollard, S. (1982), *The Wasting of the British Economy*, London, Croom Helm.

Porter, J. (1965), *The Vertical Mosaic*, Toronto University Press.

Poulantzas, N. (1973), 'The Problem of the Capitalist State', in J. Urry and J. Wakeford (eds), *Power in Britain*, London, Heinemann, pp. 291-305.

Poulantzas, N. (1975), *Classes in Contemporary Capitalism*, London, New Left Books.

Poulantzas, N. (1977), 'The New Petty Bourgeoisie', in A. Hunt (ed.), *Class and Class Structure*, London, Lawrence & Wishart, pp.113-24.

Power, M. (1975), 'Women's Work is Never Done – by Men: A Socio-economic Model of Sex-typing in Occupations', *Journal of Industrial Relations*, 17, 3, pp.225-39.

Prais, S.J. (1976), *The Evolution of Giant Firms in Britain: A Study of the Growth of Concentration in Manufacturing Industry in Britain 1909-70*, London, Cambridge University Press.

Pryor, F. (1973), *Property and Industrial Organization in Communist and Capitalist Countries*, Bloomington, Indiana University Press.

Przeworski, A. (1977), 'Proletariat into Class: The Process of Class Formation from Karl Kautsky's "The Class Struggle" to Present Controversies', *Politics and Society*, 7, pp.343-401.

Pugh, D.S. and Hickson, D.J. (1976), *Organizational Structure in its Context: The Aston Programme I*, London, Saxon House.

Purdy, D. (1981), 'Government–Trade Union Relations: Towards a New Social Contract', in D. Currie and R. Smith (eds), *Socialist Economic Review 1981*, London, Merlin Press, pp.191-208.

Radice, H. (ed.) (1975), *International Firms and Modern Imperialism*, Harmondsworth, Penguin.

Ratcliff, R. (1980), 'Banks and Corporate Lending: An Analysis of the Impact of the Internal Structure of the Capitalist Class on the Lending Behaviour of Banks', *American Sociological Review*, 45, 4, pp.553-70.

Regini, M. (1983), 'The Crisis of Representation in Class-oriented Unions: Some Reflections on the Italian Case', in S. Clegg, G. Dow and P. Boreham (eds), *The State, Class and the Recession*, London, Croom Helm, pp.239-56.

Regini, M. and Esping-Andersen, G. (1980), 'Trade Union Strategies and Social Policy in Italy and Sweden', *West European Politics*, 3, 1, pp.107-23.

Reich, M., Gordon, D.M. and Edwards, R.C. (1973), 'Dual Labor Markets: A Theory of Labor Market Segmentation', *American Economic Review (Papers and Proceedings)*, 63, 2, pp.359-65.

Reid, I. (1981), *Social Class Differences in Britain* 2nd edn, London, Grant McIntyre.

Ricardo, D. (1819), *On the Principles of Political Economy and Taxation*, 2nd edn, London, John Murray.

Rimmer, M. (1972), *Race and Industrial Conflict*, London, Heinemann.

Ritti, R.R. (1971), *The Engineer in the Industrial Corporation*, New York, Columbia University Press.

Roberts, K., Cook, F.G. and Semeonoff, E. (1977), *The Fragmentary Class Structure*, London, Heinemann.

Robinson, J. (1935), 'Beggar-my-neighbour Remedies for Unemployment', *Collected Economic Papers: Volume Four* (1973), Oxford, Blackwell, pp.229-40.

Robinson, J. (1954), 'The Production Function and the Theory of Capital', in *Collected Economic Papers: Volume Two* (1960), Oxford, Blackwell, pp.114-31.

Robinson, J. (1958), 'Full Employment and Inflation', in *Collected Economic Papers: Volume Two* (1960), Oxford, Blackwell, pp.271-9.

Robinson, J. (1966), 'Kalecki and Keynes', in T. Kowalik *et al.* (eds), *Problems of Economic Dynamics and Planning: Essays in Honour of Michal Kalecki*, Oxford, Pergamon Press, pp.335-41.

Robinson, J. (1971), *Economic Heresies: Some Old-fashioned Questions in Economic Theory*, London, Macmillan.

Robinson, J. (1972), 'The Second Crisis of Economic Theory', *American Economic Review (Papers and Proceedings)*, 62, 2, pp.1-10.

Robinson, J. (1973), 'What Has Become of the Keynesian Revolution?', in J. Robinson (ed.), *After Keynes*, Oxford, Blackwell, pp.1-11.

Robinson, J. (1974), *History Versus Equilibrium*, London, Thames Polytechnic.

Robinson, J. (1976a), 'The Age of Growth', *Challenge: The Magazine of Economic Affairs*, 19, 2, pp.4-9.

Robinson, J. (1976b), 'Michal Kalecki: A Neglected Prophet', *New York*

Review of Books, 23, 3, pp.28-30.

Robinson, J. (1977), 'Michal Kalecki and the Economics of Capitalism', *Oxford Bulletin of Economics and Statistics* (special issue: *Michal Kalecki Memorial Lectures*), 39, 1, pp.7-17.

Robinson, J. (1979), 'Misunderstandings in the Theory of Production', in *Further Contributions to Modern Economics*, Oxford, Blackwell, pp.135-40.

Robinson, J. and Eatwell, J. (1973), *An Introduction to Modern Economics*, Maidenhead, Berks, McGraw-Hill.

Robinson, J. and Wilkinson, F. (1977), 'What Has Become of Employment Policy?', *Cambridge Journal of Economics*, 1, 1, pp.5-14.

Rolfe, H.A. (1967), *The Controllers: Interlocking Directorates in Large Australian Companies*, Melbourne, Cheshire.

Rose, M. (1979), *Servants of Post-industrial Power? 'Sociologie du Travail' in Modern France*, London, Macmillan.

Rose, R. (ed.) (1980), *Challenge to Governance: Studies in Overloaded Policies*, London, Sage.

Roslender, R. (1981), 'Misunderstanding Proletarianization: A Comment on Recent Research', *Sociology*, 15, 3, pp.428-30.

Ross, A.M. and Hartman, P.T. (1960), *Patterns of Industrial Conflict*, New York, Wiley.

Ross, G. (1978), 'Marxism and the New Middle Classes: French Critiques', *Theory and Society*, 5, pp.163-90.

Ross, G. and Jenson, J. (1983), 'Crisis and France's "Third Way": Genesis, Implementation and Contradictions of a Left Strategy out of Economic Crisis', *Studies in Political Economy: A Socialist Review*, 11, pp.71-103.

Rostow, W.W. (1978), *The World Economy: History and Prospect*, Austin, University of Texas Press.

Rowthorn, B. (1977), 'Inflation and Crisis', *Marxism Today*, 21, 11, pp.326-33.

Rowthorn, B. (1980), 'Imperialism in the Seventies – Unity or Rivalry?', in *Capitalism, Conflict and Inflation: Essays in Political Economy*, London, Lawrence & Wishart, pp.48-78.

Rowthorn, B. (1982), 'Britain and Western Europe', *Marxism Today*, 26, 5, pp.25-31.

Roy, W.G. (1981a), 'From Electoral to Bureaucratic Politics: Class Conflict and the Financial-Industrial Class Segment in the United States, 1886-1905', in M. Zeitlin (ed.), *Political Power and Social Theory: A Research Annual*, Greenwich, Conn., JAI Press, pp.173-202.

Roy, W.G. (1981b), 'The Process of Bureaucratization in the US State Department and the Vesting of Economic Interests, 1886-1905', *Administrative Science Quarterly*, 26, 4, pp.419-33.

Roy, W.G. (1981c), 'The Vesting of Interests and the Determinants of Political Power: Size, Network Structure and Mobilization of American Industries, 1886-1905', *American Journal of Sociology*, 86, pp.1287-1310.

Royal Commission on Australian Government Administration (1976), *Main Report*, Canberra, Australian Government Publishing Service.

Rubery, J. (1978), 'Structured Labour Markets, Worker Organization and Low Pay', *Cambridge Journal of Economics*, 3, pp.17-36.

Rubinstein, W.D. (1974), 'Men of Property: Some Aspects of Occupation, Inheritance and Power among Top British Wealth Holders', in P. Stanworth and A. Giddens (eds), *Elites and Power in British Society*, Cambridge University Press, pp.144-69.

Rutigliano, E. (1977), 'The Ideology of Labor and Capitalist Rationality in Gramsci', *Telos*, 31, pp.91-9.

Salaman, G. (1979), *Work Organizations: Resistance and Control*, London, Longman.

Salaman, G. (1981), *Class and the Corporation*, London, Fontana.

Salaman, G. and Thompson, K. (1978), 'Class Culture and the Persistence of an Elite: The Case of Army Officer Selection', *Sociological Review*, 26, pp.283-304.

Samuelson, P. (1973), *Economics*, New York, McGraw-Hill.

Scase, R. (ed.) (1980), *The State in Western Europe*, London, Croom Helm.

Scase, R. (1982), 'The Petty Bourgeoisie and Modern Capitalism: A Consideration of Recent Theories', in A. Giddens and G. Mackenzie (eds), *Social Class and the Division of Labour: Essays in Honour of Ilya Neustadt*, Cambridge University Press, pp.148-61.

Scase, R. and Goffee, R. (1980), *The Real World of the Small Business Owner*, London, Croom Helm.

Scase, R. and Goffee, E. (1982), *The Entrepreneurial Middle Class*, London, Croom Helm.

Scherer, F.M. (1970), *Industrial Market Structure and Economic Performance*, Chicago, Rand McNally.

Schloss, D.F. (1898), *Methods of Industrial Remuneration*, London, Williams & Norgate.

Schmidt, M.G. (1982), 'The Role of Parties in Shaping Macroeconomic Policy', in F.G. Castles (ed.), *The Impact of Parties: Politics and Policies in Democratic Capitalist States*, London, Sage (European Consortium for Political Research), pp.97-176.

Schmitter, P.C. (1974), 'Still the Century of Corporatism?', in P.C. Schmitter and G. Lehmbruch (eds), *Trends Towards Corporatist Intermediation*, London, Sage, pp.7-52.

Schmitter, P.C. (1979), 'Modes of Interest Intermediation and Models of Societal Change in Western Europe', in P.C. Schmitter and G. Lehmbruch (eds), *Trends Towards Corporatist Intermediation*, London, Sage, pp.63-94.

Schmitter, P.C. and Lehmbruch, G. (eds) (1979), *Trends Towards Corporatist Intermediation*, London, Sage.

Schumpeter, J.A. (1939), *Business Cycles: A Theoretical, Historical and Statistical Analysis of the Capitalist Process*, 2 vols, New York, McGraw-Hill.

Schumpeter, J.A. (1943), *Capitalism, Socialism and Democracy*, London, Allen & Unwin.

Scott, J. (1979), *Corporations, Classes and Capitalism*, London, Hutchinson.

Scott, J. (1982), 'Property and Control: Some Remarks on the British Propertied Class', in A. Giddens and G. Mackenzie (eds), *Social Class and the Division of Labour: Essays in Honour of Ilya Neustadt*, Cambridge University Press, pp.228-47.

Scott, J. and Hughes, M. (1976), 'Ownership and Control in a Satellite Economy: A Discussion from Scottish Data', *Sociology*, 10, 1, pp.21-41.

Seccombe, W. (1974), 'The Housewife and her Labour under Capitalism', *New Left Review*, 83, pp.3-24.

Seccombe, W. (1975), 'Domestic Labour – A Reply to Critics', *New Left Review*, 94, pp.85-96.

Sengenberger, W. (1975), *Arbeitsmarktstruktur: Ansäkze zu einem Modell des Segmentierten Arbeitsmarkts*, Frankfurt, Aspekte.

Sengenberger, W. (1978), *Die Gespaltene Arbeitsmarkt: Probleme der Arbeitsmarktsegmentation*, Frankfurt, Campus.

Shalev, M. (1979), 'The Strike: Theoretical and Empirical Studies of Industrial Conflicts across Time and Nations', unpublished PhD thesis, University of Wisconsin.

Sharp, N. (1969), 'Editorial: Hegemony, Theory and Programme', *Arena*, 20, pp.2-4.

Sheriff, P.E. (1974), 'Unrepresentative Bureaucracy', *Sociology*, 8, 3, pp.447-62.

Shorter, E. and Tilly, C. (1974), *Strikes in France, 1830-1968*, Cambridge University Press.

Silverman, D. and Jones, J. (1976), *Organizational Work*, London, Collier-Macmillan.

Simon, H.A. (1952), 'Decision-making and Adminstrative Organization', in R.K. Merton, A.P. Gray, B. Hockey and H.C. Selvin (eds), *Reader in Bureaucracy*, New York, Free Press, pp.185-94.

Simon, H.A. (1976), *Administrative Behaviour*, 3rd edn, New York, Free Press.

Simpson, D. (1983), *The Political Economy of Growth: Classical Political Economy and the Modern World*, Oxford, Blackwell.

Sinfield, A. (1976), 'Unemployment and the Social Structure', in G.D.N. Worswick (ed.), *The Concept and Measurement of Involuntary Unemployment*, London, Allen & Unwin, pp.221-46.

Singh, A. (1977), 'UK Industry and the World Economy: A Case of Deindustrialization?', *Cambridge Journal of Economics*, 1, 2, pp.113-36.

Skidelsky, R. (ed.) (1977), *The End of the Keynesian Era: Essays on the Disintegration of the Keynesian Political Economy*, London, Macmillan.

Sklar, H. (ed.) (1980), *Trilateralism: the Trilateral Commission and Elite Planning for World Management*, Boston, South End Press.

Smelser, N.J. (1959), *Social Change in the Industrial Revolution*, University of Chicago Press.

Smith, A. (1961), *An Enquiry into the Nature and Causes of the Wealth of Nations* (1776), ed. B. Mazlish, Indianapolis, Bobbs-Merrill Educational Publishing.

Smith, N.R. (1967), *The Entrepreneur and his Firm: The Relationship Between Type of Man and Type of Company*, Michigan, Bureau of Business and Economic Research, University of Michigan.

Smith, T.C. (1955), *Political Change and Industrial Development in Japan: Government Enterprise 1868-1880*, Stanford University Press.

Sofer, C. (1970), *Men in Mid-career*, Cambridge University Press.

Sohn-Rethel, A. (1978), *Intellectual and Manual Labour: A Critique of Epistemology*, London, Macmillan.

Sonquist, J.A. and Koenig, T. (1976), 'Examining Corporate Interconnections through Interlocking Directorates', in T.R. Burns and W. Buckley (eds), *Power and Control: Social Structures and their Transformation*, London, Sage, pp.53-83.

Spence, A.M. (1973), 'Job Market Signalling', *Quarterly Journal of Economics*, 87, pp.355-74.

Stanworth, M.J.K. and Curran, J. (1976), 'Growth and the Small Firm: An Alternative View', Journal of Management Studies, May, pp.95-110.

Stanworth, P. and Giddens, A. (1974), 'An Economic Elite: A Demographic Profile of Company Chairmen', in P. Stanworth and A. Giddens (eds), *Elites and Power in British Society*, Cambridge University Press.

Stark, D. (1980), 'Class Struggle and the Transformation of the Labor Process: A Relational Approach', *Theory and Society*, 9, 1, pp.89-130.

Steindl, J. (1966), 'On Maturity in Capitalist Economies', in T. Kowalik *et al.* (eds), *Problems of Economic Dynamics and Planning: Essays in Honour of Michal Kalecki*, Oxford, Pergamon Press, pp.423-32.

Stening, B.W. and Wai, W.T. (1984), 'Interlocking Directorates among Australia's Largest 250 Corporations, 1959/79', *Australian and New Zealand Journal of Sociology*, 20, 1, pp.47-55.

Stephens, J.D. (1979), *The Transition from Capitalism to Socialism*, London, Macmillan.

Stevens, M. (1981), *The Big Eight*, New York, Macmillan.

Stone, K. (1974), 'The Origin of Job Structures in the Steel Industry', *Review of Radical Political Economics*, 6, pp.113-73.

Stretton, H. (1980), 'Future Patterns of Taxation and Public Expenditure in Australia', in J. Wilkes (ed.), *The Politics of Taxation*, Sydney, Hodder & Stoughton, pp.43-81.

Strinati, D. (1982), *Capitalism, the State and Industrial Relations*, London, Croom Helm.

Sweet. T.G. and Jackson, D. (1978), 'The Classification and Interpretation of Strike Statistics: An International Comparative Analysis', *The University of Aston Management Centre Working Paper Series*, no. 97.

Szymanski, A. (1975), *The Capitalist State and the Politics of Class*, Cambridge, Mass., Winthrop Publishers.

Szymanski, A. (1979), 'A Critique and Extension of the Professional-Managerial Class', in P. Walker (ed.), *Between Labor and Capital*, Boston, South End Press, pp.49-65.

Tarling, R. and Wilkinson, F. (1977), 'The Social Contract: Post-war Incomes Policies and their Inflationary Impact', *Cambridge Journal of*

Economics, 1, 4, pp.395-414.
Taylor, F.W. (1967), 'Shop Management' (1903), reprinted in F.W. Taylor, *Scientific Management*, New York, Norton.
Taylor, M. and Thrift, N. (1980), 'Organization, Location and Political Economy: Towards a Geography of Business Organizations', paper presented at Commission on Industrial Systems, Fujiyoshida Business Meeting, August.
Therborn, G. (1976), *Science, Class and Society: On the Formation of Sociology and Historical Materialism*, London, New Left Books.
Therborn, G. (1977), 'The Rule of Capital and the Rise of Democracy', *New Left Review*, 103, pp.3-41.
Therborn, G. (1978), *What Does the Ruling Class Do When it Rules? State Apparatuses and State Power under Feudalism, Capitalism and Socialism*, London, New Left Books.
Therborn, G. (1979), 'Enterprises, Markets and States: A First, Modest Contribution to a General Theory of Capitalist Politics', paper presented at the Moscow International Political Science Association Congress, August.
Therborn, G. (1983), 'Why Some Classes Are More Successful than Others', *New Left Review*, 138, pp.37-55.
Thomas, A.B. (1978), 'The British Business Elite: The Case of the Retail Sector', *Sociological Review*, 26, pp.305-26.
Thompson, E.P. (1968), *The Making of the English Working Class*, Harmondsworth, Penguin.
Thompson, E.P. (1971), 'The Moral Economy of the English Crowd in the Eighteenth Century', *Past and Present*, 50, pp.76-136.
Thompson, E.P. (1978), *The Poverty of Theory and Other Essays*, London, Merlin Press.
Thompson, G. (1977), 'The Relationship between the Financial and Industrial Sector of the United Kingdom Economy', *Economy and Society*, 6, 3, pp.235-83.
Thompson, J.D. (1967), *Organizations in Action*, New York, McGraw-Hill.
Thompson, J.D. and McEwan, W.J. (1958), 'Organizational Goals and Environment', *American Sociological Review*, 23, pp.23-31.
Thrift, N.J. (1983), 'On the Determination of Social Action in Space and Time', *Environment and Planning: Society and Space*, 1, 1, pp.23-58.
Tomasson, R.F. (1970), *Sweden: Prototype of Modern Society*, New York, Random House.
Tomlinson, J. (1982), *The Unequal Struggle? British Socialism and the Capitalist Enterprise*, London, Methuen.
Touraine, A. (1971), *The Post-industrial Society: Tomorrow's Social History: Class, Conflicts and Culture in the Programmed Society*, New York, Random House.
Tribe, K. (1975), 'Capitalism and Industrialization', *Intervention*, 5, pp.23-37.
Urry, J. (1981), *The Anatomy of Capitalist Societies: The Economy, Civil Society and the State*, London, Macmillan.
Useem, M. (1978), 'The Inner Group of the American Capitalist Class',

Social Problems, 25, pp.225-40.
Useem, M. (1979), 'The Social Organization of the American Business Elite and Participation of Corporate Directors in the Government of American Institutions', *American Sociological Review*, 44, pp.553-72.
Useem, M. (1980), 'Corporations and the Corporate Elite', in A. Inkeles, M.J. Sindser and R.H. Turner (eds), *Annual Review of Sociology*, 1980, 6, pp.41-77.
Useem, M. (1982), 'Classwide Rationality in the Politics of Managers and Directors of Large Corporations in the United States and Great Britain', *Administrative Science Quarterly*, 27, 2, pp.199-226.
Useem, M. and McCormack, A. (1981), 'The Dominant Segment of the British Business Elite', *Sociology*, 15, 3, pp.381-406.
Veblen, T. (1921), *The Engineers and the Price System*, Boston, Heubsch.
Vernon, R. (1971), *Sovereignty at Bay*, New York, Basic Books.
Wachtel, H.M. (1974), 'Class Consciousness and Stratification in the Labor Process', *Review of Radical Political Economics*, 6, 1, pp.1-15.
Wainwright, H. (1978), 'Women and the Division of Labour', in P. Abrams (ed.), *Work, Urbanism and Inequality: UK Society Today*, London, Weidenfeld & Nicolson, pp.160-205.
Wallerstein, I. (1974), *The Modern World System: Capitalist Agriculture and the Origins of the European World Economy in the Sixteenth Century*, London, Academic Press.
Wallerstein, I. (1979), *The Capitalist World Economy*, Cambridge University Press.
Wallerstein, I. (1980), 'The Future of the World Economy', in K. Hopkins and I. Wallerstein (eds), *Processes of the World System*, London, Sage, pp.167-80.
Ward, A. (1975), 'European Capitalism's Reserve Army', *Monthly Review*, 26, 6, pp.31-41.
Watts, H.D. (1980), *The Large Industrial Enterprise: Some Spatial Perspectives*, London, Croom Helm.
Webb, S. and Webb. B. (1924), *The History of Trade Unionism*, London, Longman.
Webber, D. (1982), 'Combatting and Acquiescing in Unemployment? Crisis Management in Sweden and West Germany', *West European Politics*, 6, 1, pp.22-43.
Weber, M. (1923), *General Economic History*, trans. F.H. Knight, London, Allen & Unwin.
Weber, M. (1947), *The Theory of Social and Economic Organization*, trans. by T. Parsons and A.M. Henderson, New York, Free Press.
Weber, M. (1968), *Economy and Society: An Outline of Interpretive Sociology*, ed and introd. by G. Roth and C. Wittich, New York, Bedminster Press.
Weber, M. (1976), *The Protestant Ethic and the Spirit of Capitalism*, trans. by T. Parsons, London, Allen & Unwin.
Weber, M. (1978), *Economy and Society: An Outline of Interpretive Sociology*, 2 vols, G. Roth and C. Wittich (eds), Berkeley, University of California Press.

Wedderburn, D. (1972), 'Inequality at Work', in P. Townsend and N. Bosanquet (eds), *Labour and Inequality*, London, Fabian Society, pp.174-85.

Weick, K.E. (1969), *The Social Psychology of Organizing*, Reading, Mass., Addison-Wesley.

Weisskopf, T. (1981), 'The Current Economic Crisis in Historical Perspective', *Socialist Review*, 57, pp.9-53.

Wells, D. (1981), *Marxism and the Modern State: An Analysis of Fetishism in Capitalist Society*, Brighton, Harvester.

Wenger, W.G. (1980), 'The Transmutation of Weber's *Ständ* in American Sociology and its Social Roots', in S.G. McNall and G.N. Howe (eds), *Current Perspectives in Social Theory: a Research Annual*, Greenwich, Conn., JAI Press, pp.357-78.

Westergaard, J.H. (1965), 'The Withering Away of Class: A Contemporary Myth', in P. Anderson and R. Blackburn (eds), *Towards Socialism*, London, Fontana, pp.77-113.

Westergaard, J.H. (1972), 'Sociology: The Myth of Classlessness', in R. Blackburn (ed.), *Ideology in Social Science: Readings in Critical Social Theory*, London, Fontana, pp.119-63.

Westergaard, J.H. (1977), 'Class, Inequality and Corporatism', in A. Hunt (ed.), *Class and Class Structure*, London, Lawrence and Wishart.

Westergaard, J. and Resler, H. (1976), *Class in a Capitalist Society: A Study of Contemporary Britain*, Harmondsworth, Pelican.

Westney, D.E. (1980), 'Patterns of Organizational Development in Japan: The Spread of the Incorporated Enterprise 1888-1918', in D. Dunkerley and G. Salaman (eds), *The International Yearbook of Organization Studies 1980*, London, Routledge and Kegan Paul, pp.142-56.

Wexler, P. (1982), 'Structure, Text and Subject: A Critical Sociology of School Knowledge', in M.W. Apple (ed.), *Cultural and Economic Reproduction in Education: Essays on Class, Ideology and the State*, London, Routledge & Kegan Paul, pp.275-303.

Wheelwright, E.L. (1957), *Ownership and Control of Australian Companies*, Sydney, Law Book Company.

Wheelwright, E.L. (1970), *Overseas Investment in Australia*, Sydney, Department of Adult Education, University of Sydney.

Wheelwright, E.L. (1974), *Radical Political Economy: Collected Essays*, Sydney, Australian and New Zealand Book Company.

Wheelwright, E.L. (1980), 'The Age of the Transnational Corporations', in G. Crough, T. Wheelwright, and T. Wilshire (eds), *Australia and World Capitalism*, Ringwood, Penguin, pp.123-36.

Wheelwright, E.L. and Miskelly, J. (1967), *Anatomy of Australian Manufacturing Industry*, Sydney, Law Book Company.

Whitley, R.D. (1973), 'Commonalities and Connections among Directors of Large Financial Institutions', *Sociological Review*, 21, pp.613-32.

Whitley, R.D. (1974), 'The City and Industry: The Directors of Large Companies, their Characteristics and Connections', in P. Stanworth and A. Giddens (eds), *Elites and Power in British Society*, Cambridge University Press, pp.65-80.

Wild, R.A. (1978), *Social Stratification in Australia*, Sydney, Allen & Unwin.

Wildavsky, A. (1964), *The Politics of the Budgetary Process*, Boston, Little, Brown.

Wildsmith, J.R. (1973), *Managerial Theories of the Firm*, London, Martin Robertson.

Wilenski, P. (1980), 'Discussion' (rejoinder to D.A. Kemp's 'Taxation: The Politics of Change') in J. Wilkes (ed.), *The Politics of Taxation*, Sydney, Hodder & Stoughton, pp.311-13.

Wilkinson, F. (1981), *The Dynamics of Labour Market Segmentation*, London, Academic Press.

Williams, C. (1981), *Open Cut: The Working Class in an Australian Mining Town*, Sydney, Allen & Unwin.

Williams, R. (1961), *The Long Revolution*, London, Chatto & Windus.

Willis, P. (1977), *Learning to Labour: How Working Class Kids Get Working Class Jobs*, Westmead, Saxon House.

Willoughby, J. (1982), 'The Changing Role of Protection in the World Economy', *Cambridge Journal of Economics*, 6, 2, pp.195-211.

Wilson, H.T. (1977), *The American Ideology: Science, Technology and Organization as Modes of Rationality in Advanced Industrial Societies*, London, Routledge & Kegan Paul.

Wilson, H.T. (1983), 'Technocracy and Late Capitalist Society: Reflections on the Problem of Rationality and Social Organization', in S. Clegg, G. Dow and P. Boreham (eds), *The State, Class and the Recession*, London, Croom Helm, pp.152-238.

Winch, P. (1958), *The Idea of a Social Science and its Relation to Philosophy*, London, Routledge & Kegan Paul.

Wolff, J. (1977), 'Women in Organizations', in S. Clegg and D. Dunkerley (eds), *Critical Issues in Organizations*, London, Routledge & Kegan Paul, pp.7-20.

Wood, S. (1980), 'Corporate Strategy and Organization Studies', in D. Dunkerley and G. Salaman (eds), *The International Yearbook of Organization Studies 1980*, London, Routledge & Kegan Paul, pp.52-71.

Wood, S. (ed) (1982), *The Degradation of Work? Skill, Deskilling and the Labour Process*, London, Hutchinson.

Worswick, G.D.N. (1977), 'Kalecki at Oxford, 1940-44', *Oxford Bulletin of Economics and Statistics* (special issue: *Michal Kalecki Memorial Lectures*), 39, 1, pp.19-29.

Wright, E.O. (1976), 'Class Boundaries in Advanced Capitalist Societies', *New Left Review*, 98, pp.3-41.

Wright, E.O. (1978), *Class, Crisis and the State*, London, New Left Books.

Wright, E.O. (1979), 'Intellectuals and Class Structure of Capitalist Society', in P. Walker (ed.), *Between Labor and Capital*, Boston, South End Press, pp.191-211.

Wright, E.O. (1980a), 'Varieties of Marxist Conceptions of Class

Structure', *Politics and Society*, 9, 3, pp.323-70.

Wright, E.O. (1980b), 'Class, Occupation and Organization', in D. Dunkerley and G. Salaman (eds), *The International Yearbook of Organization Studies 1979*, London, Routledge & Kegan Paul, pp.1-30.

Wright, E.O. (1980c), 'Class and Occupation', *Theory and Society*, 9, pp.177-213.

Wright, E.O. (1983), 'Capitalism's Futures', *Socialist Review*, 68, 13, 2, pp.77-126.

Young, M. and Wilmott, P. (1957), *Family and Kinship in East London*, London, Routledge & Kegan Paul.

Zald, M. (1969), 'The Power and Functions of Boards of Directors', *American Journal of Sociology*, 75, pp.97-111.

Zeitlin, M. (1974), 'Corporate Ownership and Control: The Large Corporation and the Capitalist Class', *American Journal of Sociology*, 79, pp.1073-119.

Zeitlin, M. (1976), 'On Class Theory of the Large Corporation: Response to Allen', *American Journal of Sociology*, 81, pp.894-903.

Zeitlin, M., Ewen, L.A. and Ratcliff, R.E. (1974), ' "New Princes" for Old? The Large Corporation and the Capitalist Class in Chile', *American Journal of Sociology*, 80, pp.87-123.

Zeitlin, M., Newman, W.L. and Ratcliff, R.E. (1976), 'Class Segments: Agrarian Property and Political Leadership in the Capitalist Class of Chile', *American Sociological Review*, 41, pp.1006-29.

Zimbalist, A. (ed.) (1979), *Case Studies on the Labor Process*, New York, Monthly Review Press.

Zweig, F. (1961), *The Worker in an Affluent Society*, London, Heinemann.

Zweig, F. (1976), *The New Acquisitive Society*, London, Barry Rose.

Author Index

Subject Index

interests, 7, 11, 23, 24, 32, 43, 49, 50, 53, 55, 59, 62, 67–8, 88, 115, 116, 120, 123, 124, 126, 132, 133–4, 142, 146, 147, 149, 160, 165, 167, 168, 169, 170, 171, 172, 177, 178, 187, 188, 189, 190, 200–1, 202, 207, 216, 223, 233, 237, 248, 251, 256, 258, 259, 260–75, 277–81, 284, 285, 286, 289, 290, 293, 332, 334, 340, 369, 370, 373, 384, 385, 386, 389, 390; outside the enterprise, 62
interlocking directorships, 106–7, 122–35
interlocks, 77, 107
intermediate small firms: loyal opposition, 79–80; satellites, 79–80
intermediate strata, 171, 172, 176
intermediation, 201, 265, 266, 267
International Labour Organization (ILO), 253
International Monetary Fund (IMF), 288, 258, 363
internationalization of capital, 101–3, 356–8, 361–4
intervening locations, 144
intervention, 20, 270, 319, 320, 322, 325, 327, 329, 330, 338, 342, 365, 366, 380, 390; see also government intervention, state intervention
interventionism, 8, 389
intraorganizational conflict, 109–12
investment, 2, 17, 18, 22, 23–4, 47, 67, 70, 72, 77, 88–9, 90, 98, 112, 154, 231, 236, 245, 259, 286, 287–8, 297, 298, 301, 302, 303, 304, 305, 306, 307, 308, 309, 310, 317, 318, 320, 334, 343, 344, 348, 361, 363, 367, 373, 374, 375, 376, 380, 381, 382, 383, 389, 390
'invisible hand', 7, 8, 24
Ireland, 254, 255, 348
Israel, 225
Italy, 80, 83, 95, 156, 161, 253, 254, 255, 256, 333, 338, 350

Japan, 72, 74–6, 83, 95–7, 126, 245, 254, 255, 333, 344, 345, 347, 348, 349, 350, 351, 352, 353, 358
joint stock companies, 60, 75, 87, 105–8

Kaleckian theory, 287, 302–11, 343, 367, 380
Kampuchea, 270
Keynesian: theory, 21, 24, 287, 298–302, 322, 327, 334, 335, 339; welfare state, 330–1, 333
Keynesianism, 298–302, 309, 311–14, 316–17, 319, 322, 323, 324–5, 329–35, 336, 347, 360, 365
knowledge, 146, 150, 173, 174, 195, 197
kokata, 96, 110

Labor and Monopoly Capital, 238–42
labour, 2, 9, 12, 14, 18, 19, 21, 24, 25, 29, 37, 40–50, 58, 63, 67, 85, 86, 92–105, 166, 186, 190, 201, 238, 240, 242, 250, 259–69, 274, 286, 289, 293, 294–5, 305, 307, 310, 314, 315, 316, 320, 322, 325, 329, 331, 332–3, 334, 335, 336, 339, 340, 341, 344, 362, 367, 373, 374, 380, 381, 386, 388, 389, 390
labour exchange, 268
labour governments, 131, 288, 358, 360
labour market(s), 43–4, 53–4, 63, 65, 92, 139, 168, 178, 194, 207, 209, 214–31, 245, 260, 265, 267–8, 293, 305, 334, 340, 359, 377, 378, 380, 386; dual, 110, 218–23, 248; internal, 153, 219, 222, 223, 224, 227, 228, 230, 232, 233, 245, 252; primary sector, 179, 219–20, 222–3, 231, 372; secondary sector, 179, 219–20, 222, 226, 227, 228, 229, 372; segmentation, 49, 148, 179, 190, 194, 209, 214, 216, 222–31,

For Product Safety Concerns and Information please contact our EU
representative GPSR@taylorandfrancis.com
Taylor & Francis Verlag GmbH, Kaufingerstraße 24, 80331 München, Germany

www.ingramcontent.com/pod-product-compliance
Lightning Source LLC
Chambersburg PA
CBHW050555270326
41926CB00012B/2063